NOBODY'S STORY

THE NEW HISTORICISM: STUDIES IN CULTURAL POETICS
Stephen Greenblatt, General Editor

NOBODY'S STORY

~

THE VANISHING ACTS OF WOMEN WRITERS IN THE MARKETPLACE, 1670–1820

CATHERINE GALLAGHER

University of California Press
Berkeley · Los Angeles

This book is a print-on-demand volume. It is manufactured using toner in place of ink. Type and images may be less sharp than the same material seen in traditionally printed University of California Press editions.

University of California Press
Berkeley and Los Angeles, California

© 1994 by Catherine Gallagher

First Paperback Printing 1995

Library of Congress Cataloging-in-Publication Data

Gallagher, Catherine.
    Nobody's story : the vanishing acts of women writers in
the marketplace, 1670–1820 / Catherine Gallagher.
        p.   cm. — (The New historicism : 31)
    Includes bibliographical references and index.
    ISBN 0-520-20338-0 (alk. paper)
    1. English literature—Women authors—History and
criticism.   2. Women and literature—Great Britain—
History—18th century.   3. Women and literature—Great
Britain—History—17th century.   4. Women and
literature—Great Britain—History—19th century.
5. Feminism and literature—Great Britain—History.
6. Literature publishing—Great Britain—History.
7. Women authors, English—Economic conditions.
8. Sex role in literature.   I. Title.   II. Series.
PR113.G35   1994
820.9'9287'09032—dc20   94-9208

Printed in the United States of America

To Marty

Contents

Acknowledgments

This study owes a great deal to the many friends and colleagues who read and commented on the various chapters: Elizabeth Abel, Janet Adelman, John Bender, Heather Glenn, Steven Knapp, Jayne Lewis, Jerome McGann, D. A. Miller, Felicity Nussbaum, Robert Post, Hilary Schor, George Starr, and Bernard Williams. I am also thankful to the students in my 1990 graduate seminar on eighteenth-century British women writers, to the scholars at various universities who gave me the opportunity to develop these ideas in the form of public lectures, and to the audiences who corrected my numerous mistakes and helped me focus the argument. Thanks are also due to the superb young scholars who served as research assistants on this project, Nora Johnson, Simon Stern, and Kate McCullough; as general organizer, collaborator, and author of many a footnote, Elizabeth Young was much more than a research assistant. Stephen Greenblatt, Thomas Laqueur, and Michael Rogin inspired, encouraged, and helped revise each chapter in succession, and Kim Chernin read the first draft of the completed book and told me what it said; to these four steadfast friends I am deeply indebted.

My mother, Mary Sullivan, and my mother-in-law, Sari Jay, helped and encouraged me, and my daughter Shana Gallagher's growing interest in feminism and representation made this project seem increasingly close to home. I am also grateful to my daughter Rebecca Jay, whose loving companionship and good-humored patience sustained me. Finally, to my husband, Martin Jay, I owe an inestimable debt of gratitude. He was the first and most critical reader of each chapter, and he has provided the emotional as well as intellectual support that made the book's completion possible.

The National Endowment for the Humanities, the John Simon Guggenheim Memorial Foundation, the University of California, and Clare Hall, Cambridge, all generously subsidized this study.

I would also like to thank the British Library, the Cambridge University Library, and the Houghton Library at Harvard University for their hospitality.

A portion of Chapter 1 was first published in *Last Laughs: Perspectives on Women and Comedy,* ed. Regina Barreca (New York: Gordon and Breach, Science Publishers, 1988). A part of Chapter 3 first appeared in *Eighteenth-Century Studies* 23:4 (1990): 502–21; and a portion of Chapter 6 was published in *Nineteenth-Century Contexts* 12:1 (Spring 1988): 11–19.

Introduction

I was strongly advised against calling this book "Nobody's Story" because the title, it was feared, would suggest exactly the sort of study this is not: one lamenting the unjust absence of women from the eighteenth-century literary canon. Let it be known at the outset, therefore, that the "nobodies" of my title are not ignored, silenced, erased, or anonymous women. Instead, they are literal nobodies: authorial personae, printed books, scandalous allegories, intellectual property rights, literary reputations, incomes, debts, and fictional characters. They are the exchangeable tokens of modern authorship that allowed increasing numbers of women writers to thrive as the eighteenth century wore on.

Nobody was not on my mind when I began this study. Noticing that the appearance of what was called "female authorship" in the late seventeenth and eighteenth centuries coincided with the appearance of a literary marketplace, I set out to show that many women writers emphasized their femininity to gain financial advantage and that, in the process, they invented and popularized numerous ingenious similarities between their gender and their occupation. Far from disavowing remunerative authorship as unfeminine, they relentlessly embraced and feminized it. And, far from creating only minor and forgettable variations on an essentially masculine figure, they delineated crucial features of "the author" for the period in general by emphasizing their trials and triumphs in the marketplace. This book, in short, began by describing the reciprocal shaping of the terms "woman," "author," and "marketplace."

At the outset, my objective was to show the extreme plasticity of these terms as well as their interrelations. I was inspired by studies in the history of sexuality, which point to the mid-eighteenth century as a watershed of European discourse on the topics of sexuality and gender, a time when the very meaning of "woman" underwent a drastic revision.[1] I was also deeply impressed by recent accounts of eighteenth-century economic changes that stress the revolution in credit and the proliferation of both debt and "paper" property.[2] A few historians even suggest that these concurrent shifts in the organization and meaning of both gender differences and marketplace transactions were connected.[3] A small group of new economic literary critics, moreover, had been exploring the relations between literary and economic exchange,[4] while feminist theorists had renewed interest in the topic of the exchange of women.[5] Stimulated by these historiographical and theoretical developments, I wanted to know how women writers integrated the changing concept of woman into their authorial personae, how they connected it to the discourse of marketplace exchange, and how prevalent notions of authorship were altered in the process.

Consequently, I chose five writers to represent five different stages of authorship in the marketplace: Aphra Behn (1640–1689), Delarivier Manley (1663–1724), Charlotte Lennox (1729–1804), Frances Burney (1752–1840), and Maria Edgeworth (1768?–1849).

1. The most thorough account of this revision is Thomas Laqueur, *Making Sex: Body and Gender from the Greeks to Freud* (Cambridge: Harvard Univ. Press, 1990).

2. Three books on this topic have especially influenced me: J. G. A. Pocock, *Virtue, Commerce, and History: Essays on Political Thought and History, Chiefly in the Eighteenth Century* (Cambridge: Cambridge Univ. Press, 1985); John Brewer, *The Sinews of Power: War, Money and the English State, 1688–1783* (New York: Knopf, 1989); and Peter de Bolla, *The Discourse of the Sublime: Readings in History, Aesthetics and the Subject* (Oxford: Basil Blackwell, 1989).

3. Pocock and de Bolla, for example, explore the uses of gender in economic discourse.

4. Examples of this new economic criticism include Marc Shell, *The Economy of Literature* (Baltimore, MD: Johns Hopkins Univ. Press, 1978), and *Money, Language, and Thought: Literary and Philosophical Economies from the Medieval to the Modern Era* (Berkeley: Univ. of California Press, 1982); Kurt Heinzelman, *The Economics of the Imagination* (Amherst: Univ. of Massachusetts Press, 1980); Jean-Joseph Goux, *Freud, Marx: Economie et symbolique* (Paris: Editions de Seuil, 1973), and *Les iconoclastes* (Paris: Editions de Seuil, 1978), parts of which have been recently combined, translated, and published as *Symbolic Economies: After Marx and Freud*, trans. Jennifer Curtiss Gage (Ithaca, NY: Cornell Univ. Press, 1990); Walter Benn Michaels, *The Gold Standard and the Logic of Naturalism: American Literature at the Turn of the Century* (Berkeley: Univ. of California Press, 1987); and Jean-Christophe Agnew, *Worlds Apart: The Market and the Theater in Anglo-American Thought, 1550–1750* (Cambridge: Cambridge Univ. Press, 1986).

5. See especially Gayle Rubin, "The Traffic in Women: Notes on the 'Political Economy' of Sex," in *Toward an Anthropology of Women*, ed. Rayna R. Reiter (New York: Monthly Review Press, 1975); and Luce Irigaray, "Commodities among Themselves," in *This Sex Which Is Not One*, trans. Catherine Porter and Carolyn Burke (Ithaca, NY: Cornell Univ. Press, 1985).

These five writers are commonly acknowledged to have been widely read, and all were formally innovative. Their popularity and influence give their careers representative status. Initially, I noticed that the "feminine" aspects of their authorial personae only intensified contradictions implicit in authorship generally. Hence, although this book concentrates on women as representatives of the condition of the author in the eighteenth century, it does not claim that they belonged to a separate tradition. Rather, it takes them to be special in their extreme typicality and describes the metamorphoses of authorship as seen through the magnifying glass of women's careers.

As I watched these metamorphoses take shape, I noticed recurrently that women, authorship, and marketplace exchange had—literally—*nothing* in common.[6] In Aphra Behn's play *The Lucky Chance*, for example, the early modern concept of female "nothingness," which refers to both women's presumed genital lack and their secondary ontological status in relation to men, overlaps with the conceptual disembodiment that all commodities achieve at the moment of exchange, when their essence appears to be an abstract value. This nothingness, placed at the center of both femaleness and commodity exchange, the playwright further linked to her own elusive and disembodied persona. These layered nothings, which I first encountered in Behn's works, seemed even more insistently present in Delarivier Manley's scandalous court chronicles, where political writing, especially in its gossipy female form, is likened to deficit spending.

In Manley's works, though, the nothingness also seemed to contain at least the potential for a new and more positive form: the form of the fictional Nobody, a proper name explicitly without a physical referent in the real world. While analyzing the differences between the scandalous court chronicles of the 1710s and the novels of the mid-eighteenth century, I found myself tracing the appearance of a fourth concept in addition to the three—woman, author, and marketplace—that I had set out to track. I was following the emergence into public consciousness of a new category of dis-

6. For an excellent discussion of the importance of the concept of nothing to the development of money, representation, and subjectivity, see Brian Rotman, *Signifying Nothing: The Semiotics of Zero* (New York: St. Martin's Press, 1987). My debt to this study would be difficult to overestimate.

course: fiction. Like most literary critics, I had hitherto taken fiction for granted as a constant feature of the textual landscape, but when I began to look closely at the recognized early eighteenth-century discursive options, I noticed that it was barely visible. As far as the reading public and most writers were concerned, narrative came in two forms: referential truth telling and lying. In cultures where the concept of fiction is firmly in place, however, it constitutes an easily recognizable alternative. To be sure, the absence of the category did not necessarily indicate the absence of the thing. Literary historians have quite rightly pointed to numerous pre-eighteenth-century writings that can now be called fictional: romances, fables, some allegories, fairy stories, dramas, narrative poems—in short, all forms of literature that were not taken to be the literal truth but that apparently had no particular intention to deceive. Before the mid-eighteenth century, though, there was no consensus that all those genres shared a common trait; instead they were classified according to their implied purposes (moral fables, for example), their forms (e.g. epic), or their provenance (e.g. oriental tales). That discursive category we now call fiction was a "wild space," unmapped and unarticulated.[7]

Nobody was the pivot point around which a massive reorientation of textual referentiality took place, and the location of this pivot was the mid-eighteenth-century novel. Far from being the descendant of older overtly fictional forms, the novel was the first to articulate the idea of fiction for the culture as a whole. I realized that what Ian Watt called "formal realism" was not a way of trying

---

7. My argument does not deny that there were occasional quite sophisticated discussions of fiction (under different names) prior to the mid-eighteenth century. Aristotle is, of course, the locus classicus; Sir Philip Sidney's *Defence of Poesy* is another obvious case in point. Most Renaissance writers, however, followed Aristotle in linking the fictional to the heroic, and none of them succeeded in creating a cultural consensus on the nature and legitimacy of fiction. By the early eighteenth century, when Joseph Addison published his essay on the pleasures of the imagination in the *Spectator* (see esp. numbers 416–21), he could rely on a cultured understanding of the difference between a fiction and a lie, and he did not need to engage in an explicit defense. However, his division of poetic subjects into the sublime, the beautiful, and the marvelous, as well as his penchant for drawing examples from Homer and Virgil, points to an underlying assumption that fiction is justified when it represents heroic idealizations. Fiction as an independent category of discourse, disjoined from any particular content, was not yet fully realized even in Addison's treatise. It is a generalized understanding of the status of fiction that concerns me here.

to hide or disguise fictionality; realism was, rather, understood to be fiction's formal sign.[8] Eighteenth-century readers identified with the characters in novels *because* of the characters' fictiveness and not in spite of it. Moreover, these readers had to be taught how to read fiction, and as they learned this skill (it did not come naturally), new emotional dispositions were created.

Nobody was crucial to the development of the literary market-place as well. My analysis of the careers of Charlotte Lennox and Frances Burney links new concepts of literary property, a new attribution of innocence to authors (especially female authors), and the circulation of fictional entities through the culture. In analyzing the transition from Behn's and Manley's authorial personae, who were often disguised, disreputable scandalmongers, to Lennox's and Burney's, who were genuine, proper purveyors of original tales, I noticed that the later authors stressed their renunciation of personal satire and slander. That is, the explicit fictionality of their works initially recommended them as wholesome goods. But the novel soon came under attack as an unruly medium; readers, it was increasingly noted as the century wore on, could not be counted on to disengage themselves from Nobody. Consequently, each generation of writers felt called upon to reform the genre by encouraging an affective pulsation between identification with fic-tional characters and withdrawal from them, between emotional

8. Watt, *The Rise of the Novel: Studies in Defoe, Richardson and Fielding* (Berkeley: Univ. of California Press, 1957). In the 1980s many new accounts of the "rise of the novel" were published, but few of them challenged Watt's category of "formal realism," and none suggested that realism was an indicator of fiction. The recent studies that have been most influential are Nancy Armstrong, *Desire and Domestic Fiction: A Political History of the Novel* (New York: Oxford Univ. Press, 1987); Lennard J. Davis, *Factual Fictions: The Origins of the English Novel* (New York: Columbia Univ. Press, 1983), and *Resisting Novels: Ideology and Fiction* (New York: Methuen, 1987); Terry Castle, *Masquerade and Civilization: The Carnivalesque in Eighteenth-Century English Culture and Fiction* (Stanford, CA: Stanford Univ. Press, 1986); Michael McKeon, *The Origins of the English Novel, 1600–1740* (Baltimore, MD: Johns Hopkins Univ. Press, 1987); John Bender, *Imagining the Penitentiary: Fiction and the Architecture of Mind in Eighteenth-Century England* (Chicago: Univ. of Chicago Press, 1987); J. Paul Hunter, *Before Novels: The Cultural Contexts of Eighteenth-Century English Fiction* (New York: Norton, 1990). Davis and McKeon notice that the novel marks a new stage of explicit fictionality in narrative, but Davis is too censorious of this development to analyze it fully, and McKeon, whose focus is the epistemology rather than either the ontology or the affective force of the novel, allows his insights to remain scattered. I am indebted to all these studies, but I remain convinced that the novel can be seen in historical perspective only when the powerful novelty of its fictionality is recognized.

investment and divestment. The constant need, created by fiction itself, to revise the genre into an ever more efficient exercise in self-control further stimulated the market and inspired numerous women writers to come to the novel's rescue. The works of Frances Burney and Maria Edgeworth exemplify alternative modes of formal rectification. Both writers claimed to remedy the mistakes of earlier fiction, to encourage new forms of identification that would annul the consequences of past overidentification.

~

The terms "woman," "author," "marketplace," and "fiction," sharing connotations of nothingness and disembodiment, reciprocally defined each other in the literature analyzed here. To say that they defined each other is to renounce at the outset any single cause for the changes they underwent. For example, although this book describes the economic conditions of authors, it does not use the economy as a stable explanatory "base" on which their careers can be firmly situated. Indeed, as my title implies, the literary marketplace, described here in several of its eighteenth-century phases, is often the setting for what might be called the authors' vanishing acts. It is a place where the writers appear mainly through their frequently quite spectacular displacements and disappearances in literary and economic exchanges. Hence the marketplace is not so much the *cause* of the phenomenon of female authorship as its point of departure.

To concentrate on the elusiveness of these authors, instead of bemoaning it and searching for their positive identities, is to practice a different sort of literary history. But it is not to abandon the tasks of historical analysis altogether, for the vanishing acts themselves are discoverable only as historical occurrences. I describe the disappearances by offering plausible and multifaceted accounts of their exigencies and mechanisms; in turn, these accounts create images of the departed in the act of dematerializing. To be sure, the images are not entirely of my own manufacture: they are partly, I believe, the conscious artifices of the women whose works form the core of this study. And they, of course, were not creating ex nihilo but were molding the material already designated "female author" to their own economic and literary ends. Centuries of literary history and criticism have also made these apparitions visible and, at least in the case of Frances Burney and Maria Edgeworth, have given them such a semblance of substance that they hardly seem spectral at all. In contrast, the elusiveness of the authorial personae of Aphra Behn, Delarivier Manley, and Charlotte Lennox is partly determined by their having almost vanished from literary history in the nineteenth and early twentieth centuries.

It would be perverse of me to claim that Edgeworth should seem as remote and ultimately unavailable as Behn. Edgeworth, after all, left a voluminous correspondence, the reminiscences of dozens of friends and acquaintances, estate ledgers, memoirs, and so forth, whereas Behn left scarcely any information about herself. It would surely be outlandish to complain that we know too much about Maria Edgeworth's life to be able to view her, properly, as a rhetorical effect. I am claiming, however, that the Edgeworth we can construct from the historical record seems to have been convinced that the creature she called her "author-self" was an entity distinct from her individual personal identity. This book examines the writers' "author-selves," not as pretenses or mystifications, but as the partly disembodied entities required by the specific exchanges that constituted their careers.

The author-selves, therefore, are also partial Nobodies, but their nobodiness differs from that of fictional characters. There is understood to be no particular, embodied, referent in the material world for the proper name of a fictional character; but the names of these author-selves refer to entities that are neither identical to the writers nor wholly distinct from them. They are rhetorical constructions, but constructions that playfully point to their role in keeping the physical writers alive. I argue, further, that the authorial Nobodies of Aphra Behn and Delarivier Manley anticipated many of the characteristics of explicit, fictional Nobodies. Fictional characters developed partly out of the artful employment of female authorial personae in the works of early modern writers. I also argue that once fiction became explicit and Nobody's characteristics could be fully developed, new possibilities of disembodiment appeared for the author as well.

～

Some of these possibilities resemble those that have already been described by critics working on the connections between literature and the history of sexuality, especially Nancy Armstrong and Jane Spencer.[9] These critics stress that the new cultural power of women, beginning in the mid-eighteenth century, was part of the consolidation of middle-class hegemony. Although women writers gained acceptance and prestige, becoming the spokeswomen for cultural change, these critics argue that they did so only by constructing a discourse that "reformed" women by locking them into a disciplinary domestic sphere. Armstrong and Spencer identify a discursive break prior to the 1740s: on the "before" side is the aristocratic model of woman, political, embodied, superficial, and amoral; on the "after" side is the middle-class model, domestic, disembodied, equipped with a deep interiority and an ethical subjectivity.

This study, however, argues that different as the completed authorial personae of the pre- and post-1740 authors may be, their components are surprisingly similar. The "nothingness" of Aphra Behn's author-whore has a great deal in common with the "Nobody" of the moralistic novelists. Authors on both sides of the mid-century revolution in sensibility, in quite dissimilar social and economic conditions and across a range of discourses, portrayed themselves as dispossessed, in debt, and on the brink of disembodiment. How can we explain the continuities, as well as the historical ruptures, in the rhetoric of female authorship?

First, the recurrent features of these authorial profiles might easily be seen as manifestations of the persistent imbalance of power, especially economic power, between the sexes. Indeed, some people might simply attribute these features to the persistence of patriarchy. For example, all the women in this study combine their rhetoric of authorship with one of dispossession. The combination takes different forms and answers to different exigencies in each career, but the presentation of authorship as the effect of the writer's inability to *own* the text remains constant and is explicitly linked to the author's gender.

My concentration on gender in this study attests to the weight I give the persistence of patriarchal assumptions. But even if that persistence, which ensured the secondary status of women and their economic powerlessness, explains the writers' experience of

---

9. See Armstrong, *Desire and Domestic Fiction;* and Spencer, *The Rise of the Woman Novelist: From Aphra Behn to Jane Austen* (Oxford: Basil Blackwell, 1986).

dispossession, it does not explain the cultural desire to have that experience articulated. Indeed, it cannot account for the appearance of female authorship in the first place. Nor can the remnants of patriarchy be used to explain the universality of the theme of dispossession in the rhetoric of authorship generally; male authors also frequently stressed that their work and their authorial personae could circulate only because they had sold them. In comic, pathetic, heroic, and even tragic forms, authors of both sexes called attention to their existence in and through their commodification and their inseparability from it. The rhetoric of female authorship differs, in this regard, from that of authorship in general by exaggerating and sexualizing the common theme.

The very commonness of the theme, though, might lead one to conclude that its recurrence is due to the continuities of capitalist commodification. This study will partly justify such a conclusion, but in a form so heavily qualified and transposed that the adjective "capitalist" might seem unrecognizable. First, we must take into account the ways in which the economics of eighteenth-century authorship depart from capitalist models. Despite the (slow) growth of the market, for example, authors were dependent on patronage until the end of the century, although the forms of patronage continually changed. Most authors, moreover, neither alienated their labor by writing, for a fixed wage, whatever the bookseller ordered nor played the role of the independent producer, going to market with a secure possession; that is, the classic models of industrial and artisanal production do not apply.

Moreover, if we look closely at these authors' rhetoric of alienation, we see that it contradicts the classic Marxist formulation of the capitalist appropriation of surplus value. Instead of assuming the labor theory of value on which the Marxist understanding rests, their rhetoric stresses that value is an effect of exchange, not production. As authors, they imply, they themselves are effects of exchange. They do not present their texts as places where they have stored themselves, nor do they portray their authorship as an originary activity of creation. Hence the rhetoric of "dispossession" in their texts is sometimes ecstatic (as in Aphra Behn's preface to *Oroonoko*) and often comic. Even when their tone is more mournful, in the second half of the century, they seem fascinated by the paradox that the copyright, their former "property," was no property at all but a mere ghostly possibility. They seem to revel in the mystery of having sold something (the right to publish a work) that was only technically theirs (since they did not have the means of publication).

Indeed, these authors commonly figured their labor as the accumulation of credit rather than the production of property. And this idea, especially in the last half of the century, led to another difficulty: if one lived on credit, then one was in debt. The consequences of this reasoning are most fully explored in the last two chapters of the book, which discuss the careers of Frances Burney and Maria Edgeworth. Both authors stressed the superfluity of their fictional representations and indicated that the more credit they gained by writing them, the more they owed their public. They both, moreover, linked this escalating sense of the author-self's indebtedness to the pressure of a seemingly unpayable daughterly obligation to their fathers. In this layering of literary, patriarchal, and economic exigencies, the idea of debt began to dominate their authorial representations.

The predominance of debt in the rhetoric of authorship, a predominance that increased in women's texts as the century went on, reminds us that England in the eighteenth century was a society living on debt, and not on the production of consumer commodities. It should also remind us, though, that texts are odd commodities, because they compound the paradoxes of the commodity form. In the rich description Marx gives of that form in the first chapter of *Capital*, he notes that a commodity is normally composed of a material substance and what appears to be an abstract, immaterial value (an exchange value). In that form of mystification he calls "commodity fetishism," the origin of the exchange value in human labor is forgotten, and that value comes to seem the dominant "essence" of the thing in the marketplace. Both the potential use value of the thing and the human relations of production and exchange are then obscured by the dominance of the exchange value. *Capital* is an attempt to demystify the commodity, to unveil the origin of the exchange value in labor, to explain how that origin is warped by the appropriation of surplus value in production, and hence to demonstrate that the abstract, immaterial essence of the commodity is really a material social relationship after all. Marx, although his answer to the question of how commodities are assigned abstract values in the marketplace differs from that developed by the classical political economists, certainly follows their lead in concentrating on labor and thereby stressing the ultimate materiality of exchange value.

One need not agree with Marx's solution to the puzzle of commodities, one need not even think of commodities as a problem that requires a solution, to be struck by the power of his description of the form, especially the commodity's wavering between materiality and ideality. As long as it is in the marketplace—that is, as long as it is a commodity—the item's materiality is constantly on the brink of disappearing, being replaced and represented by a mere notation of value, such as money. That is, in the marketplace as Marx and the political economists tended to conceive of it, the commodity had to have a material form, but that was not what really mattered about it at the moment of exchange.

With the exception of Maria Edgeworth, the authors studied in this book neither adhered to nor anticipated the political economists' or Karl Marx's productivist explanations of how commodities become fungible; nevertheless, the process of disembodiment in the marketplace is a recurrent theme in their work and an important element in their construction of authorship. Their treatment of it often shows the overlap between the wavering immaterial materiality of commodities in general and that of texts. Like the commodity, the text must take a material form, yet the text's "materiality," even more than the commodity's, is only tenuously connected to its value, either its exchange value qua text (an entity different from a book, which is only an instance of a text) or its more elusive "literary" value. If we can speak of the "use value" of a text, moreover, we certainly cannot equate that with the paper, print, binding, and so forth, that make up the books. The text, in other words, multiplies the loci of the split between matter and value, and at each locus materiality slips away or is translated into ideas and yet persists.

The recurrence of dematerialization and rematerialization, like that of dispossession and debt, might be attributed, then, to something that seems more abstract than either patriarchy or the marketplace: textuality itself. Some might say that the texts in this study, simply because they are texts, frequently canvass the ways materiality ceases to matter but is nevertheless indispensable. Texts are not only strange commodities but also strange entities that can never be neatly divided between matter and idea. The textual "signifier," the sound or graphic form conventionally attached to a particular idea to create a word, cannot be naively regarded as matter. Rather, it is what spoils the distinction between things and ideas, the material and the ideational.

Several of the women authors in this study repeatedly identify not only their texts but also their authorship with the vacillating materiality of the signifier. They make this identification more frequently, emphatically, and affirmatively than do their male counterparts. Hence, they seem to offer some empirical grounds for those deconstructive-feminist theories that, by privileging the signifier, explore the similarities between textuality and femininity.[10] I have drawn extensively on these ideas and have simultaneously emphasized their historical contingency.

That the most popular women writers in this period openly link their authorship to the flickering ontological effect of signification suggests that the linking is a strategy for capitalizing on their femaleness. The overlapping of femininity and the signifier, like many other ways of coupling women and writing, proved profitable. I invite the reader to enjoy these constructions, savor their ironies, analyze their mechanisms, and discern their complex exigencies; I do not recommend *believing* in them as universal truths. "Caveat emptor" is the motto of this study.

10. The many influential books of feminist deconstructionists include Barbara Johnson, *A World of Difference* (Baltimore, MD: Johns Hopkins Univ. Press, 1987); Mary Jacobus, *Reading Woman: Essays in Feminist Criticism* (New York: Columbia Univ. Press, 1986); and Peggy Kamuf, *Signature Pieces: On the Institution of Authorship* (Ithaca, NY: Cornell Univ. Press, 1988).

1

Who Was That Masked Woman?

The Prostitute and the Playwright
in the Works of Aphra Behn

Musing in 1821 on the vagaries of literary fashion, Walter Scott tells a story about his great aunt, who at the age of eighty wanted to reread a work of Aphra Behn's that she remembered finding delightful in her youth.

> One day she asked me, when we happened to be alone together, whether I had ever seen Mrs. Behn's novels—I confessed the charge.—Whether I could get her a sight of them?—I said, with some hesitation, I believed I could; but that I did not think she would like either the manners, or the language, which approached too near that of Charles II's time to be quite proper reading.

But the "good old lady" insisted.

> So I sent Mrs. Aphra Behn, curiously sealed up, with "private and confidential" on the packet, to my gay old grand-aunt. The next time I saw her afterwards, she gave me back Aphra, properly wrapped up, with nearly these words: "Take back your bonny Mrs. Behn; and, if you will take my advice, put her in the fire, for I found it impossible to get through the very first novel. But is it not," she said, "a very odd thing that I, an old woman of eighty and upwards, sitting alone, feel myself ashamed to read a book which, sixty years ago, I have heard read aloud for the amusement of large circles, consisting of the first and most creditable society in London?"[1]

Behn's book occasions the old woman's astonishment at her younger self and the society that bred her; her question reverberates with the shock of personal and cultural discontinuity, suddenly perceived. We can easily imagine her fragile sense of identity as

1. From a letter to Lady Louisa Stuart quoted in John Gibson Lockhart, *Memoirs of the Life of Sir Walter Scott*, rpt. in 5 vols. (New York, 1910), vol. 3, pp. 596–97.

she recalls herself publicly applauding what any proper lady, by the standards of the late eighteenth century, should instinctively have recognized as depraved. Such a "change of taste," Scott explains in his commentary on this story, "takes place insensibly without the parties being aware of it." The cultural revolution that Scott's great aunt "insensibly" lived is registered only retrospectively, as a deeply private, self-revelatory sense of shame. The story itself, by giving us three moments in the "life" of Aphra Behn's book, plots the development of this shamed self-consciousness as a shift from the public to the private consumption and eventual suppression of certain kinds of literature. His great aunt remembers public readings, probably in the 1730s,[2] whereas Scott himself, born in 1760, was no doubt introduced to Behn as a semipornographic writer whose works, though still in circulation, needed to be labeled "private and confidential" and had to be "curiously sealed" (a phrase that nicely catches the stimulating effect of the book's slide into contraband). Finally, the old lady returns the book, this time truly under wraps ("properly wrapped"), and advises that it circulate no more. Her uncanny private experience leads to the resolve that this book never be shared, that the intense sense of shame, which she recognizes as inappropriate to her privacy, remain utterly her own.[3]

For Scott himself the incident seems not to have such complex personal resonances. He recounts it mainly as an instance of the secret, "insensible" nature of any "change of taste." In most cases, Scott explains, such changes are arbitrary, mere matters of fashion, unpredictable and unaccountable; in the specific case of Aphra Behn, the change reflects progress. The increasingly private and shamefaced reading of Behn represents for Scott "the gradual improvement of the national taste and delicacy." Nevertheless, he concludes enigmatically, "The change that brings into and throws out of fashion particular styles of composition, is something of the same kind." The instability of Behn's reputation, its peculiar vulnerability to fluctuations in the social mores governing sexual propriety, shows the close link between feminine works and

2. Behn's *Love-Letters between a Nobleman and His Sister*, for example, was issued in book form in 1735.

3. On the categorization of Behn's work as pornographic, see Naomi Jacobs, "The Seduction of Aphra Behn," *Women's Studies* 18 (1991): 395–403.

ephemeral ones. It is not surprising, then, that Scott's tone in telling the story of his great aunt's embarrassment is one of detached amusement.

Walter Scott and his great aunt were not the last commentators to reflect on the phenomenon of Aphra Behn in just these ways. Her works have been objects of both outrage and urbane antiquarian curiosity, and we are still pondering the mystery and significance of her career. If her success later seemed inexplicable to Walter Scott's great aunt, who actually experienced it, how much more mysterious must it seem to us, who must reconcile it with both the disappearance of her works from the canon and our belief in a strong prejudice against women writers in the seventeenth century. Hence, we still marvel at her incredible early acclaim; it strains our historical imagination and our sense of cultural continuity to realize that, after Dryden, Behn was the most prolific and probably the most popular writer of her time, with at least eighteen plays, several volumes of poetry, and numerous works of fiction that were in vogue for decades after her death. She was second only to Dryden also in the number of her plays (four) that were produced at court.[4] Moreover, the other Restoration playwrights to whom we might compare her, the men whose works were regularly produced by one of the two playhouses, had advantages of education and family that Behn lacked. According to her biographer Maureen Duffy, "Most were of the gentry or nobility, and almost all had university or Inns of Court education."[5] In contrast, Aphra Behn's origins are obscure, and we are hard-pressed to explain how such a sociological anomaly achieved such cultural prominence.[6]

4. Fidelis Morgan, ed., *The Female Wits: Women Playwrights of the Restoration* (London: Virago, 1981), p. 12. For a brief comparison of the careers of Dryden and Behn, see Deborah C. Payne, "'And Poets Shall by Patron-Princes Live': Aphra Behn and Patronage," in *Curtain Calls: British and American Women and the Theater, 1660–1820,* ed. Mary Anne Schofield and Cecilia Macheski (Athens: Ohio Univ. Press, 1991), p. 107.

5. *The Passionate Shepherdess: Aphra Behn, 1640–1689* (London: Cape, 1977), p. 104.

6. There are competing early accounts of Behn's birth and social status. Her two most recent biographers draw very different conclusions from the evidence. Assuming that her maiden name was Johnson and that she was born around 1640 in Kent, Maureen Duffy thinks she was the daughter of Bartholomew Johnson, yeoman, and Elizabeth, née Denham, daughter of a "gentleman." Angeline Goreau makes the same initial assumptions but suggests that Behn was the illegitimate daughter of Lady Willoughby, whose husband was founder and governor of the English

If Scott's story only increases our wonder at Behn's success by assuring us that even one who had experienced it could not make sense of it half a century later, his letter nevertheless wraps the odd facts in a more familiar narrative. By linking Behn's decline to "improvements" in "delicacy," Scott gives us a succinct index of the pace of cultural change in the mid-eighteenth century and suggests the impact of that change on standards of decency for women writers in particular. Indeed, stories like Scott's have made Behn into a symbol for those vicissitudes of female literary reputation that are caused by changes in ideas of sexual propriety. Many students who cannot name a single work by Aphra Behn are quick to identify her as the excessively risqué "first Englishwoman to earn her living by her pen." No other author has the very fact of her initial market success so prominently in the forefront of her reputation that it often obscures everything else about her works. Everything, that is, except the infamous "bawdiness" that accounts, it seems, for both their contemporary success and their unacceptability to readers in the prudish centuries that followed. The history of Behn's reception, in short, is better known than her works, and it would be no exaggeration to say that she has become *the* figure for the volatility of the marketplace in women's literature.[7]

colony of Surinam. See *Reconstructing Aphra: A Social Biography of Aphra Behn* (New York: Dial, 1980), p. 13. This account would explain Behn's superior education and her trip to that colony. Both versions of her birth are highly speculative, and we simply do not know how she received her education or her introduction to literary and theatrical circles. Sara Heller Mendelson places her date of birth in the late 1640s; see *The Mental World of Stuart Women: Three Studies* (Brighton: Harvester, 1967), pp. 116–17. Earlier biographies of Behn include George Woodcock, *The Incomparable Aphra* (1948; rpt. as *The English Sappho* [Montreal: Black Rose, 1989]); and Frederick M. Link, *Aphra Behn* (New York: Twayne, 1968).

7. For a concise overview of Behn's career, see Janet Todd's introduction to *The Works of Aphra Behn*, ed. Todd, vol. 1 (Columbus: Ohio State Univ. Press, 1992), pp. ix–xxxv. Mary Ann O'Donnell surveys Behn's career and includes a selection of her work in "Tory Wit and Unconventional Woman: Aphra Behn," in *Women Writers of the Seventeenth Century*, ed. Katharina M. Wilson and Frank J. Warnke (Athens: Univ. of Georgia Press, 1989), pp. 349–72. For a variety of recent critical approaches to Behn's writing, see Ros Ballaster, *Seductive Forms: Women's Amatory Fiction, 1684–1740* (Oxford: Clarendon Press, 1992), pp. 69–113; Bernard Duyfhuizen, "'That Which I Dare Not Name': Aphra Behn's 'The Willing Mistress,'" *ELH* 58 (1991): 63–82; Judith Kegan Gardiner, "The First English Novel: Aphra Behn's *Love Letters*, the Canon, and Women's Tastes," *Tulsa Studies in Women's Literature* 8 (1989): 201–22; Dorothy Mermin, "Women Becoming Poets: Katherine Philips, Aphra Behn, Anne Finch," *ELH* 57 (1990): 335–55; Jacqueline Pearson, "Gender and Narrative in the Fiction of Aphra Behn," parts 1 and 2, *Review of English Studies* 42 (1991): 40–56 and 179–90; Jane Spencer, *The Rise of the Woman Novelist: From Aphra Behn to Jane Austen*

Aphra Behn herself initiated this emphasis on her struggles in the marketplace. In the very midst of her success she complained about a double standard in judging plays. For example, an oft quoted passage from the epistle to *Sir Patient Fancy* (1678) claims she had been censured for using language that any male playwright might use with impunity.[8] Following Behn's lead, and citing numerous contemporary attacks on both her character and works, her biographers have concluded that Behn's popularity was gained despite a heavy handicap imposed by her sex.[9]

However, the double standard Behn complains of did not seem to discourage attendance at her plays, nor is there much evidence that it forced her to change her style or to leave off writing plays in order to take up the less "public" genre of romance. There is a gap in her production of new plays between 1682 and 1685 during which she seems to have written a great many tales, but when she opened a new play in 1686, *The Lucky Chance*, it turned out to be as full of cuckolding and witty double entendre as anything she ever wrote. Behn was rewarded for this play with both a successful run and a predictable return of criticism, which she immediately used

---

(Oxford: Basil Blackwell, 1986), pp. 42–52; Dale Spender, *Mothers of the Novel: 100 Good Women Writers before Jane Austen* (London: Pandora, 1986), pp. 47–66; George Starr, "Aphra Behn and the Genealogy of the Man of Feeling," *Modern Philology* 87 (1990): 362–72; Janet Todd, *The Sign of Angellica: Women, Writing and Fiction, 1660–1800* (London: Virago, 1989), pp. 69–83; Donald R. Wehrs, "Eros, Ethics, Identity: Royalist Feminism and the Politics of Identity in Aphra Behn's *Love Letters*," *Studies in English Literature, 1500–1900* 32 (1992): 461–78; and the anthologies *Curtain Calls*, esp. essays by Frances Kavenik, Jessica Munns, Deborah C. Payne, and Rose Zimbardo; and *Fetter'd or Free? British Women Novelists, 1670–1815*, ed. Mary Anne Schofield and Cecilia Macheski (Athens: Ohio Univ. Press, 1986), esp. essays by Jerry C. Beasley and Robert Adams Day. For a detailed bibliography of scholarship on Behn, see Mary Ann O'Donnell, *Aphra Behn: An Annotated Bibliography of Primary and Secondary Sources* (New York: Garland, 1986).

8. "I printed this play with all the impatient haste one ought to do, who would be vindicated from the most unjust and silly aspersion . . . ; *That it was Bawdy*, the least and most excusable fault in the men writers to whose plays they all crowd, as if they came to no other end than to hear what they condemn in this." To accept this complaint at face value, as Goreau does on pp. 233–34, one must ignore other evidence. First, in 1678 Behn was not singled out for chastisement because she was a woman; other playwrights were as heavily criticized that year. See Arthur H. Scouten and Robert D. Hume, "Restoration Comedy and Its Audiences, 1660–1776," in *The Rakish Stage: Studies in English Drama, 1660–1800*, ed. Robert D. Hume (Carbondale: Southern Illinois Univ. Press, 1983), pp. 56–64. Second, in concentrating on Behn's complaint about her play's reception, we overlook both its good run and its remaining in the repertory until 1692.

9. See especially Goreau's chapter 11, "Success and Attack," pp. 207–35.

as the occasion for her finest self-defense, a fiery, defiant "epistle to the reader." Granted, the last play produced during her lifetime, her commedia dell'arte farce *The Emperor of the Moon*, might have been taken as evidence of moral reformation; it offended no one. The bawdy, satirical Behn, though, was resurrected in the posthumous production of *The Widow Ranter*; this play, however, received a relatively lukewarm reception because, a contemporary commentator suggested, "our Author" was dead and unable to supervise or cast the production.[10]

Even in the next century, although there was certainly a gradual insistence on sexual propriety in the theater, it developed slowly and applied to male as well as female playwrights. As Scott's great aunt testifies, Behn was a highly respected author until the middle of the eighteenth century, and her plays received the same posthumous treatment as her "nouvelles." Curiously, throughout the first half of the eighteenth century audiences seem to have accepted in old plays what they condemned in new ones. Hence, *The Rover*, certainly one of Behn's bawdiest plays, was a staple of the repertory until the 1760s. *The London Stage* records productions for almost every year between 1703 and 1743, when the productions began tapering off over two decades before disappearing altogether.[11] But the same pattern applies to a "classic" like Ben Jonson's *Epicoene*. Apparently, when standards of propriety became stricter, old plays were at first exempt and were then condemned in a heap, without distinguishing between Jacobean and Restoration, male and female authors.[12]

Since the evidence does not support the contention that Behn's

10. The dedication to the 1690 edition of the play complains that "the Play had not that Success which it deserv'd. . . . The main fault ought to lye on those who had the management of it. Had our Author been alive she would have Committed it to the Flames rather than suffer'd it to have been Acted with such Omissions as was made. . . . And Lastly, many of the Parts being false Cast, and given to those whose Tallants and Genius's Suited not our Authors Intention." *The Works of Aphra Behn*, ed. Montague Summers (London, 1915), vol. 4, pp. 221–22. Unless otherwise noted, subsequent quotations form Behn's works are from this edition, hereafter cited as *Works*.

11. *Index to the London Stage, 1660–1800*, ed. William Van Lennep, Emmett L. Avery, Arthur H. Scouten, George Winchester Stone, Jr., and Charles Beecher Hogan, compiled by Ben Ross Schneider, Jr. (Carbondale: Southern Illinois Univ. Press, 1979), p. 61.

12. See Scouten and Hume, "Restoration Comedy and Its Audiences, 1660–1776," pp. 64–81.

career was hindered by general prejudices against either women playwrights or bawdy women playwrights, one might justifiably suspect that the author's complaints and her adversaries' insults were pieces of an elaborate rhetorical interaction that dictated the very terms in which she was conceived. As we will shortly see, Behn's prologues and prefaces were often artfully constructed in a rhetorical tradition that required her defamation. This is not to say that the defamation never took place, that it was a mere trope; it is only to say that Behn depended and capitalized on it. She especially depended on getting a barrage of abuse from wits of a rival political stripe, for, as we will see in Chapter 2, such harassment vouched for her effectiveness as a Tory writer. For the most part, men of her own party supported Behn staunchly, and if we simply count contemporary male judgments of her in print, we find that instances of praise outnumber those of blame by at least ten to one.[13] To understand this first female authorial success, we must enumerate the many cultural desires she satisfied.

I will be arguing that Behn's career was both enabled and shaped by a certain conjunction of Restoration theatrical, rhetorical, sexual, political, and economic exigencies. Laments about the obnoxious material necessities of one's career or the utter prostitution of one's rivals' careers were the normal language of the Restoration author's self-representations. These, in turn, can best be understood as instances of complicated arguments about the relationship between property and selfhood. Behn often feminized these concerns and created a novel authorial identity in doing so, but she was no more *impeded* by them than was Dryden or Wycherley. They formed the discourse that called her authorship into being and made her the great success she was.

In examining Behn's use of her gender to present herself as an author in the marketplace, we will encounter a set of Restoration paradoxes pertaining to authorship and self-ownership generally. These paradoxes are not unique in Behn's self-representations, but her gender gave them unusual depth and resonance. This chapter concerns itself primarily with the theatrical representation of the author; it shows why and how she staged her simultaneous pres-

13. For an itemized list of contemporary references (1677–1700), see O'Donnell, *Aphra Behn: An Annotated Bibliography of Primary and Secondary Sources*, pp. 327–43.

ence and absence in the theater, audaciously using the metaphor of the author as prostitute to create distinctions between the obliging playwright and the withholding private person, the woman's body and her self, the stage and real life. She fabricated the impression of a continuous but mysterious authorial identity—never actually embodied on the stage but persisting and transforming itself from play to play—and aligned this idea of authorship with the "no thing" of female sex. The next chapter considers the representation of the author in print; it probes the mystique of a bodiless medium that holds out promises of sovereignty and anonymity in the midst of commodification. Behn typically encapsulates these themes in the figure of the author-monarch, and hence her romance of the sovereign in the marketplace, *Oroonoko*, is interpreted here as an absolutist fantasy of disembodiment through representation and exchange.

Together the chapters contend that Behn created a complex authorial identity by drawing on seemingly irreconcilable metaphors—the author as prostitute and the author as monarch—that, despite their apparent incompatibility, lead into surprisingly similar explorations of the anomalies of Restoration authorship. Each metaphor rendered that authorship problematic in a different way, but from both Behn emerges as the heroine-victim of the marketplace, utterly sold yet pristinely unsoiled because able to separate herself from her physical being. This paradoxical effect, I will argue, is her ultimate and most compelling achievement as well as her most enduring commodity.[14]

~

We have little documentary evidence about the financial details of Aphra Behn's career. Indeed, it is difficult to locate and describe something we might feel justified in calling a literary marketplace in the late seventeenth century. "Literary marketplace" implies the existence of a mass of buyers of printed works large enough both to offset the costs of producing the books (including the cost of

14. For different interpretations of Behn's self-presentation as commodity, see Elin Diamond, "*Gestus* and Signature in Aphra Behn's *The Rover*," *ELH* 56 (1989): 519–41; and Todd, *The Sign of Angellica*, pp. 69–83.

paying the author) and to return a profit to the bookseller. But the high cost of printing in the late seventeenth century and the relatively small reading public meant that book publishing was not yet an industry based on this sort of market. The costs of publication were still often met by private persons, and profits on sales went to the bookseller. Many authors, then, were still paid by wealthy individuals, and most were not paid at all. The financial innovation during this period was the growth of subscription publication, a form of collective patronage that is sometimes seen as a step toward an actual literary marketplace, but individual patronage also persisted.[15] Aphra Behn's generation is said to be the first in which the "professional writer" appeared, but we should not conclude from that commonplace that authors had suddenly been freed from patronage and were relying on the favor of some anonymous "public."[16]

Behn does not seem to have taken advantage of subscription publication, and although she published many volumes, she could not have supported herself on her income from books. The minimum standard rate for a play manuscript was only £10,[17] so even in her most prolific play-writing year, 1682, she might not have made more than £30 from the publication of her plays. In 1684 we

15. For an assessment of the evidence that Behn might have had income from patrons in the 1680s, see Payne, "'And Poets Shall by Patron-Princes Live': Aphra Behn and Patronage," in *Curtain Calls*, pp. 105–19.

16. Relevant accounts of the London book trade in this period include Terry Belanger, "Publishers and Writers in Eighteenth-Century England," in *Books and Their Readers in Eighteenth-Century England*, ed. Isabel Rivers (New York: St. Martin's Press, 1982), pp. 1–25; John Feather, "British Publishing in the Eighteenth Century: A Preliminary Subject Analysis," *Library* 8 (1986): 32–46; Frank Arthur Mumby, *Publishing and Bookselling* (London: Cape, 1930); Marjorie Plant, *The English Book Trade: An Economic History of the Making and Sale of Books* (London: Allen and Unwin, 1965); Graham Pollard, "The English Market for Printed Books," *Publishing History* 4 (1978): 7–48; William Roberts, *The Earlier History of English Bookselling* (1889; rpt. Detroit: Gale, 1967), chapter 4; Kathleen M. Lynch, *Jacob Tonson: Kit-Cat Publisher* (Knoxville: Univ. of Tennessee Press, 1971); and Shirley Strum Kenny, "The Publication of Plays," in *The London Theatre World, 1660–1800*, ed. Robert D. Hume (Carbondale: Southern Illinois Univ. Press, 1980), pp. 309–36.

17. John Wilson Bowyer claims that this was the normal rate for a play (*The Celebrated Mrs. Centlivre* [Durham, NC: Duke Univ. Press, 1952], p. 98), but Maureen Duffy, assuming that Behn was paid as much or more for plays as for volumes of poetry, estimates £20–30 (*The Passionate Shepherdess*, p. 204). Duffy, though, is making guesses on the basis of Behn's arrangements with Jacob Tonson; the booksellers for most of her plays dealt in far cheaper wares. See Payne, "'And Poets Shall by Patron-Princes Live': Aphra Behn and Patronage," pp. 108–09.

find her writing to her publisher Tonson to ask for a £5 increase in her payment for a volume of poems. If we estimate that she earned between £20 and £30 for each volume of poetry and prose, her peak earning year for printed matter would probably have been 1685, when she might have made £90, but for many years she would have had no income at all.

When we speak of Behn making her living by her pen, then, we do not mean she made a living primarily from having books published. Like most of the age's "professional writers"—by which most historians seem to mean people who had no means of livelihood other than writing—Behn was a playwright partly because the structure and financing of drama allowed for the support of writers. The theater as an institution changed abruptly when, after a twenty-year hiatus, it was restored along with the monarchy. The changes made playwriting a more independent, lucrative, and chancy activity than it had been. Earlier playwrights had either been members of the theater companies that produced their scripts and therefore simply shared in the companies' profits, often while performing other tasks as well as writing, or, like Ben Jonson, were heavily reliant on aristocratic or royal patronage. In contrast, Restoration playwrights were paid the receipts (above the house charges) for the third day's performance of their plays.[18] Each playwright was generally attached to one of the two theater companies licensed to operate in London, though the writers tended not to be on salary or to own shares.[19] Behn's letter to Tonson claims that in the 1670s playwrights could borrow from the company, but apparently even this practice was discontinued in the 1680s.[20] Consequently, if a play was not popular enough to hold the stage for three days, the playwright got nothing; if it lasted until the "author's benefit" performance, the playwright's fee would be

18. If the play was very popular, a sixth-night benefit might also be added. For a history of the development of this mode of payment, see the introduction by Emmett L. Avery and Arthur H. Scouten to *The London Stage. Part I: 1660–1700*, ed. William Van Lennep (Carbondale: Southern Illinois Univ. Press, 1965), pp. lxxix–lxxxiv.

19. There were exceptions to this rule. Dryden and Settle, for example, were both sharers in the King's Company. See *The London Stage. Part I: 1660–1700*, p. lxxii.

20. "I have been without getting so long yt I am just on ye poynt of breaking, especially since a body has no creditt at ye playhouse for money as we usd to have, fifty or 60 deepe, or more," she wrote to Tonson in 1684. The letter is in the Folger Library now. It was printed in the *Gentleman's Magazine* 5 (1836): 481–82.

roughly proportionate to the play's reputation, based on its first and second nights' reception. The London theatergoing population was small enough for word-of-mouth reporting to spread rapidly through the potential audience. Hence, as numerous commentators have noted, Restoration playwrights were far more dependent financially on the success of individual plays than their Renaissance predecessors had been, with their share in the general profits of the company.

Playwriting had through this process also become a better differentiated activity, for which the writer seemed to receive money almost directly from a grateful audience. This "professionalization" produced a more personal relationship between playwright and audience than had previously existed. The author's benefit night provided an opportunity for rewarding or punishing playwrights quite specifically.[21]

The audience that gave or withheld this support was by no means a cross section of London's general population, but neither was it the tiny and homogeneous coterie that literary historians of a generation ago seem to have imagined. At the two licensed playhouses, the King's Company and the Duke's Company, both of which produced Aphra Behn's plays, audiences were arranged in four sections, according to a description of 1699.[22] There was an "upper gallery" where servants stood. Below that were boxes, "one peculiar to the King and Royal Family, and the rest for the Persons of Quality." Then there was the middle gallery, "where the Citizens Wives and Daughters, together with *Abigails*, Serving-men, Journey-men and Apprentices commonly take their Places, and now and then some disponding Mistresses and superannuated Poets." Finally, there was the pit, inhabited by "*Judges, Wits*, and *Censures* . . . in common with . . . the *Squires, Sharpers, Beaus, Bullies* and *Whores*, and here and there an extravagant *Male* and *Female Cit.*" It is estimated that with both theaters running, daily audiences would

---

21. The highest income recorded for a third night is Shadwell's £130 for *The Squire of Alsatia* in 1668. Perhaps we can estimate that Behn took in around £50 on successful benefit nights and also received handsome gifts from the nobles to whom she dedicated the printed books of the plays. See Duffy, p. 204, and the introduction to *The London Stage. Part I: 1660–1700*.

22. *The Country Gentlemen's Vade Mecum* is the source of the description that follows; it is quoted in Peter Holland, *The Ornament of Action: Text and Performance in Restoration Comedy* (Cambridge: Cambridge Univ. Press, 1979), p. 15.

have been between three and five hundred, although the capacity of the theaters was closer to one thousand. Peter Holland tells us these numbers indicate that theatergoers were "a substantial proportion of the wealthy," including aristocrats, gentlefolk, and comfortable bourgeois citizens, with a sprinkling of the lower classes among them.[23] Moreover, it appears to have been an audience full of habitual, rather than occasional, playgoers; Samuel Pepys's practice of attending the theater, indeed attending the same production, more than once a week was common. Holland claims that "any play that ran for more than four or five nights must have been playing to an audience many of whom were seeing it for the second or third time."[24] We might also conclude that a third-night audience for a very popular play must have contained many returnees.

The theater, then, does begin to look like a peculiarly intimate market for literary wares, "public" because anyone with the price of admission could attend, but by no means anonymous. The more one reads accounts of theatrical London in the 1670s and 1680s, the more one senses both the momentous theatricality and the personal immediacy of the exchange between playwright and "public." Dryden's epilogue to *Sir Martin Mar-all* captures these qualities exactly:

> But when the Curtain's down we peep, and see
> A Jury of the Wits who still stay late,
> And in their Club decree the poor Plays fate;
> Their verdict back is to the Boxes brought,
> Thence all the Town pronounces it their thought.[25]

That immediate judgment after the fall of the curtain, with the company lingering onstage to listen, could bring a full house on the third night, with many of the "wits" returning to reward the playwright. Behn's prologues also frequently remind the audience of its duty to the playwright in particular. The prologue to *Abdelazer*, for example, complains,

23. Holland, p. 17.
24. Holland, p. 17. On the Restoration audience, see also Harold Love, "Who Were the Restoration Audience?" *Yearbook of English Studies* 10 (1980): 21–44; and Robert D. Hume and Arthur H. Scouten, "'Restoration Comedy' and Its Audiences, 1660–1776," in *The Rakish Stage*, pp. 46–81.
25. *The Works of John Dryden* (Berkeley: Univ. of California Press, 1966), vol. 9, p. 209.

You come not sharp, as you are wont, to Plays;
But only on the first and second Days.[26]

By thus frequently recurring to the simultaneously public and personal nature of the exchange between author and audience, the playwrights staged versions of the mutual obligation between themselves and their public, several of which will be discussed in this chapter. All the versions, however, stressed that the audience was being asked to respond immediately, indeed to make its response a part of the theatrical event, and to be mindful of the playwright as a distinct individual.

This sense of personal mutual obligation played out in public was only increased by the many opportunities for patronage that lingered in the third-night system. Indeed, the very name of the event, the author's benefit (sometimes also referred to as the gift), reveals its association with patronage in the period. Moreover, the "benefit" was particularly linked to women, since the concept of allocating the profits of certain performances to specified groups or individuals originated as a way of bestowing a "gift" on "the women of the house," the actresses.[27] Hence the author's benefit had overtones of gallantry as well as patronage, and Behn, as we will see, reminded her audience of the former. Authors could also make use of individual patrons under the third-night system by selling them expensive seats. Occasionally a fashionable patron could announce that he or she would attend the play on the third night, and the theater would be filled with playgoers who actually had come to see the patron.[28] The system also allowed for adverse attention from the great: eminent individuals could loudly cry down a play and others would follow suit. Sometimes powerful cliques managed to disrupt and spoil performances so thoroughly that the plays failed.[29] In short, the relative social diversity of the

---

26. *Works*, vol. 2, p. 7.

27. See *The London Stage. Part I: 1660–1700*, p. lxxix, where Samuel Pepys's diary for September 28, 1668, is quoted: "Knepp's maid comes to me, to tell me that the women's day at the playhouse is to-day, and that therefore I must be there to increase their profit . . . the house, for the women's sake, mighty full."

28. *The London Stage. Part I: 1660–1700* gives several instances of this form of patronage. See pp. lxxxi–lxxxii.

29. The only example we have of successful factional opposition to a play by Behn concerns the revision of *The Younger Brother* staged in 1695 by Charles Gildon. Gildon complained that "I may reasonably impute its miscarriage to some Faction

Restoration audience did not mean that plays prospered or failed on the basis of an undifferentiated, impersonal "public" opinion.[30]

Words like "professionalization" and "marketplace," while not altogether inaccurate in this case, can therefore be rather misleading unless we understand the jointly theatrical and personal nature of the third night. Moreover, it is only as part of this specialized financial arrangement that we can fully appreciate Aphra Behn's construction of her various authorial personae. Like other Restoration playwrights, Behn presents herself as a person to whom something is owed individually; she tries to engender a relationship of mutual obligation that will bring in an audience on the third night. Also like her fellow playwrights, she insists on her struggle against the staleness of theatrical effect that might arise from the very continuity of personality she stresses. She presents herself as a playwright whose credit is based on a personal appeal, the appeal of the familiar author to whom the theatrical habitué is obliged, but who consequently must work to keep herself interesting, to dispel the boredom of familiarity. But unlike other Restoration playwrights, in constructing the first of her personae to be analyzed here, she uses explicitly and shockingly feminine tropes.

～

Conscious of her historical role, Aphra Behn introduced to the world of English letters the professional woman playwright as a newfangled whore. This persona has many functions in Behn's work: it titillates, scandalizes, arouses pity, and indicates the perils of public identity and the poignancy of authorship in general. The author-whore persona is the central figure in a dark comedy Behn played throughout her career, a comedy in which she exposes the bond between the liberty the stage offered women and their confinement behind both literal and metaphorical vizards. I will begin

---

that was made against it, which indeed was very Evident on the First day, and more on the endeavours employ'd, to render the Profits of the Third, as small as possible" (dedication to *The Younger Brother; or, the Amorous Jilt* [London, 1696], n.p.). Aphra Behn had been dead for six years by this time, so the faction must have been formed against Gildon, who would have had the third day's profits as the play's reviser.

30. Goreau, *Reconstructing Aphra*, discusses Restoration stage financing, pp. 122–23.

exploring the development of this persona in several short pieces: the epistles to *The Dutch Lover* (1673) and *Sir Patient Fancy* and the prologue to her first play, *The Forced Marriage* (1670). I will then describe the theatrical and larger cultural contexts informing the author-whore persona; and, finally, I will discuss one of her later plays, *The Lucky Chance*.

Introductory epistles to the printed plays, whether addressed to the general reader or a patron, created authorial effects very different from those produced by the plays' spoken prologues and epilogues. Normally appearing after the author's benefit night, the printed introductions cannot be seen as part of the immediate solicitation of the audience for support. Nevertheless, they were crucial to creating a sense of a "real" person behind the play and thus contribute importantly to the development of a long-term relationship between public and playwright, a sense of obligation that carried over from play to play. Behn's first such self-presentation, the epistle to *The Dutch Lover*, was continuous with the portrayals of the playwright in the early prologues and epilogues; this Aphra Behn, in a sustained tone of comic raillery, insists on her feminine seductiveness and the levity of her enterprise:

> Good, Sweet, Honey, Sugar-Candied Reader,
>   Which I think is more than anyone has called you yet, I must have a word or two with you before you advance into the Treatise; but 'tis not to beg your pardon for diverting you from your affairs, by such an idle Pamphlet as this is, for I presume you have not much to do and therefore are to be obliged to me for keeping you from worse employment.[31]

The comic feminine persona in this discourse is an adaptation of one that harks back at least to Chaucer's Wife of Bath; it is ribald, debunking, racy, digressive, and slightly madcap. Perhaps because it employs such obvious comic conventions and emphasizes its own inauthenticity, however, it proved less powerful than the rhetoric that emerged five years later, in the epistle to *Sir Patient Fancy*. This is the first of the epistles to be taken by commentators as an expression of Behn's actual sentiments. It is not a comic seduction but a complaint against what Behn presents as her ill-

---

31. *Works*, vol. 1, p. 221.

treatment at the hands of some female critics. She addresses her female readers here, claiming that the ladies should have been *particularly* forgiving of the play's bawdiness, for

> they ought to have had good Nature and justice enough to have attributed all its faults to the Authours unhappiness, who is forced to write for Bread and not ashamed to owne it, and consequently ought to write to please (if she can) an Age which has given severall proofs it was by this way of writing to be obliged, though it is a way too cheap for men of wit to pursue who write for Glory, and a way which even I despise as much below me.[32]

In addressing the ladies, Behn invokes the anomaly of her economic situation, its pathetic inappropriateness to an implied womanly norm. That very anomaly, however, is founded on the condition Behn shares with the ladies she addresses: a lack of independent property that obliges all women to earn their livelihood by pleasing men. Behn appeals to ladies for understanding because her very deviation from their pattern reveals a common female condition: she "ought . . . to please (if she can)." In the author's case, this shared condition enforces impropriety; it is only proper that she be improper, for what she "ownes" is only her lack of property. This is the unhappy situation of the prostitute, but Behn insists it is not a blamable one. Indeed, she describes it to prove her innocence; by selling bawdiness and then complaining of the necessity to do so, she assures her female readers that there is an innocent self above the exchange. Authorship for the marketplace and selfhood are here dissevered, for the author that can be inferred from the work is merely a "way of writing" dictated by the age, an alienable thing outside and beneath the true self. But it is precisely this severing, this inauthenticity, that is supposed to *oblige* the audience, to make them feel an obligation to the compromised author.

The effect of an authentic female self that Aphra Behn produces in such passages is based on the very need to sell her constructed authorial self. By making her authorial self an emanation of the marketplace, then, she saves this putative authentic self from

32. *Works*, vol. 4, p. 7.

contamination. The implied author of the plays is fashioned in the service of the male audience's fancy; but the implied author of the epistle claims to be Aphra Behn's unexchangeable, but also largely unrepresentable, self. Each of these authors is, in essence, an effect of the other, although the illusion created is that of the ontological priority of the woman who regrets her misrepresentations. All we know of this woman, however, are those misrepresentations, for in the case of the female author, as in the case of the prostitute, self-sale creates the illusion of an unknowable authenticity by never giving anything away, both in the sense of refusing to give free gratification and in the sense of refusing self-revelation. The epistle stresses that the professional woman author as prostitute is internally divided: what can be seen of her is never what she is, but the theatrical inauthenticity of what can be seen implies the existence of some hidden woman directing the drama of her self-sale.[33]

Behn was certainly not the only writer to create such a split persona. In the Restoration it seems to have been quite common to advertise that plays in general and comedies in particular were not the expression of the author's "true" self, but were instead a means of "obliging" the audience. Dryden, for example, although constantly thrusting the poet's skill into the consciousness of both auditors and readers of his plays, distinguishes between his personal taste and that which he adopts to please his audience. In his preface to *The Indian Emperour*, he declares,

> My chief endeavours are to delight the Age in which I live. If the humour of this, be for low Comedy, small Accidents, and Raillery, I will force my Genius to obey it, though with more reputation I could write in Verse. I know I am not so fitted by Nature to write Comedy: I want that gayety of humour which is required to it. My Conversation is slow and dull, my humour Saturnine and reserv'd: In short, I am none of those who endeavour to break Jests in Company, or make reparties, so that those who decry my Comedies do me no injury, except it be in point of profit.[34]

33. For a contrasting interpretation, one that offers a sanitized version of Behn's authorial personae in the prologues, epistles dedicatory, and epilogues, see Cheri Davis Langdell, "Aphra Behn and Sexual Politics: A Dramatist's Discourse with Her Audience," in *Drama, Sex and Politics*, ed. James Redmond (Cambridge: Cambridge Univ. Press, 1985), pp. 109–28.
34. *The Works of John Dryden*, vol. 9, pp. 7–8.

Here we have another wide gap between the obliging comedy writer and the self ("those who decry my Comedies do *me* no injury"), but the self is certainly not the elusive creature glimpsed only fleetingly in Behn's prologues. Instead, the numerous prologues and critical essays that introduce the first editions of Dryden's plays present the man behind his "profit" as a consistently serious-minded critic capable of passing negative judgments on his own plays but nevertheless condescending to please the audience. Dryden gives us his true mind at great length, and the wider the gap between that critical tone and the comic work, the more the audience feels itself indebted for the favor of having been humorously indulged by such a fiercely penetrating and learned man.

Dryden's rhetoric of authenticity, then, resembles Behn's in splitting the true poetic self from the comic playwright but differs from hers in actualizing and elevating his real, judgmental, self. Dryden is both known and known to be superior to his audience. "I made the Town my Judges," he declares in the preface to *The Wild Gallant*, and since his audience judges only by his fiat, he is not really imagined to be at their mercy. Rather, the very act that creates the gap between Dryden and the comic writer seems to be yet another instance of Dryden's superiority. The authentic Behn in the epistles to her early plays, on the other hand, breaks with her comic persona only momentarily to reveal the self-pity in every woman who must sell herself. Unlike Dryden, she is not above her audience; their obligation to her stems not from her condescension but from her regrettable feminine dependence on their approval.

The theme of the writer's self-alienation had already been made explicitly sexual in the spoken prologues to Behn's early plays, but in these the interaction between playwright and audience remained comically and excessively theatrical. Prologues and epilogues were not always written by the author of the play, but they were nevertheless often about the author. Unlike forewords and epistles to the printed plays that aimed at authenticity, prologues and epilogues often created the author as a merely theatrical persona; they pushed into the foreground the author who stages herself and discourses waggishly on the nature of her exchange with the audience. They were often directed very pointedly at the third night. The author's inventiveness in presenting new perspectives on this exchange, in dramatizing herself and the audience's obligation in new terms, was one of the skills deserving recompense.

Behn's femaleness gave her unique opportunities for self-presentation in her prologues and epilogues. The first prologue of her career incorporates standard conventions and carries them a step further by inviting the audience, through the metaphor of prostitution, to reflect on the self-alienation, and hence theatricality, of exchange in general. This prologue to *The Forced Marriage* (1670) is staged not only as a novel presentation of a playwright, but also as a *staged* novelty in which the author wittily allows her strategies to be laid bare so ostentatiously that the revelation of the strategy itself seems strategic. The prologue presents Aphra Behn's playwriting as an extension of her erotic play. In it, a male actor pretends to have temporarily escaped the control of the intriguing female playwright; he comes onstage to warn the gallants in the audience of their danger. This prologue added a sexual dimension to the Restoration convention of betraying the playwright: the comic antagonism between playwright and audience also becomes a battle in the war between the sexes. Playwriting, the actor warns, is a new weapon in woman's amorous arsenal. She will no longer wound only through the eyes, through her beauty, but will also use wit to gain a more permanent ascendancy.

> Women those charming victors, in whose eyes
> Lie all their arts, and their artilleries,
> Not being contented with the wounds they made,
> Would by new stratagems our lives invade.
> Beauty alone goes now at too cheap rates
> And therefore they, like wise and politic states,
> Court a new power that may the old supply,
> To *keep* as well as gain the victory:
> They'll join the force of wit to beauty now,
> And so *maintain* the right they have in you.

Here, woman's playwriting is wholly assimilated to the poetic conventions of amorous battle that normally informed lyric poetry. If the male poet had long depicted the conquering woman as necessarily chaste, debarring (and consequently debarred from) the act of sex itself, then his own poetry of lyric complaint and pleas for kindness could only be understood as attempts to overthrow the conqueror. Poetry in this lyric tradition is a weapon in a struggle that takes as its ground rule a woman's inability to conquer through sexual consummation: for the doing of the deed would be the undoing of her power.

Aphra Behn's first prologue stretches this lyric tradition to incorporate theater. Just as in lyric poetry, writing becomes part of a larger erotic contest. The woman's poetry, however, cannot have the same *end* as the man's. Indeed, according to the prologue, ends, in the sense of terminations, are precisely what a woman's wit is directed against. Writing is certainly on a continuum here with sex, but instead of leading to the act in which the woman's conquest is overturned, playwriting extends the woman's erotic power beyond the moment of sexual encounter. The prologue thus situates the drama inside the conventions of male lyric love poetry but then reverses the chronological relationship between sex and writing; the male poet writes before the sexual encounter, the woman between encounters. She thereby actually creates the possibility of a woman's version of sexual conquest. The woman now can have a "right" in the man that is not automatically self-canceling. She will not be immediately conquered and discarded because she will maintain her right through her writing. The woman's play of wit is the opposite of foreplay; it is a kind of afterplay specifically designed to resuscitate desire and keep a woman who has given herself sexually from being traded in for another woman. If the woman is successful in her poetic exchange, the actor warns the gallants, then they will no longer have the freedom of briskly exchanging mistresses:

> You'll never know the bliss of change; this art
> Retrieves (when beauty fades) the wandring heart.

Thus writing retroactively enables sex by ensuring its continuance, a point emphasized by the fusion of military and commercial metaphors. That is, war in the prologue is not a contest ending in a mere moment of conquest; rather, it resembles a battle for commercial advantage. Motivated in the first place by an unfavorable balance of trade ("Beauty alone goes now at too cheap rates"), it is designed not to destroy the enemy but to establish a monopoly, another sense of "right," on a growing number of sexual exchanges.

Aphra Behn, then, inaugurated her career by taking up the role of the seductive lyric poet. The drama the audience is about to see is framed by the larger drama of erotic exchange between a woman writer and a male audience. This prologue does what so many Restoration prologues do, makes of the play a drama within a drama, a series of conventional interactions inside another series of conventional interactions. But the very elaborateness of this staging, combined with the novelty of its metaphor, makes the love battle itself (the thing supposedly revealed) seem a strategic pose in a somewhat different drama. What kind of woman would stage her sexual desire as her primary motivation? The answer is a woman who might be suspected of not having any real affection, a woman for whom professions of amorousness and theatrical inauthenticity are the same thing: a prostitute.

Finally, just in case anyone in the audience might have missed this analogy, a dramatic interruption occurs, and the prologue becomes a debate about the motivation behind all this talk of strategy. The actor calls attention to the prostitutes in the audience, who were generally identified by their masks, and characterizes them as allies of the playwright, jokingly using their masks to expose them as spies in the amorous war:

> The poetess too, they say, has spies abroad,
> Which have dispers'd themselves in every road,
> I' th' upper box, pit, galleries; every face
> You find disguis'd in a black velvet case,
> My life on't; is her spy on purpose sent,
> To hold you in a wanton compliment;
> That so you may not censure what she's writ,
> Which done they face you down 'twas full of wit.

At this point, an actress comes onstage to refute the suggestion that the poetess's spies and supporters are prostitutes. Returning to the conceits linking money and warfare, her speech thus enacts the denial of prostitution that was all along implicit in the trope of amorous combat. She claims that the legion of the playwright's supporters, unlike prostitutes,

> scorns the petty spoils, and do prefer
> The glory not the interest of war.
> But yet our forces shall obliging prove,
> Imposing naught but constancy in love:
> That's all our aim, and when we have it too,
> We'll sacrifice it all to pleasure you.

What the last two lines make abundantly clear, in ironically justifying female promiscuity by the pleasure it gives to men, is that the prologue has given us the spectacle of a prostitute dramatically denying mercenary motivations.

The poetess, like the prostitute, is she who "stands out," as the etymology of the word "prostitute"[35] implies, but it is also she who is masked. Indeed, as the prologue emphasizes, the prostitute is she who stands out by virtue of her mask. The dramatic masking of the prostitute and the stagy masking of the playwright's interest in money are parallel cases of theatrical unmasking in which what is revealed is the parallel itself: the playwright is a whore.

When we put the spoken prologue to *The Forced Marriage* together with the printed epistle to *Sir Patient Fancy,* we notice that they both imply a woman hidden behind her own representations. In the prologue and the epistle the explanations for Aphra Behn's authorship are the two usual excuses for prostitution: addressing herself to the women, she claims the motive of want; addressing herself to the men, she claims the motive of love, but in a way that makes the claim seem merely strategic. The two motivations can be arranged into a narrative. Driven by financial necessity, the mistress pretends to take an amorous interest in her lover, to be desirous, like the lyric poet, simply of erotic intercourse. At the same time she might, as she implies in the epistle, despise the entire interaction. What all this amounts to is the dramatization of her lack of self-representation, which then implies that her true self is the sold self's seller. She thus implies the existence of an unseeable selfhood through the flamboyant alienation of her language.

~

Hence Aphra Behn managed to create the effect of a distinctively female integrity out of the very metaphor of prostitution. In doing so, she capitalized on a commonplace slur that probably kept many less ingenious women out of the theatrical and literary marketplaces. "Whore's the like reproachful name, as poetess—the luck-

35. From *pro,* meaning "before," and *statuere,* meaning "to set up or place." To prostitute is thus to set something, oneself perhaps, before someone else to offer it for sale.

less twins of shame," wrote Robert Gould in 1691.[36] The equation of poetess and "punk" (in the slang of the day) was inescapable in the Restoration. A woman writer could either deny it in the content and form of her publications, as did Katherine Philips, or she could embrace it, as did Aphra Behn. But she could not entirely avoid it. For the belief (Gould again) that

> Punk and Poesie agree so pat,
> You cannot well be *this*, and not be *that*

was held independent of particular cases. It rested on the evidence neither of how a woman lived nor of what she wrote. It was, rather, an a priori judgment applying to all cases of female public language. As Angeline Goreau, one of Aphra Behn's biographers, has pointed out, the seventeenth-century ear heard the word "public" in "publication" very distinctly, and hence a woman's publication automatically implied a public woman.[37] The woman who shared the contents of her mind instead of reserving them for one man was literally, not metaphorically, trading in her sexual property. If she was married, she was selling what did not belong to her, because in *mind and body* she should have given herself to her husband. In the seventeenth century, "publication," Goreau adds, also meant sale due to bankruptcy, and the publication of the contents of a woman's mind was tantamount to the publication of her husband's property. In 1613 Lady Elizabeth Cary, in a strikingly inconsistent act, published these lines on marital property rights, publication, and female integrity:

> Then she usurps upon another's right,
> That seeks to be by public language graced;
> And tho' her thoughts reflect with purest light

36. *Satirical Epistle to the Female Author of a Poem called "Sylvia's Revenge"* (London, 1691). The poem acknowledges that the lines paraphrase one of Rochester's poems, and the sentiment is a commonplace. The lines are also quoted by Goreau, p. 311.

37. This discussion is heavily indebted to Goreau, esp. pp. 144–62. Goreau and I cite much of the same evidence but draw very different conclusions. Goreau writes that Behn "savagely resented" the charge of immodesty and makes no references to the playwright's own sly uses of the author-whore metaphor. For a discussion of Behn's self-presentation that recognizes her use of this trope, see Duffy, *The Passionate Shepherdess*, esp. pp. 94–104. For more general discussions of the metaphor of prostitution in women's writing in the period, see Janet Todd, *The Sign of Angellica;* and Jacqueline Pearson, *The Prostituted Muse: Images of Women and Women Dramatists, 1642–1737* (New York: St. Martin's Press, 1988).

> Her mind, if not peculiar, is not chaste.
>   For in a wife it is no worse to find
>   A common body, than a common mind.[38]

Publication, adultery, and trading in one's husband's property could all be thought of as the same thing as long as the female self remained an indivisible unity. As Lady Cary explained, the idea of a public mind in a private body threatened to fragment female identity, to destroy its wholeness:

> When to their husbands they themselves do bind,
> Do they not wholly give themselves away?
> Or give they but their body, not their mind,
> Reserving that, tho' best, for other's prey?
>   No, sure, their thought no more can be their own
>   And therefore to none but one be known.

The unique unreserved giving of the woman's self to her husband is the act that keeps her whole. Only in this singular and total alienation does the female self maintain its complete self-identity.

It was precisely this ideal of an integrated woman, preserved because *wholly* given away, that Aphra Behn sacrificed to create a different idea of identity, one complexly dependent on the necessity of multiple exchanges. She who is able to repeat the action of self-alienation an unlimited number of times is she who is constantly there to regenerate, possess, and sell a series of provisional, constructed identities. Self-possession and self-alienation, then, are two sides of the same coin; the repeated alienation verifies the still maintained possession. In contrast, the wife who gives herself once and completely, and thus has no more property in which to trade, attains a whole inviolate selfhood by ceasing to possess herself. She can *be* herself because she has given up *having* herself. Further, as Lady Cary's lines make clear, if a woman's writing is an authentic extension of herself, then she cannot have alienable property in that without disintegrating.

Far from denying these assumptions, Aphra Behn's early au-

38. *The Tragedie of Mariam, the Faire Queene of Jewry* (London, 1613), lines 1237–48. These lines are spoken by the play's "chorus," and Barbara Kiefer Lewalski maintains that in Senecan dramas such as *Mariam*, the chorus's opinion is often not definitive: "[T]he chorus is expected to speak from a partial, not an authoritative, vantage point." See *Writing Women in Jacobean England* (Cambridge: Harvard Univ. Press, 1993), p. 198.

thorial persona and much of her comedy are based on them. Like her contemporaries, she presented her writing as part of her sexual property, not just because it was bawdy, but because it was hers. All her properties, like those of other women, were the *potential* property of another; she could either reserve them and give herself whole in marriage, or she could barter them piecemeal, accepting self-division to achieve self-ownership and forfeiting the possibility of marriage. In this sense, Aphra Behn's self-presentation fits into the most advanced seventeenth-century theories about the self: it closely resembles what C. B. Macpherson has called "possessive individualism,"[39] in which property in the self both entails and is entailed by the parceling out and serial alienation of the self. For in this theory property, by definition, is alienable. Aphra Behn's, however, is a gender-specific version of possessive individualism, one constructed in opposition to the very real alternative of keeping oneself whole by renouncing any claim in the self. Because the husband's right of property was in the whole of the wife, the prior alienation of any part of her had to be seen as a violation of either actual or potential marital propriety. As we will see in analyzing *The Lucky Chance*, Behn belabors this opposition between woman as inalienable and woman as alienable property in order to prepare for a comic collision of the two concepts. Nevertheless, their opposition was assumed in the period, and hence a woman who, like Aphra Behn, embraced possessive individualism, even if she was single and never bartered her sexual favors, could do so only with a consciousness that she thus contradicted the notion of female identity on which legitimate sexual property relations rested.

Publication, apart from the contents of what was published, ipso facto implied the divided, doubled, and ultimately unavailable self whose female prototype was the prostitute. By flaunting her self-sale, then, Aphra Behn embraced the title of whore; by writing bawdy plays that she then partly disclaimed, she capitalized on her

39. See C. B. Macpherson, *The Political Theory of Possessive Individualism: Hobbes to Locke* (Oxford: Clarendon Press, 1962). Although ultimately this chapter challenges Macpherson's characterization of the political implications of the theory of possessive individualism, his remains a useful description of the model of personhood that Behn develops in her writing. For a critique of Macpherson see J. G. A. Pocock, "Authority and Property: The Question of Liberal Origins," in *Virtue, Commerce, and History: Essays on Political Thought and History, Chiefly in the Eighteenth Century* (Cambridge: Cambridge Univ. Press, 1985), pp. 51–71.

supposed handicap. Finally, she even used this persona to make herself seem the prototypical writer, and in this effort she certainly seems to have had the cooperation of her male competitors. Thus, in the following poem, William Wycherley slyly acknowledges that the sexual innuendos about Aphra Behn rebound on the wits who make them. The occasion of the poem was a rumor that the poetess had gonorrhea. Wycherley emphasizes that the "Sappho of the Age" is more public than any normal prostitute, that her fame grows as she loses her fame, and that the rate of the author-whore is cheaper than that of her sister punk. But he also stresses how much more power the poetess has since in the world of wit, as opposed to the world of sexual exchange, use increases desire, and the author-whore accumulates men instead of being exchanged among them:

> More Fame you now (since talk'd of more) acquire,
> And as more Public, are more Mens Desire;
> Nay, you the more, that you are Clap'd to, now,
> Have more to like you, less to censure you;
> Now Men enjoy your Parts for Half a Crown,
> Which, for a Hundred Pound, they scarce had done,
> Before your Parts were, to the Public known.[40]

Appropriately, Wycherley ends by imaging the whole London theatrical world as a sweating house for venereal disease:

> Thus, as your Beauty did, your Wit does now,
> The Women's envy, Men's Diversion grow;
> Who, to be Clap'd, or Clap you, round you sit,
> And, tho' they Sweat for it, will crowd your Pit;
> Since lately you Lay-in, (but as they say,)
> Because, you had been Clap'd another Way;
> But, if 'tis true, that you have need to Sweat,
> Get, (if you can) at your New Play, a Seat.

If Aphra Behn's sexual and poetic parts are the same, then the wits are contaminated by her sexual distemper. Aphra Behn and her fellow wits infect each other: the theater is her body, the play is a case of gonorrhea, and the cure is the same as the disease.

Given the general delight of the Restoration in equating mental,

40. William Wycherley, *Miscellany Poems*, in *The Complete Works of William Wycherley*, ed. Montague Summers (London, 1924), vol. 3, pp. 155–56.

sexual, and theatrical "parts" and its frequent likening of writing to prostitution and playwrights to bawds, one might argue that if Aphra Behn had not existed, the male playwrights would have had to invent her in order to increase the witty pointedness of their cynical self-reflections. For example, in the prologue written to Behn's posthumously produced *Widow Ranter,* the actor chides the self-proclaimed wits for contesting the originality of one another's productions and squabbling over literary property. Drawing on the metaphor of literary paternity, he concludes:

> But when you see these Pictures, let none dare
> To own beyond a Limb or single share;
> For where the Punk is common, he's a Sot,
> Who needs will father what the Parish got.[41]

These lines would lose half their mordancy if the playwright were not Aphra Behn, the poetess-punk, whose offspring cannot seem fully her own but whose right to them cannot be successfully challenged, since her promiscuous literary intercourse would make disputes about fatherhood unresolvable. By literalizing and embracing the playwright-prostitute metaphor, therefore, Aphra Behn was distinguished from other authors, but only as their prototypical representative. She became almost an allegorical figure of authorship for the Restoration, the writer and the strumpet muse combined. Even those who wished to keep the relationship between women and authorship strictly metaphorical were fond of the image: "What a pox have the women to do with the muses?" asks a character in a play attributed to Charles Gildon. "I grant you the poets call the nine muses by the names of women, but why so? . . . because in that sex they're much fitter for prostitution."[42] Given the ubiquity of the metaphor, it seems almost inevitable that Behn should have obliged the age by "owning" it.

Aphra Behn, therefore, created a persona that skillfully intertwined the age's available discourses concerning women, property, selfhood, and authorship. She found advantageous openings where other women found repulsive insults; she turned self-divi-

---

41. *Works*, vol. 4, p. 224.
42. The lines are spoken by Critick, the comically negative wit in *A Comparison between the Two Stages* (London, 1702). The other characters in the play defend the writers under discussion, who are Mary Pix and Delarivier Manley.

sion into identity and impropriety into property. To understand her plays, we first have to understand these paradoxical relationships she helped construct between the female self and her written representations. However, we also have to remind ourselves once again that the primary nexus of exchange constituting these plays was not publication but theatrical production. Although these two phenomena were closely related in the period, they were not identical, and for a fuller view of the creation of Behn's authorial persona, we must return to the particularities of the Restoration stage, especially its staging of the female.

~

In thus shifting our perspective, we are not entirely turning away from the topos of prostitution. If the simple combination of female-ness and authorship implied prostitution, female authorship for the stage entailed it doubly. We need hardly rehearse here all the well-known associations between prostitution and the theater, from the Middle Ages, when women were explicitly barred from the stage in England to keep them from using it as a platform for solicitation, to the Restoration, when they appeared as professional actresses but were still often connected in the public mind with the prostitutes who had made the theater their haunt through all the centuries that denied women the boards.

If seventeenth-century texts about the theater often assume that actresses are actual or potential prostitutes, texts about prostitution are altogether certain that whores were essentially actresses or, more precisely, rhetoricians and actresses combined. The anonymous *Whores Rhetorick* (1683) stresses that the essence of prostitution is not exchanging sexual favors for money but dissimulating affection in words and actions. The old bawd in the first of the *Rhetorick*'s dialogues instructs the novice:

> Interest is the subject of this art; and what ever an insatiable avarice can either pretend to, or desire, may be included in the object thereof. Invention is principally necessary in this Art, to frame new pretexts, and a diversity of expression, with reference to the circumstances of person, time and place: and to impose probabilities, or even things utterly false, as certain, and true. A good memory is requisite to

avoid contradictions, and those inconveniences, the repetition of the same frauds and artifices would infallibly produce.[43]

The bawd continues through the divisions of oration, elocution, and the doctrine of tropes and figures ("only I omit the barbarous . . . names"). The whore's behavior, like her language, the bawd stresses, must be entirely illusionary: "[Y]ou must put on a seeming modesty, even when you exercise the most essential parts of your Profession: you must pretend a contempt of money, that your most amorous caresses are purely the effects of love; . . . your whole life must be one continued act of dissimulation." Prostitutes clustered around the theater because there they learned the romantic parts that played well with their "cullies" or gallants, according to John Dunton's *Night-Walker; or, Evening Rambles in Search after Lewd Women*, a series of pamphlets published in 1696–97. The clients themselves, in the following account of a theater-frequenting whore, seem in search of a dramatic, as much as a sexual, experience:

> I use to be attended with a fine Spark, who uses to ask me, How I lik'd the Play to Day, and then we pass our Censures upon every one's part, admiring such a one's sweet Voice, another's fine Meen and noble Deportment, the witty Replies of a third, the surprizing-ness of the Plot and the delicate Turns and great Thoughts in the Prologue and Epilogue, and after we had drank plentifully then my Gallant and I used to fancy our selves the Lovers represented in the Play, he would damn himself if I was not as amiable an Object in his sight as ever Cassandra was in the Eyes of her Orondates, or Cleopatra in the Esteem of her Anthony, and a thousand such soft and charming Expressions: And on the other hand; I would tell him, That he was as lovely in my Eyes as Orondates was to Cassandra, or Anthony to Cleopatra, and this gave our Pleasures high Gust and Relish.[44]

If prostitution, then, was often imagined as acting, to unmask an actress as a prostitute was simply to reveal her as an actress. What was essential to both arts, indeed what collapsed them into one,

---

43. *The Whore's Rhetorick: Calculated to the Meridian of London and Conformed to the Rules of Art. In Two Dialogues* (London, 1683; rpt. New York: I. Obolensky, 1961), p. 46.

44. John Dunton, *The Night-Walker; or, Evening Rambles in Search after Lewd Women, with the Conferences Held with Them, etc.*, no. 3 (November 1696), pp. 16–17.

was the successful maintenance of a gap between self-representation and the "real" woman.[45]

In Behn's first prologue, this way of conceiving of actresses and
prostitutes is assumed. It is the actress who intervenes to save the
playwright from identification with the prostitutes in the audience,
but as we have seen, it is also the actress who, by theatrically
disclaiming mercenary motives, helps establish another aspect of
that identification: its reliance on concealment. The actress, like the
prostitute, is always playing roles, even when she is playing the
role of the actress distinguishing herself from the prostitute. Behn's
identification with the actress, then, is another way of thematizing
the self-division of the woman in the marketplace, of reminding
the audience that self-reserve is the condition of self-sale.

The actress, however, is more than just a metaphor for the
playwright; she is also the playwright's proxy. She speaks the author's words, bodies forth her ideas. She stands in relation to the playwright as body to mind, and, as we are about to see, part of the
thrill of Aphra Behn's plays in the Restoration seems to have been
the combined novelty of a literally feminine body representing,
standing for, a "really" feminine mind.[46] Hence, although the idea
of concealment, of an internal difference, is implicit in Behn's very
identification with the actress, so too is an idea of revealing sameness. A real woman on the stage speaks the words of a real woman
playwright; like represents like.

In general, Restoration playwrights seem to have done all they
could to capitalize on the new spectacle of the female body onstage.
In the Renaissance, physical femaleness had been represented by
low stature, high voices, and women's clothes. The bodies onstage
had all been male; femaleness had been a costume, a way of
disguising the actual body. As if to emphasize their break with the
past in this regard, Restoration comedy writers took every opportunity to demonstrate that their women's bodies were real by
undressing them, presenting them in dishabille, or showing off

45. For a much more thorough discussion of contemporary discourse on prostitution, see James Grantham Turner, "Sex and Consequence," *Review* 11 (1989):
133–77.
46. For a discussion of this reality effect in the staging of Restoration actresses,
even in male-authored plays, and its reliance on the prostitute-actress connection,
see Katherine Eisaman Maus, "'Playhouse Flesh and Blood': Sexual Ideology and
the Restoration Actress," *ELH* 46 (1979): 595–617.

their legs in pantaloon parts. Indeed, pantaloon parts were a favorite spectacle because they so neatly reversed the cross-dressing of the Renaissance stage and showed the Restoration's superiority in being able to costume and undress simultaneously. The epilogue to Dryden's *Secret Love*, for example, comments on the eroticism of physical female presence, enhanced by the woman's being dressed (or rather undressed) in tights. The cross-dressed actress addresses the audience:

> What think you Sirs, was't not all well enough,
> Will you not grant that we can strut, and huff?
> Men may be proud, but faith for ought I see,
> They neither walk, nor cock, so well as we.
> . . . .
> Oh would the higher Powers be kind to us,
> And grant us to set up a female house.
> Wee'l make our selves to please both Sexes then,
> To the Men Women, to the Women Men.
> Here we presume, our Legs are no ill sight,
> And they would give you no ill Dreams at night.
> In Dream's both Sexes may their passions ease,
> You make us then as civil as you please.[47]

This epilogue cleverly stresses both the reality of the female body on the stage and its status as a body of representation, both a spectacular literal presence and an invitation to imaginative embellishment onto which even masculinity might be grafted. But adding masculine costumes to feminine bodies on the Restoration stage was not the simple inversion of adding feminine costumes to masculine bodies on the Renaissance stage, because Renaissance actors had put on skirts whereas Restoration actresses took them off. In short, on the Restoration stage, the act of imagination was supposed to accompany the revelation, not the concealment, of the actual body.

The difference between the two theaters in this regard is neatly summarized by Davenant's revision of *The Tempest*. As Dryden explained, Davenant wished to "complete" Shakespeare's play by inventing a "counterpart to Shakespeare's Plot, namely that of a Man who had never seen a Woman."[48] That is, Davenant, somewhat

47. *The Works of John Dryden*, vol. 9, pp. 202–03.
48. Dryden's preface to his own *Tempest; or, the Enchanted Island*, in *Complete Works*, vol. 10, p. 4.

oddly imagining that Miranda had never laid eyes on any man at all, gave her a lover who, like the early Restoration playgoer, had never before had the theatrical spectacle of an actual woman. The Restoration playwright thus revised the Renaissance to make the revelation of woman the wonder. The brave new world of the Restoration stage was indeed the female body.[49]

Behn turned this innovation to her special advantage in several ways. According to Peter Holland, she made the spectacle of the undressed woman one of her hallmarks. In ten of Behn's comedies, he claims, there are eighteen "discovery" scenes of undressing, dressing, or going to bed, and almost all of these involve women: "No other dramatist is even half as preoccupied with bedroom scenes."[50] Such a preoccupation certainly justifies Pope's famous couplet on Behn:

> The stage how loosely does Astraea tread
> Who fairly puts all characters to bed![51]

The lines are not so much a sexist slur motivated by the double standard as a simple recognition of what made Behn's plays stand out for her contemporaries: far more than her male colleagues, she exploited the spectacle of the undressed body and incessantly presented the scene of sexuality itself. One of the commodities, then, that Behn consistently promises and delivers is the female body in a particularly "literally" exposed state.

As I suggested earlier, part of the power of such moments must have been that they were a staging of a female by a female, increasing the effect of literalness, of reality, or at least of a symbolic economy in which things are represented by things like themselves.

49. Of course, some older plays completely lost their point under these circumstances. The Restoration fashion for exposing women's legs lasted well into the eighteenth century and led one director, for example, in 1776 to cast a woman in the role of Jonson's Epicoene; when she removed her skirts, revealing not the boy the script called for but a woman in boy's tights, "the audience felt themselves rather trifled with than surprized." See *Ben Jonson: Volume 1*, ed. and introd. Brinsley Nicholson and C. H. Herford (New York: Scribner's, 1957), pp. 113–14.

50. Holland, *The Ornament of Action*, p. 41. For an analysis of Behn's use of breeches parts, see Frances M. Kavenik, "Aphra Behn: The Playwright as 'Breeches Part,'" in *Curtain Calls*, pp. 177–92.

51. "First Epistle of the Second Book of Horace. To Augustus," in *Alexander Pope: Collected Poems*, ed. Bonamy Dobree and introd. Clive T. Probyn (London: J. M. Dent, 1987), p. 300. The context of these lines is a general satire on comedy, and Behn is one of several instances of "how seldom even the best succeed."

The female character is created by a female writer and represented on the stage by a female actress. Thus Pope can imagine that it is Behn herself who loosely treads the stage, even as he distinguishes between the playwright and the characters by turning the former into a kind of procuress or perverse "mother" putting her characters to bed. The more literal-minded Robert Gould in "The Play-house. A Satyr" flatly equates the spectacle of the actress who plays Lady Galliard in *The City Heiress* with the character and both with Behn:

> the lewd Widow comes, with brazen face
> Just reeking from a Stallion's rank embrace.[52]

Such a bare equation of author and character may seem naive, cruel, and slanderous to us now, but it was similar to, and probably motivated by, the writer-actress-character identification that Behn exploited.

Although satires like Pope's and Gould's reveal something important about Behn's unique procedures and appeal, they ignore Behn's skill at playing with the decorum of the stage without ever allowing the levels of representation to collapse. Her care to distinguish between actresses and characters, between literal bodies and what they represent, for example, is evident even in her staging of the exposed body. The bedroom scenes that abound in her comedies are, appropriately, "discoveries" (scenes upstage, furthest from the audience) that are in progress when the curtain opens to "discover" them. Behn, therefore, even as she thus increased the sensation of voyeurism, kept her undressed actors upstage, apparently to keep them in character, to keep them from being confused with actors whose "undress" was supposed to designate that they were temporarily out of character, that is, playing the role of the actor. As Holland explains, "the Restoration styles of forestage acting encouraged the identification of actor and character simultaneously far more than does upstage acting."[53] Behn's exploitation of the body, then, relied on the very distinction of symbolic levels that it threatened to collapse.

The distinctions among playwright, actress, and character were

---

52. In *Poems Chiefly Consisting of Satyrs and Satyrical Epistles* (London, 1689), rpt. in Montague Summers, *The Restoration Theatre* (New York: Humanities Press, 1964), p. 305.
53. Holland, p. 42.

similarly crucial to Behn's mode of self-presentation. As we have already noticed, Restoration playwrights needed to make themselves prominent in the imagination of the audience. For example, in his "Defence of an Essay of Dramatique Poesie" Dryden insists on the preeminence of the poet in the audience's experience of the play. Refuting the idea that "a Play will . . . be supposed to be a composition of several Persons speaking *ex tempore*," he claims, "a Play is suppos'd to be the work of the Poet, imitating, or representing the conversation of several persons."[54] Dryden's is not an expressive aesthetic; the playwright does not represent himself. Nevertheless, the play is *his* work of representation and must be viewed as such. This emergence of the poet in the foreground of the audience's consciousness as a being distinguishable from both the object and the theatrical means of representation is, as I have already noted, the basis of the playwright's entitlement to a separate benefit. Like her male colleagues, Behn had to create a separate, authorial, persona, but her work, unlike theirs, relied for its novelty and power partly on an identification of heroine, actress, and playwright. Behn, then, had a delicate representational task to perform: she had to draw a sense of her difference out of the very materials of her identification. The self-presentation we have been tracing through the metaphors of prostitution and acting was partly a solution to this problem. Her identification with the prostitute and actress signals her ultimate elusiveness, the difference between what she is and what she seems, even as it tells the audience what she is "like." Her relationship to the actress is like the prostitute's relationship to her own body: the mask that hides the face signals the availability of the body but also implies the impenetrability of the controlling mind.

~

It is in Behn's comedies that these relationships are most complexly enacted and that the perils of such a means of authorial empowerment come into view. Through their exploration of the relationships between women and property, the plays examine the dynamics of

54. *The Indian Emperour; or, the Conquest of Mexico by the Spaniards,* in *The Works of John Dryden,* vol. 9, p. 6.

desire, gratification, and representation. If the poetess-punk is she who is identified by her disguise, she whose nature is marked by her mask, whose mode of self-representation is that of hiding to produce desire, then the implied "real" self is both a phenomenon created by representation and one implying its limits. The poetess is by definition the person not representing herself, the person behind representation. She inspires desire through disguise, and hence it is not *she*, properly speaking, who is the object of desire. And yet she is the implied first cause of desire as well as its epiphenomenon. This authorial self in the land of Aphra Behn's representations is a mere shadow, darkened with the sense of exclusion, with a sense that her involvement is predicated on her "nothingness," her absence from the scene. The sold self's seller, the exchanger on the other side of representation, "Aphra Behn" is often felt as just a suggestion of a lack of gratification.

This hint of authorial dissatisfaction should not be confused with the disapproval of turning women into items of exchange that is so often expressed by characters in the comedies.[55] *The Lucky Chance*, which will serve here as Behn's exemplary comedy, all too readily yields a facile, right-minded thematic analysis centering on women and property exchange. The play's three plots can easily be seen as variations on this theme: Diana is being forced into a loveless marriage with a fop because of her father's family ambition. Her prepossession in favor of the young Bredwell is ignored in the exchange. Diana's father, Sir Feeble Fainwood, is also purchasing himself a young bride, Leticia, whom he has tricked into believing that her betrothed, who had been banished for fighting a duel, is dead. Julia, having already sold herself to another rich old merchant, Sir Cautious Fulbank, is being wooed to adultery by her former lover, Gayman. All three women are both property and occasions for the exchange of property: Diana is part of a financial arrangement between the families of the two old men, and the intended bridegroom, Bearjest, sees her merely as the embodiment of a great fortune; Leticia is bought by "a great jointure"; and

55. For overviews of the theme of forced marriage in Behn's plays, see Marc Lussier, "'The Vile Merchandize of Fortune': Women, Economy, and Desire in Aphra Behn," *Women's Studies* 18 (1991): 379–93; and Jessica Munns, "'I by a Double Right Thy Bounties Claim': Aphra Behn and Social Space," in *Curtain Calls*, pp. 193–210.

though we know, interestingly, nothing of Julia's motives, we are told that she had also married for money. It is easy, then, to make the point that the treatment of women as property is the problem that the play's comic action will set out to solve. Women as forms of property and items of exchange, whether they married for property, like Leticia and Julia, or were married, like Diana, for dowry, seem to be the play's point of departure, and the urge to break that identification seems, on a casual reading, to license the play's impropriety. One could even redeem the old men's *giving* of all the women to their lovers in the end by pointing out that this is, after all, a comedy, a form that requires female desire to flow through established channels.

This superficial thematic analysis of *The Lucky Chance* fits in well with the image of Aphra Behn her most recent biographers promote: that of an advocate of "free love" in every sense of the phrase and a heroic defender of the right of women to speak their own desire. However, such an interpretation does not bear the weight of the play's structure or remain steady in the face of its ellipses, nor can it sustain the pressure of the play's images. For the moments of crisis in the play are not those in which a woman becomes property, but those in which a woman is burdened with a selfhood that can be neither represented (a self without properties) nor exchanged. They are the moments when the veiled woman confronts the impossibility of being represented and hence of being desired.

Before turning to those moments, though, I will outline the larger organizational features of the play that complicate its treatment of the link between women and property. First, we should notice the emphatic way in which the plots are disconnected in their most fundamental logic. The plots of Diana and Leticia rely on the idea that there is an irreversible moment of matrimonial exchange after which the woman is "given" and cannot be given again. Thus the action is directed toward thwarting and replacing the planned marriage ceremony, in the case of Diana, and avoiding the consummation of the marriage, in the case of Leticia. However, the interaction of even these two plots oddly affects the very sense of urgency that each plot individually tries to elicit; how can we see the marriage ceremony as the crucial, irretrievable step in Diana's plot if Leticia, who has just taken the same step, is somehow still marriageable? That is, both plots contain a logic of crisis, but they are slightly mutually disorienting because of their different accounts of just what is critical.[56]

Yet even more devastating to our sense that these actions signify is their alternation with Julia's adultery plot. Julia has crossed all the thresholds and is still somehow free to dispose of herself. The logic on which her plot is based seems to deny that there are critical or irremediable events in female destiny. Hence, in the scene directly following Leticia's intact deliverance from Sir Feeble Fainwood's bed and Diana's elopement with Bredwell, we find Julia resignedly urging her aged husband to get the sex over with and then stop meddling with the affairs of her heart: "But let us leave this fond discourse, and, if you must, let us to bed."[57] Julia proves her self-possession precisely by her indifference to the crises structuring Diana's and Leticia's experiences.

On the one hand, Julia's plot could be seen to undercut the achievement of resolution in the other plots by implying that there was never anything to resolve: the obstacles were not real, the crises were not crises, the definitive moment never did and never could arrive. But on the other hand, we could argue that the crisis plots drain the adultery plot not only of moral credibility but also of dramatic interest, for there seems to be simply nothing at stake in Julia's plot. Indeed, Julia's plot seems itself to be bent on making this point, turning, as it so often does, on attempts to achieve things that have already been achieved or gambling for stakes that have already been won. These two responses, however, tend to cancel one another, and we cannot conclude that either plot logic renders the other nugatory. *The Lucky Chance* achieves its effects,

---

56. Susan Staves has noted that this casual attitude toward marriage vows is a distinguishing feature of much Restoration comedy; she examines "how weak the traditional obligations imposed by the religious vows of marriage could seem when the individuals they joined could not respect each other." See *Players' Scepters: Fictions of Authority in the Restoration* (Lincoln: Univ. of Nebraska Press, 1979), chapters 3 and 4; the quotation is on p. 180. See also Harold Weber, *The Restoration Rake-Hero: Transformations in Sexual Understanding in Seventeenth-Century England* (Madison: Univ. of Wisconsin Press, 1986); and John Harrington Smith, *The Gay Couple in Restoration Comedy* (Cambridge: Harvard Univ. Press, 1948). On Behn's adaptation from Fletcher of these conventions regarding marriage in *The Lucky Chance*, see Kavenik, "Aphra Behn: The Playwright as 'Breeches Part,'" pp. 178–80.

57. *The Lucky Chance; or, an Alderman's Bargain* (performed first in 1686), in *The Female Wits*, ed. Morgan, p. 135. Subsequent quotations from this edition are cited parenthetically in the text.

rather, by presenting, alternately, the problem and its seeming nonexistence. The imminent danger of becoming an unwilling piece of someone else's property is at once asserted and denied.[58]

The alternation of assertion and denial emphasizes the discontinuity between the two "resolutions" of women's sexual identity that I discussed earlier: one in which the giving of the self intact is tantamount to survival; the other in which the self is maintained in a series of exchanges. This very discontinuity, as I have already pointed out, is part of a discursive pattern of juxtaposition. The proof of self-ownership is repeated self-sale; hence Julia needs no exculpating story of deceit or coercion to explain her marriage to Sir Cautious. But the complete import of what she does, both of what she sacrifices and what she gains, can only be understood against the background of a story like Leticia's that imagines the alternative of a marriage that maintains the whole self.

Each story thus highlights the assumptions of the other through juxtaposition. Nevertheless, our inability to perceive these plots within a single dramatic perspective reveals the oppositional relationship between the two seventeenth-century versions of the female self as property discussed earlier in this chapter. Built into this very disjunction, therefore, is a complicated explanation of why women cannot cease to be property. In the play, the exchange, by women themselves or by someone else, of women as property appears inevitable, and the action revolves around the terms of exchange. The crisis plots, of which Leticia's is the most important, posit wholeness as the precondition of exchange and as the result of its successful completion. The unitary principle dominates the logic of this plot and also, as we are about to see, the language of its actors and its representational rules. Julia's plot, in contrast, assumes not only the fracturing and multiplication of the self as a condition and result of exchange but also the creation of a second order of reality: a reality of representations through which the characters simultaneously alienate and protect their identities.

The disjunction in the deep assumptions of the plots, then, is accompanied by the second general formal feature I will discuss

58. For a discussion of women and exchange in two other Behn plays, see Lussier, "'The Vile Merchandize of Fortune': Women, Economy, and Desire in Aphra Behn."

before turning to the topic of feminine representation: the split in representational procedures that can be detected in the very first scene, where it differentiates the characters of the leading men. In the play's opening speech, Bellmour enters, complaining that the law has stolen his identity, has made him a creature of disguise and the night. His various complaints in the scene cluster around a central fear of de-differentiation, of the failure properly to distinguish essential differences. Thus it is the

> rigid laws, which put no difference
> 'Twixt fairly killing in my own defence,
> And murders bred by drunken arguments,
> Whores, or the mean revenges of a coward
> (p. 76)

that have forced his disguise, his alienation from his own identity. That is, the denial of the true, identity-ensuring, difference (that between duelers and murderers) necessitates false difference, disguises, and theatrical representations that get more elaborate as the plot progresses. The comedy is this series of disguises and spectacles, but its end is to render them unnecessary by the reunion of Bellmour with his proper identity and his proper wife.

The very terms of Bellmour's self-alienation, moreover, emphasize stable identity and sameness by assuming that like must be represented by like. Bellmour has taken a life in a duel, and for that he is deprived of the life he thought he would lead. He has destroyed a body with his sword, and for that a body that belongs to him, Leticia's, will be taken from him also, through puncturing. Even the comic details of Bellmour's reported death are consonant with this mode of representation:

RALPH: Hanged, Sir, hanged, at The Hague in Holland.

BELLMOUR: For what, said they, was he hanged?

RALPH: Why, e'en for high treason, Sir, he killed one of their kings.

GAYMAN: Holland's a commonwealth, and is not ruled by kings.

RALPH: Not by one, Sir, but by many. This was a cheesemonger, they fell out over a bottle of brandy, went to snicker snee, Mr. Bellmour cut his throat, and was hanged for't, that's all, Sir.

The reductio ad absurdum of like representing like is the common-wealth in which everyone is a king. Within this comically literalist system of representation Bellmour is imagined to have had his neck broken for slitting the throat of a cheesemonger. It is no wonder that the climax of Bellmour's performance is a simulation of the exchange of like for like. As Sir Feeble Fainwood approaches the bed on which he intends to deflower Leticia, asking her, "What, was it ashamed to show its little white foots, and its little round bubbies?" Bellmour comes out from between the bed curtains, naked to the waist. And, all the better to ward off that which he represents, he has Leticia's projected wound painted on his own chest and a dagger ready to make another such wound on Sir Feeble. The whole representational economy of this plot, therefore, has an underlying unitary basis in the notion that things must be paid for in kind. Even Leticia's self-sale seems not to be for money but for the jewelry to which she is often likened.

Like Bellmour, Gayman also enters the first scene in hiding, "wrapped in his cloak," but the functional differences between the two kinds of self-concealment are soon manifested. The end of Gayman's disguises is not the retrieval of his property but the sexual use of what he thinks is the property of others: "Are you not to be married, Sir?" asks Bellmour. "No Sir," returns Gayman, "not as long as any man in London is so, that has but a handsome wife, Sir" (p. 77). He attempts, not to reestablish essential differences, but rather to blur them. "The bridegroom!" exclaims Bellmour on first seeing Sir Feeble. "Like Gorgon's head he's turned me into stone." "Gorgon's head," retorts Gayman, "a cuckold's head, 'twas made to graft upon" (p. 79). Gayman's dizzying swiftness in extending Bellmour's metaphor speaks a desire to destroy the paired stability of exchanges. Looking at the bridegroom's head, Bellmour sees an image of immobilizing female sexuality, the Gorgon. Thus the bridegroom represents the alienated sexuality of Leticia. Gayman disarms this image by decking it with horns to introduce the idea that if Leticia has been unfaithful, she may, by continuing on the same course, be persuaded by Bellmour to cuckold Sir Feeble. But this seems no solution at all to Bellmour, since it only further collapses the distinction between lover and husband, merging him with Sir Feeble at the moment he agrees to the alienation of "his" sexual property right in Leticia: "What, and let him marry her! She that's mine by sacred vow already! By heaven it would be flat adultery in her!" (p. 80). "She'll learn the trick," replies Gayman, "and practice it the better with thee." The destruction of the "true" distinctions between husband and lover, cuckold and adulterer, proprietor and thief is the state for which Gayman longs.

Bellmour's comedy, then, moves toward the reinscription of true difference through the creation of false differences; Gayman's comedy moves toward the erasure of true differences through the creation of false samenesses. Gayman is in disguise because he cannot bear to let Julia know that he is different from his former self. He wishes to appear before her always the same, to hide the new fact of his poverty. He tries to get money from his landlady so that he can get his clothes out of hock and disguise himself as himself to go on wooing Julia. On the same principle of the efface-ment of difference, Gayman later tries to pass himself off as Julia's husband when he, unbeknownst to her, takes the old man's place in bed.

Moreover, just as the false differences of Bellmour's comedy conform to a unitary like-for-like economy of representation, the false samenesses of Gayman's plotting are governed by an economy of representation through difference, the most obvious example of which is the use of money. Money in this plot often represents bodies or their sexual use, and such exchanges generally emphasize the differences between the body and money. For example, in the scene of Gayman's two prostitutions (the first with his landlady and the second with his unknown admirer) the difference between the women's bodies and the precious metals they can be made to yield is the point of the comedy. The landlady is herself metamor-phosed into iron for the sake of this contrast: Gayman describes her as an iron lady who emerges from her husband's blacksmithing shop. She is then stroked into metals of increasing value as she yields "'postle spoons and caudle cups" that Gayman exchanges for gold. But Gayman's expletives remind us that this sexual al-chemy is being practiced on an unsublimable body that constantly sickens the feigning lover with its stink. Even more telling is the continuation of this scene in which Gayman receives a bag of gold as advance payment for an assignation with an anonymous woman. Here the desirability of the gold (associated with its very anonymity) immediately implies the undesirability of the woman who sends it:

> Some female devil, old and damned to ugliness,
> And past all hopes of courtship and address,
> Full of another devil called desire,
> Has seen this face, this shape, this youth,
> And thinks it's worth her hire. It must be so.
>
> (p. 94)

Of course, as this passage emphasizes, in both cases the women's money, which indicates Gayman's sexual worthiness, again marks a difference, the difference in the desirability of the bodies to be exchanged.

The freedom and perils, especially the perils for women, that such systems of representation through difference introduce into erotic life are explored in the conflict between Julia and Gayman. And that exploration returns us to the issue of feminine authorial representation. Julia, like many of Aphra Behn's heroines, confronts a familiar predicament: she wishes to have the pleasure of sexual intercourse with her lover without the pain of losing her honor. "Honor" is not a matter of conscience in the play, since secret actions are outside its realm. Rather, to lose honor is to give away control over one's public representations. Hence, in the adultery plot, as opposed to the crisis plot, women's bodies are not the true stakes; representations of bodies, especially in money and language, are the focal points of conflict.

Gayman's complaint against Julia, for example, is that she prefers the public admiration of the crowd, which she gains through witty language ("talking all and loud" [p. 99]), to the private "adoration" of a lover, which is apparently speechless. Julia's retort, however, indicates that it is Gayman who will betray the private to public knowledge for the sake of his own reputation. It is Gayman who will "describe her charms,"

> Or make most filthy verses of me
> Under the name of Cloris, you Philander,
> Who, in lewd rhymes, confess the dear appointment,
> What hour, and where, how silent was the night,
> How full of love your eyes, and wishing mine.

We have, by the way, just heard Gayman sing a verse about Cloris's wishing eyes to his landlady. To escape being turned into someone else's language, losing the ability to control her own public self-presentation, Julia subjects herself to a much more radical sever-ance of implied true self from self-representation than Gayman could have imagined. At once gratifying her sexual desire and preserving her honor, she arranges to have Gayman's own money (in some ways a sign of his desire for her) misrepresented to him as payment for sexual intercourse with an unknown woman.

Julia, then, hides behind the anonymity of the gold that passes between them, relying on its nature as a universal equivalent for desire, universal and anonymous precisely because it does not resemble what it stands for and can thus stand for anything. But in this episode, she is erased by the very anonymity of the repre-sentation. For as we have already seen, Gayman takes the gold as a sign of the difference between the woman's repulsiveness and his own desirability. Apparently, moreover, this representation of her undesirability overwhelms the tactile experience itself, so that when they finally couple, Gayman does not actually have Julia but rather another version of his landlady. As he later reluctantly describes the sightless, wordless encounter to Julia (whom he does not suspect of having been the woman), "She was laid in a pavilion all formed of gilded clouds which hung by geometry, whither I was conveyed after much ceremony, and laid in a bed with her, where, with much ado and trembling with my fears, I forced my arms about her." "And sure," interjects Julia aside to the audience, "that undeceived him." "But," continues Gayman, "such a carcass 'twas, deliver me, so shrivelled, lean and rough, a canvas bag of wooden ladles were a better bedfellow." "Now, though, I know that nothing is more distant than I from such a monster, yet this angers me," confides Julia to the audience, "'Slife, after all to seem deformed, old, ugly." The interview ends with Gayman's final misunderstand-ing: "I knew you would be angry when you heard it" (p. 118).

The extraordinary thing about this interchange is that it does not matter whether Gayman is telling the truth about his sexual expe-rience. The gold may have so overwhelmed his senses as to make Julia feel like its opposite: a bag of wooden ladles rather than precious coins; and, indeed, the continuity of images between this description and Gayman's earlier reactions to women who give him money tends to confirm his sincerity. The bag of ladles reminds us of the landlady, who was also a bag, but one containing somewhat more valuable table utensils: "'postle spoons and caudle cups." However, Gayman, to prevent Julia's jealousy, may be lying about his experience. Either way, Julia was missing from that experience. Whether he did not desire her at all or desired her as someone else is immaterial; what Julia feels as she sees herself through this doubled representation of money and language is the impossibility of keeping herself to herself and truly being gratified as at once a subject and object of desire.

This economy of difference, in which Julia's representations are not recognizably hers, leaves her in a state of unexchangeability. The drive for self-possession removes her "true" self from the realms of desire and gratification. Because she has not given herself away, she finds that her lover has not been able to take her. Surprisingly, however, the play goes on to overcome this difficulty, not by taking refuge in like-for-like exchanges, but by remaining in the economy of difference until Julia seems able to adjust the claims of self-possession and gratification.

The adjustment becomes possible only after Julia has been explicitly converted into a commodity worth three hundred pounds. The process leading up to this conversion merits our scrutiny. Gayman and Sir Cautious are gambling; Gayman has won three hundred pounds and is willing to stake it against something of Sir Cautious's:

SIR CAUTIOUS: I wish I had anything but ready money to stake: three hundred pound, a fine sum!

GAYMAN: You have moveables Sir, goods, commodities.

SIR CAUTIOUS: That's all one, Sir. That's money's worth, Sir, but if I had anything that were worth nothing.

GAYMAN: You would venture it. I thank you Sir. I would your lady were worth nothing.

SIR CAUTIOUS: Why so, Sir?

GAYMAN: Then I would set all 'gainst that nothing.

SIR CAUTIOUS: What, set it against my Wife?

GAYMAN: Wife, Sir! Ay, your Wife.

SIR CAUTIOUS: Hum, my Wife against three hundred pounds! What, all my Wife, Sir?

GAYMAN: . . . Why, Sir, some part of her would serve my turn.

Sir Cautious begins this dialogue with a comical identification of everything with its universal equivalent, money. Everything he owns is convertible into money; hence, he believes that money is the real essence of everything that is not money. Hence, everything is *really* the same thing—money. For Sir Cautious the economy of difference collapses everything into sameness. The only thing that is truly different, then, must be "nothing," a common slang term for the female genitals. One's wife is this nothing because she is at once female and, in the normal course of events, not a commodity: "Why, what a lavish whoremaker's this? We take money to marry our wives but very seldom part with 'em, and by the bargain get money" (p. 126). Her usual nonexchangeability for money is what makes a wife different from a prostitute; it is also what makes her the perfect nothing to set against three hundred pounds. We could say, then, that Julia is here made into a commodity only because she is not one. She differs from everything that is worth anything and thereby becomes the principle of universal difference for her husband. She is a cipher that can safely stand in for any of Sir Cautious's other things, which are all "money's worth, Sir." She is, then, a kind of counter-money that takes the place of all the exchangeable things without exactly becoming one of them. As a principle of universal difference, a "nothing," she paradoxically seems ideally suited to be exchanged for the universal equivalent, money. However, this very exchangeability then blurs the distinction between the counter-money and money itself, the distinction that motivated the exchange in the first place.

Hence, Sir Cautious finds himself in a logical double bind and is unable to rest content with his bargain. What originally distinguishes his wife, or her "part," from the rest of his property is her putative inalienability. As a merchant, Sir Cautious imagines that owning something gives him the right to sell it. He defines ownership as an absolute property right to do whatever he chooses with his belongings. It is this relatively "new" way of conceptualizing property that leads him to see everything as money, for the exchangeability of things is the ultimate proof that they belong to him.[59] The one thing in which Sir Cautious seems to have a property right that denies rather than entails marketability is Julia's "part." For a woman, if she can be conceived of as property at all, is a very anomalous sort of property in Sir Cautious's mental universe. She can only "belong" to a man under heavily qualified notions of ownership. Under the strictest patriarchal rules whereby a woman could be conceived of, in Lady Cary's words, as "wholly" given "away," the property rights of the male in the female could never be absolute, for the father, who had the right to exchange her, could not have the right to possess her sexually, and the husband, who had the right to possess her, could not have the right to exchange her. It is the paradox of such an inalienable property that traps Sir Cautious. If he owns Julia's "part," he should be able to exchange it, like any other possession, for money; but if he exchanges it for money, he fears that Julia will no longer be *his* wife. The concept of an inalienable property is foreign to him, but its very incomprehensibility makes it the only kind of property he can imagine as "nothing."

What we have here, then, is the comic collision of possessive individualism with the very idea of marital propriety, a collision that wipes out all Sir Cautious's claims to property in Julia. Moreover, the episode decisively links Julia's liberation with the triumph of representation through difference. Her prostitution parallels Gayman's, in which, as we have seen, money also marked difference. But the sequels of the two scenes are strikingly dissimilar. Gayman is once again in Julia's bed, but his, rather than her, identity is supposedly masked. Whereas in the first encounter Gayman went to bed with what he thought was an old woman, in the second, Julia goes to bed with what she thinks is her old husband. The difference between these two scenes in the dark as they are later recounted stems from the relative inalienability of male sexual identity. Even in the dark, we are led to believe, the

59. On the growth of this notion of property in seventeenth-century England, see both Macpherson and Joyce Oldham Appleby, *Economic Thought and Ideology in Seventeenth-Century England* (Princeton, NJ: Princeton Univ. Press, 1978). For a consideration of the politics of the mobility of property, see Pocock, "The Mobility of Property and the Rise of Eighteenth-Century Sociology," in *Virtue, Commerce, and History*, pp. 103–23.

difference between men is sensible because their selfhood is not easily effaced: Gayman says,

> It was the feeble husband you enjoyed
> In cold imagination, and no more.
> Shyly you turned away, faintly resigned . . .
> Till excess of love betrayed the cheat.
> (p. 139)

Gayman's body, even unseen, is not interchangeable with Sir Cautious's. Unlike Julia's body, Gayman's will undo the misrepresentation; no mere idea can eradicate this palpable sign of identity, the tumescent penis itself. Hence, when Gayman takes Sir Cautious's place in bed, he does not really risk what Julia suffered earlier: "after all to seem deformed, old, ugly." Gayman's self will always obtrude into the sphere of representation—another version of the ladle, but one that projects from the body instead of being barely discernible within it.

This inalienable masculine identity, although it seems at first Gayman's advantage, is quickly appropriated by Julia, who uses it to secure at once her own good reputation and complete liberty of action. Once again we are given a scene in which the speaker's sincerity is questionable. When Gayman's erection reveals his identity, Julia appears outraged at the attempted deception: "What, make me a base prostitute, a foul adult'ress? Oh, be gone, dear robber of my quiet" (p. 139). We can only see this tirade as more deceit on Julia's part, since we know she tricked the same man into bed the night before. Indeed, Gayman himself knows the truth at this point in the play. But since her deceit was not immediately discovered and his was, she is able to feign outrage and demand a separation from her husband. The implication, although once again it cannot be represented, is that Julia has found a way to secure her liberty and her "honor" by maintaining her misrepresentations.

It is, then, precisely through her nullity, her nothingness, that Julia achieves a new level of self-possession along with the promise of continual sexual exchange. But this, of course, is an inference we make from what we suspect Julia of hiding: her pleasure in Gayman's body, her delight that she now has an excuse for separating from her husband, her intention to go on seeking covert pleasure. All of this is on the other side of what we see and hear; it consequently conjures the shadow of the controlling but unrepresentable woman. This shady effect also constitutes our idea of the author of *The Lucky Chance*, a being who appears as an afterimage of her disappearance. The very shadiness allows us to imagine her as at once triumphantly elusive and poignantly dissatisfied, as heroine and victim of her exchanges. She is herself the nothing that might equal anything.

Hence, for all her staginess and explicit sexuality, the Aphra Behn of the comedies might nonetheless be seen as a kind of "Nobody." Associating herself with tokens of internal division (prostitutes, actresses, commodities) or with emblems of blank anonymity (money and the "nothing" of women's genitals), she eludes our desire for a positive identification. Although I will argue in later chapters that "Nobody" achieves both her explicitly "fictional" nature and her full stature only with the ascendancy of the novel in the middle of the eighteenth century, we can already see in Aphra Behn's comic authorial persona that "Nobodiness" appears when the topics of femaleness and commercial exchange are combined in the rhetoric of authorship.

2

The Author-Monarch
and the Royal Slave

Oroonoko *and the*
Blackness of Representation

Prostitution was not Behn's only metaphor for authorship. In the early eighties, the prologues and epilogues to her works featured a different figure: the author-monarch. The royalist politics of her most popular comedies during these years—*The Rover, Part II* (1681), *The City Heiress* (1682), *The Roundheads* (1682), *The False Count* (1682)—carried over into her self-presentations, especially into the presentations of the financial exchange between herself and her audience. The playhouse audience became the object of raillery for its stinginess and low tastes; and the playwright implies that just as she has been loyal to her king, the audience should reform and be loyal to her.

Although it is clear from both the success of these comedies and the abuse the Whig playwrights heaped on Behn during this period that her audience was indeed large and loyal, the conceit of the epilogue to *The Rover, Part II* is that the playgoers, like a Whiggish parliament, are on the verge of rebellion:

Poets are Kings of Wit, and you appear
A Parliament, by Play-Bill, summon'd here;
When e're in want, to you for aid they fly,
And a new Play's the Speech that begs supply:
But now—
The scanted Tribute is so slowly paid,
Our Poets must find out another Trade;
They've tried all ways th'insatiate Clan to please,
Have parted with their old Prerogatives,
Their Birth-right Satiring, and their just pretence
Of judging even their own Wit and Sense;
And write against their Consciences, to show

How dull they can be to comply with you.
. . . .
And yet you'll come but once, unless by stealth,
Except the Author be for Commonwealth.[1]

The monarch and the whore might seem incompatible metaphors for authorship, the monarch stressing the masculine qualities of commanding presence and forthright self-expression and the whore stressing the feminine modes of manipulative invisibility and deceptive disguise. Indeed, Behn sometimes figured the adoption of her political persona as putting off the mask of the prostitute, a "true," full revelation of the real author: "*The Vizor's off*," declares the actress who recites the epilogue to *The Roundheads*,

> and now I dare appear.
> High for the Royal Cause in Cavalier;
> Tho once [I seemed] as true a Whig as most of you,
> Cou'd cant, and lye, preach, and dissemble too:
> So far you drew me in, but faith I'll be
> Reveng'd on you for thus debauching me:
> . . . .
> For since I cannot fight, I will not fail
> To exercise my Talent, that's to rail.[2]

It seems as though self-expression has been achieved through politics. Shady difference, anonymity are banished and identity emerges into the light. The actress, probably in tights,[3] unmasks and exposes herself as a cavalier, and the cavalier, like the playwright, is a simulacrum of the monarch. Thus the new persona seems to deemphasize Behn's gender;[4] although it could easily be heard as a double entendre, her complaint against those who "come but once" (that is, who fail to return on the third night) is not that

1. *The Rover; or, the Banish'd Cavaliers, Part II*, in *The Works of Aphra Behn*, ed. Montague Summers (London, 1915), vol. 1, pp. 212–13. Unless otherwise noted, subsequent quotations from Behn's works are from this edition, hereafter cited as *Works*.

2. *The Roundheads; or, the Good Old Cause*, in *Works*, vol. 1, p. 424.

3. See Frances M. Kavenik, "Aphra Behn: The Playwright as 'Breeches Part,'" in *Curtain Calls: British and American Women and the Theater, 1660–1820*, ed. Mary Anne Schofield and Cecilia Macheski (Athens: Ohio Univ. Press, 1991), pp. 177–92.

4. The king did not entirely replace the prostitute as a figure of the author; Behn used both figures during the last seven years of her career. For another discussion of Behn's change of persona, see Deborah C. Payne, "'And Poets Shall by Patron-Princes Live': Aphra Behn and Patronage," in *Curtain Calls*, pp. 116–17.

they have deserted an inventive and entertaining woman who depends on them, but that they are refusing to defer to a superior wit who had, moreover, in her own political deportment set them an example of proper loyalty.

Despite these differences, however, Behn's author-monarch retains many of the prostitute's characteristics. The gender contrast between the two figures, for example, was not stable. Although always abstractly masculine, the monarch could legitimately be played by a woman, and the likening of women's rights to the rights of monarchs was a chivalric cliché often used in Behn's career to beg applause. We should also note that this courtly trope had bawdy undertones since "quean" was the age's most widespread slang term for "whore." These rather stiff lines from one of the epilogues (written by "a Friend"), for example, would probably have been heard as "gallant" in both senses of the word:

> [M]y Sex's Cause,
> Whose Beauty does, like Monarchs, give you Laws,
> Should now command, being join'd with Wit, Applause.[5]

The fair sex's demand for approval, like the monarch's, is based, not on an exchange between equal individuals, but on a God-given right.[6]

Whatever ideal rights monarchs and "queans" had, in the prologues and epilogues to Behn's political comedies they are always financially at the mercy of their subjects. Because the monarch, like the prostitute, appears in the prologues and epilogues only in this

---

5. *Abdelazer; or, the Moor's Revenge,* in *Works,* vol. 2, p. 98. It should also be noted that men generally delivered the prologues, while women were assigned the epilogues so that they could appeal to the audience's gallantry and not just their judgment in begging applause.

6. I have tried to demonstrate elsewhere that some seventeenth-century women writers, most notably Margaret Cavendish, duchess of Newcastle, converted this courtly language into a new rhetoric of femininity, stressing the absolute "singularity" of the female, her right to an autotelic, nonrelational, self-referential, and literary existence. In her writings, as in Behn's, the woman-monarch metaphor seems at first designed to provide an identity, but its paradoxes become quickly apparent. A representational economy of sameness, by creating a *mise en abyme,* finally has the effect of hollowing out the writer's selfhood, of making it seem every bit as elusive as that of Behn's masked lady. Fantasies of absolutism, carried to their logical conclusion, tended to enlarge rather than fill the void of female identity. See "Embracing the Absolute: The Politics of the Female Subject in Seventeenth-Century England," *Genders* 1 (1988): 34–54.

context of want, Behn's rhetoric of absolutism begins to sound like a bargaining position, a language *of* rather than *against* marketplace exchange. The absolute prerogative may be asserted as a birthright that should "naturally" free one from negotiation. However, since the occasion of the assertion is the negotiation of an exchange, the right that is claimed must be one that has already been violated. The metaphor, therefore, ennobles the author by providing a reference point against which her dependence on the audience appears unnatural; but that reference point, the monarch's "natural" right, must already have been denied by the time it is invoked.

In the prologue to *The False Count*, for example, the monarch of wit has been forced into the "Whiggery" of writing a farce:

> Our Author, as you'll find it writ in Story,
> Has hitherto been a most wicked Tory;
> But now, to th' joy o'th'Brethren be it spoken,
> Our Sister's vain mistaken Eyes are open;
> And Wisely valuing her dear Interest now,
> All-powerful Whigs, converted is to you.
> . . . .
> We have fitted you with one today,
> 'Tis writ as 'twere a Recantation Play;
> Renouncing all that has pretence to witty,
> T'oblige the Reverend Brumighams o'th'City.[7]

The theme of the split author is as evident in this self-presentation as it was in the prefatory epistle to *Sir Patient Fancy.*[8] Although the "real" author behind the "interested" one has definable qualities, such as true wit and royalism, these have already been sacrificed to the theatrical marketplace, where the audience is now expected to pay its due to both her natural superiority and her condescension. Hence, although the monarch seemed at first an alternative persona to the prostitute, one offering the possibility of representation through sameness, he/she turns out to be another internally divided figure. Just as the real woman could only be inferred from her misrepresentations, the real monarch, with his "divine" rights, becomes a rhetorical effect of the needy monarch searching for a bargaining position.

7. *The False Count; or, a New Way to Play an Old Game,* in *Works,* vol. 3, pp. 99–100.
8. See Chapter 1, pp. 16–18.

During the years when the political comedies were produced, the spectacle of the needy monarch was at the center of the severest political crisis of Charles II's reign: the exclusion crisis. The immediate allusion in Behn's prologues was no doubt to the 1681 decision of the Commons to refuse all supply to the crown until Charles assented to the Exclusion Bill, which would have barred the succession of Catholics and hence of Charles's brother, James. Charles ultimately ended the crisis that year, not by capitulating (parting with the old Prerogatives, to paraphrase Behn), but by dissolving Parliament and ruling without it for the rest of his reign, financed by French subsidies. The topic of the prologues, then, the contrast between the author-monarch's rights and wherewithal, was inspired by the spectacle of the actual sovereign in the political marketplace.[9]

The scandalous contrast between old prerogatives and new poverty, however, was even starker for the author than for the monarch because the playwright's equivalent of dissolving Parliament would only be "to find out another Trade." Thus Behn's prologues further ironically contrast the recent actions of the poet-monarch with those of the actual king, announcing that the former has been ignominiously subdued by her audience's financial pressure, whereas the latter scorned the demands of the Commons. By the end of the prologue to *The False Count*, the author, in order to remain in the theater, has become a counter-example to the heroic Charles; she is almost a parodic carnival queen, even though she makes it clear that this, too, is just a comic pose. The possibility of finding wealthy allies, patrons on whom one could depend, just as Charles was depending on the French to establish his independence from the Commons, was no doubt the implied alternative to authorial Whiggery.[10]

Thus, Behn's political persona, by figuring the contrast between the ideal of an absolute sovereignty beyond exchange and the reality of utter dependence on one's inferiors, provided a more explicit rhetoric of dissatisfaction with the marketplace than had the prostitute persona. Simultaneously, though, the political em-

9. On the financial instability of the king, see Payne, "'And Poets Shall by Patron-Princes Live': Aphra Behn and Patronage," p. 106.

10. For an investigation of Behn's patronage possibilities, see Payne, pp. 105–19.

phasis was calculated to give Behn a marketplace advantage. The exclusion crisis was accompanied and preceded by a series of plots, counter-plots, and sham plots that kept the polity both excited and polarized for several years, during which playwrights made themselves into political personages to attract interest and audience loyalty. The theaters, like the monarchy, had fallen on hard times; indeed, the companies finally merged in 1682, when it seemed that London could only support one stage. Like other playwrights under such conditions, Behn probably thought it wise to cultivate the patronage of the great on political grounds rather than rely on the playgoing audience, no matter how loyal. All these circumstances underscore what the prologues reveal: that the antimarketplace rhetoric of absolutism is itself a commercial strategy.

It would be possible to explore the dramatic elaboration of these themes in Behn's political comedies, especially in both parts of *The Rover* and *The City Heiress*. One might show, for example, that in these plays the cavalier ("A Cavalier was but a Type of Tory"[11]) is locked in amorous combat with either a prostitute or a woman who wishes, like the prostitute, to reserve her selfhood and use her representations to her best advantage. In each case the cavalier seems to unmask her by eliciting her true desire. But in each case, too, the cavalier prostitutes himself, accepting money for sex, marrying for money, or joining forces with the prostitute. His language of wit and honor turns out to be itself a form of dissimulation. Thus the king's representative, the cavalier, conquers the prostitute only by changing places with her.

The comedies, though, are not the best examples of Behn's writing on the relationship between sovereignty and the marketplace, which is far more extensively and seriously explored in her most famous prose narrative, *Oroonoko; or, the Royal Slave.*[12] As the

11. *Roundheads*, p. 425.
12. *Oroonoko* is the one text that kept Behn's name in the literary histories of the late eighteenth century and the nineteenth. Even the Victorians praised it: "When Mrs. Behn's shortcomings are remembered against her, 'Oroonoko' should be put to her credit; it is instinct with real feeling and womanly sympathy" ("Our Early Female Novelists," *Cornhill Magazine* 72 [1895]: 590). Each century seems to have been able to reconcile this one story with its ideas of what a woman writer should accomplish. Late seventeenth- and early eighteenth-century readers saw it primarily as a heroic love story, complete with a royal protagonist, who performs deeds of superhuman strength and stoically suffers unbelievable torments for the sake of his honor. For these readers, Oroonoko's slavery is significant primarily because it

very phrase "royal slave" implies, Oroonoko's tragedy is his commodification. His story elaborates the dark side of the marketplace in persons; in *Oroonoko*, trade in bodies cannot be comically redeemed, as it was in *The Lucky Chance*. Nevertheless, Oroonoko,

---

illustrates that nobility is inborn and manifests itself even under the most adverse circumstances. Later eighteenth- and nineteenth-century commentators, like the Victorian quoted above, read *Oroonoko* as a sentimental tale expressing sympathy for oppressed people in general and slaves in particular. After 1850 it became common to compare it to *Uncle Tom's Cabin* and read it as an emancipationist tract. See, for example, "England's First Lady Novelist," *St. James Magazine* 7 (1863): 854. Twentieth-century commentators have concentrated on the work's satire of European civilization, reading it as a descendant of Montaigne's "Of Cannibals" and an ancestor of Rousseau's *Second Discourse*. This lineage partly accounts for the work's popularity in France; see, for example, Bernard Dhuicq, "*Oroonoko*: Expérience et création," in *Mémoire et création dans le monde anglo-américain aux XVIIe et XVIIIe siècles*, Société d'Etudes anglo-américaines des XVIIe et XVIIIe siècles (Strasbourg: Univ. of Strasbourg, 1983), pp. 41–47. Satiric readings of the work interpret slavery as an instance of the corruptions of commercial society in general, so that Oroonoko himself is seen not as the oppressed slave but as the "natural man," the necessary satiric foil to civilization. See, for example, Peter J. Weston, "The Noble Primitive as Bourgeois Subject," *Literature and History* 10 (1984): 59–71. For a study of the tale that locates it at the beginning of the sentimental novel tradition and emphasizes Behn's gender, see George Starr, "Aphra Behn and the Genealogy of the Man of Feeling," *Modern Philology* 87 (1990): 362–72. Most recent criticism of *Oroonoko* has focused on racial and gender issues. See, for example, Ros Ballaster, "New Hystericism: Aphra Behn's *Oroonoko*: The Body, the Text and the Feminist Critic," in *New Feminist Discourses: Critical Essays on Theories and Texts*, ed. Isobel Armstrong (New York: Routledge, 1992), pp. 283–95, and Ballaster, *Seductive Forms: Women's Amatory Fiction, 1684–1740* (Oxford: Clarendon Press, 1992), pp. 94–99; Laura Brown, "The Romance of Empire: *Oroonoko* and the Trade in Slaves," in *The New Eighteenth Century: Theory, Politics, English Literature*, ed. Felicity Nussbaum and Laura Brown (New York: Methuen, 1987), pp. 41–61; Margaret W. Ferguson, "Juggling the Categories of Race, Class and Gender: Aphra Behn's *Oroonoko*," *Women's Studies* 19 (1991): 159–81; Moira Ferguson, "*Oroonoko*: Birth of a Paradigm," *NLH* 23 (1992): 339–59; Beverle Houston, "Usurpation and Dismemberment: Oedipal Tyranny in *Oroonoko*," *Literature and Psychology* 32 (1986): 30–36; Jacqueline Pearson, "Gender and Narrative in the Fiction of Aphra Behn," part 2, *Review of English Studies* 42 (1991): 184–90; Jane Spencer, *The Rise of the Woman Novelist: From Aphra Behn to Jane Austen* (Oxford: Basil Blackwell, 1986), pp. 47–52; and Dale Spender, *Mothers of the Novel: 100 Good Women Writers before Jane Austen* (London: Pandora, 1986), pp. 60–64. Relevant discussion of *Oroonoko* may also be found in Robert L. Chibka, "'Oh! Do Not Fear a Woman's Invention': Truth, Falsehood, and Fiction in Aphra Behn's *Oroonoko*," *Texas Studies in Literature and Language* 30 (1988): 510–37; George Guffey, "Aphra Behn's *Oroonoko*: Occasion and Accomplishment," in *Two English Novelists: Aphra Behn and Anthony Trollope*, Papers read at a Clark Library Seminar, May 11, 1974, by George Guffey and Andrew Wright (Los Angeles: Clark Library, 1975); Katharine M. Rogers, "Fact and Fiction in Aphra Behn's *Oroonoko*," *Studies in the Novel* 20 (1988): 1–15; and William C. Spengemann, "The Earliest American Novel: Aphra Behn's *Oroonoko*," *Nineteenth-Century Fiction* 38 (1984): 384–414. Unlike the plays, then, this tale has attracted readers in almost every generation and has accumulated a body of historical meanings that is a significant part of Behn's posthumous adventures in the literary marketplace.

like Julia, is a creature conceived entirely within such a market-place. Both the prostituted wife and the enslaved king, by virtue of their oxymoronic nature, are ideal commodities.

As ideal commodities, moreover, each emphasizes a different aspect of Behn's vendable authorship. Chapter 1 concentrated on theatrical exchange and the representation of the emphatically female author through the presence of female bodies on the stage. This chapter concentrates on a far more disembodied form of representation and a less insistently gendered authorial persona. However, what was said in Chapter 1 about the interpenetration of femininity and commodification should still be borne in mind, for it helps explain why Behn, of all Restoration writers, would connect the author with a *sold* king.

That Behn should give her most thoughtful consideration to the issue of sovereignty in the marketplace in a nontheatrical form is significant in light of the prologues discussed earlier. Theatrical representation was consistently characterized there and elsewhere in her work as inimical to sovereign authorial selfhood. In contrast, her various remarks on her reasons for publishing her plays link the medium of print to authorial supremacy. Hence, before turning to *Oroonoko*, I would like to describe the characteristics of author-ship that Behn associated with her dissemination in the disembod-ied, inky darkness of print. For Oroonoko is associated with Behn's authorship not only through his kingly commodification but also through his very blackness.

~

Shortly after Behn started using the monarch-author metaphor, she stopped being a prolific playwright. After 1682 only two new plays were produced in her lifetime: *The Lucky Chance* in 1686 and *The Emperor of the Moon* in 1687. It is improbable that, like Charles II, she had come across a secure source of income, for her letter to Tonson in 1684, discussed in Chapter 1, indicates that she was suffering financially. Almost all the playwrights were. In 1683 Dryden was complaining bitterly of debt and a vastly reduced income, Otway was almost starving to death, and Wycherley was in debtors' prison.[13] Behn, like the other poets, turned to writing occasional political poetry, translations, miscellanies, and prose narratives. She no doubt also sought patronage all the more assiduously.

In addition to the diminished demand for plays, from which all the authors suffered, Behn might have had special reasons for avoiding the stage. In 1682 one of her prologues, which "reflected" on the duke of Monmouth (Charles's illegitimate and soon-to-be openly traitorous son), seems to have displeased the king, and a warrant was issued for her arrest under the libel law. Although there is no record of an actual arrest or prosecution, the warrant might have made the theater seem a more dangerous arena than before. Hence, Behn might have sought the potentially greater anonymity of the print medium. Her massive *Love-Letters between a Nobleman and His Sister* (1684–87), for example, also "reflected" on Monmouth and others of his circle, but part 1 was published anonymously. Moreover, there is evidence that Behn was ill during these years, and hence she may have lacked the stamina required of Restoration playwrights, who were often involved in casting the plays, altering them during rehearsals, and generally struggling to see that they were well produced.[14]

Behn's sense of her medium, therefore, was shifting away from theatrical production toward print, and the shift probably intensified her concern with the issue of authorial sovereignty in the marketplace. Even quite early in her career, Behn had contrasted print with theatrical performance and (unexpectedly, given the comparatively small income books provided) extolled the power of the printed word and its superior ability to communicate the author's intentions and designs. One of the themes of Behn's forewords to the printed editions of her plays is that publication shows the reader just what the writer had in mind, without the distorting effect of playgoers' noise or actors' quirks. Over the printed edition, she suggests, the mind of the author has sovereign control; other people's collaborations and interferences are minimal, and hence the printed text is the real play, disseminated for careful and private

13. Angeline Goreau, *Reconstructing Aphra: A Social Biography of Aphra Behn* (New York: Dial, 1980), p. 253.
14. Emmett L. Avery and Arthur H. Scouten, introduction to *The London Stage. Part I: 1660–1700*, ed. William Van Lennep (Carbondale: Southern Illinois Univ. Press, 1965), pp. clii–cliii.

perusal. It is the objective evidence that she sends into the world to establish supremacy over works that have been appropriated and "marred" by actors or misinterpreted in the reports of critics. "I Printed this Play with all the impatient haste one ought to do, who would be vindicated from the most unjust and silly aspersion,"[15] begins the epistle to *Sir Patient Fancy.* What the printed text will represent perfectly and directly, she claims, is the author's individual design, her intellectual conception. She asks her readers not to be swayed by reports of the performance but rather to take the printed play "into their serious Consideration in their Cabinets."

Thus print is presented as a superior medium because it is relatively independent of time and place. Since it is explicitly opposed to live actors performing for an often raucous and crowded audience, its appeal seems based on its transcendence of these physical conditions, which had obstructed the public's view of the author's thought. Indeed, the preface to *The Lucky Chance* implies that the excitement of the moment in the theater overwhelms the audience's judgment: "I cannot omit to tell you, that a Wit of the Town, a friend of mine at Wills Coffee House, the first Night of the Play, cry'd it down as much as in him lay, who read it and assured me he never saw a prettier Comedy."[16] The medium of bodies striding about and speaking on a stage, which Behn skillfully exploited, is potentially an impediment to authorial communication:

> Know then that this Play was hugely injur'd in the Acting, for 'twas done so imperfectly as never any was before, which did more harm to this than it could have done to any of another sort; the Plot being busie . . . and so requiring a continual attention, which being interrupted by the intolerable negligence of some that acted in it, must needs much spoil the beauty on't.[17]

15. *Works,* vol. 4, p. 7.
16. *Works,* vol. 3, p. 187.
17. *The Dutch Lover,* in *Works,* vol. 1, pp. 224–25. Shirley Strum Kenny gives other examples of "the battles of actors and authors over the text" (p. 316). She quotes a satirical scene from Richard Sheridan's *The Critic* in which the character of the author laments the destruction of his play in performance and consoles himself with the thought of print: "The pruning knife—zounds the axe! why, here has been such lopping and topping, I shan't have the bare trunk of my play left presently.— Very well, Sir—the performers must do as they please, but upon my soul, I'll print every word" (quoted on p. 317 of "The Publication of Plays," in *The London Theatre World, 1660–1800,* ed. Robert D. Hume [Carbondale: Southern Illinois Univ. Press, 1980], pp. 309–36).

The dense, embodied nature of theatrical production seems peculiarly unsuited to the representation of that mental essence, the playwright's intention, whereas the comparatively disembodied marks on the page are imagined as transparent revelations of her design. Hence, she claims that she should be judged only after "reading, comparing . . . thinking."[18] Through print readers can separate themselves from the crowd and find, in private places and moments, the author's intended meaning.

By stressing the speed and extent of her textual dissemination, Behn's epistles make it clear that she is contrasting *printed,* and not just written, representation with performance. Her need quickly to counteract mangled performances or false rumors of her plays puts a certain emphasis on the technology of rapid and standardized reproduction.[19] Moreover, only through print publication could she even conceive of herself as an author with the power to make a direct textual appeal to the public: a set of discrete but anonymous individuals, each of whom would possess other books with which to compare and judge hers.[20]

The epistles to the plays, therefore, demonstrate a high level of consciousness of print as a separate and superior form of representation, one that allowed the author a sovereign control and gave her thoughts a disembodied, almost unmediated, presence in the public mind. Nevertheless, the printed plays remained an after-effect, or epiphenomenon, of theatrical production; they derived their peculiar charm and also their raison d'être from the shortcomings of performance. Moreover, we should bear in mind that the epistles helped create the sense of obligation on the part of play-goers that might be redeemed on future third nights. Hence print and performance are peculiarly enmeshed in the marketplace of the theater.

18. *Works,* vol. 3, p. 185.
19. Shirley Strum Kenny points out that "most plays of the period have the appearance of hasty and careless printing. . . . The kinds of error corrected most frequently suggest that printinghouse personnel, not authors, read proof. . . . The important thing was not neatness or accuracy but speed" ("The Publication of Plays," p. 319).
20. On the relationship between new forms of individualism and print technology, see Elizabeth L. Eisenstein, *The Printing Revolution in Early Modern Europe* (Cambridge: Cambridge Univ. Press, 1983), pp. 50–58. My remarks on the general features of print culture throughout this chapter are heavily indebted to part 1 of Eisenstein's book.

When Behn turned to publishing prose narratives that were independent of her theatrical career,[21] another potentially advantageous aspect of print emerged: anonymity. The ultimate unknowability of the prostitute had always been part of the allure of Behn the playwright, but her first prose narrative, the initial volume of the *Love-Letters between a Nobleman and His Sister*, was anonymous in the more usual sense of being unsigned. We do not know how many of Behn's other stories were intended for anonymous publication, since all but two of them, *The Fair Jilt* and *Oroonoko* (both 1688), were published posthumously by editors and booksellers who capitalized on her name. Internal evidence, drawn primarily from the narrative personae, suggests that some of them were to have been anonymously or pseudonymously published.

Even if Behn intended to publish these works under her own name and draw, as she did in *Oroonoko*, on her established reputation as a playwright, a leitmotif linking written representation and anonymity runs through the stories. The narrators, for example, are even more shadowy than the protean designer of the majority of the comedies, and their obscurity paradoxically enhances the effect of authorial control and independence. The tales stress that all written communication takes place in the dark, which is only intensified by publication. Such a darkness, however, is also presented as the natural element of authorial transfiguration.

21. I do not call Behn's stories novels in this study because I prefer to reserve that term for self-proclaimed fictional works. Critics have argued that *Oroonoko* strongly resembles a novel because of its uncertain veracity: thus Lennard Davis, for example, argues that "every turn reveals fact warped into fiction which turns back upon itself to become fact," while Robert L. Chibka, agreeing with Davis, claims that "the novel is a form of discourse that suspends its readers on a knife-edge between belief and disbelief" (see Lennard J. Davis, *Factual Fictions: The Origins of the English Novel* [New York: Columbia Univ. Press, 1983], p. 110; and Chibka, "'Oh! Do Not Fear a Woman's Invention': Truth, Falsehood, and Fiction in Aphra Behn's *Oroonoko*," p. 513). These arguments do not persuasively link *Oroonoko* to the novel. When the conventions of novelistic form are truly in place, we do not wonder about a book's referentiality. In contrast to Chibka and Davis, I argue that the truth-falsehood byplay marks *Oroonoko* as, at best, a proto-novel. For other discussions of genre in Behn's tales generally and *Oroonoko* specifically, see Frederick M. Link, *Aphra Behn* (New York: Twayne, 1968), chapter 8; Michael McKeon, *The Origins of the English Novel, 1600–1740* (Baltimore, MD: Johns Hopkins Univ. Press, 1987), pp. 111–13; Rogers, "Fact and Fiction in Aphra Behn's *Oroonoko*," pp. 1–15; Paul Salzman, *English Prose Fiction, 1558–1700: A Critical History* (Oxford: Clarendon Press, 1986), chapter 17; and Spengemann, "The Earliest American Novel: Aphra Behn's *Oroonoko*," pp. 392ff. Both Chibka and Davis also provide excellent accounts of the veracity issue in the novel and its importance for narrative structure.

Behn's narrators, to be sure, are not the faceless, third-person, omniscient storytellers invented by later generations of writers. In accordance with the conventions of the seventeenth century, almost all of them intermittently use the first person, especially to explain how they came by their knowledge of the story. In the very process of explaining themselves, however, the narrators often become mysterious. The following passage from *Love-Letters between a Nobleman and His Sister* is typical of these first-person statements: "I have heard her page say, from whom I have had a great part of the truths of her life, that he never saw Sylvia in so pleasant a humour all his life before, nor seemed so well pleased, which gave him, her lover [the page], a jealousy that perplexed him above any thing he had ever felt from love; though he durst not own it."[22] At first glance, the passage seems to reveal the narrator; however, it actually serves to obscure her.[23] Her information comes from servants, who, moreover, like the page mentioned here, long to be actors in the drama they are only allowed to observe. She moves mysteriously below stairs, collecting information like a spy.

Often allied in this with the frustrated and relatively anonymous instruments of the main characters (Sylvia's page has no name), Behn's narrators are sometimes associated with a marginality that becomes sinister. One such instance is particularly interesting in connection with *Oroonoko*. In "The Unfortunate Bride; or, the Blind Lady a Beauty," the narrator claims that much of her information comes indirectly from a black woman, Mooria, who not only longs to be the object of the hero's love but also steals his letters to his mistress and forges letters to drive the lovers apart. The story makes the lady's blackness a metaphor for her "dark designs" and for her means of accomplishing them: stealing the writings of others and writing "in a disguised hand." The black lady, in other words, is an inky creature who separates people from their written representations and plunges them into obscurity. She is more designing than the narrator and more adept than any other character at achieving her designs by textual misrepresentation.

Although in Behn's stories there are several such designing

---

22. *Love-Letters between a Nobleman and His Sister,* introd. Maureen Duffy (London: Virago, 1987), p. 405.
23. *Love-Letters* sometimes presents the narrator as masculine, but in the third volume, a feminine persona is consistently used.

women, who manipulate the action by disguising their "hands," Mooria is the only one who *embodies* this form of power. The darkness of her skin is associated with invisibility and magical powers of transformation; that is, her black body seems a metaphor for the disembodying potential of writing. The very ink that allows graphic representation, and the consequent dissociation of bodies and language, seems to cover Mooria herself.

Since Mooria's skin becomes an emblem of the disembodying power of writing, for which the blackness of ink is a related sign, her darkness suggests by association the "anonymous hand" par excellence: print, the medium of the story's dissemination. Print intensified anonymity simply by increasing standardization, making the graphemes relatively interchangeable regardless of their origin, and by wide dissemination, which broke the link common in scribal cultures between texts and specific places where they could be read. The more identical copies of a text there were, the less that text seemed to occupy any particular location, and the less it seemed the physical emanation of any body. The figure of the black woman combines the blackness of racial difference, the obscurity of the narrative "I" in this particular story, and the potential erasure of the writer through the "anonymous hand" of publication.[24]

However, since our modern notion of the author is itself a feature of print culture, we must acknowledge that the disembodiment of the writer in the standardized, multiplied, and widely disseminated text was the condition of her appearance as an *author*. As Elizabeth Eisenstein shows, "Until it became possible to distinguish between composing a poem and reciting one, or writing a book and copying one; until books could be classified by something other than incipits;[25] the modern game of books and authors could not be

24. As we might also have predicted, the black lady of this story identifies all these aspects of difference with female desire. As in *The Lucky Chance*, the very principle of difference, and hence, paradoxically, of interchangeability, is the "nothing" of female sexuality, whose obscurity is stressed in yet another seventeenth-century slang term for the female sexual part: "the black ace" (Goreau, *Reconstructing Aphra*, p. 232). In *The Lucky Chance*, however, the "nothing" is "but a part" of Julia, whereas the black lady is the black ace writ large. Hence, in the act of identifying her source, the narrator of "The Unfortunate Bride" implies that to appear in print is to reach some apotheosis of femaleness by not appearing at all.

25. Scribal copies generally did not have title pages; instead they opened with

played."[26] The potential anonymity realized in the figure of Mooria, therefore, was merely the underside of that seemingly unmediated and purely mental presence that Behn celebrated in the epistles to the printed edition of her plays.

This same paradoxical effect vis-à-vis the author—that decreased physical proximity enabled increased mental intimacy—was also built into the property exchanges that accompanied the production of the books. There was no third night in the print shop, no specific time and place for gathering to reward the author. The printed work appeared before public and patron only after it had ceased to be the exchangeable property of the author. The books that came out during Behn's lifetime were printed under the Licensing Act of 1662, which gave the court of the Stationers' Company, that is, the guild of printers and booksellers, control over the printing of texts entered in the company's register. Behn sold her manuscripts, the only actual commodities she ever owned, to booksellers, who sometimes traded on her name and sometimes did not; but she never trafficked in the right to print her text, since that was brought into being only when the bookseller registered the work.[27] Hence Behn, unlike authors after the passage of the 1710 Copyright Act, never had potential property in the text, as distinct from the physical manuscript. She had no share of the income from the book's sales, and the only hope for remuneration after publication

conventional phrases or incipits, a word deriving from the commonplace opening phrase "Incipit Liber" (Here begins the book).

26. Eisenstein, p. 84.

27. The question of common law copyright prior to 1710 is vexed. Some historians have claimed that before the Statute of Anne the author was assumed to be a common law owner of a literary work, but the case for such a view is very weak. See Frank Arthur Mumby, *Publishing and Bookselling* (London: Cape, 1930), pp. 169–71; and Joseph Loewenstein, "For a History of Literary Property: John Wolfe's Reformation," *ELR* 18 (1988): 389–412. For a refutation of this view, see Mark Rose, *Authors and Owners: The Invention of Copyright* (Cambridge: Harvard Univ. Press, 1993). The copyright and a script of the work were both called the copy, indicating that someone who managed to procure a copy of the text that had not been registered had the right to copy it. For a lucid discussion of the complex relationship between the laws governing the book trade and the actual practices of London booksellers, see Graham Pollard, "The English Market for Printed Books," *Publishing History* 4 (1978): 7–48. Useful analyses of print culture in this era may also be found in Julie Peters, "The Bank, the Press, and the Illusory 'Return of Nature': On Currency, Print, and Dramatic Property in the 1690s"; and Gerald M. MacLean, "Class, Gender, and the Progress of Property: Scattered Speculations on Print Culture in Seventeenth-Century England," unpublished conference papers, Center for Seventeenth- and Eighteenth-Century Studies, University of California, Los Angeles, 1990.

was founded on a dedicatee's generosity. Nevertheless, the author seemed to participate quite cheerfully in the process that turned her physical product, the manuscript, into the multiple standard copies that she praised as the carriers of her true design, for the less Behn owned it, the more perfectly it conformed to her intention. The sale of the manuscript and the inconceivability of any property in the text were indeed forms of alienation from the work, but they were also the conditions of what Behn seemed to imagine as her ghostly endurance in the text. The appearance of the multiplied, perfected text magnified her lack of dependence on any particular material object. The more standardized and impersonal the medium became, the more sovereign the creating mind appeared.[28] The delivery of the manuscript to the bookseller, the alienation of one's "hand" and the first occasion of payment to the author, was also the first step in liberating the text from graphic contingency. A second step, at which the author normally received the balance of the money due from the bookseller, was the return of the corrected proofs, a hybrid of anonymous print and authorial marks signaling progress toward an ever more readable copy. Finally, the reproduction and sale of the *identical text* in numerous copies provided proof of the ideas' transcendent nonmateriality, their escape from the physical accidents of place and time,[29] and therefore of their substantive likeness to the immaterial and immortal mind they represented.[30]

28. Critics of Elizabeth Eisenstein have pointed out that many early modern writers complained about the inaccuracy of print and the tendency of printers to introduce changes as well as to make errors. We have no warrant, however, for believing that Behn shared these grievances. Rather, the internal evidence suggests that she thought publication superior to performance as a means of conveying her conceptions. She was fortunate to have a reliable bookseller, Jacob Tonson, to look after the publication of her tales and poetic works. For a description of Behn's booksellers, see Payne, "'And Poets Shall by Patron-Princes Live': Aphra Behn and Patronage," p. 109.

29. See Eisenstein's remarks on the preservative powers of print, pp. 78–88, where she explains that wide dissemination became the means of making the text imperishable. "The notion that valuable data could be preserved best by being made public, rather than by being kept secret, ran counter to tradition," she claims, and was still controversial in the eighteenth century. Behn, however, seems to have been quite secure in the belief that publication would make her words immortal.

30. When Walter Benjamin argues in his famous essay "The Work of Art in the Age of Mechanical Reproduction" that the artwork loses its aura when it is reproduced and disseminated en masse, he fails to distinguish between books and texts.

Such a notation of a transcendent text, elevated above all materiality, preceded print; but print paradoxically gave material evidence for a text surpassing all copies. The potential for seemingly infinite reproduction obviated the possibility of equating the text with any, or for that matter all, of its instantiations. Behn imagines that through such wide dissemination her ideas can be anywhere and yet nowhere in particular. Like other seventeenth-century writers,[31] she seems fascinated with not only the appearance of the anonymous hand but also the gap between the physical act of writing and the immaterial result. Hence she confesses the haste of the book's composition in the dedication to *Oroonoko*—"I writ it in a few hours . . . I never rested my pen a moment"[32]—even as she contrasts the ephemeral, bodily labor to the eternal, static, spiritual product: "[Poets] draw the nobler part, the soul and mind; the pictures of the pen shall out-last [the drawing] of the pencil, and even worlds themselves." Oddly, Behn used her preoccupation with her pen—she frequently thematized the physical production of words—to remind us that writing is not really a graphic art. The black ink that outshines the "pencil" marks of the visual artist signifies the incorporeal and immortal, not only because it "draw[s] the nobler part," but also because the text perpetuated in print

---

Thus he does not acknowledge that mechanical reproduction results in a new auratic emanation, even if it is one that is easily detachable from the physical book itself. Stephen Greenblatt comes closer to the argument I am making here in his chapter "The Word of God in the Age of Mechanical Reproduction," where he argues that the wide dissemination of the published English Bible gave the English a far more powerful sense of the immediate presence of God's word than could have been provided by the scarcer and more "auratic" scribal copies. ·Although he does not emphasize the distinction between the physical book and the abstract text, he implies it when he notes that "the power of the English Bible was at its height precisely in the years when copies were publicly burned by the authorities" (*Renaissance Self-Fashioning: From More to Shakespeare* [Chicago: Univ. of Chicago Press, 1980], p. 96).

31. Not until the Restoration did writers explore the implications of communicating with readers through print. Although the technology was two hundred years old by 1660, Dryden seems to have been the first author to notice its impact. "Dryden is among the first English writers to understand, at least implicitly, the conditions imposed on a literature that is primarily printed and read . . . where books and writing are the main instruments of transmission," claims James Engell in *Forming the Critical Mind: Dryden to Coleridge* (Cambridge: Harvard Univ. Press, 1989), p. 22.

32. *Oroonoko and Other Stories*, ed. and introd. Maureen Duffy (London: Methuen, 1986), p. 25.

seems to rise above its own graphics. The blackness of ink, therefore, paradoxically seems to presage even its own disappearance,
a disappearance that Oroonoko ultimately achieves.

~

The relationship of blackness, authorship, textuality, exchange, and
transcendence helps explain why Behn's most sustained work on
heroic kingship should make black the color of both exchange and
sovereignty. In *Oroonoko* Behn breaks the traditional Western metaphoric connection between black bodies and moral degeneracy
that she had drawn on in characterizing Mooria, and blackness
takes on unprecedented meanings, including representation itself,
kingship, exchange value, and the paradoxes of absolute property.

Oroonoko seems the polar opposite of "The Unfortunate Bride."
The narrator not only claims her authorial identity and her personal
experience of the events but also gives herself an important role
in the story and hence a sustained presence.[33] She identifies herself as Aphra Behn, a writer already known to the public as a
playwright, whose established reputation should guarantee her
veracity. She even discusses her next play, stressing that, like
Oroonoko, it is based to some extent on her life experience: "Colonel
Martin [was] a man of great gallantry, wit, and goodness, and
whom I have celebrated in a character of my new comedy, by his
own name, in memory of so brave a man."[34] Clearly, she highlights personal-authorial continuity as a guarantee of the tale's
authenticity.

This stress on the work as an expression of the author's identity
has a parallel in the metaphoric use of blackness. Whereas in "The
Unfortunate Bride" the narrator's anonymity seemed intensified by

33. This presence is not unusual in stories about the wonders of the New World,
where narrators routinely felt obliged to claim that they were eyewitnesses of the
events they relate. Most of the evidence, though, does point to Behn's presence in
Surinam in the early to mid 1660s; see Rogers, "Fact and Fiction in Aphra Behn's
Oroonoko," pp. 1–3. For discussion of the critical controversy over Behn's eyewitness
status, see Chibka, "'Oh! Do Not Fear a Woman's Invention': Truth, Falsehood, and
Fiction in Aphra Behn's *Oroonoko*," pp. 510–13.

34. *Oroonoko; or, the Royal Slave: A True History*, in *Oroonoko, the Rover, and Other
Works*, ed. Janet Todd (London: Penguin, 1992), p. 132. Subsequent quotations from
this edition are cited parenthetically in the text.

the "dusky" obscurity of Mooria, the narrative's source, in *Oroonoko* the gleaming blackness of the eponymous hero corresponds to the narrator's heightened presence. If Mooria's color emphasized her invisibility and that of the narrator, Oroonoko's radiates, illuminating the narrator's identity. He is blacker than the black lady—indeed he is blacker than anybody—but that does not make him "dusky." Instead, it makes him brilliant: "His face was not of that brown, rusty black which most of that nation are, but a perfect ebony, or polished jet" (pp. 80–81). He is not a *brown* black, but a black black. Behn's distinction between brown blacks and black blacks departs from the convention of representing sub-Saharan native people, who, according to Winthrop Jordan, were normally all described as absolutely black: "blacke as coles," as one voyager to Guinea put it a century earlier.[35] By making complete blackness a distinguishing characteristic of the noble Oroonoko, Behn attached a positive aesthetic value to the skin color: the brown blacks are dull, but the shiny black black reflects light.[36] Even when he was dressed in slave's clothes, Oroonoko's gleaming blackness "shone through all" (p. 108). The lustrous quality of the hero's blackness, which is "so beyond all report," requires the eyewitness reporting of a known author; Aphra Behn, therefore, must emerge from her obscurity and explain the circumstances of her witnessing. In short, the hero's blackness calls the authorial persona into existence.

As a character, Behn is also clearly paralleled with Oroonoko.[37]

---

35. Jordan, *White over Black: American Attitudes toward the Negro, 1550–1800* (Chapel Hill: Univ. of North Carolina Press, 1968), p. 5.

36. In a footnote Jordan names several later writers who celebrate "the Negro's jet blackness," but Behn's is the earliest instance by over thirty years. Jordan, p. 10 n. 23. Lines 16–20 from Milton's *Il Penseroso*, which Jordan does not cite, might be taken as a precedent:

> Black, but such as in esteme
> Prince Memnon's sister might beseem
> Or that starred Ethiop queen that strove
> To set her beauty's praise above
> The sea nymphs, and their powers offended.

The mythical nature of these beings and their allegorical use as illustrations of the attractiveness of Melancholy's blackness, however, disqualify them as representations of seventeenth-century Africans.

37. For analyses of the narrator-hero relationship, see Martine Watson Brownley, "The Narrator in *Oroonoko*," *Essays in Literature* 4 (1977): 174–81; Ferguson, "Juggling the Categories of Race, Class and Gender: Aphra Behn's *Oroonoko*," pp. 165–66; Pearson, "Gender and Narrative in the Fiction of Aphra Behn," part 2, pp. 184–90;

Like him, she arrives a stranger in Surinam but is immediately recognized as superior to the local inhabitants; like him, she appears a shining marvel when she travels to the Indian village; and like his words, hers are always truthful. As narrator, she repeatedly identifies herself as the well-known author Aphra Behn to vouch for the otherwise incredible brightness of Oroonoko. The sustained authorial presence in this book is thus closely connected to the black hero's luster; as the story moves forward, narrator and hero polish each other's fame. Although in the beginning Oroonoko had the misfortune "to fall in an obscure world, that afforded only a female pen to celebrate his fame" (p. 108), by the end the narrator presumes to hope "the reputation of my pen is considerable enough to make his glorious name to survive to all ages" (p. 141).

Hence through an intensification of blackness, hero and narrator emerge into the light. Like Behn's forewords to her plays, this process can be read as a full-blown celebration of the bright, transcendent possibilities inherent in print, possibilities that Mooria only darkly suggested. Oroonoko resembles the mystical body of the text.[38] His blackness is a luminous emanation of the author that gleams forth from multiple inscriptions.

Such an interpretation of this "admirably turned" (p. 80) ebony figure is consonant with one of Oroonoko's most remarked features: he is densely overwritten. Indeed, the narrator seems quite self-consciously to present her hero's story as a layering of narrative conventions. She moves from her de rigueur promise to tell the unadorned truth in the opening paragraph into a brief wonders-of-the-New-World passage whose extreme conventionality has often been noted. Indeed, she notes it herself on the second page when the wonders turn into London's stage spectacles, and the authenticity of her story momentarily depends on its "intertextual" relationship to one of Dryden's plays: "I had a [suit of feathers made by the Indians] presented to me, and I gave them to the King's Theatre; it was the dress of the Indian Queen, infinitely admired by persons of quality; and was inimitable." The momen-

---

Spencer, *The Rise of the Woman Novelist*, pp. 47–52; and Starr, "Aphra Behn and the Genealogy of the Man of Feeling," pp. 362–68.

38. For a fascinating discussion of the parallels between kingship and textuality in the early modern period, see David Lee Miller, *The Poem's Two Bodies: The Poetics of the 1590 Faerie Queene* (Princeton, NJ: Princeton Univ. Press, 1988).

tary uncertainty about which Indian queen is being referred to, a queen of the Indians who owned the dress or Dryden's stage heroine, only emphasizes the lack of distinction between the two possible meanings. As a real Indian artifact transferred to the stage, the dress authenticates both. Readers can be assured of the truth of Behn's claims because their own eyes have seen such things on the stage. The early part of Oroonoko's story is no less dependent on references to the theater and on the self-conscious employment of courtly intrigue conventions to familiarize and authenticate the action. And the brief idyll of the middle section is similarly realized through reference to a literary model; when Oroonoko and his wife, Imoinda, are reunited, Oroonoko's English protector and putative master, looking on, "was infinitely pleased with this novel" (p. 112). One could continue to multiply the evidence, for the last half of Oroonoko's history is particularly thickly encrusted with tragic references and is highly wrought in the histrionic codes of heroic drama.[39]

This dense literary artificiality has exasperated some modern readers of *Oroonoko* and has been the chief evidence in the twentieth century for the story's inauthenticity.[40] The stress on Oroonoko's conformity to literary conventions, however, was probably intended to make him seem believably noble. The narrator proves the hero's greatness by showing how closely he adhered to heroic models. The sense that Oroonoko was made up of myriad literary conventions would have made him familiar and hence credible to contemporary readers, for real heroic action was necessarily imitative.[41] The resolute intertextuality of the narrative was not a failure of imagination but rather a proof that the author deserved fame because she had a legitimately heroic story that was recognizable as such only because it conformed to other such representations.

We can read Oroonoko's gleaming blackness, then, as a celebration of inscription without turning it into a self-reflective modern

39. In 1696 Thomas Southerne turned the story into just such a play, which, in various versions, was a staple of the eighteenth-century repertory.

40. See, for example, Ernest Bernbaum, "Mrs. Behn's *Oroonoko*," in *Anniversary Papers by Colleagues and Pupils of George Lyman Kittredge* (Boston: Ginn and Co., 1913).

41. On *Oroonoko*'s relation to heroic drama, see Brown, "The Romance of Empire: *Oroonoko* and the Trade in Slaves," pp. 48–51.

text. However, a danger lurks in such a reading. If Oroonoko's blackness becomes mainly an allegory of textuality, even with such historical and formal qualifications as have been introduced, we lose sight of the phenomenal wonder that empowers the text in the first place. Unless we acknowledge that Oroonoko's blackness refers most importantly to racial difference and indeed is dependent on a stock response of racial prejudice in the reader, we cannot explain what is so wonderful about him and so meritorious in the author. The reader is frequently invited to marvel that Oroonoko, *although black*, behaves like a conventional European tragic hero. Hence passages such as the following rely for their sense of the marvelous on the very racial prejudice they seem to dispel:

> His nose was rising and Roman, instead of African and flat. His mouth, the finest shaped that could be seen; far from those great turned lips, which are so natural to the rest of the Negroes. The whole proportion and air of his face was so noble, and exactly formed, that, bating his colour, there could be nothing in nature more beautiful, agreeable and handsome. . . . Nor did the perfections of his mind come short of those of his person; for his discourse was admirable upon almost any subject; and whoever had heard him speak, would have been convinced of their errors, that all fine wit is confined to the white men, especially to those of Christendom; and would have confessed that Oroonoko was as capable even of reigning well, and of governing as wisely, had as great a soul, as politic maxims, and was as sensible of power, as any prince civilized in the most refined schools of humanity and learning, or the most illustrious courts. (p. 80)

Oroonoko is a wonder because blackness and heroism are normally thought to be mutually exclusive qualities; indeed, the passage asserts that they normally *are* mutually exclusive. Only in his differences from other Africans does Oroonoko achieve heroism, but in his blackness his heroism partakes of the marvelous. His is a "beauty so transcending all those of his gloomy race, that he struck an awe and reverence, even in those that knew not his quality; as he did in me, who beheld him with surprise and wonder" (p. 79). Thus his color, as a sign of racial difference, itself reminds us that all his features differ from those "which are so natural to the rest of the Negroes."

Oroonoko's blackness must therefore be seen as at once authentically and unnaturally African. It is the exotic trait that makes his story worth writing, the feature that makes him unprecedented as hero, and hence a wonder. However, it is also the feature that necessitates such an energetic marshaling of heroic literary precedents. Both hero and writer must overcome his blackness, which "naturally" threatens to become the condition of his obscurity even though it also makes him worthy of fame. The author packs Oroonoko so densely with heroic reference as to prove him wonderful, making his very blackness shine. Blackness as racial difference at once helps explain why Oroonoko's color gleams with "unnatural" intertextuality and reveals how such gleaming redounds to the glory of the author.

Oroonoko's blackness, a "natural" physical indication of racial difference, even inferiority, is transubstantiated textually into a wonderful sign of heroic distinction. It is thus highly appropriate that descriptions of Oroonoko's and Imoinda's heroic bodies should emphasize their artificiality; they are not so much bodies of flesh and blood as pieces of polished handiwork. "The most famous statuary could not form the figure of a man more admirably turned from head to foot" is the sentence that precedes the description of Oroonoko's color as "not of that brown, rusty black which most of that nation are, but a perfect ebony, or polished jet." Readers are called on here to put the actual African bodies they might have seen (the *brown* black ones) out of mind and substitute for them statues of ebony. Indeed, when Oroonoko alights at Surinam dressed in his "dazzling habits" to be gazed at in his journey to his new home by the whites and the merely "brown" blacks, he resembles nothing so much as the statue of a magus. These common Africans eventually greet him as king and even, in a scene that fuses Christ child and magus, fall to worshiping him as divine when he finally arrives at his destination.

Imoinda's body is also artifactual, but in a slightly different way. At first she is described merely as a female version of Oroonoko; the allusions are appropriately classicized to suggest a female divinity: "To describe her truly, one need say only, she was female to the noble male; the beautiful black Venus, to our young Mars" (p. 81). Her features, like his, are to be imagined as European, and the description of the pair of lovers might well have evoked images of Jonson's *Mask of Blackness,* or of the actors and actresses in blackface and lavish costumes who played the "kings" and "queens" of Africa and India in the lord mayors' pageants.[42] Such figures would have been quite appropriate to the court intrigue section of the novel. However, after Imoinda has been sold into slavery, has had her name changed to Clemene (as Oroonoko has his changed to Caesar), and emerges into our view through the eyes of the white colonists, her body undergoes a fabulous transformation:

> Though from her being carved in fine flowers and birds all over her body, we took her to be of quality before, yet, when we knew Clemene was Imoinda, we could not enough admire her.
>
> I had forgot to tell you, that those who are nobly born of that country, are so delicately cut and raced all over the fore-part of the trunk of their bodies, that it looks as if it were japanned; the works being raised like high point round the edges of the flowers. (p. 112)

This abrupt scoring of Imoinda's body, so strongly and clumsily marked in the text ("I had forgot to tell you") coincides with the narrator's re-vision of her as at once slave and romantic heroine, "Clemene" and Imoinda. Appropriately, Imoinda's body is not just transformed textually, through metaphor, but is supposed to have been transformed materially into an artificial decorative object of exotic origin; she is "japanned," like a highly varnished and intricate piece of oriental carving. And yet she is not quite statuary in this description because the plasticity and pliancy of actual flesh as well as its susceptibility to wounding, scarring, and discoloration are invoked by the description. Finally, the reference to "high point" makes Imoinda's flesh into its own laced clothing.[43] Her body becomes a fabric for representing other things; it is inscribed.

---

42. For a description of the blackface characters in the lord mayor's pageants, see Anthony Gerard Barthelemy, *Black Face, Maligned Race: The Representation of Blacks in English Drama from Shakespeare to Southerne* (Baton Rouge: Louisiana State Univ. Press, 1987), chapter 3. For other possible references in Imoinda's iconography, see Ferguson, "Juggling the Categories of Race, Class and Gender: Aphra Behn's *Oroonoko*," p. 181 n. 49.

43. The Reverend Richard Hakluyt, indeed, calls this kind of African body carving a form of "branched damaske" and says that it takes the place of clothing (*Principal Navigations, Voyages, Traffiques and Discoveries of the English Nation*, 12 vols. [Glasgow: James Maclehose and Sons, 1903–05], vol. 4, p. 62). For other discussions of the insistent physicality of Imoinda and its hint of a conflict between the narrator and this black heroine, see Ballaster, "New Hystericism: Aphra Behn's *Oroonoko*," pp. 290–93; and Ferguson, "Juggling the Categories of Race, Class and Gender: Aphra Behn's *Oroonoko*," pp. 170–71.

The descriptions thus stress the exotic artificiality of both Oroonoko and Imoinda, but the decoration of Imoinda suggests that her sublimation, the process of becoming art, is accomplished on her body. That is, the reader's experience of flesh is not· altogether banished from Imoinda's description, as it is from Oroonoko's. Even more obtrusively than Oroonoko's, Imoinda's is a body of representation. However, we are required, in this revision of her halfway through the story, to imagine her skin as the material out of which the representations are made. Oroonoko, on the one hand, is a completed representation; the African body is useful to his description only as contrast. Imoinda, on the other hand, reminds us that such refinement uses up bodies. Consequently, her image directs us to a consideration of the full relationship between Oroonoko and the commonplace "brown" Africans in the tale.

~

The overwrought artificiality of Oroonoko, symbolized by the gleaming blackness of his body, not only sets him apart from his countrymen but also suggests the two ways in which he absorbs and represents them: through kingship and commodification. On an abstract level, one could point to a structural homology between Oroonoko's unnatural blackness and kingship as it was conceived from the late Middle Ages through the seventeenth century.[44] Just as Oroonoko can be seen as the mystical body of the text, that which outlives myriad graphic instantiations to become the repository of overlapping forms of heroism; and just as his heroism, like the book's textuality, both depends on and is poised against blackness—the blackness of print, the blackness of racial difference (both, in turn, concepts abstracted from physical objects)—so kingship was perceived as a mystical body standing above and incor-

---

44. I am not arguing here that Oroonoko is supposed to be any particular king or all the Stuarts collectively. Rather, Oroonoko, although he may indeed bring to mind certain Stuarts, is the symbol of an entity that is itself symbolic, kingship, and represents a seventeenth-century revision of that entity. For arguments that detect likeness with the Stuart kings, see Guffey, "Aphra Behn's *Oroonoko*: Occasion and Accomplishment," pp. 3–41; and Brown, "The Romance of Empire: *Oroonoko* and the Trade in Slaves," pp. 57–59.

porating all bodies in the realm but also outliving them and thus proving the realm's continuity through time.

In Ernst Kantorowicz's well-known account of this concept, the mystical body of the king both depends on physical bodies and is contrasted to them.[45] Since all the realm's bodies are imagined to be incorporated in one, with the king as the head, all are imagined to be, in some sense, the bodies of the king; and yet in no physical body, not even his own, is true kingship completely contained, for the king's physical body, subject to decay and death, merely represents the immortal kingship that temporarily inhabits it. How the king's physical body represented kingship was a subject of some debate, especially in the years preceding and following the regicide, which Parliament justified by claiming in effect that *it* was the mystical body of the king, and Charles I's body was that of an enemy to the "real" sovereign. Such a radical splitting off of the actual and mystical bodies, however, was abnormal, and the explicit ideology of a high Tory like Behn would have held that the king's actual body, as long as it breathed, was the sacred and unique incarnation of the realm's mystical incorporation. Nevertheless, the king's two bodies were conceptually separable, and in *Oroonoko* they emphatically come apart so that the body of kingship itself, like the text, achieves a kind of incorporeality.

The narrator often refers to Oroonoko's kingship as if it were comparable to normal European models. In the initial description quoted earlier, for example, her stress on his heroism culminates in the greatest wonder of all, which her European readers would have found most difficult to believe: "That Oroonoko was as capable even of reigning well, and of governing as wisely . . . as any prince civilized in the most refined schools of humanity and learning, or the most illustrious courts." It is not surprising that such an ideal of princely capability would be figured in a bloodless statue of a body, one contrasted to living bodies and made imperishable through metaphors, for Behn in this figure represents not just a king, but kingship. As a specimen of a mere African king, we are given Oroonoko's grandfather, who is "a man of a hundred and

45. I give in this paragraph a schematic summary of the intricate and complicated arguments described by Kantorowicz in *The King's Two Bodies* (Princeton, NJ: Princeton Univ. Press, 1957).

odd years old" (p. 79) but who, far from having any marks of immortality about him, is senile and sexually impotent. Moreover, the actual king's body is indistinguishable from the bodies of his subjects; to get his first glimpse of Imoinda, he dresses himself as the "slave and attendant" of a "man of quality" (p. 84) and is wholly successful in this disguise. This king's body, then, is to be imagined as one of that mass of brown black bodies that Oroonoko's unnatural blackness is defined against.

Even though the king's actual and mystical bodies seem thus separated in Oroonoko's home kingdom, Oroonoko's blackness is nonetheless defined against the mass of African bodies as an abstracted essence of them, as if his blackness were the sum and intensification of their lesser darkness. The mystical body of kingship continues to represent even that against which it is defined, the physical bodies that constitute the realm, and the physical bodies are incorporated into the mystical body. Oroonoko's representation conforms to the imaginative pattern informing centuries of monarchist thought, pageantry, state organization, criminal law, family relations, and so forth; it was the common cultural property of the time.

Such a pattern of thinking, however, does not fully account for the representation of kingship in *Oroonoko*, for it does not explain why the salient physical attribute of the African bodies that is abstracted, refined, and intensified in Oroonoko's body should be their darkness. Of all the attributes of their bodies, why this one? In making her hero darker than his subjects, Behn departed radically from the traditional portrayal of the noble African or Moor,[46] who was usually painted white. Of course, we have already partly answered this question in discussing textuality and racial difference, but neither of those issues comprehends Oroonoko's princeliness, his relationship to his subjects. Why should the sign of his kingship be a body from which everything that is African is explicitly banished except a hue that can only abstractly be described as "black"?

The answer lies in Oroonoko's subjects, who, unlike those of a modern European king, are also his commodities. The narrator

---

46. See Barthelemy's discussion of the contrast between the heroic white Moor and the villainous black Moor in George Peele's *Battle of Alcazar* (1589), pp. 75–81.

painstakingly explains that the word "black" distinguishes the bodies of people who can be bought and sold from those of people who cannot. To a twentieth-century reader the history of slavery makes this linkage obvious, but in the seventeenth century, before racial ideologies of slavery developed fully and as the institution itself was being racialized, it bore reiterating.[47] The word "blacks" first appears in *Oroonoko* in contrast not to "whites" but to natives of Surinam, who are "a reddish yellow" (p. 76). These last, we are told, are not used as slaves because, through their fishing, hunting, and industry, they supply the colony with such necessities that they must be lived with in "perfect tranquillity, and good under-standing" (p. 77).[48] Hence "Negroes, black-slaves altogether," are imported. "Black" here differentiates the body of the African from that of the Native American; it signifies that one has been made a commodity, and the other has not. Because this "blackness" is the mark of commodification, we are then told, everything else about these bodies becomes indistinguishable:

> Those who want slaves, make a bargain with a master, or captain of a ship, and contract to pay him so much apiece, a matter of twenty pound a head. . . . So that when there arrives a ship laden with slaves, they who have so contracted, go aboard, and receive their number by lot; and perhaps in one lot that may be for ten, there may happen to be three or four men; the rest women and children. (p. 78)

The twenty pounds paid, then, is for a "black" body, regardless of any other physical characteristic. Nor will any other color suffice, as the case of the Frenchman, seized along with Oroonoko but turned loose because of his color, makes clear. "Black" is a word that is used to describe a skin tone differing from all others that allows a body to have an abstract exchange value independent of any of its other physical qualities.

47. For various accounts of why and how Africans came to be the enslaveable race, see Jordan, *White over Black*, esp. pp. 91–101; Barbara Fields, "Ideology and Race in American History," in *Region, Race, and Reconstruction*, ed. J. Morgan Kousser and James M. McPherson (New York: Oxford Univ. Press, 1982); David Brion Davis, *The Problem of Slavery in Western Culture* (Ithaca, NY: Cornell Univ. Press, 1966), p. 178; and William D. Phillips, Jr., *Slavery from Roman Times to the Early Transatlantic Slave Trade* (Minneapolis: Univ. of Minnesota Press, 1985), p. 184.

48. The narrator is not always consistent on this point. On at least one occasion she speaks of "Indian slaves," but she seems to use that term loosely as a synonym for "lowly servant." She never describes the commodification of Indians.

"Black," then, is connected to bodies but is also an abstraction from them signifying exchangeable value. It is not so much descriptive of the skin as of the difference between African skin and all other skin that has arbitrarily come to take on the meaning of exchange value per se. Hence the narrator immediately becomes chary of using it as a "literal" term describing bodies. "Coramantien," we are told, is "a country of blacks *so called*" (p. 78, emphasis mine), that is, a country of people one could call black and thus exchange for twenty pounds apiece.[49] But the narrator explicitly rejects this designation "black," as we have already seen, to describe the literal color of the African body, whose physicality is merely brown. "Black" identifies the commodity value of the slave body, its exchangeability for twenty pounds, as opposed to its physicality.

Thus the terrifying condition of slavery—having an African body that could be called "black"—is transfigured in this novel into a gleaming vision of disembodied value in the figure of Oroonoko's kingly blackness. Oroonoko's utterly unnatural body is the only one in which the word signifying exchangeability, "black," and the actual color of the body coincide. Only in his body is value realized as blackness. The intrinsic, nonnegotiable kingship of Oroonoko is thus paradoxically figured in the same blackness that designates the principle of exchange itself.

The superimposition of kingship and exchange, odd as it might at first appear, was not uncommon. Money, after all, was similarly a representation of exchange value underwritten by the idea of the English state's sovereignty, the mystical body of kingship. Although the relationship between the sovereign power and money was substantially revised in the seventeenth century, and the last decade saw a strong parliamentary attempt to discount the "extrinsic" value that money received from its association with sovereignty, the very agitation of the issue would have given the relationship a pronounced ideological importance.[50] What is odd about

49. In fact, Coramantien was not a country at all but a port on the Gold Coast where the English had a trading station. According to Rogers, though, planters in America generally referred to Gold Coast Africans as Coramantiens (Rogers, "Fact and Fiction in Aphra Behn's *Oroonoko*," p. 6).

50. For the larger political implications of the debate over money at the end of the seventeenth century, see Joyce Oldham Appleby, *Economic Thought and Ideology in Seventeenth-Century England* (Princeton, NJ: Princeton Univ. Press, 1978), pp. 236–41. Appleby argues that "Locke's denial of the extrinsic value of coin carried with it

Oroonoko's depiction of this relationship is its insistence on the exchangeability of the subjects themselves for money. Exchange value and kingship are both realized in *Oroonoko* at the vanishing point of the African bodies, the moments when the king sells his subjects.

The kingship represented in Oroonoko, then, cannot be explained simply by noting that the king's mystical body underlay commerce; it is, rather, related to developments in the ideology of absolutism that reimagined the king's sovereignty as an absolute *property* right in the bodies of his subjects. It is to this notion of sovereignty that I now turn.

~

As I remarked in analyzing *The Lucky Chance*, the idea of property as an absolute right to dispose of something in any way one saw fit—to use it, destroy it, alienate it through exchange, and so forth— was still not fully developed in English law in the seventeenth century. Nevertheless, such an idea of property underlay the vast expansion of trade during that century, and the desire of subjects to have greater dominion over their property came into conflict with what some saw as increasing claims of the crown for dominion. Conversely, some advocates of monarchical "absolutism" argued that the secure property rights of Englishmen would prevent the king from becoming a despot, but even here the complete freedom of a subject to dispose of his own goods and the power of the monarch are counterpoised. To dissociate absolute individual property claims from the claims of absolute monarchy, however, would be mistaken, for the two were sometimes powerfully conjoined.[51] Indeed, never was the ideological connection closer than

a limitation of government in economic affairs" (p. 237). She also quotes John Briscoe's 1696 attack on the state's power to fix the value of money, an attack phrased in language peculiarly relevant to *Oroonoko*: "[As] it is a mark of slavery, so is it the means of poverty in a State, where the Magistrate assumes a Power to set what price he pleases on the Publick Coin: It is a sign of Slavery, because the Subject in such Case lives merely at the Mercy of the Prince, is Rich, or Poor, has a Competency, or is a Begger, is a Free-Man, or in Fetters at his Pleasure" (p. 237).

51. The once widely held view that the Whigs represented the interests and ideology of trade while the Tories stood for an older aristocratic order that shunned commerce is no longer tenable. The most concise statements revealing the errors and simplifications of this position are J. G. A. Pocock's "Mobility of Property and

during the exclusion crisis of 1679–81, when the most famous work of Robert Filmer, *Patriarcha*, originally written in the 1640s, was published and widely cited to defend James's right to the throne. *Patriarcha* bases kingship itself on God-given, patriarchal ownership of the bodies of the subjects. The king's divine rights, Filmer argued, no matter how severely qualified by the customs and laws of modern nations, derived ultimately from his private property right in these bodies, his right to dispose of them in any way he saw fit. Any legitimate limitation on this right, he argued further, was to be construed as self-imposed by the king.

Filmer's defense of absolutism, John Locke pointed out in the first of his *Two Treatises of Government*, essentially turned subjects into slaves:[52]

> This *Fatherly Authority* then, or *Right of Fatherhood*, in our Author's sense is a Divine unalterable Right of Sovereignty, whereby a Father or a Prince hath an Absolute, Arbitrary, Unlimited, and Unlimitable Power, over the Lives, Liberties, and Estates of his Children and Subjects; so that he may take or alienate their Estates, sell, castrate, or use their Persons as he pleases, they being all his Slaves, and he Lord or Proprietor of every Thing, and his unbounded Will their Law.[53]

---

the Rise of Eighteenth-Century Sociology" and "Authority and Property: The Question of Liberal Origins," in *Virtue, Commerce, and History: Essays in Political Thought and History, Chiefly in the Eighteenth Century* (Cambridge: Cambridge Univ. Press, 1985), pp. 103–24 and 51–72. They show the strong connections between absolutist ideology in the seventeenth century and the spread of a notion of property as that which can be exchanged. To be sure, a Tory ideology grew up in the 1690s and the early eighteenth century that vociferously opposed this idea of property, but Pocock, again, has shown that the Toryism of Harley and St. John descends from theorists like Locke as opposed to absolutists. There is, then, no ideological contradiction between Behn's Restoration Court Toryism and her presentation of Oroonoko as a heroic warrior *and* slave-trader. The general intellectual history is complicated by the identification of slavery sometimes as a characteristic of precommercial societies; in *Oroonoko*, however, slavery is presented not as a semifeudal but as a fully commercial institution. That is, exchange, rather than mere ownership, is its essence. Tory writers such as Behn often complained that Whig "tradesmen" had reduced all issues of honor to those of barter, but as we have already seen in *The Lucky Chance*, the opposition comically collapses. In *Oroonoko*, too, the oppositions between war and commerce, possession and exchange collapse, but the effect is at once tragic and transcendent.

52. Indeed, Filmer's argument gave them a status lower than that of slaves under English law, for even slaves were deemed to have something like a natural right to life, and in many of the English colonies (including Surinam) they could own property themselves.

53. *Two Treatises of Government: A Critical Edition*, ed. and introd. Peter Laslett

Filmer thus pressed a claim of unlimited private property, and Locke refuted that claim in order to promote "the older and more traditional constitutionalist or consent theory of government."[54] Filmer made not only all property ultimately the property of the king but also all proprietors, arguing that they held their very lives as well as their livelihoods by royal gift.

Without implying that Aphra Behn had actually read *Patriarcha* or that Filmer's formulations per se directly influenced her thinking, I would suggest that *Oroonoko*'s royalism, imagined through the institution of slavery, is Filmeresque.[55] I would also venture, however, that the tale, because it depicts kingship as the absolute ownership of others, whose essence is the right to exchange or destroy them, constantly renders problematic what it takes for granted: that someone can be owned, even by himself.

The narrator never claims that the subjects of the kingdom of Coramantien are slaves of their king, but the distinction between subject and slave is often blurred. The slaves Oroonoko trades in are supposed to be prisoners of war, in conformity with traditional European ideas of how slaves might legitimately be acquired. Because Oroonoko conquered them and could have put them to death, their lives are forfeit to him, and hence he can spare them and make them the property of others. Slavery, then, is legitimate because it is incidental to war. But Coramantien is also presented as a place where war is the only enterprise and slaves the only commodity,

---

(Cambridge: Cambridge Univ. Press, 1960), *First Treatise*, chapter 2, section 9, pp. 9–10.

54. James Tully, "The Framework of Natural Rights in Locke's Analysis of Property: A Contextual Reconstruction," in *Theories of Property: Aristotle to the Present*, ed. Anthony Parel and Thomas Flanagan (Calgary: Wilfrid Laurier Univ. Press, 1979), p. 119. For other contributions to the debate about sovereignty and the rise of absolute property, see Alan Ryan, *Property and Political Theory* (Oxford: Basil Blackwell, 1984), pp. 14–48; J. G. A. Pocock, "The Mobility of Property and the Rise of Eighteenth-Century Sociology"; and G. E. Aylmer, "The Meaning and Definition of 'Property' in Seventeenth-Century England," *Past and Present* 86 (1980): 87–97.

55. I mean that Behn's articulation of kingship and property in subjects is similar to Filmer's although not necessarily derived from his. It is not clear how widely influential *Patriarcha* was in the 1680s; but it certainly stands in the ideological terrain of the decade as a landmark that allows us to locate the general vicinity of Behn's tale. For a contrasting view of Oroonoko as the Lockean bourgeois subject, see Weston, "The Noble Primitive as Bourgeois Subject." For a shrewd discussion of a possible link between *Oroonoko* and a Hobbesian view of the world, see Starr, "Aphra Behn and the Genealogy of the Man of Feeling."

for that nation is very warlike and brave, and having a continual campaign, being always in hostility with one neighbouring prince or other, they had the fortune to take a great many captives; for all they took in battle, were sold as slaves, at least, those common men who could not ransom themselves. (pp. 78–79)

In this account, war seems incidental to the slave trade rather than vice versa. Moreover, as the story progresses, we are told often of attendants, mistresses, friends, and even wives who are sold as slaves. Although it is a dishonor for a subject to be sold into slavery, the king has a right to make such a sale, and we are told that every husband has the right either to take the life of his wife or to sell her. The kingdom is imagined to work on patriarchal principles closely resembling those that Filmer describes, with the members of each family living only by the father's sufferance, and the king, as the father of all, holding the same absolute power to dispose of all his subjects: "for they pay a most absolute resignation to the monarch" (p. 83). The real status of a subject, therefore, is that he may at any moment be converted into a commodity.

Indeed, the proof of the monarch's power is precisely in such acts of alienation, for merely to keep and use a slave, as one would any other servant or subordinate, is not to assert fully one's right of ownership. Hence, the slaves Oroonoko encounters in Surinam recognize him as king because he had previously sold them:

[T]hey all came forth to behold him, and found he was that prince who had, at several times, sold most of them to these parts; and, from a veneration they pay to great men, . . . they all cast themselves at his feet, crying out in their language, "Live, O King! Long live, O King!" And kissing his feet, paid him even divine homage. (p. 109)

Kingship, the right of ownership, and the act of exchange entail each other so closely in *Oroonoko* that they are virtually identical. It is consistent with this logic that kingship should be painted black, the color of exchange. It also follows that the representative of kingship, identified by this color more perfectly and conspicuously than anyone, should ultimately be himself taken for a commodity in the very trade he practiced.

If Oroonoko's abduction and sale seem inevitable, however, the logic of this version of absolutism must be deemed highly paradoxical. If absolute kingship is ownership and absolute ownership is exchange, we are returned to the paradox we encountered at the climax of *The Lucky Chance:* the enduring, stable possession of a person, even of oneself, becomes a near impossibility. Sovereignty keeps sliding into self-alienation, and keeping someone entails the renunciation of property claims. Before his betrayal and enslavement, for example, when Oroonoko wishes to keep a captive with him, he essentially frees him:

> This Jomoan afterwards became very dear to him . . . so that he never put him amongst the rank of captives as they used to do, without distinction, for the common sale or market, but kept him in his own court, where he retained nothing of the prisoner but the name, and returned no more into his own country. (p. 100)

The pattern of freeing a slave to keep him is repeated several times in the novel. After abducting Oroonoko, the ship's captain makes a pretense of freeing him to keep him from killing himself, and Trefry, Oroonoko's "master" in Surinam, also assures the hero that he is free ("had only the name of slave") in order to live with him in peace. The assertion of sovereign possession, on the other hand, is the prelude to loss.[56]

Perhaps the most complex variation on this theme is the drama surrounding the possession of Imoinda, for in *Oroonoko,* as in *The Lucky Chance,* the paradoxes of absolute property in persons become most starkly apparent precisely where in the culture at large the property relation would be deemed most "natural": in the relation of husband and wife. Imoinda's possession is problematic from the outset. Plighted to Oroonoko, she is appropriated by his grandfather, the king, but the old man cannot consummate the relationship by "possessing" her sexually. Aware of the king's impotence, Oroonoko continues to consider her his and succeeds in possessing her clandestinely, whereupon the lovers are discovered, and Oroonoko must flee. Up to this point, the story is an utterly conventional intrigue plot, but here the slave market intervenes, giving the old man an unusual means of proving that Imoinda is actually his: he sells her. This act eventually, after Oroonoko's enslavement, reunites the lovers, but their second marriage, which

---

56. For an exploration of this paradox in *Uncle Tom's Cabin,* see Walter Benn Michaels, *The Gold Standard and the Logic of Naturalism: American Literature at the Turn of the Century* (Berkeley: Univ. of California Press, 1987), pp. 101–05.

takes place when they are both "slaves in name only," exacerbates the problems of possession. For Imoinda and Oroonoko slavery means nothing but potential commodification; they are not forced to labor, and their activities are almost completely unrestricted. However, as long as they remain in Surinam, they are officially Trefry's property and hence vulnerable to sale. As soon as Imoinda becomes pregnant, this state of affairs becomes intolerable to Oroonoko, for the prospect of fathering a child while officially a slave, while his patriarchal right is legally violable, makes him suddenly aware that Imoinda's body is a medium for his self-alienation. By possessing her sexually he produces another property, a child, whom he cannot legally call his own. The reappropriation through revolt of Imoinda and all the Africans he formerly sold into slavery then seems exigent, and when this plan fails, Oroonoko's only means of keeping Imoinda and his child from the market is to "free" them both from life altogether. Thus the integrity of Oroonoko's kingship is accomplished by the final "carving" of Imoinda's body:

> [T]he lovely, young and adored victim lays herself down, before the sacrificer, while he, with a hand resolved, and a heart breaking within, gave the fatal stroke, first, cutting her throat, and then severing her, yet smiling, face from that delicate body, pregnant as it was with the fruits of tenderest love. (p. 136)

This quite literal defacing of Imoinda, the lifting of her still-smiling face, as if it were a mask or portrait, off her body, is presented as the "brave and just" (p. 135) liberation of her self from the body that was perpetually exchangeable. Only through this ultimate form of alienation does Oroonoko, the king of exchange, keep her and return her to herself.

Imoinda's severed face is not the first mask to signify integrity or self-possession, for in *Oroonoko* the problem of owning extends even to one's relationship with oneself. The great Indian warriors, for example, prove their fitness for leadership by defacing themselves.[57] In the contest for generalship,

---

57. For another discussion of mutilation and self-mutilation in *Oroonoko*, see Ballaster, "New Hystericism: Aphra Behn's *Oroonoko*," p. 292.

> He, who is first . . . cuts off his nose, and throws it contemptibly on
> the ground, and the other does something to himself that he thinks
> surpasses him, and perhaps deprives himself of lips and an eye. So
> they slash on till one gives out, and many have died in this debate.
> And 'tis by a passive valour they show and prove their activity, a
> sort of courage too brutal to be applauded by our black hero; never-
> theless, he expressed his esteem of them. (p. 124)

This bizarre chopping away of bits of one's body becomes, by
the end of the story, the heroic alternative to the alienation of
marketplace exchange, which appears to require whole bodies.
Thus although the Indian's self-mutilation seems "too brutal" at
first to Oroonoko, he copies it in the sacrificial transfigurations that
are supposed to give him back his kingly sovereignty:

> "Look ye, ye faithless crew," said he, "'tis not life I seek, nor am I
> afraid of dying," and at that word, cut a piece of flesh from his own
> throat, and threw it at them, "yet still I would live if I could, till I
> had perfected my revenge. But, oh! it cannot be; I feel life gliding
> from my eyes and heart; and if I make not haste, I shall yet fall victim
> to the shameful whip." At that, he ripped up his own belly, and took
> his bowels and pulled them out. . . . (p. 138)

Later, in the actual execution scene, Oroonoko seeks the dismemberment of his entire body, which appears all the more bloodless,
inhuman, and indestructible with each partition:

> And the executioner came, and first cut off his members, and threw
> them into the fire. After that, with an ill-favoured knife, they cut his
> ears, and his nose, and burned them; he still smoked [tobacco], as if
> nothing had touched him. Then they hacked off one of his arms,
> and still he bore up, and held his pipe. But at the cutting off the
> other arm, his head sunk, and his pipe dropped, and he gave up the
> ghost, without a groan, or a reproach. . . . They cut Caesar in
> quarters, and sent them to several of the chief plantations. . . .
> (p. 140)

Although this horror was aimed at "terrifying and grieving" the
slaves "with frightful spectacles of a mangled king" (p. 140), it also
creates the spectacle of the body of kingship, which appears most
powerfully in such vanishing acts, when bodies seem at once
reduced to mere things and transcended altogether. Now deprived
of that which first constituted it—the ownership and exchange of
others—Oroonoko's kingship comes to consist in his godlike will-

ing of the piecemeal alienation of his own body. In this contradictory manner, he proves that he still owns it. Although the moment
of death is noted ("his pipe dropped, and he gave up the ghost"),
it seems just another stage in the separation of his parts. Oroonoko
undergoes an extraordinary self-division, only to become all the
more singularly immortal, for "he" is now unlocatable. The mystical
body of kingship and the actual body of Oroonoko again become
identical when the latter is fragmented and scattered. Just as the
brown bodies reached their vanishing point in Oroonoko's black
body of kingly and monetary representation, so his own body of
representation reaches its vanishing point in this dispersion.

~

By using the prostitute and the monarch as her most frequent
authorial metaphors, Behn views her authorship through Restoration concepts of self-alienation and sovereignty, that is, through
the age's self-contradictory notions about property and exchange.
Shadowy aspirations of independence from the marketplace are at
once raised and renounced in a paradoxical logic of property:
ownership of oneself and others, this logic states, entails their
commodification or annihilation. Through this reiterated recognition, Behn renders authorship, doomed to the marketplace but
struggling for sovereignty, poignant. However, the author-whore
and author-king metaphors also point toward ways in which the
author, of all traders, seems to escape the direst consequences of
the marketplace.

To demonstrate this claim, let us return to the vanishing point
of Oroonoko's body, the point at which kingship has achieved a
combined dispersion and incorporeality resembling that of the text
itself. At that moment, the narrator makes her most striking appropriation in the form of a disclaimer: "Thus died this great man,
worthy of a better fate, and a more sublime wit than mine to write
his praise. Yet, I hope, the reputation of my pen is considerable
enough to make his glorious name to survive to all ages, with that
of the brave, the beautiful and the constant Imoinda" (p. 141).
Oroonoko's "worth" demands more sublimity than she can summon, yet her own authorial reputation, itself a mystical body
existing in and between texts, will be the support of "his glorious

name." Ending the text with the word "Imoinda" reminds us of Behn's special fitness to tell this love story, her femaleness, but the effect of authorship here transcends all such physical accidents even as it takes them into account. If Oroonoko scatters his members to maintain his integrity, Behn performs a similar act of disowning the text (insisting that it is really Oroonoko's and Imoinda's) to open a rhetorical space in which she can remind us of her authorship and the obligation it imposes. In her dedication of the book to Richard Maitland, she similarly effaces herself as the principle of exchange, effecting a transfer of "the nobler part" from one great man, Oroonoko, to another: "'Tis purely the merit of my Slave that must render [the book] worthy of the Honour it begs; and the Author of that of subscribing herself, My Lord, Your Lordship's most oblig'd and obedient Servant, A. Behn."[58]

In this odd mixture of appropriation and disowning ("'Tis purely the merit of *my Slave* that must render" the book worthy of Maitland), the author trades in the "parts" she claims are not exactly hers, and thus she avoids identifying herself with her commodity. Despite the insistent presence of the first-person narrator in *Oroonoko*, then, the phenomenon of authorship per se tends to come into view as the principle of the exchange of representations. Like Sir Cautious Fulbank, the author seems to want to trade in what she does not own, and quite literally she did not own *Oroonoko* by the time the printed book appeared, begging the patronage of Maitland. Or, perhaps more precisely, the authorial effect might be likened to Sir Cautious's reasoning that one may safely trade in "nothing": commodities like Julia's "part," Oroonoko's "nobler part," and finally, his "glorious name." What, after all, is a name? "Why 'tis a word, an empty sound; 'tis breath, 'tis air, 'tis *nothing*," answers Sir Cautious. Such commodities certainly direct us to the anomalies of ownership in general. However, by insisting on the oddly evanescent materiality of these commodities and by showing that the human body disappears into them, she implies that they are the perfect "nothing" to set against all other commodities. Like authorship itself, they seem endlessly negotiable precisely because they are not really owned, and hence they make their vendor invulnerable.

58. "The Epistle Dedicatory to the Right Honourable the Lord Maitland," in *Oroonoko; or, the Royale Slave: A Critical Edition*, ed. and introd. Adelaide P. Amore (Lanham: Univ. Press of Maryland, 1987), p. 3.

Little wonder, then, that Aphra Behn seems to us both the victim and the heroine of the literary marketplace. Her two favorite personae invite exploration of the splendors and miseries of authorship as it realized itself on the stage and in print. What is the relationship between these authorial effects and the historical woman Aphra Behn? Throughout the chapter, I have implied that the historical woman was the producer of these effects, that they are therefore not to be confused with her, indeed that "she" warns us against such confusions. Simultaneously, though, I have suggested that Behn had a heightened consciousness of the connection between self-possession and self-alienation because of her experience as a woman in the literary marketplace. Even when she universalizes the paradoxes of property in the oxymoronic "Royal Slave," her insights seem grounded in the specific entanglements between women and commodities in the late seventeenth century. But because these were the entanglements of commodification, they produce an effect of emptiness when we try to reconstruct the historical subjectivity of Aphra Behn. In the first chapter of *Capital*, Marx imagines what commodities would say if they could speak. They would say that their essence is not in their matter; that it is an abstract value seemingly divorced from time and place.[59] To seek to know the interior of the commodity is thus to witness an abstraction from history. My analysis has neither exposed nor exorcised the historical woman, but has rather gained multiple perspectives on her works by composing them around the historically demarcated points where the lady vanishes.

In the chapters that follow, the self-presentations of eighteenth-century women writers will be seen to undergo alterations that are now familiar to students of English literature. The imperceptible change that Sir Walter Scott's great aunt lived through is easy to trace in what might be called the "revirginization" of the woman writer at mid-century. But through this and many other variations, the phenomenon of "Nobodiness" persists, not as an indication of the female author's lack of importance, but as a sign of her success.

59. *Capital: A Critique of Political Economy* (New York, 1906), p. 95. See also Walter Benjamin: "[T]he commodity attempts to look itself in the face. It celebrates its becoming human in the whore" ("Central Park," *New German Critique* 34 [Winter 1985]: 42).

3

Political Crimes and Fictional Alibis

The Case of Delarivier Manley

When Delarivier Manley was arrested for seditious libel in 1709, according to her later account of the inquest, fiction was her alibi.[1] She had written *Secret Memoirs and Manners of Several Persons of Quality, of Both Sexes. From the New Atalantis, an Island in the Mediterranean*, a provocative satire on the sexual irregularities and political corruptions of a number of important Whigs who then controlled the government of Queen Anne. Like an earlier work that was probably also by Manley, *The Secret History of Queen Zarah and the Zarazians* (1704), *The New Atalantis* was particularly intent upon libeling Sarah Churchill, then Lady Marlborough, and the Whig ministers closest to her. Both books were huge successes; the first went through at least six editions in as many years. *The New Atalantis* was so popular that Sarah Churchill anxiously wrote to Queen Anne, complaining that "notwithstanding the prosecution" it was being "sold at every shop."[2]

1. I am convinced by Patricia Köster's argument that there is no evidence for believing Manley's first name was Mary. See "Delarivier Manley and the *DNB*," *Eighteenth Century Life* 3 (1977): 106–11. Furthermore, I follow Fidelis Morgan's lead in spelling Manley's Christian name Delarivier because that is the way the author consistently spelled it. See *A Woman of No Character: An Autobiography of Mrs. Manley* (London: Faber and Faber, 1986), p. 14.

Information about Manley's arrest and questioning comes from two sources: Narcissus Luttrell, *A Brief Historical Relation of State Affairs* (London, 1714), pp. 505–08 and 546; and Manley's own fictionalized autobiography, *The Adventures of Rivella; or, the History of the Author of the Atalantis* (London, 1714), pp. 108–16. Excerpts from both accounts are brought together in Morgan, pp. 146–51. Manley apparently surrendered herself on October 29, 1709, after a secretary of state's warrant had been issued against her, and her publishers and printer had already been detained. She was questioned in the secretary's office; four days later the publishers and printer were discharged, but Manley remained in custody until November 7, when she was released on bail. Her trial was heard on February 11, 1710, at the Queen's Bench Court; she was discharged.

2. *Private Correspondence of Sarah, Duchess of Marlborough*, 2d. ed. (London: Henry Colburn, 1838), vol. 1, p. 237.

The prosecution was a partisan affair; the government probably hoped, in questioning Delarivier Manley about her motives, to uncover a Tory plot at the origin of *The New Atalantis*; the book would then become a Tory rather than a Whig scandal.[3] According to Manley's version of the events, written in the third person, the prosecutors pressed her to confess her political-economic motivation and to admit that she had informants in high places. Instead, she pleaded innocent on the grounds that she was merely a fiction writer:

> They us'd several arguments to make her discover who were the Persons concerned with her in writing her Books; or at least from whom she had receiv'd Information of some special Facts, which they thought were above her own Intelligence. Her Defence was with much Humility and Sorrow, for having offended, at the same Time denying that any Persons were concern'd with her, or that she had a farther Design than writing for her own Amusement and Diversion in the Country; without intending particular Reflections on Characters: When this was not believ'd, and the contrary urg'd very home to her by several Circumstances and Likenesses; she said then it must be Inspiration, because knowing her own Innocence she could account for it no other way: The Secretary reply'd upon her, that Inspiration us'd to be upon a good Account and her Writings were stark naught. She told him, with an Air full of Penitence, that might be true, but it was as true, that there were evil Angels as well as good, so, nevertheless, what she had wrote might still be by Inspiration.[4]

Such a defense, if it was indeed made, was certainly not designed to convince anyone that Manley was an isolated genius or

3. I draw this inference from Manley's description of the questioning, quoted below, and from Sarah Churchill's letter to the queen, which identifies Harley, Peterborough, and Mrs. Masham as Manley's sources of information and financial support:

> The woman that has been put upon writing it, and the printer, have been in custody, and are now under prosecution. It has appeared that she kept correspondence with two of the favourite persons in the book—my Lord Peterborough and Mr. Harley, and I think it is to be suspected that she may have had some dealing with Mrs. Masham, who is called Hilaria.

Private Correspondence of Sarah, Duchess of Marlborough, vol. 1, p. 244.

4. *The Adventures of Rivella; or, the History of the author of Atalantis with secret memoirs and characters of several considerable persons, her contemporaries* (London, 1714); rpt. in *The Novels of Mary Delariviere Manley*, ed. Patricia Köster (Gainesville, FL: Scholars' Facsimiles and Reprints, 1971), vol. 2, p. 849. Subsequent quotations from this edition are cited parenthetically in the text.

an ignorant but innocent woman merely trying to amuse herself. It was more likely a tactical ploy, calculated to confound and embarrass the prosecution as well as protect Manley's associates.[5] She makes herself liable by claiming full responsibility for the offensive book, but the very terms of her admission signal her refusal to cooperate with the prosecution. By insisting on the pure fictionality of the text, Manley both denied her sources and placed the burden of identifying the libeled persons of quality on her interrogators, who were thus tricked into attaching the scandalous stories to the names of Whig ministers, in a sense becoming parties to the libel. Her appeal to "Inspiration" was similarly disingenuous, at once evoking and mocking the idea of the isolated literary genius. The alibi of fiction thus had many uses, but deceit was not one of them. The alibi was as transparently untrue (or, since it was not intended to convince, as truly fictional) as *The New Atalantis* was transparently slanderous.

Delarivier Manley's comic-heroic version of her defense opposes the truth of a political crime to the fictionality of a fictional alibi. Indeed, the obvious fictionality of the alibi indicates the truth of the charge. Delarivier Manley's case is full of paradoxes of this sort, which I will trace to explore an extraordinary moment in the history of English women's writing, a moment when party politics, proto-fiction, the literary marketplace, and feminine sexuality became intricately entangled.

Politics was not beyond the scope of women's writing in the Restoration. Behn, for example, never hinted an awareness that there was anything inappropriate in her political advocacy. Nevertheless, we can sense in her employment of two different personae, one "feminine" and the other "political," an acknowledgment of some normal mutual exclusion belonging to the two terms. Like the work of several other seventeenth-century women, Behn's writings also hint that the very separation of femininity and politics could justify authorship.[6] Earlier in the century Margaret Caven-

---

5. For the evidence that Manley did have highly placed sources, see Gwendolyn B. Needham, "Mary de la Riviere Manley, Tory Defender," *Huntington Library Quarterly* 12 (1949): 253–88.
6. For a longer discussion of this idea in seventeenth-century women's writing, see my article "Embracing the Absolute: The Politics of the Female Subject in Seventeenth-Century England," *Genders* 1 (1988): 24–39. For further discussions of women's political writing in the seventeenth century, see Hilda L. Smith, *Reason's*

dish, for example, reasoned that since she could not be a political subject, she would rule small worlds in books, and at the end of the century Mary Astell pleaded that since she could not promote her plans for female education through the normal political channels, she resorted to the public press. When Behn announced that since she could not fight for the cavalier cause, she would rail from the stage, she used her feminine disability as a familiar warrant for public language.

We should not imagine, then, that in the seventeenth century women were either admitted to political discourse more readily or excluded from it more successfully than in the early decades of the eighteenth century. However, during Queen Anne's reign there occurred a peculiar chiasm, or intersection, of antithetical terms that distinguishes this moment of women's authorship from those that preceded and followed it: femininity became useful in political discourse by virtue of a new set of terms, overtly employed to exclude women from politics. The crossing of politics and femininity that I want to describe involves a third term, "fiction." Indeed, the figure I have in mind is a three-way cross, in which politics and fiction, starkly opposed in Delarivier Manley's trial, came to be closely identified at those rhetorical junctures where Manley's authorship was most emphatically identified as feminine.

These intersections, moreover, occurred during realignments between politics and commerce in general and politics and the literary marketplace in particular. This chapter traces three instances of such realignments. One is a new discursiveness in English politics, a redefinition of politics as public, indeed published, debate. The second is the growth of what historians have called civil humanism, an ideology that conferred a high value on personality traits cultivated both in commerce and in social intercourse between the sexes. The third is the reciprocal stimulation of the national debt and the growth of speculative finance capital. The chapter interweaves these developments to reveal both their individual and cumulative pressure on the crossings described above.

Disciples: Seventeenth-Century English Feminists (Urbana: Univ. of Illinois Press, 1982), pp. 3–17; Moira Ferguson, introduction to *First Feminists: British Women Writers, 1578–1799* (Bloomington: Indiana Univ. Press, 1985), pp. 1–50; and Barbara Kiefer Lewalski, *Writing Women in Jacobean England* (Cambridge: Harvard Univ. Press, 1993), passim.

All three of the rearticulations of politics with commerce aggravated anxieties about the possible independence of language from reality and women from men.

～

Let me continue to trace the paradox of Delarivier Manley's alibi, the alibi that continually crosses politics with fiction through the economic, political, and legal labyrinth of early eighteenth-century letters. It seems odd to come up with an alibi no one is supposed to believe, just as it seems odd to invent allegories and codes that are supposed to be transparent. This bizarre feature of Augustan literary life is normally explained as simply protection against the libel law, the use to which Manley put it at her inquest. After the Licensing Act lapsed in 1695, and before the new Copyright Act of 1710 and the Stamp Act of 1712 were passed, the English printing trade was almost entirely unregulated.[7] Because the state found itself without automatic channels of prepublication censorship, it relied all the more heavily on prosecutions for libel to control a growing press.[8] Almost anything that "reflected" on the government, the crown, the church, the Parliament, the laws, persons of quality, private persons, and so forth, could be prosecuted.[9] The libelous statements did not need to be false; indeed, they did not even need to be damaging. Merely "reflecting" on the forbidden topics was illegal. Precisely because the law was so broad, prosecutions tended to be highly factional. A Whiggish secretary, for example, might prosecute High Church Tories for defending the church against dissenting attacks because such defenses, the pros-

7. For accounts of the British printing industry, its regulation, and the general effects of the lapsing of the Licensing Act in 1695, see Marjorie Plant, *The English Book Trade: An Economic History of the Making and Sale of Books* (London: Allen and Unwin, 1965), esp. pp. 115–21; Frank Arthur Mumby, *Publishing and Bookselling* (London: Cape, 1930), esp. pp. 169–96; and Graham Pollard, "The English Market for Printed Books," *Publishing History* 4 (1978): 7–48.

8. For an overview of seditious libel prosecutions in the early eighteenth century, see Donald Thomas, *A Long Time Turning: The History of Literary Censorship in England* (New York: Routledge and Kegan Paul, 1969), pp. 34–74; and Laurence Hanson, *The Government and the Press, 1695–1763* (Oxford: Clarendon Press, 1936).

9. C. R. Kropf gives a useful summary of the law in his essay "Libel and Satire in the Eighteenth Century," *Eighteenth-Century Studies* 8:2 (1974–75): 153–68. See also Hanson, pp. 7–35.

ecutors claimed, might give the people the impression that the church was in danger and thereby spread alarm. Even zealous patriotism could thus be read as seditious libel. When we further recall that the government, itself of no party during the triumvirate period (1704–09), indicted writers of every party, it becomes clear that entering into controversy on any side could make one vulnerable to prosecution.

Why, then, we might ask, did writers not just avoid political controversy? This question also has a standard answer. It was all but impossible for a writer to stay out of politics during the period from 1695 (the discontinuance of the Licensing Act) to 1714 (the death of Queen Anne), for political controversy was virtually the only road to making either a name or a living as a writer.[10] The economics of authorship were especially precarious, for although lack of regulation swelled the population of Grub Street, it also made authors and printers powerless against pirating.[11] It is extremely difficult to calculate the incomes of the mass of writers, but the conditions of the London printing trade from 1695 to 1714 suggest a period of unusually harsh exploitation. Predictably, instances of private patronage declined every decade after 1700, although subscription publishing continued throughout the early eighteenth century and was even "democratized" by London syndicates that advertised everywhere for subscribers.[12] But in the period under discussion, no form of literary support was as widespread as party patronage. Patrons were still a necessity, but patronage tended to flow through partisan political channels. Writers were no longer fully dependent on the crown or individual aristocrats, nor could most of them yet rely on something called the

10. For discussions of this development, see David Harrison Stevens, *Party Politics and English Journalism, 1702–1742* (Madison, WI: Banta, 1916); and J. A. Downie, *Robert Harley and the Press: Propaganda and Public Opinion in the Age of Swift and Defoe* (Cambridge: Cambridge Univ. Press, 1979).

11. "In such circumstances," notes A. S. Collins, "the relation of author to publisher existed on a very insecure basis. How could a bookseller pay highly for the rights to a work whose profits another might steal from him by a cheaper edition?" (*Authorship in the Days of Johnson: Being a Study of the Relation between Author, Patron, Publisher and Public, 1726–1780* [London: R. Holden and Co., 1927], p. 8).

12. Stevens, pp. 1–4. W. A. Speck, however, points out that subscription lists were dominated by the peerage in the early eighteenth century and that subscriptions were often themselves a vehicle for political patronage. See "Politicians, Peers, and Publication by Subscription, 1700–1750," in *Books and Their Readers in Eighteenth-Century England,* ed. Isabel Rivers (New York: St. Martin's Press, 1982), pp. 47–68.

public. Rather, they found themselves indebted to new political institutions that were only beginning to organize and define themselves.

Thus there was an unprecedented politicization of authorship during this period and in politics a new reliance on writing. Writers were central to the process of party formation and to that other enormous change in British politics, the development of ministerial government. British politics were shifting, in the words of a historian of the period, "from a system based on status, in which honor and obligation were paramount," to "a system based on rewards in which patronage and principle were paramount."[13] The political patrons, the heads of parties, needed writers who could articulate and in numerous instances invent the "principles" on which the patronage depended.[14] The relationship between Robert Harley and Daniel Defoe is only the best-known instance of a generalized symbiosis between politics and authorship. The great lords who controlled the political purse strings, although constantly accused of ingratitude by their writers, in fact did subsidize the production of a large quantity of literature during this period, either by direct payment to writers or by the distribution of pensions, offices, and other places. Both politics and literature, however, were altered in the transaction.

The new public textuality of political controversy was by definition impossible to restrict to a readership actively involved in running the country. This period famously marks the beginning of a political culture in England extending far beyond the ranks of the enfranchised. The London press formed the heart of this culture, and the new politics permeated every aspect of the press, including the taste of its readership. Even that still-embryonic entity, the public marketplace in literature, then, encouraged and was itself virtually identical to the new print culture based on party and ministerial politics. The vast majority of writers in this period managed to make their way in the world only by engaging in

13. Mark Kishlansky, *Parliamentary Selection: Social and Political Choice in Early Modern England* (Cambridge: Cambridge Univ. Press, 1986), p. 225.

14. See Collins on patronage in this period, pp. 114–18 and 214–21; see also Downie's *Robert Harley and the Press* and his *Jonathan Swift, Political Writer* (London: Routledge and Kegan Paul, 1984), passim. For an overview of early eighteenth-century patronage in all the arts, see Michael Foss, *The Age of Patronage: The Arts in England, 1660–1750* (Ithaca, NY: Cornell Univ. Press, 1972).

political controversy, that is, by making themselves liable to prosecution for libel. As James Bramston facetiously asked somewhat later in the century,

Can Statutes keep the British Press in awe
When that sells best, that's most against the law?[15]

Party politics and ministerial government, the very forces that were bringing the libel prosecutions against controversial publications, were also feeding on, stimulating, and subsidizing the marketplace in those very publications.

In her political activities, Delarivier Manley was a typical Queen Anne writer. Like Richard Steele, Joseph Addison, Jonathan Swift, and Susannah Centlivre, she practiced partisan political writing because (1) it was the most popular form of writing in the incipient literary marketplace; (2) it held the additional financial advantage of sometimes commanding party patronage; and (3) party loyalty became in the late years of Anne's reign "the new criterion for activity and friendship" in literary London.[16] And certainly Delarivier Manley was in need of "friends," in the eighteenth-century sense of the term.

There is no full biography of this author,[17] but she wrote several fictionalized versions of her own story, in which she repeatedly claims that her cousin, who, becoming her guardian when her father (the lieutenant governor of Jersey) died, tricked her into a sham marriage by telling her that his former wife was dead. After spending her fortune, this cousin, whose name was also Manley, abandoned her in London. Hence she found herself, in her mid-teens, a ruined woman with an infant son. Her first "friend" was the duchess of Cleveland, who spent her declining years trying to attract aristocratic gamblers to her home, vying in this attempt with London's other great gambling establishment of the period, that of Madame de Mazarin. These two formidable former mistresses of

15. From *The Man of Taste* (1733), quoted as the epigraph to Thomas, *A Long Time Burning*.

16. Stevens, p. 17.

17. Fidelis Morgan's *A Woman of No Character* interleaves autobiographical passages from Manley's writings with Morgan's research into the author's life. It is the fullest account we have of the life and work, and most of the biographical information in this chapter is drawn from it.

Charles II were among those who provided gathering places for the newly "amphibious" English aristocracy, which after the Restoration began regularly spending part of each year in London. The gambling ladies needed young gentlewomen to entertain their guests and play at cards, and such employment probably gave Delarivier Manley access to the aristocratic gossip and political intrigue she was later to circulate in her scandal chronicles.

The duchess of Cleveland may also have provided her contacts to the London theater, where she had four plays produced after a quarrel with her patron sent her out on her own. She was not, however, a successful playwright, and she may have been somewhat nervous about the notoriety of that form of authorship. The dedication to her first printed work (1696), signed "by a gentleman," praises her plays but also claims that ladies should not write for the theater and touts the superiority of the epistolary narrative, *Letters Written by Mrs. Manley,* to which it is prefixed. Her next major work, *Queen Zarah,* appeared anonymously in 1704 and was not attributed to her until a 1711 reprinting claimed it for "the author of the *New Atalantis.*"

The libelous and political nature of Manley's writing in the Queen Anne period encouraged anonymity, thus increasing our difficulties in determining the extent of her writing. Nor is it clear exactly how or what she was paid. Although she probably did not receive much for the manuscript of *The New Atalantis,* we find her in 1711 requesting patronage from Robert Harley, earl of Oxford and head of the Tory Party:

> If your Lordship think I have been any way serviceable, however accidentally, your justice will inspire you to give me your protection; if not, I hope your generosity will incite you to reward my good endeavours, whether by some small pension . . . or some other effect of your bounty, which I humbly leave to your Lordship's choice.[18]

Swift also turned over the editorship of the *Examiner,* the Tory organ of abuse, to Manley in 1710, and one of his letters mentions the necessity of "doing something" for Mrs. Manley. She was commissioned to write other Tory pamphlets in the late years of

---

18. "Mrs. Dela Manley to [the Earl of Oxford]," British Library, Historical Manuscripts Commission, Portland Papers, 5:55.

the reign as well. Partisan works were not her only productions, but they were certainly a high percentage of her writings between 1704 and 1714.[19] Delarivier Manley was a phenomenon of the new political culture that kept the secretary of state so busy issuing warrants.

As I have pointed out, the relationship between these conditions of authorship and the style of Augustan literature is often said to be quite uncomplicated. Allegories and other stylistic disguises such as ironic inversions and numbered codes, we are told, developed as technicalities through which the penalties of the law might be evaded.[20] Certainly some techniques of the period fit this description, and writers were fond of expatiating on both their necessity and their transparency. Swift, for example, would on occasion discuss the techniques of satire as if they were quite extraneous to its substance:

> First, we are careful never to print a man's name out at length; but as I do that of Mr. St——le: So that although every body alive knows who I mean, the plaintiff can have no redress in any court of justice. Secondly, by putting cases [telling recognizable but altered stories] . . . [Lastly,] by nicknames, either commonly known or stamped for the purpose, which every body can tell how to apply.[21]

The literary techniques, in other words, were supposedly mere technicalities for avoiding arrest or hindering successful prosecution. They were legal exigencies imposed from without, not rhetorical strategies developing from within the satirical intent.

We should note that in this view technique and message, literature and politics are substantially disengaged; political satire took,

19. After the Stamp Act (1712) suppressed the periodical press and the Tories collapsed upon the death of the queen, Manley lived with the bookseller John Barber, who had published both the *Examiner* and *The New Atalantis*. Some contemporaries believed he exploited her as an author (see Morgan, pp. 155–57). Her career demonstrates the process by which the press in the unlicensed period finally increased the power of the booksellers. See Michael Harris, "Journalism as a Profession or Trade in the Eighteenth Century," in *Author/Publisher Relations during the Eighteenth and Nineteenth Centuries*, ed. Robin Myers and Michael Harris (Oxford: Oxford Polytechnic Press, 1983), pp. 37–55.

20. Kropf, "Libel and Satire in the Eighteenth Century," views the relationship between technique and libel in these terms.

21. *The Importance of the Guardian Considered*, in Jonathan Swift, *Political Tracts, 1713–1719*, ed. Herbert Davis and Irvin Ehrenpreis (Oxford: Basil Blackwell, 1953), pp. 14–15. See the discussion of this passage in Hanson, *The Government and the Press, 1695–1763*, p. 25.

for example, the form of allegorical narrative because one could always claim that the story was not meant to reflect on any real, living person or contemporary event. But to see the stylistic component of the satire simply as a hindrance to prosecution gives literary techniques the attributes of mere codes, devices wholly separable from the message, which one extracts by a process of decoding.

Literary historians have sometimes followed this line of reasoning until it yielded an explanation for the appearance of early fiction. The need for legal protection led to increasing disguises, which eventually took on a life of their own, leaving behind the context of political controversy (to which the techniques were generally irrelevant anyway) and resulting in the invention of the purely literary. *Gulliver's Travels* has been cited as an example of this development—a satirical allegory that disguised its topical reflections so successfully that it completely failed as specific satire and ended up instead as a fictional classic.[22] However, in the passage by Swift quoted above, such a development is not anticipated, for the devices described are imagined to be completely transparent, so transparent that one can hardly call them disguises of political purpose at all. Rather, like Manley's alibi of inspiration, they *indicate*, although in a supposedly arbitrary way, illicit political intentions.

That the techniques indicated rather than concealed libelous statements makes it difficult to argue that the writers were only trying to protect themselves from prosecution by allegorizing, changing names, or altering circumstances. We should note at the outset that these devices did not always protect writers and printers from either arrest or successful prosecution. But they multiplied the issues in a libel case to the advantage of the accused, and they introduced legal questions a jury, rather than the court alone, could

---

22. For example, see Thomas, *A Long Time Burning*, p. 57. See also the more sophisticated reading of Swift that regards his works as purposely elusive mockeries of the allegorizing of other writers and the allegory hunting of the prosecutors in Lennard J. Davis, *Factual Fictions: The Origins of the English Novel* (New York: Columbia Univ. Press, 1983), pp. 149–53. Bertrand A. Goldgar, however, in *Walpole and the Wits: The Relation of Politics to Literature, 1722–1742* (Lincoln: Univ. of Nebraska Press, 1976), pp. 49–63, demonstrates that parts of *Gulliver's Travels* were immediately received as obvious personal satire.

decide.[23] However, one ran an obvious risk in using such devices, for although they interfered with prosecutions, they also at times alerted prosecutors to libel in a piece of writing. Indeed, some forms of "disguising" a "reflection" could be interpreted as the culpable act itself.

The "allegorical style" favored by Manley, for example, involved telling scandalous stories about recognizable real persons, with the names and some circumstances altered. The stories were given distant historical, exotic, or mythical settings and were often interspersed with stories lacking apparent referents. The author of a 1738 book called *State Law; or, the Doctrine of Libels Discussed and Examined* explains why such "fictional" allegorizing was by no means a foolproof protection against prosecution. "[W]hat Right has the allegorical Style to escape [the law of libel]? . . . if it be the common Notion, that this Picture represents a certain Person, the Drawer is answerable for the Injury he suffers."[24] Hence the more every body alive knows who is meant, to paraphrase Swift, the more ineffective the technique is as alibi. Delarivier Manley, her printer, and her bookseller were fined, not imprisoned, but they were not exonerated, and their relatively light penalties owed more to the less Whiggish ministry that had come to power while they were out on bail than to Manley's alteration of names and places.

This technique, then, could not always be counted on as an effective technical defense. Quite the contrary, for in many cases such as Manley's it not only indicated but also constituted the crime itself. To explain, let me continue with the discussion of allegory in *State Law; or, the Doctrine of Libels:*

> If a man draws a picture of another, and paints him in any shameful Posture, or ignominious Manner, 'tho no Name be to it; yet if the Piece be such, that the Person abused is known by it, the Painter is guilty of a Libel; what then should serve in Excuse for the allegorical Libeller? Abusive Allegory in Writing, has a very near Resemblance to this satyrical Kind of Painting: The Man that is painted with Fool's Cap and Horns, is certainly abused; but, says the Painter, he is disguised [by the foolscap and horns], and how can you pretend to

23. See Kropf, pp. 157–59.
24. Quoted in Thomas, p. 58.

know him. This is the very subterfuge of the Allegorist, and ought to have the same Answer.[25]

The answer is that the disguise (foolscap and horns) *is* the slander. The allegories in Manley's works are often precisely of this abusive type. When she "disguises" Godolphin as "Volpone" or Steele as "M. Ingrat," the fictional names themselves are the guilty "reflections." Swift's "St——le" may be a neutral code and a mere technicality, but "M. Ingrat" conveys the accusation in the very name. When Manley portrays Sarah Churchill as the ravenous Queen Zarah, literally usurping the throne from the rightful monarch, such "fictionalizing" of circumstances was itself the criminal message about the duchess of Marlborough and Queen Anne. To base one's defense on the allegorical "disguise" was thus tantamount to citing the most obnoxious aspect of the crime as evidence of one's innocence.[26] The legal status of Manley's style was hence profoundly ambivalent: the style could be viewed in Swift's terms, as her alibi, or in the terms of *State Law,* as her crime. If one sees allegory as disguise, it appears to be insurance against political prosecution; but if one sees it as abuse, allegory becomes the very thing that would provoke prosecution.[27]

Although both contemporary views of allegory (as alibi and as crime) in this legal discourse cross the technique with politics, we

25. Quoted in Thomas, p. 58, as the "interpretation [of the law] accepted" when Manley was prosecuted (pp. 58–59), but Thomas does not comment on the passage or note the paradox of innuendo: that in cases of abusive allegory, the same evidence may be cited as either exonerating or incriminating.

26. For this reason Lennard Davis's very helpful discussion of the news-novel matrix is somewhat too simple. According to Davis, in the early eighteenth century one had to claim that books of "news" were fictional and works of fiction were "true." The very use of the word "fiction," however, could often be a clue to the contemporary reference of the work.

27. This same paradox applies to modern libel law. Marc A. Franklin and Robert Trager point out that in cases where plaintiffs feel themselves to have been defamed in a work of fiction by similarities between themselves and characters with other names, defendants often rest their case on the differences between the fictional characters and the plaintiffs. Among such dissimilarities are often the very bits of fiction "that prompt the defamation action." Apparently because it would be absurd to rest one's defense on such abusive details, Franklin and Trager call them "latent dissimilarities," implying that they are seldom emphasized in a defense because they form the grounds of the plaintiff's charge. Nevertheless, they are mentioned along with other differences between the plaintiff and the character as a kind of potential evidence that the statements about the character are not "of and concerning" the plaintiff. See "Literature and Libel," *Comm/Ent* 4:2 (1981–82): 212. I am grateful to Robert Post for calling my attention to this article.

should notice that *State Law's* discussion actually focuses on allegory, takes it seriously, in a way that Swift's view does not. When satirical allegory is seen as the crime, the allegorical level, the textual level of technique where the writer invents many of the very circumstances that constitute the defamation, takes on an opacity that Swift's view would deny it. It was acknowledged that such techniques marked the controversial text and thereby attracted potential readers. In Swift's description, though, one only looked for such devices in order to look through them, whereas those who recognized the abusive function of allegory like Manley's perceived the device as the controversial matter and thus bestowed on it an interest of its own. Thus we might conclude that to view allegory as a crime (not an alibi), wholly identified with political transgression, encouraged the development of techniques we now call fictional by giving them greater weight.

Let us then momentarily hold in abeyance the idea that Manley's technique protected her from prosecution and concentrate instead on how allegorical invention furthered her libelous purposes. What Manley gained from the allegorical necessity of altering and therefore inventing circumstances was a representational density that enabled especially effective libel. Manley's talent was for crafting the invented circumstances into what we would now call a "novelistically" satisfying story, one read for its own sake as well as for its scandalous referentiality. At their best, the stories of *The New Atalantis* inspired a partial disregard for veracity that allowed them to develop simultaneously toward a more specific referentiality and a more independent "fictionality."

This point will perhaps be clearer if we compare two passages from Manley's works; the first, from *Queen Zarah*, has *only* an allegorical interest and not an independent narrative one. It figures Sarah Churchill as the domineering usurper trying to "tame" a series of ministers:

> Nothing griev'd Zarah like this ungovernable Spirit of the Albigions, who wou'd not bear to think of being rid with a Side-Saddle, having had their Backs gall'd so much before in the Female Reign of Rolando [Charles II].
>
> But notwithstanding all these Difficulties, Zarah was resolved to mount on the Stirrup of Hippolito's [Marlborough's] Fame . . . and drive her Beasts forward by the help of Volpone's [Godolphin's] Rod

... by this Means she got on the Backs of the most Able Pads in the whole Kingdom . . . , some of which she rid to Death, others she jaded, and some she rides still. (1:110–11)

The episode goes on to satirize a group of noblemen in equestrian language, drawing on the iconographic trope of woman on top that was used often in the period to satirize she-favorites.[28] As a story it is competent, if commonplace, but nothing about it invites the reader to linger on the "literal" level, the invented level of fiction.

The second passage, from *The New Atalantis*, is not allegorical in the same sense. It also gives us the she-favorite on top, but it endeavors to produce its own narrative and erotic interest in doing so. In the episode the duchess *de l'inconstant*, the "disguised" duchess of Cleveland (mistress of Charles II), is being tricked by John Churchill into sleeping with his young friend Henry, Baron Dover. At this point in the story, the Churchill figure, Count Fortunatus, wishes to be free of the duchess, to whom he had been prostituting himself. The duchess approaches the bed of Fortunatus, unwilling to perceive that the youth lying before her is not her lover.

[H]e had thrown himself upon the Bed, pretending to Sleep, with nothing on but his Shirt and Night-Gown, which he had so indecently dispos'd, that slumbering as he appear'd, his whole Person stood confess'd to the Eyes of the Amorous Dutchess, his Limbs were exactly form'd, his Skin shiningly white, and the Pleasure the Ladies graceful entrance gave him, diffused Joy and Desire throughout all his Form. His lovely Eyes seem'd to be closed, his Face turn'd on one side (to favour the Deceit) was obscur'd by the Lace depending from the Pillows on which he rested; the Dutchess, who had about her all those Desires she expected to employ in the Embraces of the Count, was so blinded by 'em that at first she did not perceive the Mistake, so that giving her Eyes time to wander over Beauties so inviting, and which encreased her Flame; with an amorous Sigh, she gently threw herself on the Bed close to the desiring Youth; the Ribbon of his Shirt-Neck not tied, the Bosom (adorn'd with the finest Lace) was open, upon which she fix'd her charming Mouth, impatient, and finding that he did not awake, she raised her Head and

28. For a discussion of this trope and its functions, see Natalie Zemon Davis, "Women on Top: Symbolic Sexual Inversion and Political Disorder in Early Modern Europe," in *The Reversible World: Symbolic Inversion in Art and Society,* ed. Barbara Babcock (Ithaca, NY: Cornell Univ. Press, 1978), pp. 147–90.

laid her Lips to that part of his Face that was reveal'd: The burning
Lover thought it was now time to put an end to his pretended Sleep,
he clasp'd her in his Arms, grasp'd her to his Bosom; her own
Desires help'd the Deceit; she shut her Eyes with a languishing
Sweetness, calling him by intervals, her dear Count, her only lover,
taking and giving a thousand Kisses, he got possession of her Person
with so much transport, that she owned all her former Enjoyments
were imperfect to the Pleasure of this. (1:305–06)

It is easy to see why *The New Atalantis* was a more popular book
than *Queen Zarah*. Although *Zarah* contains some interesting stories,[29] nothing in it approaches the sheer voyeuristic eroticism of
the later satire, a voyeurism mirrored in the lascivious looking of
the duchess herself. The passage is practically a parable about the
pleasures of reading *The New Atalantis*. Because the youth on the
bed can be looked at either as a dazzling surface to be enjoyed, no
matter who he is, or as a simulacrum, an allegory, of the count,
complete erotic indulgence is licensed, which makes "all . . . former
Enjoyments . . . imperfect [compared] to the Pleasure of this." If
one really wants to enjoy the book, one should not try to sort out
the levels of referentiality but rather, like the duchess, let one's
desire aid the deceit and take one's pleasure both ways at once.
This text truly works on two levels: it can be enjoyed as mere story,
suspending the referential issue, or as defamation. Such doubleness, moreover, makes the defamation all the more pleasurable,
effective, and, indeed, *explicit*.

Thus we seem to have exactly reversed the usual explanation for
allegorical writing in the eighteenth century and the emergence of
fiction. Instead of maintaining that writers evaded the law through
allegory, we could argue that they exposed themselves to the law
through it. And instead of arguing that purely literary fictions
emerged from evasive actions, from the search for alibis, we might
argue that stories became more elaborate and interesting in them-

---

29. A comparable scene in *Queen Zarah* has Hippolito (John Churchill) encounter
the young Zarah (then Sarah Jennings) where he expects to find Clelia (the duchess
of Cleveland), but although the setting is described (actually translated directly from
Sebastian de Bremond's earlier *histoire scandaleuse, Hattigé, ou Les Amours du Roy de
Tamara* [Paris, 1676], p. 69), the young Zarah is not. Moreover, Hippolito recognizes
Zarah immediately, so that the themes of double vision and disguise are absent,
whereas they recur frequently in *The New Atalantis*. See, for example, vol. 1, pp.
662–65, as well as the passages cited at the end of this chapter.

selves and narrative technique became more "novelistic" because writers became more intent on effective political scandalmongering.

However, I do not want to hold one of these theses to the exclusion of the other. Because Delarivier Manley could vacillate between the poles of alibi and crime in developing her technique, she created a sheer excess of story, which certainly resembles our modern idea of fiction but retains the pleasurable and controversial doubleness, the special way of seeming to point "outside," that belongs to allegory.[30] The allegorical style thus met the paradoxical exigencies of her circumstances: it was partisan when viewed from one point of view, neutral when viewed from another, and remunerative when viewed from any. In a sense, then, Delarivier Manley could not lose by this crossing of politics and "fiction" in the discourse of libel.

~

It should be apparent from the passage quoted above that *The New Atalantis*'s presentation of female eroticism was at least partly re-

30. My analysis, then, breaks with the critical tradition that would characterize Manley's genre as she herself facetiously characterized it—as simply fiction. John J. Richetti's discussion of Manley in *Popular Fiction before Richardson* (Oxford: Clarendon Press, 1969), pp. 119–53, turned critical attention away from her writings as scandalous histories toward their role in the construction of the myth that female innocence is constantly besieged by an egotistical and corrupt masculinity. The mythic and the fictional are roughly equivalent concepts for Richetti, and hence Manley's works are fictional despite their contemporary referentiality. Richetti's analysis had the merit of recognizing Manley's importance in developing narrative patterns that would later be incorporated into the novel, but it also, somewhat anachronistically, imposed the concept of fiction on Manley's work retroactively. More recent discussions tend to follow Richetti's lead in this matter; Jerry C. Beasley repeats the same argument about beleaguered femininity while noting that Manley exploits the pattern for political purposes. See "Politics and Moral Idealism: The Achievement of Some Early Women Novelists," in *Fetter'd or Free? British Women Novelists, 1670–1815*, ed. Mary Anne Schofield and Cecilia Macheski (Athens: Ohio Univ. Press, 1986), pp. 223–25. Jane Spencer, *The Rise of the Woman Novelist: From Aphra Behn to Jane Austen* (London: Basil Blackwell, 1986), pp. 53–61, 113–16; Michael McKeon, *The Origins of the English Novel, 1600–1740* (Baltimore, MD: Johns Hopkins Univ. Press, 1987), pp. 232–33; and Jacqueline Pearson, *The Prostituted Muse: Images of Women and Women Dramatists, 1642–1737* (New York: St. Martin's Press, 1988), pp. 193–95, all attempt to place Manley in various typologies of narrative fiction. Even Dolores Palomo, who argues vigorously against Richetti's particular analysis, allows his generic identification to stand. Indeed, she seems almost embarrassed to mention at one point that "contemporaries recognized the authenticity of this and other stories in her secret histories, and in fact her success resulted partly from the presumption that she told real stories about real people." See "A Woman Writer and the Scholars: A Review of Mary Manley's Reputation," *Women and Literature* 6:1 (Spring 1978): 44.

sponsible for its irresistible crossing of politics and allegorical invention. To get an adequate understanding of this moment in the history of women's writing, we should briefly note how the new political culture was simultaneously making use of femininity and redefining it.

Aphra Behn's career had flourished in the somewhat libertine climate of Restoration court circles. The air of gallantry was not quickly dispelled after 1688, although the courts of William and Mary and of Anne celebrated conjugal fidelity, and Anne especially tried to punish some noblemen for ostentatiously rakish misbehavior. There is only a slight change of tone, too, in women's writing. The playwrights who followed immediately in Behn's wake—Mary Pix, Susannah Centlivre, Delarivier Manley herself—wrote a more sentimental style of comedy than had Behn, but this could be said of male playwrights as well after 1690. Nor can Manley be said to have written chaster stories than Aphra Behn. Although she did not contribute to the flood of pornographic libertine literature per se,[31] she wrote a titillating kind of amatory tale,[32] turning out dozens of stories and scandalous court chronicles compounded of seduction, adultery, incest, and betrayal. The difference between the two writers' stories is not in Manley's display of any new sense of propriety, but in her firmer subordination of the stories to a satirical political purpose; as in the excerpt from *Queen Zarah*, Manley often employed the misogynistic tropes available to such satire. Behn, even in her most satirical moments, indulged in these far less frequently.[33] In short, women's sexual and political appetites, depicted in the fiction of both writers, are made more central and problematic in Manley's satires.

Such a difference is not at all surprising, given the nature of Queen Anne's court, where women were perceived to have a distressing amount of power. A woman on the throne meant that the nobles of the household (Groom of the Stole, Mistress of the

31. Studies of this literature include Roger Thompson, *Unfit for Modest Ears: A Study of Pornographic, Obscene and Bawdy Works Written or Published in England in the Second Half of the Seventeenth Century* (London: Macmillan, 1979); and David Foxon, *Libertine Literature in England, 1660–1745* (New York: University Books, 1965).

32. For a definition of this genre, see Ros Ballaster, *Seductive Forms: Women's Amatory Fiction, 1684–1740* (Oxford: Clarendon Press, 1992), pp. 32–35.

33. If we look, for example, at Behn's presentation of Monmouth's mistress in *Love-Letters between a Nobleman and His Sister* as an instance of the woman-on-top topos, we can see how she undercuts the convention even as she uses it.

Robe, Keeper of the Privy Purse, and so forth) were also women. Moreover, Anne seems to have been especially dependent on her ladies-in-waiting, demanding what contemporaries often depicted as inappropriately intimate relationships. Since access to the queen was often thus controlled by women, the developing political parties and the increasingly powerful government ministers found themselves more than usually dependent on the favor of the ladies of the royal household.

Predictably, partisan attacks began to center on the illegitimate power these women were perceived to hold. Manley's attacks on Sarah Churchill were matched by equally outrageous Whig satires on Abigail Masham, Robert Harley's cousin, when she became the queen's favorite.[34] Like the libels on Queen Zarah, those on King Abigail, as one satirist called her, were often sexual. We might argue that this was the case simply because attacks on women's character had always been sexual. If Churchill was accused of being a whore, Masham was accused of lesbianism, and since each party needed its own female allies, making such accusations and fighting with other factions often fell to the women themselves. Thus Sarah Churchill commissioned and sang, although she did not actually write, the following ballad about her rival:

> When as Qu[een] Anne of great Renown
> Great Britain's Sceptre sway'd
> Besides the Church, she dearly lov'd
> A Dirty Chamber-Maid.
>
> O! Abi[gail] that was her Name,
> She stich'd and starch'd full well,
> But how she pierc'd the Royal Heart,
> No Mortal Man can tell.
>
> However for sweet Service done,
> And Causes of great Weight,
> Her Royal Mistress made her, Oh!
> A Minister of State.

34. See, for example, John Dunton's *King Abigail; or, the Secret Reign of the She-Favourite, Detected, and Applied: In a Sermon Upon these Words, "And Women rule over them" Isa. 3.12* (London, 1715). For a general discussion of English satires on women and English uses of Juvenalian rhetoric, see Felicity A. Nussbaum, *The Brink of All We Hate: English Satires on Women, 1660–1750* (Lexington: Univ. Press of Kentucky, 1984).

Her Secretary she was not,
Because she could not write;
But had the Conduct and the Care
Of some dark Deeds at Night.[35]

This ballad comes so close to slandering the queen herself that it reveals how active her mere femaleness was in generating the theme of perpetual sexual scandal in the political discourse of the period. The simplest way to explain the crossing of partisan politics and female eroticism, then, is to point to the coincidence of the female monarch and the rage for party.

I would like to suggest, however, that the court was more the occasion than the cause of the new emphasis on women in political discourse. J. G. A. Pocock has argued that, following the financial revolution of the 1690s, a new model of personhood emerged in England, a model he calls civil humanism, which elevated "commerce, leisure, and cultivation" over the key terms of the older-model civic humanism, "property, leisure, politics."[36] The emergent civil humanist model accepted that the worthy man would have private interests and commercial dealings as well as a private life in which he cultivated himself merely for the sake of personal cultivation; the earlier civic model eschewed commerce and justified property and leisure primarily on the grounds that they freed one for service to the state, not for the development of a multifaceted self. Pocock also points out that the new concentration on enriched private experience in social and commercial intercourse and the new tolerance for private interests among public men were not universally embraced. Although he cautions against simplistic partisan analyses, he links the new civil model to the New Whigs; in the decade that concerns us, they would have been associated with Marlborough and Godolphin, who represented the alliance between military and monied interests. Their most important writers would have included Addison and Steele. On the side of the old-style civic humanists, Pocock places politicians such as St. John and (toward the end of Anne's reign) Robert Harley. The attacks of

35. Sarah Churchill, "A New Ballad to the Tune of Fair Rosamund," quoted in David Green, *Sarah Duchess of Marlborough* (London: Collins, 1967), pp. 322–23.

36. "Virtues, Rights, and Manners," in *Virtue, Commerce, and History: Essays on Political Thought and History, Chiefly in the Eighteenth Century* (Cambridge: Cambridge Univ. Press, 1985), p. 49.

Swift and Manley (financed through Harley) on Whig corruption called into question the new ideology of civility and was linked to a coalition of country, Old Whig, and new Tory groups.

Manley's alignment politically with what Pocock calls the civic humanists, those most likely to express fears about the new toleration for private interests, partly explains the kind of satire she wrote. However, it would be difficult to place Manley squarely inside the Scriblerian milieu we associate with Swift, Pope, and Arbuthnot, for in their discourse the idea of woman often functions in ways that Manley's texts could not consistently accommodate.[37] Indeed, Manley's authorial self-presentation relies on the civil humanist ideology normally associated with her political antagonists because both she and they were reconstructing the idea of femininity explicitly in the context of exchange.

According to Pocock, contrasting conceptions of property underlay the differences between civic and civil humanists; the former stressed "possession and civic virtue" and the latter "exchange and the civilization of the passions."[38] Moreover, Pocock implies that in the Queen Anne period these different concepts of property were aligned with opposite valuations of female social discourse. This was the case because the financial revolution of the 1690s had turned the polity into a network of debtors and creditors, made the state heavily dependent on financial interests, and encouraged new habits of speculation. It was not simply the growth of the market in general but specifically the growth of the stock market in relation to the fiscal-military state that encouraged a newly positive assessment of women and new anxieties about them.[39] For the new eighteenth-century economic man, he continues, "was seen as on the whole a feminized, even an effeminate being, still wrestling with his own passions and hysterias and with interior and exterior forces let loose by his [stock market–induced] fantasies and appetites."[40]

37. For studies of "the feminine" in Swift and Pope, see Ellen Pollak, *The Poetics of Sexual Myth: Gender and Ideology in the Verse of Swift and Pope* (Chicago: Univ. of Chicago Press, 1985), passim; and Nussbaum, pp. 94–116 and 137–58.

38. "The Mobility of Property and the Rise of Eighteenth-Century Sociology," in *Virtue, Commerce, and History*, p. 115.

39. For a detailed description of this process, see John Brewer, *The Sinews of Power: War, Money and the English State, 1688–1783* (New York: Knopf, 1989).

40. "The Mobility of Property," p. 114.

Pocock thus presents those who rode the crest of that great surge in military and financial growth and publicized its benefits as centrally concerned with new representations of the feminine that might contain (in both senses of the word) the threatening excessiveness they themselves projected onto it. Often in their writings femininity is associated with the vagaries of credit itself, but it is also linked to politeness and refinement, as if the male writers were trying to reassure themselves that their own passions might be refined into rational interests.[41] Civil humanists claimed that the very thing that had liberated the passions—commercial society—would, by providing relations of confidence between men, itself refine the passions. Similarly, a freer and more "rational" intercourse between men and women in civil society would at once teach women to contain their own passions and allow men to improve that "politeness" which was to be the new support and justification for a commercial civilization. The possibility of rational intercourse with women, therefore, was often promulgated by the same men who were beginning to extol the benefits of exchange, and hence after the 1690s women's public discourse was fastened to the idea of commerce in *positive* as well as negative new ways.

This shift in British political discourse away from the Renaissance language of civic virtue and toward one of civility, cultivation, and politeness realigned the realms of public and private more profoundly and lastingly than did the rather anomalous gender relations of Queen Anne's court. However, the new alignments, even inside the ideology of civil humanism, were extremely convoluted. When Addison and Steele, for example, called for women's public language in the *Spectator*, they were encouraging not women's political involvement but rather their participation in something quite different but closely related, the construction of civil society.[42] In polite London society, women were told by the *Spectator*, they were to be part of the intercourse that created the civil gentleman, whose exchanges were no longer imagined to unfit him for political life but were rather asserted to demonstrate his credentials as a

41. The classic study of this dichotomy in the early period is Albert O. Hirschman, *The Passions and the Interests: Political Arguments for Capitalism before Its Triumph* (Princeton, NJ: Princeton Univ. Press, 1977).

42. See Kathryn Shevelow, *Women and Print Culture: The Construction of Femininity in the Early Periodicals* (London: Routledge, 1989).

cultured individual. However, the refinement of such interactions was associated with their "personal" nature, their removal from immediate connections to politics and the struggle for state power. Women, then, became important to the social identity of the political male in a new way that involved social exchange, conversation, a world of shared cultural experience not necessarily organized into the family; hence the feminine and the political were not simply opposed. At the same time, however, a man's personal cultivation could have political weight only if pursued for its own sake; the feminine and the political remained disjoined even in their mode of mutual implication. Thus although the *Spectator* encouraged its female correspondents, it did not encourage them to write about politics.

Although the *Spectator* officially placed women outside the boundaries of politics, that very position gave women writers a special political usefulness in an ideology that based political worthiness partly on personal merit, that insisted on the relevance of traits exhibited in private life to the performance of public duties, and that feminized the sphere of civil society. The political women writers who slipped most comfortably through this opening provided by the ideology of civil humanism were Whigs; I will now turn to the works of one of these, Susannah Centlivre, whose presentation of herself as a political author makes an instructive contrast to Manley's. By looking first at a writer inside the ideology of civil humanism, we can get a clearer idea of how Manley's works cut against its grain.

Centlivre claimed to be the daughter of gentlefolk of small estate and zealous Parliamentarian politics, whose property was confiscated at the Restoration. She was a strolling player, a London actress, and from 1700 to 1723 a playwright of some reputation. In 1709 she entered the lists of the polemicists on the side of the Whig supporters of the duke of Marlborough, whose conduct of the continental wars was then being sharply criticized by the Tories. For the rest of her career she vociferously opposed the Tories and supported the Protestant Succession. Married to one of the overseers of the royal kitchen who was officially called the Groom of the Mouth, she may have expected her husband's place at court to serve as a conduit of reward for her partisan writing, an expectation she facetiously attributed to him in a very late and uncharacteristically self-satirizing comic poem entitled "A Woman's Case":

> Deuce take your scribbling vein, quoth he,
> What did it ever get for me?
> Two Years you take a Play to write,
> And I scarce get my Coffee by't.
> . . . .
> . . . from your boasted Friends I see
> Small Benefit accrues to me:
> I hold my Place indeed, 'tis true;
> But I well hop'd to Rise by You.

Her contemporary biographers mention several of the gifts she received from grateful noblemen during Anne's reign, but her largest rewards no doubt derived from George I's later enthusiastic patronage of her plays.[43]

Centlivre and her male colleagues emphasized her gender. First, they presented it as a necessary counter to the writings of the women on the other side. Each party abused the other's female authors for overstepping their proper bounds, then rather inconsistently praised their own for combatting the errors of the enemy. The Whig (soon to turn Tory) hack Nicholas Amhurst thus praised Centlivre as the only loyal female writer in 1720:

> Whilst party-mad the British Fair,
> On Monarch Jemmy set their hearts,
> Despise the peaceful house-wife's care,
> and practice their seditious arts.
>
> Whilst they with lies revile the Throne,
> And with Church fears their minds perplex,
> Their follies singly you atone,
> And singly you redeem the Sex.[44]

These stanzas not only reveal the casual way in which male writers exempted their own female colleagues from the discursive limitations they declared suitable for the whole sex, but also figure

---

43. See John Wilson Bowyer, *The Celebrated Mrs. Centlivre* (Durham, NC: Duke Univ. Press, 1952), pp. 144–70, for an account of her political exploits and their rewards.
44. Quoted in Bowyer, p. 224.

women's partisan involvement as arising from infatuation or sexual longing. The Tory women of the first stanza are metaphorically bad housewives not only because they meddle in politics but also because they desire the Pretender; Centlivre becomes the good wife not by keeping still but by voicing her fidelity to the lawful monarch. In these stanzas the smitten women, pining for a man who is not their legal master, serve as a figure for the fickleness of the nation as a whole, which had become rather quickly disenchanted with George I. Desire for the Stuart Pretenders was represented as a kind of adulterous attraction throughout the first half of the eighteenth century, with Jacobite women thus serving as a very convenient target for satire and women loyal to the Hanoverians as their necessary foil.

This connection between female infatuation and politics was also prevalent in the reign of Queen Anne, and its presence in Centlivre's poetry at that time reveals a second typical use of feminine authorship. We often find women political writers themselves insisting on their own infatuation with the political leaders they supported. These coy lines from one of Centlivre's occasional poems, praising a political hero, catch the tone of the age:

> 'Tis well he's a Lord, and that I am not Fair;
> His Eyes have such Power—but I'll say no more.[45]

Such public testimonials to the personal charms of the political patron fit well into the ideology of civil humanism, with its emphasis on the private character and cultivation of the new political man. Of course, Renaissance encomia had earlier contained a similar language of praise for the nobleman's beauty and power to fascinate the writer and all other beholders, but that tradition of praise, no matter how obviously erotic, was developed within a hierarchical male structure of status and obligation that concentrated more on the hero's capacity to inspire enthusiastic obedience than on his success in eliciting desire. The male writer contemplated the personal charm of the hero as an outward sign of the fitness of the hero's power and the writer's subordination to him. Interestingly, mention of personal attractions begins to disappear from the repertoire of male encomia at just about the time it is

---

45. Quoted in Bowyer, p. 222.

picked up by women writers and converted from a statement about the awesome sway of the object to a statement explicitly about his desirability. This shift in the political meaning of male beauty from its ability to overawe the male observer to its power to create longing in the female viewer signals the new relevance in the hero of personal traits that were designated as outside official political culture and associated with femininity and chastened passions. The civil gentleman's power to fascinate women is one of the things that gives him his polite credentials, and such credentials were essential to his political success.

This sexual division of praise, in which men note the patron's civic virtues and women attest to his personal attractions, is well displayed by the editor of the Whig *Patriot* in his introduction to a Centlivre poem praising Charles, earl of Halifax, in 1714:

> Amongst these Patriots the Earl of Hallifax is one of the first, this Gentleman by the Zeal he has perpetuallo [*sic*] shewn for the Interest of his Country, and the Mild Temper with which he has bore the Insults and Pillages of Prostituted Men, has gained him as many Admirers among his Country Men, who are Honest in their Politicks, as his other Excellent Qualifications have among all Lovers and Judges of Letters. And thus far one would willingly allow: But that his Lordship should proceed so universally to be admir'd as to make even the Ladies write Panegyricks on him, is what, I fear, some of our fine Gentlemen will ill bear.[46]

Centlivre is not identified in this introduction because the claim that the writer is a "fine Lady (for I am sure she must be so by the Goodness of her Poetry and the Badness of her Spelling)" is important to the ideological pattern. Panegyrics from a party hack like Centlivre, whom Halifax rewarded with "a fine repeating Gold Watch,"[47] would hardly betoken the spontaneous outpouring of genteel female enthusiasm necessary to prove Halifax universally admired as a polished man as well as a patriot. The woman political writer had to be cast as the amateur in all senses of the word. What was desired of her was desire itself, the introduction of the passions into a proto-political civil discourse, where their regulation might also be displayed: "His Eyes have such Power—but I'll say no

46. Quoted in Bowyer, pp. 158–59.
47. Bowyer, p. 159.

more." The civil humanists, then, encouraged women's political interventions even as they presented their writings as not really political.

Manley's self-presentation as a female partisan was more complex than Centlivre's. Although she, too, found a political niche by advertising her feminine disqualifications for politics, she drew not only on the language of the civic humanists but also on that of the satirists in the civil humanist tradition exemplified by Jonathan Swift. Swift's partisan affiliations were unstable; in the very early part of Anne's reign, he was friendly with the New Whig lords of the "Junto," and found himself on the Tory side only when Robert Harley (himself of the country party) was forced by circumstances to appoint mainly Tories to the government he led between 1709 and 1714.[48] Ideologically, too, it would be a mistake to cast Swift simply as an antagonist to civil humanism. He was close to Steele and Addison before and after their factional quarrels and wrote for both the *Tatler* and the *Spectator*. Nor do we find in Swift's writing any consistent hostility toward the civil idea of refinement through linguistic interchange with women. His "Essay on Conversation" lays the period's familiar emphasis on the refinement that can only be achieved in mixed society. Nevertheless, Swift was more apt than Addison or Steele to draw on Juvenalian misogynistic rhetorical traditions in his satire. As numerous critics have recently pointed out, in satires by Swift and Pope, females often function as figures of disorder, irrationality, unruly passion, or mere triviality.[49] This satirical tradition, well established in English letters, was especially useful, as I have already pointed out, in the disturbingly feminine environment of Anne's court, where both parties used it to discredit individual women and to supply images of general corruption. Yet Delarivier Manley also wrote in this tradition; we have to ask how its rhetoric elicited her writing.

I have already mentioned that the satire on a woman in a

48. Downie, in *Jonathan Swift, Political Writer*, notes the stability of principles underlying Swift's change in party. He was always committed to the strict separation of powers entailed in the Revolution Settlement. During Anne's reign and after, that separation was championed by anticorruption Tories, such as St. John and Harley, rather than by the New Whigs.

49. For studies of the functions of "the feminine" in Swift and Pope, see Laura Brown, *Alexander Pope* (Oxford: Basil Blackwell, 1985); Pollak, *The Poetics of Sexual Myth*; and Nussbaum, *The Brink of All We Hate*.

woman's voice was particularly relished, but I have not explained why. Manley's own justification for having written *The New Atalantis* provides important clues. *The Adventures of Rivella*, the third-person autobiography from which I quoted Manley's defense at her libel hearing at the beginning of this chapter, presents a confession as well as a defense, and the confession helps us understand the terms in which Manley, as a woman, was constituted a political being. She admits that she attacked

> a Faction who were busy to enslave their Sovereign, and overturn the Constitution; that she was proud of having more Courage than had any of our Sex and of throwing the first Stone, which might give a Hint for other Persons of more Capacity to examine the Defects and Vices of some men who took a Delight to impose upon the World, by the Pretence of public Good, whilst their true Design was only to gratify and advance themselves. (2:845)

Like most writers of the period, the heroine here dignifies her partisanship as general patriotism. Her attack on Godolphin's ministry is merely a defense of crown and constitution. Here the criminal confesses the crime of libel even though she seeks to be forgiven, indeed admired, on the grounds that she committed it in the service of a higher cause. This passage, insofar as it is merely a confession and glorification of the act, is altogether standard in the political literature of the period written by both men and women. By calling partisan libel patriotic zeal, Manley gives her act a universal and ungendered significance.

But this passage departs from its own high-mindedness when the author's gender emerges. The woman "proud of having more Courage than had any of [the male] Sex and of throwing the first Stone" is a figure out of a political tradition far less polite than that of the patriotic martyr. It is only a rhetorical moment, but the phrase nevertheless conjures the common figure of disorder, the woman at the head of the mob, both allegorical and real, who casts the first stone in the riot because she is a juridical nonperson and therefore cannot be held responsible. In the very midst of claiming her political personhood, therefore, Manley raises the specter of the common disorderly woman, politically useful precisely because she cannot be taken seriously as a political agent. The author as the female of misogynist satirical literature thus intrudes on this high-minded confession, but in doing so displays both her own inappropriateness and her utility.

Moreover, the biblical echo in the phrase "throwing the first Stone" reminds us of the sexual nature of Manley's satire; it was directed, especially, against adulterous women. This rhetorical linking of the author with the mob violence of women against women would have had wide resonance in the early eighteenth century, which saw both an enormous growth in London rioting and a doubling of the percentage of rioters who were women. According to one historian,

> female rioting was focused primarily on disputes concerning sexual morality and economic issues . . . [W]omen were proportionally most frequently accused of participating in riots "about" people in the streets or in front of their houses and in riots that involved disturbing or defaming the victim, riots that often protested deviant sexual behavior.[50]

Manley thus links herself to an increasingly visible form of female public action against sexual impropriety; the association, however, further feminizes her satire and makes it seem less centrally political.

The fact that women's riots often punished sexual misbehavior did not erase their own impropriety, moreover. Nor did Manley's many claims to be a satirical scourge keep her from being perceived as a purveyor of licentiousness and a stimulator of the very passions she exposed. In the next paragraph of her confession, indeed, she seems to admit the identity of impropriety between female victim and female accuser in her own works:

> As to exposing those who had never injured her, she said she did no more by others, than others had done by her (i.e.) Tattle of Frailties; the Town had never shewn her any Indulgence, but on the contrary reported ten fold against her in Matters of which she was wholly Innocent, whereas she did take up old Stories that all the World had long since reported. (2:845–46)

The heroine is no longer in this passage a decisive individual political subject, full of patriotic fire; instead, she now depicts

50. Robert B. Shoemaker, "The London 'Mob' in the Early Eighteenth Century," *Journal of British Studies* 26 (July 1987): 285.

herself as a slandered woman who evens a score in an altogether traditionally feminine manner: she "Tattle[s] of Frailties," and tells "old Stories"; in short she gossips. This argument resembles the fiction alibi of the inquest, for it once again claims the general triviality of Manley's writing; as in her statement to the secretary of state, she is simply a woman amusing herself with a "few amorous trifles" (2:848). And although she is willing to admit in this instance that she did not completely make them up, she is no longer concerned with their objective truth, only with their prior circulation.

In Rivella's confession, then, as in her alibi, we find ourselves once again moving between political purposes and mere amusement, between high crimes and low excuses, but here the poles are clearly gendered. Once again, however, we can also observe a crossing of binary terms, the paradoxical ways in which politics and femininity implicate each other, even when womanhood is constructed within the misogynist assumptions of Augustan satire. Manley presents herself as politically useful because she is a disorderly woman vengefully gossiping about female "secrets" and therefore doing the sort of low and frivolous work considered beneath real politicians. Hence she links her book's peculiar political efficacy to its femininity, which in turn decomposes its political nature.

The confession that presents this paradox is, as I have already mentioned, completely exculpatory. As Manley moves her explanation from patriotic fervor to feminine irresponsibility, she becomes all the more "innocent" in the archaic sense of "unaccountable." As a patriot she was behaving admirably, and as a woman she could not help herself. Although the political and sexual components of the confession work against each other both logically and imagistically, each contributes a kind of innocence, and the passage, by remaining unconscious of its contradictions, tries to add the two kinds of innocence together to achieve a complete vindication. We are to see her as both a high-minded stateswoman and a passionate, unruly creature. Her complete innocence is thus based on the juxtaposition/addition of her political and sexual impulses.

We should note, though, that *The New Atalantis*'s female villains are guilty of the same crossing of feminine amorousness and politics that supposedly constitutes the author's innocence. Figures representing Lady Marlborough and the duchess of Cleveland, for example, are exposed as having a dual and contradictory political/ sexual nature that makes them doubly corrupt, whereas Manley's made her doubly innocent. We are faced in the text of *The New Atalantis*, as in the confession in *Rivella*, with an undeniable similarity between the satirist and the satirized that is partly owing, as we have seen, to the concept of womanhood supplied by the Juvenalian tradition but also derives from another source: Manley's own dependence on the very civil ideal she seems to be satirizing.

Manley's satire is internally riven by the need her female personae have to participate in the civil humanists' revision of femininity. The disorderly woman may occasionally show herself effective, but she is too self-subverting to provide Manley with a sustained authorial self. Hence the writing woman in Manley's works tends to wander the borderland between civic and civil humanism, continually crossing from one side to the other, picking up permissions and impediments from both sides, and working them into a richly self-ironizing satirical rhetoric.

Manley's errancy on the frontiers between the two ideologies is particularly apparent in her ironic treatment of the relationship between the woman writer's passions and interests. In her wandering, she often launches her attacks against the civil humanists from inside their own ideological territory. When she exposes the "secret" underside of the new idea of social privacy, the refinement of her victims as mere lechery, their valued personal intercourse as criminal conversation, their cultivation and patronage of the arts as bribery, she invokes not some civic humanist ideal of independent masculine virtue but the very ideas of cultivated exchange, especially between the sexes, that she simultaneously seems to be exposing as hypocritical. Moreover, she betrays her own self-interested reasons for subscribing to those ideas. For example, her allegorical narrator, Lady Intelligence, often makes satirical attacks that conclude with a racy, libertine one-upmanship, as in this criticism of the duke of Marlborough for not paying his mistresses directly:

> It appears strange to me [says Lady Intelligence], that considering the Count's [Marlborough's] Power and Riches, she [Daphne (Cath-

erine Trotter)] did not make her Fortune by his Fondness. But I think there yet wants an Example of elevated Generosity in him, to any of his Mistresses, tho' the World can't dispute but that he has had many: His way to pay the Favour, being to desire the Lady to study if there is any thing in his Power, by which he may oblige any Relation or Friend of hers; and that he will not fail to grant it. Thus every way a Husband of his Money, his Reputation and Grandeur procure him the good Fortune he desires: Tho' were the Ladies with whom he has a mind to converse of my Taste, they would think his own very handsome Person a Reward sufficient for all the Charms they can bestow. (1:585–86)

The passage cleverly combines charges of stinginess and corrupt influence trading as it comically implies that the duke's dealings with his mistresses should have been more commercial, indeed that in "preferring" the male relatives, thus "husbanding" his money (as she puns), the duke has been less than a perfect gentleman. But then, to demonstrate how even the language of fair exchange can and should be translated into that of taste and cultivation, Intelligence announces her own generous and tasteful willingness to make love to Marlborough for nothing. Thus the female satirist imaginatively substitutes herself for Catherine Trotter, a Whig writer of the period and the original object of the satire. The satirized are exposed as lustful and greedy under their politeness, but the satirist playfully converts her lust and ambition into an instance of Taste in Conversation. Intelligence is a figure for the author here, so the passage creates the effect of a satirist endlessly resubscribing to the values of the social interactions she mocks.

Much of the humor of *The New Atalantis* resides in these parallels and resemblances between satirized and satirist,[51] and most of them hinge on either the satirist's erotic desires or her hopes for political patronage. In some instances, the two forms of exchange are

51. The irony of *The New Atalantis* has gone largely unremarked since John Richetti directed the attention of critics to the recurrent seduction motif, thereby giving the impression that Manley's narrators vacillate between overheated prurience and outraged virtue. But in fact Manley structures her book so that the moral pretensions of the two allegorical figures, Virtue and Astrea, are frequently deflated by the interjections of the main narrator, Lady Intelligence, who is a figure for scandal itself, and Intelligence's self-interested motivations are often exposed. Two studies that have noted Manley's irony without concentrating on its self-inclusive quality are Palomo, "A Woman Writer and the Scholars: A Review of Mary Manley's Reputation"; and Janet Todd, *The Sign of Angellica: Women, Writing, and Fiction, 1660–1800* (London: Virago, 1989), pp. 84–98.

explicitly linked, and the impossibility of distinguishing between them, as in the passage quoted above, is the point of the joke. In another sequence, for example, Marlborough is accused of being stingy with both his mistresses and his writers, requiring one poet to leave a receipt for two pieces of silver paid for his panegyric. This report is immediately followed by Intelligence's panegyric to the duke of Beaumond (Henry, duke of Beaufort), whom she praises for his patriotism, generosity, and (she emphasizes) irresistible personal attractions (1:451).

Politics and femininity are thus interwoven in a series of maneuvers that depend on the terms' normative mutual exclusion. *The New Atalantis* manages to display all the available ways of crossing women and politics and then to make those crossings themselves the object of satire. Hence although femininity, like "fiction," can always be opposed to Manley's politics as its excuse, it can also be exposed as the deep truth of politics' corruption. Femininity has, in short, the same odd potential for exculpation and incrimination that we noted in the concept of "fictional" allegory. Delarivier Manley, as a Tory satirist impelled by her gender toward the rhetoric of civil humanism, was bound to use it both ways.

~

Although fiction and femininity occupy similar discursive positions vis-à-vis the concept of politics in this period (the positional parallel alone creating a strong link between them) and although in Manley's writings the libelous "fictional" material is often about female sexual misbehavior, the equivalence of "fiction" and femaleness in Augustan political discourse has a more complex logic. To understand it requires that we look at the novelty of political discourse in the period and its attendant insecurities.

As the press became an increasingly important political forum, the correspondence between the words that poured out of it and their putative referents became a topic of concern. Had politics become "mere" words? Did these words reveal anything, or did they serve as a screen behind which plotters decided the fate of the kingdom? Was political discourse "fictional"? As we will see, one strategy for answering these questions and containing their attendant anxiety was to divide political writings into the reputable and the disreputable. Foremost in the latter category were the excessively "feminine" writings of Delarivier Manley, for these were worse than mere fictions with no relationship to reality; they were scandals, *dis*creditings, that bore a potentially negative relationship to the polity.

British politics certainly did not achieve its modern form overnight with the Revolution Settlement of 1688, but by the end of Anne's reign a broad consensus had developed among the ruling classes regarding the basic institutions of the government, especially the relationships of crown, church, and Parliament. Issues that had remained open at the Restoration—whether the monarch could be a Roman Catholic, for example, or could dissolve Parliament indefinitely—were closed by the beginning of Anne's reign, and when it ended, with the Hanoverians in possession of the throne, a high degree of institutional stability had been achieved. The enormous political ferment of Anne's reign should be viewed in the context of this growing stability. Indeed, that all factions accused their adversaries of betraying the Revolution Settlement only attests to its almost universal acceptance.

Only under the conditions of a developing consensus could the publicity of political discourse, its dissemination through print, emerge. By allowing the Licensing Act to lapse in 1695, the established powers covertly admitted that public controversy would accompany the activities of governing, an admission that might not have been tolerated while the government was still seeking its own viable form. Our modern notion that politics consists in public controversy, rather than either clandestine maneuvering or sheer force of arms, was just being invented in this period, and consequently one finds in the writings of the time a sense of surprise that politics had, in fact, become a matter of representations, especially printed words.

As we have already seen, the libel laws prevented this new discursiveness from achieving full and immediate legitimacy, and one should not underestimate the widespread uneasiness during the period, the fear, partly aroused by Anne's own hostility to the house of Hanover, that the Revolution Settlement might be overturned and that the Stuarts might regain the throne or, conversely, that the separation of powers between executive and legislature was seriously threatened by corrupt patronage practices and a standing army. These were not considered issues over which reasonable men might disagree; rather, they were seen as devastating possibilities. Moreover, just as writers risked public prosecution and private cudgeling, statesmen who lost were still vulnerable to charges of treason. Robert Harley, the man who had done more than any other single individual to make politics discursive, was imprisoned in the Tower after Anne's death in 1714. We should not, therefore, imagine that tolerance had arrived suddenly, that controversy was not itself controversial, or that those who entered into the political game never staked their physical well-being.

Nevertheless, things had changed.[52] Few writers were actually imprisoned; Harley was soon released. Politics was no longer, as Thomas More had described it, "the King's games . . . played upon scaffolds." Hence, although a sense of limited danger and illicitness surrounded their activities, the writers of the period also registered a consciousness that as politics became increasingly discursive, as it became increasingly their domain, it lost some of its consequential gravity. Factions accused each other of treason and other kinds of criminality, but such accusations were generally paid in kind; the attacks were verbal and the casualties were names. Furthermore, the scandalous and satirical writing that concerns us here was often justified on the grounds that it punished "vices the law does not reach."[53] Since it was generally perceived that the "law" was increasingly reluctant to reach into political matters, punishment through print became all the more likely, but the very form of the punishment presupposed the inconsequentiality of the offense.

The literature of the period is full of verbal executions and complaints about the wounding and assassination of names, and such acts of annihilation had their corollary linguistic births. When Jonathan Swift condemned the almanac writer John Partridge to discursive nonbeing, by first predicting and then reporting Partridge's fictional death, Swift's persona Isaac Bickerstaff became a "person" with a life independent of the author's. The pseudonym seems to have propelled dozens of pamphlets into public notice before being adopted by Richard Steele. Indeed, "Bickerstaff" came

---

52. J. H. Plumb, *The Growth of Political Stability in England, 1675–1725* (London: Macmillan, 1967), is the classic study of how these changes came about.

53. This is Manley's paraphrase of Steele's justification in the *Tatler,* but it is an altogether conventional formulation drawn from classical models (1:529).

to mean "pseudonym," a name that anyone could use and all could deny. Steele often used it in order to disown it, a procedure Delarivier Manley satirized in 1711 when she wrote a mock dedication to Isaac Bickerstaff, explaining that he must be a separate person from Steele, for Steele was too honorable to have libeled her the way someone named Bickerstaff had in the *Tatler*. And so the paper identities went on multiplying, becoming in themselves a topic of discourse, as the printed punishments were meted out.

What must be kept in mind about political and other controversial writing in this period, then, is that its very novelty, combined with the anonymity and pseudonymity encouraged by the libel law, made its practitioners aware that they could create a discursive universe with little, if any, resemblance to a world outside itself. The major satires of the period attack not only specific political practices (bribery, for example) but also, as the Bickerstaff pamphlets emphasize, the production of a merely "nominal" world in print that had the capacity to displace what it purported to represent. The self-parody of many of these satires acknowledges what modern critics have often been loath to admit: that the satirists knew they were augmenting what they ostensibly attacked; that their irony is unstable because only such instability displays the ability of language to multiply nominal entities endlessly; and that they constantly played with the idea that the medium through which the new political culture was born had trapped politics itself in shadowy unreality.

Nowhere do nominal entities multiply more rapidly than in *The New Atalantis*. The book seems bent on demonstrating not only the fecundity of language but also its ability to obscure what it pretends to expose. In the first section of this chapter, I discussed the effect of doubling that the book achieves by gesturing simultaneously inward toward an admittedly fictional universe and outward toward a putatively real one. But double vision, which this book shares with all allegories, is a mild form of its usual practice, which is to produce triple, quadruple, and even quintuple vision. *The New Atalantis* goes far beyond most examples of its genre in duplicating and reduplicating its "originals" until the "persons of quality" indicated in the key seem to have multiplied into a small crowd of personae. Most allegorical satires of the period had a much simpler mode of reference. Both Manley's models and her imitators gave each satirical object a single, stable persona, so that once readers had identified the "real" person behind the disguise of character, they would not have expected that character to turn up again in yet another guise. Even Manley's *Queen Zarah* works on this one-to-one principle, which is why modern critics have praised its economy of form. In *The New Atalantis*, though, as if striving to inflate the usual economy of scandalous representation, Manley copies the same "object" onto as many as half a dozen different characters. In the first two volumes, for example, almost every time the narrator begins an anecdote that is supposed to be about the duke of Marlborough, she introduces a new persona. He is "the Great Lord in the shabby coach," Hippolito, Count Fortunatus, the Marquis of Caria, "the Shining Favorite," and the "stingiest Lord in Atalantis." The duchess of Marlborough is similarly personated as the She-Favorite, Young Jeanatin, the "Now Great Lady," and the Marchioness of Caria. *The Memoirs of Europe toward the Close of the Eighth Century*, later published as volumes three and four of *The New Atalantis*, continue this multiplication of "allegorical" personages.

One could guess at several reasons for this inflationary mode of representation. First, it makes Atalantis's court seem overgrown with corruption; instead of one stingy duke we are given six complete misers. Second, the multiplication is no doubt intended to assist the disguises and keep the reader mystified until the publication of the keys, which were sold separately a few weeks after the appearance of the books. But it also has the more subtle effect of marking the excessiveness of the genre, of emphasizing that every "allegory" is at the very least a duplication. Multiplying the paper existences merely exaggerates the inflationary aspect of the form.

That exaggeration is perhaps clearest in relation to the keys, those supplementary texts that supposedly marked the difference between fiction and scandal. We should bear in mind that the appearance of a key was not always a definitive indication of that distinction, for spurious, unauthorized keys materialized in the wake of every popular book. Keys, therefore, generally had to be greeted with a certain amount of suspicion, but the very routineness of their production testifies to the period's desire to open every book to some extra-textual reality, to read everything double. Even

A Tale of a Tub, the age's most brilliant satire on that very desire, was followed by its fraudulent key, in which every name in the text was paired with another. The rage for reference, especially for political reference, thus spawned a bizarre genre of parasitic fantasies.

The keys to Manley's works emphasize the inflationary tendencies of political allegory in a slightly different way. They were obviously authorized; although Manley perhaps did not produce them, they were issued by the publishers of the works themselves, and they served as a referential guarantee, a certification that the stories were about "real" people. Nevertheless, their relationship to the books they at once open and ground is problematic. They are, to begin with, remarkably insufficient; they identify a surprisingly small number of characters in each volume; minor representatives of the duke and duchess of Marlborough, their duplicate, triplicate, or quadruplicate personae, for example, are often not listed at all. Hence, although people eagerly awaited the keys, the experience of reading with and through them reinforces a sense of the scarcity of reference in relation to representation or, conversely, of the excess of representation in relation to reference. The very document that is supposed to ground the fictional names in an extra-textual reality emphasizes their unreasonable proliferation.

Finally, we might add, the graphic form of the keys leads us into yet another hall of mirrors, which reflects back the nominal nature of the entire enterprise. Let us look, for example, at a page from the "Key" to the first volume of the *Memoirs of Europe.* Only about half the pseudonyms in the left-hand column are paired with spelled-out names in the right-hand column; the rest are coupled with the mere traces of names, such as, "A B of C——" and "Ld Wh——n." Our care is to fill in the blanks, to make whole names out of discrete letters; hence the "D of M——n——ue" must first be translated into the "Duchess of Montague" before it can be thought to refer to a person whose title is duchess of Montague. That is, names are often indicated and deferred, not given, by the key. Even when some name is given, it is often not the name of the person implied: "Clarinda" is "Dr Egerton's Lady," and "Bartica" is "Sir Is Neuton's Niece." In the case of "Steelico" and "The Tatler," the author's proper name ("Steele," or as Swift would have put it, "St——le") even disappears into the name of a text, reversing the

Chriftopher	late Ld Clarendon
205 Publicola	Ld Nottingham
206 Catiline	Ld Wh—n
211 Theodecta	Mrs Martham
211 D of Campania	Duke of Ormond
Rutilius	Ld Gallway
213 Herminius	Mr Harley
218 Cethegus	Ld S—d—d
Cicero	Ld S—m—s
219 worn out Miftrefs	Attorney Blunts Wife, Sir Richard Fanfhaw's Daughter.
221 Pope Adrian	A B of C—
223 Tarafium	B of S—
224 B of Galatia	B of E—
228 Plato Patriarch	Dr. Sacheverel
236 Steelico	The Tatler
246 Agrippa	D of Buckingham
260 Lady of Quality Afian fide	D of Tirconnel Bow near London
266 Lovely Lady	Lady Kingfland
270 Gratian, Florella	Ld Moon, Mrs. Griffin
273 Porcia	Mrs Bovey of Gloucefterfhire
278 Julious Sergius	Ld H—l—x
279 Revd Matron	Ld Manchefter
285 Caffius	Mr Wycherly
286 Corvino	Mr Congreve
287 Maro	Mr Addifon
288 Artificial Patron	Ld Wh—n
Gallus	Mr Prior
289 Sapho younger	Mrs Bhen
Lays Charms	Mrs Trotter
290 Clarinda	Dr Egerton's Lady
Luretia	Mr Edw. Smith
Bartica	Sir If. Neuton's Niece
298 Lady well-featur'd	D of M—n—ue
Narciffus	D of G—f—n
	299 Ariadne

Key to the first volume of *The Memoirs of Europe* (1710) by Delarivier Manley. Courtesy of The Bancroft Library, University of California, Berkeley.

direction of "real" name and pseudonym altogether. The keys, in other words, open the text to an "outside" that they also continue to defer. One cannot say that the names on both sides of the page ultimately have the same status, but one can say that a simple binary opposition between fictional and real names is impossible to maintain and that as a result the problem of the relationship between names and persons is complicated rather than solved by the use of the key.

These are only a few of the many ways in which *The New Atalantis*, like other political works of the period, makes fun of itself by emphasizing its linguistic excess in relationship to what it supposedly represents. Such an emphasis is typical of Augustan satire, and Manley loads it into her narrative framework, her frequent thematization of authorship in general, and her highly ironic treatment of her own authorship. As we will see, though, Manley's selfsatirization is ingenuously confessional, thus setting *The New Atalantis* apart from other ironic narratives of the period and giving its author an almost archetypical significance.

The narrative frame of *The New Atalantis* is perhaps the most obvious instance of its insistent excessiveness. Two goddesses, Astrea and Virtue, are wandering the ancient continent of Atalantis in search of moral exempla and cautionary tales that might help Astrea's pupil, the young prince of the moon (the future Hanoverian king), to rule wisely. At the court, they commandeer the services of Lady Intelligence, Lady of the Bedchamber to the Princess Fame, who is ordered to inform them about everything they encounter. Intelligence is a teller of secrets, although, like the allegorical form in which she appears, she will often speak, as she explains, in "metaphors," and her garments are printed all over in "Hieroglyphicks." Intelligence's entry into the book self-consciously lowers its tone. The old king [William], she tells the deities, has just died, and she is hastening to spread the word, having left the new monarch and her favorite consoling themselves over two flasks of champagne (1:291). We have been delivered from the tedious moralizing of the goddesses' into the comic rhetoric of a figure who delights in scandal for its own sake, but we must nevertheless occasionally endure the goddesses' ill-fitting *sententiae* that insist on presenting themselves as the narrative's raison d'être. There is considerable humorous byplay between Astrea and Intelligence to mark the book's mismatch between didactic claims and gossipy pleasures. Astrea complains at one point that there is nothing useful in Intelligence's stories, and Intelligence greets the goddesses' disquisitions with notable ennui: "Whilst your *Eminences* are declaiming a length beyond my understanding, give me leave to get what information I can of that new adventure before us" (1:539). The framing device reminds us frequently that the moral is always in excess of the story and the story of the moral.

Intelligence, moreover, is an admittedly digressive and repetitive storyteller. Formally as well as morally errant, she "wanders from her subject" frequently and excuses herself by noting that "'tis natural to our Sex to Elope" (1:377). The particular occasion of these remarks is a segment of the narrative that brings together several of the book's inflationary devices and shows clearly how they construct the satire on political writing. Astrea and Virtue ask

Intelligence to explain a passing funeral procession. She identifies the deceased as "the richest widow in Atalantis" (Cary Coke, formerly daughter-in-law of the ———— Coke, Whig Minister of ————, according to the key), but instead of launching into the "true" story, Intelligence insists on reading a panegyric that will present the dead widow's deceased husband "in his gay cloaths." The reading of the panegyric, though, is itself delayed by a vignette about its Grub Street origins:

> I know Astrea upon the top of Parnassus often gives the Prise to the most deserving, and therefore is an undoubted Judge of good writing; but because we don't pretend much merit for this Piece, I'll only tell you, that a certain Poet who had formerly wrote some things with success, but either shrunk in his Genius, or grown very lazy, procur'd another Brother of Parnassus to write this Elegy for him, and promis'd to divide the Profit. The Reward being considerable and sweet, he defrauded the poor Labourer of his Hire, who had been content, for his advantage, to depart from the Reputation it might gain him, justly incens'd against the treachery of his Friend, he resolves to own and print this Piece in the next *Miscellanae.* (1:361–62)

The panegyric is thus framed by an acknowledgment of both its flattering falsity and its venal motivation. Moreover, the odd little window onto the scene of the feuding poets gives us both low-life comedy and the sense that the poem, jobbed out but not paid for, is entwined in a web of deceit. After reading the poem, which goes on for many pages, Intelligence compares the real character of young Coke with the "Octavio" of the elegy and finds no resemblance.

But still we have not arrived at the story of the dead widow, for she too must be introduced by her official elegist, who is once again the industrious cheated poet: "I beg your Attention for a second Performance of the same Poet, drawn in by the pretended Repentance, and reiterated Promises of his false Friend, who perhaps (and that's no wonder) may deceive him a second time" (1:370). What was promised as a scandalous history has digressed into a satire on authorship in general. Moreover, as a coterie would have immediately recognized and the larger audience have learned after the libel prosecution, the author of *The New Atalantis* was herself the pathetic hack referred to here. Indeed, the first elegy contains its own signature by climaxing with a song from "Delia":

Delia had in Apollo's Court been bred:
Nor *Afra* nor *Orinda* knew so well,
Scarce Grecian Sapho, Delia to excel:
In Strains that tell the certainty of Fate,
And the uncertainty of Human State,
Imperfect tho' I am, I will her Song relate.
(1:368)

"Delia's" own life history is told later in the volume, and she is identified in the key as Delarivier Manley. Thus, only after twenty pages of satirical reflections on Manley's own authorship—her poverty, her willingness to supply trite panegyrics for the right price, her inability to get paid—does the story of the dead widow, Cary Coke in the key, "Sacharissa" of the elegies, and "Lady SansAmant" in the long-awaited narrative, finally begin. The prelude is out of all proportion to its most obvious point: that official panegyrics tell false stories whereas secret histories tell true ones. But its subtler comment on its own context is made by this very superabundance: the marketplace spawns representations that themselves then breed, in this case multiplying the nominal existence of both the characters and the author herself.

Manley's digressions and repetitions, therefore, illustrate the comment of a character in her later *Memoirs of Europe* (first published in 1710; republished in 1716 as volumes three and four of *The New Atalantis*), that "Authors not only live upon one another, but themselves; repeat the same thing twenty times over, like an old tale told several ways" (2:715–16). Her narrators revel in the knowledge that very few events may be turned into a great many words, and that the author's living depends on producing as high a ratio between the two as possible.

As I have already indicated, this recognition was commonplace; indeed, such acknowledgments were among the differentiating marks of genuine satire in the period. Swift, for example, by implicating himself in his satire, distinguished himself from the mass of venal hacks who feigned sincerity. Thus he created, behind his various pseudonyms, a persona whose authorial heroism derived from his many demonstrations of the power of language to overwhelm the writer. The very textual self-consciousness of Swift's parodies marks his unique control over an intransigent and self-aggrandizing medium. But when Manley calls attention to the web of textuality out of which she is made, no such control is being asserted. The elegies satirized above are a case in point. They are not Swiftian parodies; that is, they are not in themselves amusing imitations of pastoral elegies designed to accentuate the form's absurdities. They do not take up a position superior to the satirized form or imply the existence of an author above the hack. Rather, they are simply mediocre elegies that the reader could easily imagine the author writing under exactly the conditions adduced to introduce them. Whereas Swift transforms through parodic imitation, Manley merely repeats herself and playfully indicates what she is doing. We are left with the impression that the author has a sense of humor about her authorial self but not, as when reading, for example, *A Tale of a Tub,* with the sense that the author can parodically subdue the conditions of authorship even while portraying their inescapability.

But if Manley does not display her superiority by her self-ironization, what does she achieve by it? We have already noted that the resemblance of satirized and satirist in Manley's work is related to its peculiar articulation of civil and civic humanist rhetoric. Ideologies and rhetorics, however, do not of themselves produce works, and the discord between competing ideological assumptions in *The New Atalantis* does not explain the lengths to which the author goes to keep us mindful of her linguistic excesses. Manley, it seems, accomplishes something rather different from a mere personal triumph. She includes herself in her satire in such a way as to figure for the age its own worst fears about the new publicity of politics. She becomes almost a willing scapegoat, a flamboyantly scandalmongering hack, whose fantasized extrusion allows for the dream of a purified political discourse that would not endanger the public credit.

For the anxiety among writers about the multiplication of nominal entities and the creation of imaginary worlds on paper was closely bound to the anxiety mentioned earlier about the new forms of paper property—bills of exchange, stocks, and shares—that St. John declared in 1710 "now increased to be almost equal to the terra firma of our island."[54] This image of paper both covering and obscuring the land, or of the production on paper of a whole new realm of questionable firmness, links the economic and literary concerns of the age. However, the link was not made simply by the repeated accusation that new forms of property were nothing but pieces of writing. There was in addition a more immediate connection between the new discursiveness of politics and the financial developments of the time, a connection that can be adumbrated by concentrating for a moment on the particular discursive excess that Manley flaunted: scandal.

"Scandalosissima Scoundrelia," as a contemporary publication dubbed Manley,[55] seems often to have represented for her contemporaries the *scandal* of scandal: the affront to propriety of publicly discrediting people in authority. Such a figure was especially necessary when almost all political writers were actually scandalmongering, when political discourse had barely entered the process of defining what would be a proper and what an improper accusation, when almost every partisan attack was ad hominem. Very little separates Swift's accusations of a conspiracy linking the Marlboroughs ("the Family"), the Whigs, the allies, and the stockjobbers in *The Conduct of the Allies* from Manley's similar accusations in her scandalous histories. The "Britain" of Swift's famous pamphlet is in many ways as outlandishly "fictional" as the continent of the New Atalantis.[56] The uncovering of treasonous plots among the great was everywhere in the political literature of the time, and each "revelation" of such secrets, no matter how patriotically framed, represented a threat to the public credit, to the credibility of the whole structure of authority.

But more specifically in this period a threat to the public credit was believed to shake the very foundations of a governmental, military, and commercial edifice based on deficit spending and investment in government bills. Even if one were critical of these interdependencies, as Manley's political allies frequently were,

54. Quoted in Downie, *Jonathan Swift, Political Writer*, p. 156.

55. *General Postscript, being an Extract of all that is most material from the Foreign and English Newspapers, with Remarks upon the 'Observator,' 'Review,' 'Tatlers,' and the Rest of the Scribblers, in a Dialogue between Novel and Scandal* (London, Sept. 27, 1709); quoted in Bowyer, p. 125.

56. Downie argues that *The Conduct of the Allies* ought to be read partly as fiction, p. 158.

diminishing the "public credit" would not have been admitted as a legitimate means of freeing the polity from the stockjobbers. "Public credit" at this time meant both the public's good opinion of the government and the commercial credit on which the government could borrow.[57] The two meanings were so intertwined that they were as yet indistinguishable, and she who publicly discredited the queen's ministers could be accused of lessening that fund of good opinion which alone inclined property toward authority.[58]

The scandalmongering woman was thus a creature displaying the dangers of the new marketplace in political literature with peculiar clarity. Her merchandise resembled an inflated paper currency: to credit it would lead to the discredit of those who held the public trust. Thus the frightening face of the goddess Credit herself, the discrediting aspect that most clearly showed her resemblance to her changeable predecessor, Fortuna,[59] was manifest in the lineaments of "Scandalosissima."

Scandal even bore what we might call a formal resemblance to the new public sources of private profit. Drawing on the public credit, it tended, like a government bill, to defer the moment of realization, the moment when the bill was redeemed or the referent became directly accessible. Each promised such a moment in the future but also delayed it. Of course, the government bill returned a profit, some form of exchangeable currency, as a result of the delay, whereas scandalous writings tended to mark the deferrals only with new pseudonyms. Nevertheless, the structural parallels persist: (1) each claimed to be grounded in a substratum of reality that guaranteed its worth and seemed to be the source of a surplus yet could not be directly tapped; (2) each became a focus for anxieties generated by new forms of private investment in government, new opportunities for using and misusing the public credit.

The more writers actually relied on scandal, the more they

57. See Peter de Bolla, *The Discourse of the Sublime: Readings in History, Aesthetics and the Subject* (Oxford: Basil Blackwell, 1989), pp. 112–40.

58. See Sir William Temple, *An Essay on the Original and Nature of Government* (1672), rpt. in *The Works of Sir William Temple*, vol. 1 (New York: Greenwood Press, 1968), pp. 23–24.

59. On the connection between Credit and Fortuna as female deities, see Pocock, "The Mobility of Property," p. 114. See also Janet Todd, *The Sign of Angellica*: "Defoe personified credit as feminine because of its link with unstable fortune and Swift attributed the Bubble to a coven of witches" (p. 20).

sought figures onto whom they could project the opprobrium of discrediting, the scandal of scandal. Manley was in many ways perfect as a receptacle for the disgust due a writer who published the misdemeanors of the great for the delectation of all classes. As I noted in the preceding section, she displayed one of her credentials for the job in *Rivella*: she was herself a scandalous woman whose secret had been exposed, to the ruin of her fame. Indeed, as she elsewhere implies, it was this ruin that made her dependent on authorship for her livelihood; scandal, that is, comes of scandal, and its matrix is the literary marketplace. Manley's repeated references in *The New Atalantis* to her hopes for patronage added yet another scandalous feature of scandal: that it springs from private interest and is indifferent to the public good. The combination of sexual scandal and venality in Manley's self-presentation made her, indeed, the archetypical "hack," for as Pat Rogers points out, that word had a gender in the early eighteenth century. Deriving originally from "hackney," or "hired horse," it was frequently applied to prostitutes. "To hack" is defined in Johnson's *Dictionary* as "to turn hackney or prostitute."[60] "Hack," then, was short for "author-whore" and had an especially appropriate ring when applied to a ruined scandalmongering woman, who pursued her own selfish commercial ends at the expense of the health of the whole body politic.

This was the image of Manley enthusiastically purveyed by her political enemies, especially those who used her methods. For example, in 1714 John Oldmixon published an imitation of *The New Atalantis* that attacked the Tory ministers and leaders of Robert Harley's government. *The Court of Atalantis; Containing a Four Years History of that Famous Island, Political and Gallant* seemed freely to admit its debt to the earlier work in its title, and it circulated the same kind of scandalous rumor that Manley turned into far more complicated narratives. But these very similarities motivated a strong repudiation of the previous work. Presenting his own text as the collected gossip of a group of aristocrats ("one of the authors is the last Earl of Dorset"), Oldmixon depicts the author of *The New Atalantis* as a "lewd" common woman, in league with a whore and

---

60. Pat Rogers, *Hacks and Dunces: Pope, Swift and Grub Street* (London: Methuen, 1980), p. 176.

a knave to take advantage of a gullible nobleman. In his portrait of the duke of Beaufort, to whom Manley had dedicated *The New Atalantis*, Oldmixon thus betrays the origins of the whole Atalantis phenomenon on which his very text depends:

> [A] She Poet made her Fulsome Addresses to the Generous Otho, who not knowing how to distinguish Flattery from Praise, was wonderfully delighted with her Fustian Compliments, and employ'd his Domestick [the poet ———] to pay her his Acknowledgements not only in her own Kind, but also in Money. The Man not considering his own character, and hers, takes that infamous Office upon him, and gives the Lewdest Wretch in the Island a Certificate of Virtue and Honour, which she exposes on all occasions; and amidst her Lewdness and Infamy, is the greatest Fury of a Zealot that ever produc'd. Thus was the unhappy Otho surrounded by persons of both Sexes, who took as little Care of his Reputation as of their own; putting him upon all the Extravagances that reduce the Noble and Rich to Poverty and Contempt.[61]

Steele also charges Manley with sexual misbehavior, venal writing, and the exercise of a dangerous control over the reputations of the great. For example, he responds to her portrayal of him as M. Ingrat in *The New Atalantis* by noting her poverty and suggesting that she was motivated by his sexual rejection of her. Manley was so much a byword of scandal that Steele could use her co-authorship of the *Examiner* to discredit Swift: "It is nothing to me whether the Examiner writes against me in the character of an estranged friend, or an exasperated mistress."[62] Even Pope, after Manley's death, used her name to protect himself from the consequences of one of his own libels. In his "Satire I" of the *Satires and Epistles of Horace Imitated*, Pope follows a stanza in praise of his own satire with two contrasting cases of female scandals:

> Slander or poison dread from Delia's rage,
> . . . .
> From furious Sappho scarce a milder fate,
> Pox'd by her love, or libell'd by her hate.[63]

61. [John Oldmixon], *The Court of Atalantis; Containing, A Four Years History of that Famous Island, Political and Gallant; Intermixt with Fables and Epistles in Verse and Prose* (London, 1714), pp. 87–88.

62. Quoted in Downie, *Jonathan Swift, Political Writer*, p. 185.

63. Pope, *Collected Poems*, ed. Bonamy Dobree and introd. Clive T. Probyn (London: J. M. Dent, 1987).

Probably neither Delia nor Sappho here would have been understood by contemporaries to refer to Manley. Everyone believed
Pope was aiming higher: Delia was thought to be the countess of
Deloraine and Sappho, Lady Mary Wortley Montagu. But when
Pope was confronted with this last supposition and asked to justify
such an affront to a great lady, he immediately took refuge in the
image of the common hack. As Lord Peterborough, who had been
commissioned by Lady Mary to speak to Pope on the subject,
reported to her ladyship:

> He said to me what I had taken the liberty to say to you, that he
> wondered how the town would apply these lines to any but some
> noted common woman; that he should be yet more surprised if you
> should take them to yourself. He named to me four remarkable
> poetesses and scribblers, Mrs. Centlivre, Mrs. Haywood, Mrs.
> Manly, and Mrs. Behn, ladies famous indeed in their generation,
> and some of them esteemed to have given very unfortunate favours
> to their friends, assuring me that such only were the objects of his
> satire.[64]

Although Pope's explanation was improbable—Eliza Haywood was
the only "common woman" of the four alive at the time the poem
was written—it demonstrates the convenience of women like Manley, whose linguistic acts, as the parallelism of Pope's line stresses,
could be made the rhetorical equivalents of venereal disease.

Of course, casting opprobrium on Manley did not protect her
detractors from the same charges. Pope satirized Oldmixon in the
second version of *The Dunciad* as a writer "Who but to sink the
deeper, rose the higher,"[65] that is, who sunk deeper into the mire
by "reflecting" on the great. Lady Mary Wortley Montagu was not
placated by Pope's explanation, and she tossed back the charge of
scandal:

> No: like the self-blown praise, thy scandal flies;
> And, as we're told of wasps, it stings and dies.
> Then whilst with coward hand you stab a name,
> And try, at least, to assassinate our fame,

64. Pope, p. 273.
65. Quoted in Rogers, p. 165.

> Like the first bold assassin's be thy lot,
> Ne'er be thy guilt forgiven or forgot.[66]

Steele was expelled from the House of Commons for "publishing Scandalous Papers, and spreading seditious Rumours about the safety of the succession."[67]

Invoking Scandalosissima, then, could not entirely save any writer's credit; to some extent all writers suffered the scandal of scandal. Manley, however, seemed actively to embrace the charge. As we have seen, she flaunted the inflationary unreality of her libels, created a narrative persona who admittedly relished scandal, and implied in her supposed autobiography that her own scandalous life was the foundation of her entire career. Moreover, and perhaps most telling, she delivered herself for prosecution as the author of *The New Atalantis*. In almost identical circumstances Swift in 1714 kept himself hidden "under the Wings of some great Men."[68] Unlike the dean of St. Patrick's, Manley seems to have had very little reputation to lose and a great deal of notoriety to gain in making herself the figure of scandal.

Manley's role in her contemporaries' discourse about authorship was, therefore, comparable to what Behn's had earlier been. Manley, like Behn, stood for those aspects of authorship that writers themselves seemed to find most troubling. Neither writer can be said to have passively suffered the opprobrium heaped on her, especially by her political enemies. Nevertheless, both writers can be said to have cooperated with their apparent detractors by partly constructing their authorial personae on a framework of commonplace insults. Just as Behn literalized the author-whore metaphor,

66. Quoted in Rogers, explanatory note under "Lady Mary Wortley Montagu," p. 274.
67. Downie, p. 189.
68. Downie, p. 190. Swift's prosecution was related to the expulsion of Steele from the House of Commons. Steele's scandalous paper had been *The Crisis*, a pamphlet deeply offensive to the government because it argued that the Protestant Succession was in danger. But after the rebuke to Steele, the government was immediately embarrassed when a member of the House of Lords presented Swift's response to *The Crisis*, *The Publick Spirit of the Whigs*, as an example of just the sort of scandalous libel the Commons had lately suppressed. The printer and publisher were taken into custody and a search was begun for the author of *The Publick Spirit of the Whigs*. But the Dean of St. Patrick's, unlike Delarivier Manley three years earlier, did not deliver himself to the authorities, for to do so would have cast the shadow of scandal across Harley's government.

Manley explicated the sexual implications of the appellation "hack." But whereas Behn presented her authorship as the commodification of "nothing," Manley went further and sold discredit (the minus sign) itself.

~

Moreover, just as Behn worked through the perils of duplicity and anonymity toward a selfhood of transcendent "nobodiness," Manley vindicated discredit as a literary practice. She did not simply absorb the charge of scandal and thereby stand as either scapegoat or reminder to the age of its own excesses; she also registered and reflected on the age's demand for and resistance to scandal, compared it to "innocent" fiction, and justified it as a rich and complex imaginative experience.

It is not hard to imagine why, under the circumstances I described in the preceding section, Manley might have wanted to explore the writing of stories without keys. Playing the age's political alter ego must sometimes have proved tedious. The conclusion of Manley's confession in *Rivella* promises just such a reformation. The narrator reports that

> [Rivella] promised not to repeat her Fault, provided the World would have the Goodness to forget those she had already committed, and that henceforward her Business should be to write of Pleasure and Entertainment only, wherein Party should no longer mingle . . . : She now agrees with me, that Politicks is not the Business of a Woman, especially of one that can so well delight and entertain her Readers with more gentle pleasing Theams. . . . (2:852–53)

That *Rivella* itself is an *histoire scandaleuse* only partially undercuts this act of contrition; after all, the author here is making promises about future books.

Some of the most interesting episodes of *The New Atalantis*, however, can also be read as reflections on the possibility of freeing narrative from political exigencies and attaching it to a "feminine" desire for pleasure. These stories depict a drive on the part of certain characters for meaningless, "fictional," forms of feminine eroticism that would escape reference, consequence, and, therefore, scandal. The characters are thus self-consciously at odds with

the text they inhabit, for they attempt to elude the rules of significance and reference established by the form of the scandalous
allegories: to be scandalous, a story must minimally be both credible
and about Somebody. In their attempt to escape these conditions
of scandalous narratability, which were also the conditions of libel,
the ladies depicted in the sequences I am about to discuss try first
to practice an incredible female eroticism and then to practice one
that involves "nobody."

The episode of the "new Cabal" is perhaps the most obvious
attempt to opt out of *The New Atalantis*'s order of signification
altogether and enter a realm explicitly equated with nonreferential
fantasy. The new Cabal, the narrator tells us, entirely excludes men
and encourages romantic attachments between women. The eroticism of this group is first aligned with fiction by being presented
as a counter-factual slander that the narrator (ironically even as she
circulates the scandal) claims she herself finds unbelievable. The
passage that introduces the group thus concentrates on their anomalous relationship to scandal; their behavior becomes notable precisely because it does not meet a usual minimal condition of sexual
scandal—credibility:

> How unfortunate are women? if they seek their diversion out of
> themselves and include the other sex, they must be Criminal? If in
> themselves . . . still they are criminal? Tho' censurers must carry
> their imaginations a much greater length than I am able to do mine,
> to explain this hypothesis with success, they pretend to find in these
> [members of the new Cabal] the vices of old Rome revived; and
> quote you certain detestable authors, who (to amuse posterity) have
> introduced you lasting monuments of vice, which could only subsist
> in imagination; and can in reality have no other foundation, than
> what are to be found in the dreams of poets. . . . (1:575–76)

Sexual misbehavior without men is here defined as ipso facto
incredible, something requiring an excessive imagination even to
contemplate, for without penises how can any violations of female
sexual integrity occur? Appealing to the phallocentric assumption
that the penis is the referential ground of all sexual "reality," the
passage feigns to exempt the new Cabal from sexual scandal on
the grounds that its imputed impropriety strains credibility. It
begins by asserting that the ladies should have escaped the conditions of scandal by ridding themselves of men and thus making

sexuality "fantastic." However, this very assertion is made within a complaint that scandal knows no bounds because even in the absence of the significant organ, an excessive imagination can supply the lack. By appropriating fantasy, "quoting you certain detestable authors," such an imagination can temporarily suspend even the rule of credibility. Hence, the passage explicitly censures neither the women nor the prosthesis of fiction, the ability to supply "in the dreams of poets" what must be lacking "in reality"; instead it censures those who cannot tell the difference between stories that have referential grounding and those that do not.[69]

If only to protect the credibility of scandal, the sequence of stories that follows this passage continually pretends the necessity of separating incredible imaginings form scandalous reports. The women, it turns out, are indeed erotically entangled with each other, but their eroticism is in its essence phantasmic. The women's actual sexual practices have the same ontological status as the poets' dreams; both are pleasurable representational excesses. Lady Intelligence, who narrates this sequence, recounts "true" stories that corroborate the poets' dreams, but even the most physical versions of this sexuality are in a deep sense imaginary, as in the story of the "witty Marchioness of Sandomire, when she used to mask her diversions in the habit of the other sex, and with her female favorite Ianthe wander thro' the Gallant Quarter of Atalantis in search of Adventures." These two pick up prostitutes who "fail not to find their account, in obliging the Marchioness's and Ianthe's peculiar taste, by all the liberties that belonged to women of their loose character and indigence."

But these adventures, we are assured, still somehow remain on a level of imaginary, voyeuristic indulgence that does not touch the great lady's sexual reality: "[They are] none that could in reality wound her chastity! Her virtue sacred to her Lord, and the marriage bed, was preserved inviolable!" Even if the assurance is read as an ironic comment on phallocentric literal-mindedness, it is also a claim that female erotic pleasure is by its very nature potentially irrelevant to the referential norm of heterosexuality that rules "the marriage bed." Since the Marchioness's vow is here very narrowly

69. For another reading of this episode, see Ballaster, *Seductive Forms*, pp. 136–42.

construed as a promise simply to preserve herself from penetration by all penises but her husband's, all the rest of her sexual experience must be beside the point. This absurdly strict phallocentrism implies a vast area of inconsequential liberty; the narrator can barely find words to indicate sexuality without penises, cannot make such sexuality significant, and hence asserts its meaningless innocence. The Marchioness's pleasure can only be credited as something outside the referential rules that give sexual activity substance and sense; that is, it can only be credited as fictional.

The fiction, however, does have a "material" basis, for the Marchioness buys the temporary fantasy of being a man. Her money puts her in the same category as the prostitutes' other customers. We might say that the Marchioness authors a fiction about her own body and then pays the prostitutes to pretend to believe it. Her money allows her to enforce a mere story as reality, but the money also substitutes for actual credibility. Money here takes away the necessity of belief and the possibility of fraud, allowing an admittedly phantasmic freedom.

The pleasure and innocence, however, are precariously predicated on an agreement to rest content with fictional representations, when properly paid for, as a secondary order of reality, neither to question their mode of (non)referentiality nor to assert them as phenomena in their own right. Hence, female sexuality in these stories is presented, not as a freestanding, independent experience, but as one that dispenses with men by substituting representations of them. The Marchioness and her money are one such representation. In a later story we are told that the ladies of the Cabal "do not in reality love Men; but doat on the Representations of *Men* in *Women*" (1:738). The women are loved neither as women nor as men but as representations. A noble widow, for example,

> fell in Love with one of the fair *Female Comedians*, when she was acting the Part of a Young *Lover* and a *Libertine*. The Widow sent for the Girl, and made her very considerable Presents, order'd her Picture, in that Dress, to be taken at length, by one of the best Hands, and carried her to remain with her . . . at her Villa. (1:739)

At length, however, the actress disappoints the lady by insisting that their play have a meaning:

> The Widow . . . assur'd her of her *Tenderness* and *Amity;* she even
> proceeded to gentle squeezes and *embraces;* nothing cou'd be more
> innocently indearing than her transports! The *Comedian* was at a loss
> to know [not] only how to merit so many favours but also the *meaning*
> of 'em. . . . [She] told the Lady she did not like those hugs and
> indearments from her own Sex . . . ; did they come from a man, she
> should be able to guess at his Design, but here she was at a loss—.
> (1:740)

The widow's behavior, indeed, has no "meaning" of the sort the
actress seeks; by insisting on one, the actress only impresses her
lack of the significant member on the widow's consciousness,
thereby putting the actress further "at a loss." By refusing to be
content with representation and play, the actress spoils the possibility of pleasure, and the widow then appropriately punishes her
by symbolically castrating her portrait, the representation of the
actress representing a man:

> When [the widow] was return'd to her House in Town, to show the
> lurkings of her malice, tho' but in Effigy, she caus'd the Comedian's
> Picture to be let down, and with her own Hand cut out the Face; so
> stamp'd upon and abus'd, sent it back to her whom it represented.
> (1:740)

Because she insisted on seeing their fiction as empty, the actress is
confronted with her own message; her face cut out of the portrait,
she becomes the blankness of representation.

In both stories, the ladies of the new Cabal pay the common
women, the prostitutes and the actress, to suspend their disbelief,
to enter the realm of erotic fantasy, where they can indulge in
blameless pleasure. Payment in both cases should take the place of
that phallic reality the women wish to occlude; economic exchange,
therefore, is the principle enabling fiction, the principle of unend-
ing substitution. It is appropriate that the more explicit marketplace relationship, the relationship with the prostitutes, yields the
more satisfying fantasy. The ambiguous monetary relationship with
the actress fails to seal off the realm of fantasy from that of reality.
The actress is portrayed as unwilling to perform offstage; she takes
the widow's presents but then does not reciprocate by maintaining
the integrity of her own epicene illusion. Instead, she insists on
looking through the representation. Her untheatrical desire to find

the reality behind the image interferes with her role and makes holes in the illusion, for the phantasmic power of marketplace exchange had not been fully and explicitly invoked.

The widow, in other words, did not fully commodify the actress, and hence she did not cleanly separate the realms of fantasy and reality. As a result, the widow and the uncooperative actress articulate what might well be seen as a conflict between starkly opposed versions of scandal and fiction. The actress, who has not been given an adequate monetary substitute for reality, tries to read the widow's play as if its whole substance resided outside itself, as if it were supposed to be merely decoded or seen through, as if it were just a screen for some "meaning" on the other side of representation. Hence, she receives, along with the picture of herself as the blankness of representation, the widow's message that the actress "had . . . made it a Scandal to her House to have such a Picture seen in it." The actress had the chance to indulge innocently in the integrated illusion of fiction but instead chose the guilty, penetrating vision of a crude form of allegorical scandal.

Such scandal, as I have noted, is not the sort comprising *The New Atalantis*, where the pleasures of the text are often likened to an erotic double vision in which characters perceive each other as simultaneously disguised and unmasked, where representation and reference try to supplement rather than supplant each other. The episode of the widow and the actress is anomalous and seems designed to reflect not only on the precariousness of "pure" fiction but also on its thinness as an imaginative experience. The widow's insistence on one-dimensional fiction seems to call forth an equally one-dimensional demand for scandalous referentiality. The latter demand might have been silenced by proper commodification, but the achieved illusion would then have been, in *The New Atalantis*'s terms, insignificant. The episode thus suggests that the new Cabal's attempt to escape from the narrative conditions of scandal through the purchase of incredible pleasures subtracts significance from fiction and play from scandal, impoverishing both.

A second set of stories at the end of *Memoirs of Europe*, the sequel to *The New Atalantis*, takes up similar issues. Once again several ladies try to escape the données of scandalous allegorical significance, but this time they try to undermine the condition that the story be about "Somebody." Once again the marketplace enables

the escape into fiction, this time by allowing the ladies to commodify themselves, to become prostitutes. The marketplace allows them
to give up their "quality" and to achieve anonymity. Thus, as they
explain, they guard their reputations while receiving "solid Pleasure." Their clients are also "Nobodies" in the world of *The New
Atalantis:* merely minor gentry without political or social significance. What the ladies claim to seek with these men is sex without
sentiment or scandal, sex that has, through the phantasmic disso-
lution of identity in economic exchange, achieved a new mode of
meaninglessness.

Safely inside their identity as commodities, however, the ladies
have no need to buy into their own fiction. Unlike the women of
the new Cabal, they seek precisely the kind of double vision that
has all along been the mode of *The New Atalantis.* "Reality" is not
occluded but transformed into an exciting fantasy, as when one of
the ladies finds a peculiar thrill in imagining her lover imagining
that she is a great lady: "He would perhaps conclude [if he saw her
in a court procession that] his lovely Courtezan was not unlike that
resplendent Lady, and long with a double Gust till the Hour of
Assignation, that he might possess the Court-Beauty in the Person
of his *Common* Charmer" (2:720). In this vignette of the lady pretending to be a prostitute and imagining her lover pretending she
is a lady, we see how the erotic pleasure of the lady's "real" situation
is discovered through the medium of fiction, but the fiction is
doubly exhilarating because it contains the scandalous truth. Furthermore, even this moment, when fictional eroticism seems to
have appropriated the lady's social-political reality and organized
it into a regime of pure pleasure, is only made possible for the
reader by its exposure and circulation through political scandal in
The New Atalantis. The "lady" who was trying to avoid scandal is
revealed as "D. of M——e" in the key, alias Mary Montagu (née
Churchill), daughter of the Marlboroughs.

In addition to exploring the nature of fiction and its link to the
marketplace, then, the stories of the new Cabal and the feigned
courtesans also seem to stress both the inescapability of scandal
and its superiority, as a multidimensional literary genre, to nonreferential fiction. By dramatizing the women's resistance to political
scandal, *The New Atalantis* plays out and discredits what it identifies
as the feminine impulse toward pure fiction while at the same time

it appropriates imaginary devices as its own proper techniques. The attempted resistance nevertheless stands as a reminder of the tension between fiction and femininity, on the one hand, and politics, on the other. That tension was the essence of the impropriety Delarivier Manley sold; it allowed her to become, through the transformative medium of the literary marketplace, a notorious Nobody.

4

Nobody's Credit

Fiction, Gender, and Authorial Property
in the Career of Charlotte Lennox

Charlotte Lennox's first novel appeared in 1750.[1] Although it drew on episodes in the author's life and its title, *The Life of Harriot Stuart, Written by Herself*, feigned autobiography, the book made few serious demands on the public's credit; in the main,[2] it was obviously nobody's story, just an innocent female fiction. By mid-century, innocence had, at least ostensibly, become a hallmark of women's writing, one intimately connected both with the nonreferential, hence nonscandalous, "pure" fiction they supposedly produced, and with the nonlibidinous, sexually passive "nature" they newly claimed.

We might interpret the Ivy Lane Club's "whole night of festivity" (initiated by Samuel Johnson and recorded by Sir John Hawkins) to greet "the birth of Mrs. Lenox's first literary child" as a celebration of the innocence of the new representative woman writer, or literary lady:[3]

> The place appointed was the Devil tavern, and there, about the hour of eight, Mrs. Lenox and her husband, and a lady of her acquantance [*sic*], now living, as also the [Ivy Lane] club, and friends to the number of twenty, assembled. Our supper was elegant, and Johnson had directed that a magnificent hot apple-pye should make a part of it, and this he would have stuck with bay-leaves, because, forsooth, Mrs. Lenox was an authoress, and had written verses; and further,

1. The date on the title page of *The Life of Harriot Stuart* is 1751, but December 1750 seems to have been its actual date of publication. See Miriam Rossiter Small, *Charlotte Ramsay Lennox: An Eighteenth Century Lady of Letters* (New Haven, CT: Yale Univ. Press, 1935), p. 10 n. 38.
2. The novel contained one scandalous segment attacking the character of Lady Isabella Finch, Lennox's former patroness.
3. The phrase, purportedly Samuel Johnson's, is reported in Sir John Hawkins, *The Works of Samuel Johnson*, quoted in Small, p. 10.

he had prepared for her a crown of laurel, with which, but not till he had invoked the muses by some ceremonies of his own invention, he encircled her brows. The night passed, as must be imagined, in pleasant conversation, and harmless mirth, intermingled at different periods with the refreshments of coffee and tea. About five, Johnson's face shone with meridian splendour, although his drink had been only lemonade; but the far greater part of us had deserted the colours of Bacchus, and were with difficulty rallied to partake of a second refreshment of coffee, which was scarcely ended when the day began to dawn.[4]

Almost everything in this description—the analogy to a childbirth vigil, the inclusion in the company of not only the lady novelist's husband but also another lady ("now living"—as if available to testify to the wholesomeness of the proceedings), the homely and noninebriating refreshments (hot apple pie, lemonade, tea, and coffee), the good-natured rationality of the pastimes—attest to Mrs. Lennox's utter respectability and to the perfectly honorable sentiments of the company of men gathered around to pay her tribute.

Indeed, the ceremony seems to have been designed to conjure up and exorcise the unsavory associations that had attached themselves to female authorship. The "place appointed was the Devil tavern," and Johnson insisted that the festivities continue until dawn, as if to assert that *his* club, despite all received notions, could spend a "whole night" in a tavern in mixed company without compromising the women. Literary London, the gesture implies, even in its hideaways, was a fit place to entertain women as authors and ladies. Mrs. Lennox, receiving the bays *twice* from the hand of Johnson—one sprig, housewifely stuck in an apple pie, the other placed on her brows—is a fit symbol for the respectable domestication of female authorship that both complemented and guaranteed Johnson's high "notion of the dignity of literature."[5]

Sir John Hawkins's account, though, even as it draws our attention to the inversions accomplished by the ceremony, closes on an odd note: "I well remember, at the instant of my going out of the

4. Quoted in Small, pp. 10–11. For a thorough assessment of the reliability of this narrative, see James L. Clifford, "Johnson's First Club," in *Evidence in Literary Scholarship: Essays in Memory of James Marshall Osborn*, ed. René Wellek and Alvaro Ribeiro (Oxford: Clarendon Press, 1979), pp. 197–213.

5. Boswell, *Life of Johnson*, vol. 3, ed. George Birkbeck Hill and revised by L. F. Powell (Oxford: Clarendon Press, 1934), p. 310.

tavern-door, the sensation of shame that affected me, occasioned not by reflection on any thing evil that had passed in the course of the night's entertainment, but on the resemblance it bore to a debauch."[6] Exorcisms, after all, must recall the demons they attempt to expel; "the resemblance . . . to a debauch," integral to the enterprise of purging, itself produced an involuntary "sensation of shame." Extruded as she was, the apparition of the author-whore continued to haunt the site.

Moreover, she would not be eradicated if those present merely stressed the new authors' chastity and the moral seriousness of their works, for women writers had more than a legacy of sexual laxity to live down. They also had to provide a counter-image to the mercenary, selfish, disorderly, and politically opportunistic scandalmongers of the previous generation. This chapter will focus initially on the political and economic transformation of the authoress in the mid-eighteenth century. The story of her sexual reformation has already been well told elsewhere as a chapter in the history of the idea of "woman." Most accounts of the rise of the female novelist have understandably stressed the abrupt transformation in English manners and sexual mores that made mid-eighteenth-century writers disown such forebears as Aphra Behn and Delarivier Manley.[7] They have shown that women's authorship was both stimulated and regulated by sudden developments in the history of sexual difference: an unprecedented acceleration in the gendering and separation of public and private spheres; the notion that modesty, chastity, and unselfishness come "naturally" to women; and the claim that women qua women might therefore be entitled to some cultural authority.[8] I wish to supplement and complicate this story by examining the authoress's reformation at

6. Quoted in Small, p. 11.

7. The fullest account of this change can be found in part 1 of Jane Spencer, *The Rise of the Woman Novelist: From Aphra Behn to Jane Austen* (Oxford: Basil Blackwell, 1986). Other recent accounts include Janet Todd, *The Sign of Angellica: Women, Writing and Fiction, 1660–1800* (London: Virago, 1989), esp. pp. 101–45; and Cheryl Turner, *Living by the Pen: Women Writers in the Eighteenth Century* (New York: Routledge, 1992), pp. 31–59. These books fill in the transitional history between Manley and Lennox, which is left out of my own account, by detailing the contributions of such early standard-bearers of respectability as Elizabeth Rowe and Penelope Aubin.

8. On the general change in the "nature" of womanhood, see Thomas Laqueur, *Making Sex: Body and Gender from the Greeks to Freud* (Cambridge: Harvard Univ. Press, 1990), pp. 149–92.

the discursive intersection of several other key terms which, like "woman," were undergoing revision in the mid-eighteenth century: "authorship," "sympathy," and "fiction." In exploring each of these terms, I will focus on a set of connections between property and propriety that will in turn explain why female *authorship*, as opposed to other kinds of activity, and why fiction writing, as opposed to other kinds of authorship, gained cultural prestige in this period. To put it more succinctly, I hope to explain why the rise of the respectable female writer was concurrent with the rise of the novel.

~

Charlotte Lennox's career was shaped by a double "separation of spheres": (1) the formation of a specifically female-centered domestic enclave in contradistinction to the masculine public realms of politics and business, and (2) the creation of a separate and especially "dignified" class of authors, who could be distinguished from venal flatterers and party hacks. These two developments were similar in that ladies and literary gentlemen alike became too good to be put to everyday political use. A new disinterestedness and high-mindedness was imputed to women as a sex and to "men of letters" as a profession. The ancient contention that women were too passionate and unreasonable for state business was increasingly and paradoxically supplemented with the assertion that they were too virtuous to engage in political maneuvering and self-promotion. Similarly, the author underwent a transformation from the rather dangerous and unstable political operator of Queen Anne's reign to either a dispassionate Olympian observer or a disdainful judge of a political world that was morally far beneath him. In both developments, moreover, we should note the rising cultural stock of private experience. The private home was gradually being recognized and valued as *the* institution of moral formation, and the *retired* poet became an exemplum of authorial integrity.[9]

To be sure, the virtues of women and authors were asserted in superficially contrasting terms. As Nancy Armstrong has demonstrated, the discourse concerning women's virtue in the eighteenth

9. See Robert Folkenflik, "Patronage and the Poet-Hero," *Huntington Library Quarterly* 48 (1985): 363–79.

century to some extent suppressed the connection between women and property.[10] The dignity of authorship, however, was frequently proclaimed on the basis of new relationships between authors and property. Since the first of these developments has been described by many books on women writers, I will turn to the rhetoric of authorship, preoccupied as it then was with the connection between property and propriety.

The separation of the sphere of men of letters from that of statesmen was in effect a separation of authors from their former patrons. This was often conceived as the severance of an old property relation and the establishment of a new one: authors were no longer to be the creatures of the great but were instead to be their own men. "All that men of power can do for men of genius is leave them at their liberty," wrote Thomas Gray at mid-century.[11] Bertrand A. Goldgar has detailed the intricate political developments that brought about this stress on authorial self-possession. He has shown how writers gradually became alienated from the centers of power during Walpole's administration.[12] George I's accession ended the vigorous party strife of Queen Anne's reign; the Tories were no longer viable, and many former Whig writers found themselves suffering from what they considered malign neglect under Walpole's government. An assemblage of resentful wits who had previously been political opponents thus looked back nostalgically to the days of party patronage under Halifax and Harley, idealizing those earlier politicians as disinterested supporters of literature for its own sake. Writers, they claimed, had been valued for their wit and capacity for independent thought, whereas Walpole hired the cheapest, dullest, and most servile hacks he could find. Walpole's treatment of writers, moreover, was said to be of a piece with the crudity and corruption of his entire administration.[13] The cessation of party patronage for the major writers

10. Nancy Armstrong, *Desire and Domestic Fiction: A Political History of the Novel* (New York: Oxford Univ. Press, 1987). Armstrong develops this thesis primarily in the first two chapters of her study, pp. 28–95.

11. *Memoirs of the Life and Writings of Mr. Gray* (York, 1775), p. 238. See Robert Folkenflik's discussion of this passage in "Patronage and the Poet-Hero," pp. 368–69.

12. *Walpole and the Wits: The Relation of Politics to Literature, 1722–1742* (Lincoln: Univ. of Nebraska Press, 1976).

13. In fact, the Walpole ministry spent an unprecedented £20,000 per annum on

of the period helped create a specifically literary opposition to the government: an opposition claiming to represent "letters" as a social counterforce to unscrupulous politics. Moreover, the rhetoric of this opposition, despite its frequent references to the golden age of patronage, emphasized the proud independence, the uncompromising self-ownership, of the true wits.

Thus the independent, patronless, author became the poet-hero of the age, an image that reached grandiose proportions in Pope's self-presentations.[14] Witness, for example, this epitaph on himself:

> Heroes, and kings! your distance keep:
> In peace let one poor poet sleep,
> Who never flatter'd folks like you:
> Let Horace blush, and Virgil too.[15]

The condemnation of Virgil here is complicated, for Pope is drawing on a Virgilian trope to make his point; he is both invoking classical precedents for heroizing retired independence and calling attention to the superior completeness of his self-ownership. At mid-century Johnson, in his celebrated letter to Lord Chesterfield (1755), made a similar allusion. Rebuking the aristocrat's insolent, patronizing appropriation of the *Dictionary*, Johnson wrote:

> The shepherd in Virgil grew at last acquainted with Love, and found him a native of the rocks. Is not a patron, My Lord, one who looks with unconcern on a man struggling for life in the water and, when he has reached ground, encumbers him with help? The notice which you have been pleased to take of my labours, had it been early, had been kind; but it has been delayed till I am indifferent and cannot

political publications, not only supporting friendly writers but also sometimes buying the silence of opposition critics. See Paul J. Korshin, "Types of Eighteenth-Century Patronage," *Eighteenth-Century Studies* 7:4 (1974): 462.

14. See Folkenflik for Pope's importance in establishing this poetic persona. Pope, however, benefited greatly from the early eighteenth century's most popular form of patronage—subscription publishing. See Matthew Hodgart, "The Subscription List for Pope's *Iliad*, 1715," in *The Dress of Words*, ed. R. B. White, Jr. (Lawrence: Univ. of Kansas Press, 1978), pp. 25–34; W. A. Speck, "Politicians, Peers, and Publication by Subscription, 1700–1750," in *Books and Their Readers in Eighteenth-Century England*, ed. Isabel Rivers (New York: St. Martin's Press, 1982), pp. 47–48.

15. *Alexander Pope: Collected Poems*, ed. Bonamy Dobree and introd. Clive T. Probyn (London: J. M. Dent, 1987), p. 124.

enjoy it, till I am solitary and cannot impart it, till I am known and do not want it.[16]

The patronless poet, though, as Johnson's rhetoric stresses, had become virtuous through privateness and privation, through being relegated to a private station, and through suffering a lack of property. At once denied and liberated from the service of great men, he presents himself as "poor" but honorably free from debt: "I hope it is no very cynical asperity," Johnson continues, "not to confess obligation where no benefit has been received, or to be unwilling that the public should consider me as owing that to a patron, which providence has enabled me to do for myself." Johnson, the pattern modern author, acknowledged a debt only to God; otherwise, he claimed to be his own man.

Owning himself, however, was no easy matter. The middle decades of the eighteenth century were not a period of expansion for the book trades,[17] so when Johnson arrived in London in the later 1730s, he took almost any literary work he could get, writing prefatory essays, biographies, travel accounts, occasional poetry, and reports of parliamentary debates.[18] With none of Pope's disdain for the hack, Johnson almost immediately began harping on his own hardships and describing "the laborious drudgeries which [authors] are forced to undergo in the recess of Parliament, or in a time of inaction, to give expression to wornout thoughts, to say something when they have nothing to say, and to find, in the most barren months, some field of praise or satire as yet untouched."[19] On the basis of this same dreary workfulness, he claims in the same 1739 essay, "The character of an author must be allowed to

16. The letter is reprinted in numerous places, among them John Wain, *Samuel Johnson* (New York: Viking, 1974), p. 176.

17. See Jim Mitchell, "The Spread and Fluctuation of Eighteenth-Century Printing," in *Studies on Voltaire and the Eighteenth Century* 230 (1985): 305–21. For a discussion of the possible effects of this stagnation on Johnson's attitude toward Grub Street as opposed to Pope's, see Alvin Kernan, *Printing Technology, Letters and Samuel Johnson* (Princeton, NJ: Princeton Univ. Press, 1987), pp. 60–62.

18. See Edward A. Bloom, *Samuel Johnson in Grub Street* (Providence, RI: Brown Univ. Press, 1957), for a full account of Johnson's career as a journalist. One should especially note that Johnson was willing to take on political work; the distinction between letters and politics in the 1730s and 1740s was not as firm as Johnson later made it seem.

19. Quoted in Bloom, p. 12.

imply in itself something amiable and great."[20] In his self-characterizations and his numerous literary biographies, Johnson created the writer's life as one long heroic struggle against almost impossible economic odds.

Charlotte Lennox's own career fits this pattern of praiseworthy distress quite well. She was born abroad sometime during the decade preceding 1730; the daughter of an army officer, she spent part of her childhood in colonial New York. The date of her father's death and her arrival in England are said to be the same, but neither is exactly placed. In 1747 she published a volume of poetry, dedicated to her acknowledged patron, Lady Isabella Finch. Like Johnson's, however, her patron disappointed her; and like Johnson, Lennox later took a public revenge, attacking the lady as a false friend of the arts in a scandalous episode of *The Life of Harriot Stuart*. She briefly tried acting before writing her first two novels, and the enormous success of the second, *The Female Quixote*, led to a stream of commissions from her bookseller, Andrew Millar, that continued for over a decade. Between 1749 and 1764, according to her biographer, "almost every year . . . marks the publication of some work by her. Four of these were translations, two were partly translation but contained some independent writing; the rest were her own compositions."[21] Like Johnson, she was a versatile general author who produced poetry, essays, a short-lived periodical, literary criticism, translations, and novels on demand. What she could not seem to do, despite her talent, popularity, and hard work, was make a comfortable living; her struggle to support herself certainly won her the admiring help of Johnson and several other men of letters, but her correspondence records her constant economic insecurity.

She called her steady employment "slavery to the booksellers" when soliciting the help of a prospective patron in 1760,[22] and her complaint is typical of "independent" authors in the mid-eighteenth century.[23] It was a time of extreme caution among booksell-

20. Quoted in Bloom, p. 12.
21. Small, *Charlotte Ramsay Lennox*, p. 31.
22. The letter, to the duchess of Newcastle, is quoted in Small, p. 28.
23. James Ralph, for example, compared the author, who, like Lennox, wrote for the booksellers, to "the Slave in the Mines": "Both have their tasks assigned them alike: Both must drudge *and* starve; and neither can hope for Deliverance" (*The Case of Authors by Profession or Trade Stated* [London: R. Griffiths, 1758], p. 22).

ers, who operated on very narrow profit margins and were unwilling to gamble large amounts in "copy money" for new and untried compositions.[24] In the 1750s, booksellers seem even to have preferred publishing "old" to new novels, a somewhat paradoxical turn of events given that a novel's appeal, as the name of the incipient genre implies, was supposed to be based on its novelty. John Feather gives us the traditional wisdom: "From the trade's point of view, the significance of the novel lay not in its literary merit but in its essential triviality. It was seen as an ephemeral production to be read once and then forgotten. This meant that, once the demand had been created, a continuous supply of new novels was needed to fill it."[25] But either the trade had not yet caught on to the advantages of such planned obsolescence or the assumed demand had not yet been created by the 1750s, for the number of books published between 1740 and 1752 that literary historians now classify as "novels" fell significantly, and the number of new novel titles dropped steeply. Novels constituted approximately 4 percent of all titles printed between 1740 and 1760, a steadiness due, again, to the reprinting of old titles rather than to a constant turnover.[26] It was not, therefore, a propitious time to begin a novel-writing career, and, indeed, few women took on the challenge. According to statistics compiled by Judith Phillips Stanton, only six women novelists began their publishing careers in the 1750s, as opposed to ten in the 1740s and seventeen in the 1760s.[27]

24. As Terry Belanger points out, "Standard theology, standard history, standard editions of the classics, standard works of practical instruction and standard English authors tended to have long and relatively secure sales; and to a considerable extent, the aspiring eighteenth-century author attempting to get a book published (except at his own expense) was competing with the collective backlist of the whole London trade" ("Publishers and Writers in Eighteenth-Century England," in *Books and Their Readers in Eighteenth-Century England*, ed. Isabel Rivers [New York: St. Martin's Press, 1982], p. 16).

25. *A History of British Publishing* (London: Croom Helm, 1988), p. 97.

26. James Raven, introduction to *British Fiction, 1750–1770: A Chronological Check-List of Prose Fiction Printed in Britain and Ireland* (London: Associated Univ. Presses, 1987), pp. 9–10. Counting only novels that identified themselves as such, Michael Crump comes up with much smaller numbers, but no evidence of an increase in the percentage of all books published between 1740 and 1760. See "Stranger than Fiction: The Eighteenth-Century True Story," in *Searching the Eighteenth Century: Papers Presented at the Symposium on the Eighteenth Century Short Title Catalogue in 1982*, ed. M. Crump and M. Harris (London: British Library, 1983), pp. 61–62.

27. "Statistical Profile of Women Writing in English from 1660 to 1800," in *Eighteenth-Century Women and the Arts*, ed. Frederick M. Keener and Susan E. Lorsch (New York: Greenwood Press, 1988), p. 251. I have been unable to find comparable

According to Cheryl Turner, between 1740 and 1760 the annual total of women's novels never exceeded four.[28]

It is not surprising, then, that Millar was reluctant to publish *The Female Quixote* in 1752.[29] After its huge success he commissioned other works by "the Author of *The Female Quixote*," as Lennox signed herself, but since he already owned the copyright to her best-selling work (there were three editions and four printings in eleven years), he probably saw no reason to pay her large sums for the rights to lesser books. We can only speculate about the actual amounts, but in general copyrights to fiction were sold at extremely low prices. One historian tells us that

> by the 1780s the leading novel publisher, William Lane, was paying his authors £10–20 for outright purchase of the manuscript. But both then, and it is safe to assume, in the earlier decades, a payment of half-a-guinea per volume was the final offer to many an untried novelist . . . [C]ontractual agreements almost never considered the future success of a work.[30]

Hence, although Lennox was among the twenty best-selling novelists between 1750 and 1770,[31] constant economic distress was her lot, and she seems to have always been hatching schemes to end the drudgery of her "independence": subscription editions of her works, a theatrical benefit, a government annuity for herself, or a place for her husband. Most of these projects failed, and contemporary accounts of Lennox consistently present her as an undeservedly impoverished woman. Just two years after her greatest success Henry Fielding mentioned her in the *Journal of a Voyage to Lisbon* as "the inimitable and shamefully-distressed author of the

---

statistics for male novelists in the period, but James Raven demonstrates that 14 percent of the new works of imaginative literature published between 1750 and 1769 are known to be by women, and women seem to have made up a fairly steady 17 percent of novelists in the period (Raven, p. 18). This is a smaller percentage than other historians have claimed, but Raven's numbers seem the most precise and reliable.

28. *Living by the Pen*, p. 35.

29. See the correspondence between Lennox and Samuel Johnson prior to the novel's publication, reprinted in "The Lennox Collection," ed. Duncan Isles, *Harvard Library Bulletin* 18 (October 1970): 339–40, esp. item 4.

30. Raven, pp. 23–24. See also Cheryl Turner, *Living by the Pen*, pp. 113–14, for the range of prices of copyrights for women's novel manuscripts during the eighteenth century.

31. Raven, p. 14.

Female Quixote,"[32] and Johnson sounded the same note in 1775 when he wrote "Proposals for Printing by Subscription, dedicated to the Queen, a new and elegant Edition of the Original Works of Mrs. Charlotte Lennox": "She hopes . . . that she shall not be considered as too indulgent to vanity, or too studious of interest, if, from that labour which has hitherto been chiefly gainful to others, she endeavours to obtain at last some profit for herself and her children."[33]

At the end of this chapter, I will look at the feminization of Lennox's "distress" in the rhetoric of her contemporaries, but here I wish to emphasize that the mixture of victimization and heroism in these quotations is common to the period's discourse about authors. Sometime between Pope's *Dunciad* (1729) and Johnson's life of Savage (1744), Grub Street had become pathetic, and its pathos was closely intertwined with its dignified "independence." No longer the haunt of libelers and rogues, it harbored a new breed of worthy starvelings.

Behind the descriptions of proudly poor, dispossessed, and thereby dignified authors stood a background of beliefs about authorial property rights. What, after all, would be so pathetic about Charlotte Lennox's labor being "chiefly gainful to others" if there was no presumption that she had some "natural" right to profit from her productions? The rhetoric of dispossession and dignity relied on the rather new idea that authors had some legally recognized vendable property that served as the basis of their livelihood. An incipient concept of intellectual property was provided by the 1710 Statute of Anne, often called the first copyright law in English history, which both implied that copyright might be a property and vested it originally in the author. The Licensing Act that had lapsed in 1695 had granted the "copy," or right to print a book, to the member of the Stationers' Company who registered its title. How the manuscript, which was also sometimes called the "copy," came into the possession of the bookseller or printer was a moot question.[34] No law for the regulation of the press previous to

32. Quoted in Small, *Charlotte Ramsay Lennox*, p. 14.
33. Quoted in Small, p. 44.
34. Some historians have claimed that prior to 1710 the author was assumed to be a common law owner of a literary work, but the case for such a view is weak. See Frank Arthur Mumby, *Publishing and Bookselling* (London: Cape, 1930), pp. 169–

1710 made any mention of an author's rights or property, and hence the Statute of Anne might be said to have initiated the idea that texts, as opposed to manuscripts, were exchangeable commodities belonging ultimately to their authors by virtue of being "the product of their learning and labour."[35] Most historians agree that the drafters of the statute intended merely to guard against piracy and booksellers' monopolies; the presumption was that authors, having no means to produce their own books, would sell their copyright to booksellers, who would enjoy the sole right to copy and sell the book for a period of fourteen years, at which time the copyright would revert to the author to be sold again. But although the establishment of copyright as an author's right was originally intended merely to secure the property of booksellers, the interpretations of the law increasingly stressed the author's prerogative.[36] Hence, even though the statute left a number of complicated issues—the nature of property in a copyright, its tenure, the conditions of its infringement, and the definition of the author— unsettled, it can nevertheless be said to have initiated the legal notion that authors have a transferable right to control the printing and dissemination of their works.[37]

71; and Joseph Loewenstein, "For a History of Literary Property: John Wolfe's Reformation," *ELR* 18 (1988): 389–412. For a refutation of this view, see Mark Rose, "The Author in Court: *Pope v. Curll* (1741)," *Cultural Critique* 21 (Spring 1992): 197–217. On copyright, see also Chapter 2, note 27.

35. This phrase is from an early draft of the law quoted by John Feather in "The Book Trade in Politics: The Making of the Copyright Act of 1710," *Publishing History* 8 (1980): 35.

36. Lyman Ray Patterson, in *Copyright in Historical Perspective* (Nashville, TN: Vanderbilt Univ. Press, 1968), puts the matter concisely:

> The statutory copyright provided in the Statute of Anne was a publisher's copyright; but the act was construed to have provided an author's copyright. . . . This development had little to do with the Statute of Anne itself; but because the act provided for copyright, and the statutory copyright it provided later came to be an author's copyright, the inevitable conclusion was that the statutory copyright was originally designed to be an author's copyright. (p. 144)

37. In addition to the works already cited, information on the Statute of Anne comes from Benjamin Kaplan, *An Unhurried View of Copyright* (New York: Columbia Univ. Press, 1967), pp. 1–38; Ian Parsons, "Copyright and Society," in *Essays in the History of Publishing in Celebration of the 250th Anniversary of the House of Longman, 1724–1974*, ed. Asa Briggs (London: Longman, 1974), pp. 31–60; Marjorie Plant, *The English Book Trade: An Economic History of the Making and Sale of Books* (London: Allen and Unwin, 1965), pp. 99–121; Harry Ransom, *The First Copyright Statute: An Essay on an Act for the Encouragement of Learning, 1710* (Austin: Univ. of Texas Press, 1956); Mark Rose, *Authors and Owners: The Invention of Copyright* (Cambridge: Harvard

Both the idea that authors should be their own people and the idea that they are the original owners of their copyrights indicate that their new dignity, the insistence on their worth and the unfairness of their lot was intertwined at mid-century with their characterization as dispossessed proprietors. But exactly what was their proprietary right based on? In cases where authorship might be contested, what would define it? When one looks at the decisions handed down under the Statute of Anne in early copyright disputes, one is struck by the emphasis the courts placed on "invention" or "originality" as the definitive characteristic of authorship. To be sure, "the law follows a highly subjective theory of originality that often surprises, and sometimes shocks, those encountering it for the first time," as one modern commentator has remarked.[38] For example, in 1720, the bookseller who owned the copyright of Dr. Thomas Burnet's Latin work *Archaeologiae Philosophicae* tried to stop the publication of an English translation, but the court of Chancery ruled that a translation "may be called a different book, and the translator may be said to be the author" because he had invented a new form for the ideas.[39] To question whether the plaintiff's rights had been infringed, therefore, was to question whether a translator was an author and, in turn, to ask whether the translator had originated or invented something. In this case, it was decided that the translator was an author even though he had not originated the ideas, for he had conceived a new form, and *"forma dat esse rei."* Invention was also found to be the crucial criterion of authorship in cases involving abridgment; books that were only superficially changed or "colourably shortened" were judged to be piracies, but "a fair abridgement . . . may with great propriety be called a new book, because not only the paper and print, but the *invention,* learning, and judgment of the author [abridger] is shown in them."[40]

Univ. Press, 1993); and Trevor Ross, "Copyright and the Invention of Tradition," *Eighteenth-Century Studies* 26:1 (1992): 1–27. Not all contemporaries thought that *property* rights per se were involved in the copyright disputes of the mid-century; numerous pamphlets insist that copyright is a *monopoly,* as opposed to a property, right. This was, indeed, the main argument against holding it in perpetuity.

38. William S. Strong, *The Copyright Book: A Practical Guide* (Cambridge: MIT Press, 1990), p. 3.

39. This case and the two that follow are discussed by Kaplan, pp. 10–12.

40. Kaplan, pp. 10–11.

Determining "wherein consists the identity of a book"[41] became a task of discovering authorship, which in large part became the task of discovering "invention." As the century progressed, copyright disputes became occasions for articulating even more radical notions of originality than have ever been incorporated in the law itself. In 1769, for example, one justice suggested copyright should protect the *ideas* of the work, and hence that the requirement of invention might not be satisfied by mere reformation or rewording, although he simultaneously admitted that ideas, divorced from the particulars of their expression, "were 'quite wild' and incapable of *indicia certa*."[42] The question whether an author was commonly, if not legally, definable as someone whose *thoughts* are original had, however, been broached, and the affirmative response was to gain wider acceptance over the next two centuries.

It is not surprising, then, that a similar valorization of unprecedented, unique conceptualization appeared in numerous discussions of literature. Indeed, literary criticism at mid-century was often an inquiry into what could properly be attributed to various writers as their own inventions, as if the critics, like the courts, had been set the task of ferreting out infringements of literary property. Charlotte Lennox's *Shakespeare Illustrated* is an excellent example of this genre; it even addresses itself to its dedicatee, the Right Honorable John, earl of Orrery, as "that Judge whom Pliny himself would have wished for his Assessor to hear a literary Cause."[43] Its preface (which was, ironically enough in a work so punctilious about attribution, probably written by Johnson) flatly states that poets must be rated according to their powers of "Invention":

> [A]nd of all the Degrees of Invention, the highest seems to be that which is able to produce a Series of Events. It is easy when the thread of a Story is once drawn to diversify it with Variety of Colours. . . . To tell over again a Story that has been told already, and to tell it better than the first Author is no rare Qualification; but to strike out the first Hints of a new Fable . . . is the utmost Effort of the human Mind.[44]

41. This phrase, from the case of *Millar v. Taylor*, is quoted by Kaplan, p. 12.
42. Kaplan, p. 14.
43. *Shakespeare Illustrated* (London, 1753), p. vii.
44. *Shakespeare Illustrated*, pp. iv–v.

Shakespeare, it turns out, seldom succeeded in this supreme authorial "Effort" of fictionalizing, of making up new stories. Of course, the application of this mid-eighteenth-century standard of inventiveness to Shakespeare was wildly anachronistic; for Shakespeare and his contemporaries, poetic "Invention" referred to a particularly vivid use of language that could make events and people distant in time and space seem present to the hearer. "Invention" referred to the almost hallucinatory power of poetic figures. For example, when the chorus longs for "a Muse of fire, that would ascend / The brightest heaven of invention" at the beginning of *Henry V*, the speech in no way indicates a desire to make up a new story. Instead, "invention" would retrieve the heroic past in its intensity: "Then should the warlike Harry, like himself, / Assume the port of Mars" (*The Life of Henry the Fifth*, Prologue, 1–6). The lines are, to be sure, sophisticated almost to the point of obscurity about the issue of mimesis; they express a wish to watch Harry play himself playing Mars. All this representational play, though, is purported to originate, not in the playwright's invention, but in the historical actors and events themselves. By 1753, however, "invention" had become closely associated with "the Fiction of a Tale,"[45] and hence Lennox devoted herself to the "originals" of Shakespeare's plays. She translated the "novels and romances" she considered his primary sources and then went on to demonstrate how seldom the bard had been "able to produce any Thing by [his] own Imagination."[46]

The concept of literary property, then, can be said to have promoted that of "Invention," which in turn found its apotheosis in the idea of pure fabulation, or original fiction writing. For if the story itself and the vehicle of its language, if both "idea" and "expression," were invented, authorship became incontestable. To be sure, there was no general pressure to turn all authorship into fiction writing; historians, for example, were not expected to prove themselves authors by making up stories. But even among historians, a modern emphasis on originality of conception and the

45. *Shakespeare Illustrated*, p. xi. This section of the preface concedes that Shakespeare's genius was for verisimilitude rather than invention, but such a distinction would not have been comprehensible in the Renaissance, when verisimilitude was the aim of invention.

46. *Shakespeare Illustrated*, pp. v–vi.

discovery of "new" facts distinguish eighteenth-century authors. "[T]he Fiction of a Tale" was not the only mark of invention, but it did provide a particularly thorough and incontrovertible claim to that authorial activity which determined the singular identity of a work.

Copyright law and criticism, moreover, were not the only places where legal and literary concerns converged to favor fiction as an indisputable authorial property. The slow decline of the *roman scandaleux,* its gradual replacement by narratives without keys, also illustrates the separation of spheres and the new authorial will to property. When Delarivier Manley defended herself against libel by claiming that the stories of *The New Atalantis* were entirely her own invention, pure fiction innocent of reference and hence of political import, she was, even if only facetiously, making a claim to private property. If she had invented her stories instead of appropriating and circulating someone else's, she should be found innocent. A story that was nobody's could also be hers; one that reflected on somebody, however, made her authorship at once criminal and doubtful, at once libelous and unoriginal. Although prosecutions for seditious libel were not officially concerned with violations of privacy, attacks on scandalmongers like Manley often stressed that they had taken liberties with the characters and reputations of "persons of quality" and were therefore guilty of personal injury or theft.

Indeed, that invention, property, and authorial innocence were closely linked in the early eighteenth century indicates a complicated interaction between criminal and property law. Foucault's influential argument that the early modern imperative to identify authors actually derived from the needs of state censors could be maintained in the English case only if one were willing to follow an extremely circuitous path of causation.[47] The drafters of unsuc-

47. In his influential essay "What Is an Author?" Michel Foucault makes a strong link between censorship and the invention of the author, but he seems to be generalizing from the French case. Foucault's essay is in *Textual Strategies: Perspectives in Post-Structuralist Criticism,* ed. Josué V. Harari (Ithaca, NY: Cornell Univ. Press, 1979), pp. 141–60. For responses to Foucault on the French situation, see Molly Nesbit, "What Was an Author?" *Yale French Studies* 73 (1987): 229–57; and Carla Hesse, "Enlightenment Epistemology and the Laws of Authorship in Revolutionary France, 1777–1793," *Representations* 30 (1990): 109–32. See also Martha Woodmansee, "The Genius and the Copyright: Economic and Legal Conditions of the Emergence

cessful Parliamentary bills between 1695 and 1710 often linked copyright and criminal liability, and Defoe's *Essay on the Regulation of the Press* (1704) argued that the libel law itself implied authorial rights: "For if an Author has not the right of a Book, after he has made it, and the benefit be not his own, and the Law will not protect him in that Benefit, 'twould be very hard the law should pretend to punish him for it."[48] Defoe's position here is the opposite of Manley's, since it claims that criminal prosecution assumes an intimate proprietary connection between authors and their works even when the works are libelous.

The 1710 statute, however, actually initiated a significant break between the legal issues of censorship and authors' rights; John Feather, indeed, argues that the 1710 legislation had wide appeal because it did not involve "the delicate and unpopular area of censorship."[49] Since, as we saw in the preceding chapter, all parties and factions routinely violated the law, no one had an interest in strengthening it; that is, although everybody wanted some libels suppressed, nobody in 1710 was very keen to suppress libel itself. Defoe may have articulated a common way of reasoning from criminal liability to authorial propriety, but the legislative history presents us with a full stop between the author-as-libeler and the author-as-proprietor, between the issues and practices shaping Manley's career and those shaping Lennox's.

What Johnson called the "Age of Authorship" was thus not the straightforward outcome of a disciplinary procedure; rather it appears to have been the result of the state's unwillingness to censor, which left the Stationers' Company without an external regulatory means to enforce copyright and keep the trade profitable. Hence the book trade supported the Statute of Anne, which accidentally thrust authorship into the foreground of disputes over copyright, thereby privileging "invention" and hence downgrading scandal, the mere repetition of what Delarivier Manley had called "old tales."

---

of the 'Author,'" *Eighteenth-Century Studies* 17:4 (1984): 425–48; and Mark Rose, "The Author as Proprietor: *Donaldson v. Becket* and the Genealogy of Modern Authorship," *Representations* 23 (1988): 51–85.

48. *An Essay on the Regulation of the Press* (London, 1704; rpt. Oxford: Basil Blackwell, 1948), pp. 27–28.

49. "The Book Trade in Politics: The Making of the Copyright Act of 1710," p. 37.

This complicated process, coinciding with the decrease in political patronage, further reduced the rewards of libel. The cultural imperative not to infringe on the property of others and a widening notion of what "property" might be—words, ideas, characters, sentiments, stories—helped suppress coded promises to reveal secret histories while it fostered new forms of authorial credibility. Manley's alibi of nonreferentiality thus presaged and blended with a slightly later celebration of fiction as a form of writing deriving wholly from the author's imagination and therefore belonging to him or her in a peculiarly strong sense. Invention and originality, the talents associated with fiction writing, increasingly came to signal both innocence and entitlement.

A concern for authorial property, for attaching stories firmly to individual authors and detaching them from "originals" outside the text, therefore, led to a de-emphasis on the historical truth of a story and a concomitant stress on its originality, its fictionality. For the first time in the history of English letters, the historical untruth of a story could become an asset if one presented it as an instance of "the utmost Effort of the human Mind." Thus did a new respectability, deriving from the prestige of authorial property, attach itself to fiction as a category, partially obscuring what had hitherto seemed obvious: that the best stories were true ones.

～

Thus far I have argued, first, that the heroizing of writers in the mid-eighteenth century was closely intertwined with contemporary attempts to identify the property of authorship and, second, that a new valuation of fiction emerged from this discursive nexus. Useful as this analysis may be in explaining why Johnson and Lennox made the claims they did for fiction, it does not, however, help us understand why their claims were so readily honored. We need to ask what purposes, besides the validation of authorship itself, the advancement of fiction served. After all, it would be farfetched to suggest that readers began to prefer fiction to scandal simply because they wanted to savor the originality of a bona fide author. This section of the chapter, therefore, addresses itself to the reader's, rather than the author's, sense of propriety and its affiliations with the eighteenth-century ethical discourse about sympathy. I do not leave behind the issue of property but merely shift its location.

My discussion of the promotion of fiction through copyright disputes has tended to take the category of fiction for granted, to assume that there was always a branch of letters distinguished by its overt renunciation of particular referential truth claims. Recent historians of the novel, however, have shown that the concept of fiction, far from being a universal cultural category, developed slowly in early modern Europe, that the immediate predecessors of the novel—romances, secret histories, and memoirs—often claimed historical veracity, and that until the mid-eighteenth century, there was no widely employed means of distinguishing between a fiction and a lie. Indeed, the problem of differentiating kinds of untruth has generally plagued historians of the novel. In his introduction to *A Check List of English Prose Fiction, 1700–1739,* William Harlin McBurney admits that he included works claiming to be true as long as he judged them to be "full of improbable lies."[50] But fiction writing cannot be said to exist as a marked and recognized category in a culture until it can be effortlessly distinguished from lying. As Michael McKeon has exhaustively demonstrated, the terms for such a distinction were available in late seventeenth- and early eighteenth-century England, but they were seldom used.[51] The discourse of fiction, therefore, was awaiting not so much the requisite conceptual tools as some cultural imperative to use them.

Once we recognize that it is rare to find cultures where the category of fiction is strongly marked and valued as such, and that in British history the category does not precede but is rather coterminous with the rise of the novel, the history of that genre raises new questions. Because histories of the novel long assumed that its genealogy lay in fictional forms, they tended to focus on the issue of realism. Where, they asked, did the taste for *realistic* novelistic fiction come from?—as if a taste for fiction already existed. But once we see that the novel derives from forms that were not at the time understood to be fictional, we must address a prior

50. *A Check List of English Prose Fiction, 1700–1739* (Cambridge: Harvard Univ. Press, 1960), p. ix.
51. McKeon, *The Origins of the English Novel, 1600–1740* (Baltimore, MD: Johns Hopkins Univ. Press, 1987), pp. 25–64.

question. We should ask, not why the novel became the preferred form of fiction, but why fiction became a preferred form of narrative.

Both Lennard Davis and Michael McKeon have recently helped rephrase the question in these terms, and each has contributed important answers. Davis, denying that the novel developed primarily out of the romance and asserting that its origins lay in what he calls the "news-novel matrix"—the tangled mass of journalism, scandal, and political and religious controversy we examined in Chapter 3—points to the legal and political pressures that eventually legitimized fiction.[52] McKeon, on the other hand, adheres to the romance-novel connection and identifies a dialectical development in romance that created an imperative for verisimilitude, which is imagined to be at once fictional and "truthful," in accordance with a newly expanded idea of truth. The movement from romance to novel, according to McKeon, rests on an underlying epistemological shift from truth-as-historical-accuracy to truth-as-mimetic-simulation. It was the widespread acceptance of verisimilitude as a form of truth, rather than a form of illusion or lying, that made fiction a category and simultaneously founded the novel as a genre. Verisimilitude is the leading term in McKeon's account; there is no realized prior category of fiction to which mimetic realism is added to produce the novel. Rather, the legitimation of the verisimilar (as opposed to the historical) allowed the separation of the fictional from the historical components of the romance and the development of the former as The Novel.[53]

My own argument is deeply indebted to those of Davis and McKeon, but it focuses on some crucial, indeed definitive, aspects

52. *Factual Fictions: The Origins of the English Novel* (New York: Columbia Univ. Press, 1983), pp. 25–70.
53. McKeon, esp. pp. 39–64. Recent works on the origins of the novel that inform this discussion are, in addition to the books by Lennard Davis and Michael McKeon, Robert W. Uphaus, ed., *The Idea of the Novel in the Eighteenth Century* (East Lansing, MI: Colleagues Press, 1988); J. Paul Hunter, *Before Novels: The Cultural Contexts of Eighteenth Century English Fiction* (New York: Norton, 1990); Armstrong, *Desire and Domestic Fiction;* John Bender, *Imagining the Penitentiary: Fiction and the Architecture of Mind in Eighteenth-Century England* (Chicago: Univ. of Chicago Press, 1987); Frances Ferguson, "Rape and the Rise of the Novel," *Representations* 20 (1987): 88–112; Homer Obed Brown, "Of the Title to Things Real: Conflicting Stories," *ELH* 55 (1988): 917–54; Lennard J. Davis, *Resisting Novels: Ideology and Fiction* (New York: Methuen, 1987); Ralph W. Rader, "The Emergence of the Novel in England: Genre in History vs. History of Genre," *Narrative* 1:1 (1993): 69–83; and Robert Folkenflik, "The Heirs of Ian Watt," *Eighteenth-Century Studies* 25:2 (1991–92): 203–17.

of the novel that they largely ignore. Fiction no doubt renounces "historical" truth claims and replaces them with mimetic ones; this axiom would hold whether the nonfictional predecessor of the novel is news, scandal, or romance. However, as we saw in the preceding chapter, the tension between factuality and verisimilitude, between history and mimesis, could have been resolved in various ways or could simply have been left unresolved as the incommensurable layers of "allegorical" representation. Fiction writers, though, did more than admit their narratives lacked historical accuracy; after all, the authors of personal satire and scandalous "allegories" had gone that far and had, on occasion, achieved a high level of verisimilitude. But they were not, properly speaking, novelists, because their stories, whether pretending to exact historical accuracy or not, claimed to be about somebody, whereas the writers of admitted fictions professed to be telling nobody's story, that is, to be telling the stories of people who never actually lived. The most radical and least explored distinction between prenovelistic and novelistic narratives is that the former often claim particular extra-textual reference for their proper names and the latter normally do not.[54] A few seventeenth- and early eighteenth-century narratives were forthrightly fictional, just as some late eighteenth-century stories insisted on their referentiality, and still others asked the reader to switch back and forth between referential and nonreferential assumptions. There was no sudden novelistic revolution that purged English narrative of somebody and replaced him or her with nobody. Nevertheless, in the middle decades of the century, fictional nobodies became the more popular and respectable protagonists.

In those decades, though, it was by no means taken for granted that everyone would want to read stories about nobody. Arabella,

---

54. For a lucid philosophical discussion of the reference of proper names in fiction, see Richard Rorty, "Is There a Problem about Fictional Discourse?" in *Funktionen des Fiktiven* (Munich: Wilhelm Fink Verlag, 1983), pp. 67–93. Rorty concludes that a Parmenidean insistence on reference creates a problem about fiction, but that the problem would be avoided if one were consistently to view "language as behavior governed by conventions, like games, and to see 'reference' in terms of conventions which must be obeyed if one is to make a successful move in the game" (p. 71). Rorty also points out, however, that although different uses of "reference" are merely conventional, the move of claiming "no referent" constitutes the language game called "literature" in the modern period (pp. 92–93).

the heroine of Charlotte Lennox's *Female Quixote*, articulates this reluctance and expresses common eighteenth-century objections to the new kind of narrative:

> [H]e that writes without Intention to be credited, must write to little Purpose; for what Pleasure or Advantage can arise from Facts that never happened? What Examples can be afforded by the Patience of those who never suffered, or the Chastity of those who were never solicited? . . . When we hear a Story in common Life that raises our Wonder or Compassion, the first Confutation stills our Emotions, and however we were touched before, we then chase it from the Memory with Contempt as a Trifle, or with Indignation as an Imposture.[55]

Arabella's two main challenges—that self-proclaimed fictions can neither instruct nor *move* the hearer—are met by her interlocutor in the novel with classic mid-century assertions of the peculiar truth and pleasure of the verisimilar. But there is a mismatch between the objections and their refutation, for Arabella has asked why one should care about people who never existed, not why one should take aesthetic pleasure in a well-accomplished mimesis. To respond that the accuracy of the mimesis is the foundation of the emotional response, and the emotional response is therefore a register of artistry, is to miss the force of Arabella's question: Why introduce disbelief simply to suspend it, however artfully, in the interest of creating what Arabella calls "Compassion"?

For "Compassion," after all, was generally acknowledged to be the end of fiction. As we have often been told, fiction in the eighteenth century was believed to be an important tool for inculcating moral sentiments.[56] It was thought to allow the exercise of

55. Charlotte Lennox, *The Female Quixote*, ed. Margaret Dalziel (Oxford: Oxford Univ. Press, 1989), pp. 376–77. Subsequent quotations from this edition are cited parenthetically in the text.

56. The secondary literature on this topic is extensive. For recent studies see John Mullen, *Sentiment and Sociability: The Language of Feeling in the Eighteenth Century* (Oxford: Oxford Univ. Press, 1988); Janet Todd, *Sensibility: An Introduction* (New York: Methuen, 1986); Fred Kaplan, *Sacred Tears: Sentimentality in Victorian Literature* (Princeton, NJ: Princeton Univ. Press, 1987); David Marshall, *The Figure of Theater: Shaftesbury, Defoe, Adam Smith, and George Eliot* (New York: Columbia Univ. Press, 1986), and *The Surprising Effects of Sympathy: Marivaux, Diderot, Rousseau, and Mary Shelley* (Chicago: Univ. of Chicago Press, 1988). Although these books include many discussions of the links between eighteenth-century novels and moral sense philosophy, they tend not to ask why *fiction*, as opposed to another form of narrative, should have seemed to have a peculiar affinity with sympathetic sensibilities.

sympathy, that process by which one feels the joys and sufferings of another and may thereby be motivated to perform benevolent actions. Sympathy and the imagination, then, were linked in some ethical systems, and certain historians of the novel argue that the new cultural prestige of fiction depended on this link. Fiction, the argument assumes, makes it easy to appropriate another's point of view, to sympathize. But why?

Arabella's objection calls this assumption into question by pointing out that we might expect to find our emotions "stilled" if we understand that their objects do not have, and never have had, any actual existence like our own. And Arabella was by no means unique in her opinion; it is common to find early and mid-eighteenth-century commentators taking it for granted that a real hero would be easier to feel compassion for than a fictional one: "To pity a feign'd Hero," as one "novelist" expressed it, "is commendable, because it is a sure Argument that Compassion would not be wanting to a real one."[57] The link between fiction and sympathy was often made during the period in these negative terms: only someone with sympathy to spare would be able to spend any on "a feign'd Hero." Fiction was thus not always conceived as a natural stimulus to sympathy; often it was seen as a test of how far one could extend compassion. Could it be extended to a paradoxical sympathy with nobody? If so, might not the very ambiguity of the phrase "sympathizing with nobody" warn us away from such an exercise? As Arabella and a good many other eighteenth-century skeptics were fond of remarking, there is something absurd about making up people to sympathize with. Why not just sympathize with the people who were already there?

I think that there is an answer to this question, that, pace Arabella's objections, Nobody was a more likely candidate for sympathy in this period than almost anybody else. To answer Arabella, I would like to turn briefly to David Hume's *Treatise of Human Nature*, where we will find the link between fiction and sympathy that usually goes without saying. I have chosen *A Treatise* not because it was an influential work in the eighteenth century (it

---

57. *The Unfortunate Duchess; or, the Lucky Gamester. A novel, founded on a true story* (London, 1739), quoted in Michael Crump, "Stranger than Fiction: The Eighteenth-Century True Story," p. 67.

was not) but because literary critics are fond of quoting it to prove that eighteenth-century people believed that they naturally took on the emotional coloring of their human environment through the automatic operations of sympathy: "So close and intimate is the correspondence of human souls," wrote Hume, "that no sooner any person approaches me, than he diffuses on me all his opinions, and draws along my judgment in a greater or lesser degree."[58] Such passages have made it easy for commentators to cite Hume as an "optimistic" moral philosopher who claimed there were no obstacles to fellow feeling.[59] I will instead follow the lead of those writers who have stressed the problematic nature of Humean sympathy,[60] noting that the philosopher's discussions of the concept are intricately interlaced with his discussions of property. Property, indeed, is an important brake on the dynamic of sympathy, and it can also be identified as the invisible link between sympathy and fiction. Hume's *Treatise* reveals why fictional characters were uniquely suitable objects of compassion. Because they were conjectural, suppositional identities *belonging* to no one, they could be universally appropriated. A story about nobody was nobody's story and hence could be entered, occupied, identified with by anybody.

Significantly, Hume's most extensive discussion of sympathy is inserted into the section of the *Treatise* dealing with pride and humility, the passions that he claims take the *self* as their object. Sympathy occurs smoothly and seems automatic when its object is the joy or sorrow of a member of our own family or a business partner, someone who, in the common parlance of the time, would be said to "belong" to us; it is not a self-forgetting process. Interwoven as it is with the possibility of knowing another mind, it is nevertheless self-referring. As Hume tersely reasons: "In sympathy there is an evident conversion of an idea into an impression. This

---

58. *A Treatise of Human Nature*, ed. L. A. Selby-Bigge (Oxford: Clarendon Press, 1968), p. 592. Subsequent quotations from this edition are cited parenthetically in the text and notes.

59. See, for example, Kaplan, *Sacred Tears*, esp. pp. 18–20 and 25–27.

60. For example, Jerome Christensen, *Practicing Enlightenment: Hume and the Formation of a Literary Career* (Madison: Univ. of Wisconsin Press, 1987). Christensen's description of Hume's alternate involvement in and detachment from the passions has helped me formulate the idea of emotional "practice." See also Carol Kay, *Political Constructions: Defoe, Richardson, and Sterne in Relation to Hobbes, Hume, and Burke* (Ithaca, NY: Cornell Univ. Press, 1988).

conversion arises from the relation of objects to ourself. Ourself is always intimately present to us" (p. 320). That which is originally a distant, unemotional idea, in other words, becomes present by being folded in to that which is always present to us: our "impression" of ourselves. To sympathize is to expand this impression called the self to include impressions originally experienced as mere ideas of another's self.

Sympathy, then, is not an emotion about someone else but is rather the process by which someone else's emotion becomes our own. It is the conversion of the *idea* of someone else's passion into a lively *impression* of that passion, which is indistinguishable from actually feeling the passion oneself. Sympathy does not occur immediately, but is rather accomplished in three stages: (1) certain *sense data* (melancholy looks, open wounds, mournful language) communicate an *idea* of someone else's emotional state (unhappiness); (2) that idea becomes vital, forceful, and present through the operation of one or more relational principles linking sufferer and perceiver (cause and effect, contiguity and resemblance) and is thereby converted into an *impression* (impressions differ from ideas only in force and vivacity) of the other's emotion; (3) the impression (or vivacious perception) can, under certain conditions, be "so enlivened as to become the very *sentiment* or passion" (p. 319).

Such is the process by which sense (seeing the tears of another) leads to sentiment (feeling sad oneself); and according to Hume human beings are generally vulnerable to this form of emotional contagion. But the *Treatise* also strenuously insists that the process is rarely completed. It is especially likely to remain incomplete when the original sufferer is most clearly perceived to be somebody unrelated to us. The conversion of idea into sentiment, on the other hand, is most likely to occur when all three relational principles operate in a way that obscures the "otherness" of the original sufferer. In the case of human beings, Hume says, the relational principle of resemblance always operates: other people are always to some extent like us. But this is normally an insufficient basis for sympathy. Contiguity, mere physical proximity, is a somewhat stronger relational principle, but strongest of all is cause and effect, under which Hume classifies family relations and property relations (p. 310). "All these relations, when united together," Hume explains, "convey the impression or consciousness of our own person to the idea of the sentiments or passions of others, and makes us conceive them in the strongest and most lively manner" (p. 318).

In short, we are most likely to experience the emotions of other people when those other people already belong to us. Sympathy is normally that process by which the emotions of those who are related to us come to be experienced by us as our own. What happens to the otherness of the other people in this process, an otherness already blurred by the relationships described? Do we become more mindful of their separate realities? Not really, and this is the paradox of Humean sympathy: another's internal state becomes "intimately present" only by losing its distinct quality of belonging to somebody else. "I cannot feel an emotion," writes Hume, "without it becoming in some sense my own." That is, when the process occurs, the very relationships of ownership on which it depends seem at once stretched out of recognizable shape and reasserted. I feel your emotion because you are already in some sense mine, but once the feeling is mine, it is no longer distinguished by being yours.

As one of Hume's commentators has pointed out, his concept of sympathy does not, strictly speaking, imply any increase in regard for the person sympathized with. Páll S. Árdal, indeed, comes up with an extreme illustration of how the process Hume calls sympathy might rather be expected to produce selfishness: if you have a desire for a glass of whiskey, he reasons, and I sympathize with you in a Humean fashion, all that's been accomplished is that I want a glass of whiskey, too.[61] The likely outcome of my sympathizing with your yearning for a glass of whiskey is thus that I will try to get one for myself, not that I will try to satisfy you. My idea of your desire may have been the original stimulus, but by the time that the idea has been enlivened into my sentiment, you have become irrelevant. This illustration may give us an odd and in some ways distorting angle on Hume's version of sympathy, but it also allows us to see how easily the process he describes under that name might be expected to aggrandize the self and its properties, even as it unsettles the concept of a bounded, stable ego.

61. Páll S. Árdal, *Passion and Value in Hume's Treatise* (Edinburgh: Edinburgh Univ. Press, 1966), p. 46.

We might argue, then, that Humean sympathy is complete when it dispenses with its original "object," the original sufferer. I sympathize with the sentiments of others by making them mine; and the conditions for such an appropriation must be there at the outset: the person who originally feels them must somehow "belong" to me. Otherwise my senses will not travel the pathway to sentiment. Hume baldly claims that at first the passions with which we eventually sympathize "appear . . . in *our* mind as mere ideas, and are conceived to belong to another person, as we conceive of any other matter of fact" (p. 319). In other words, as long as the emotions are "conceived to belong to another person," they are rather cold, lifeless ideas; sympathy occurs when they lose this quality of belonging exclusively to another. As long as we perceive just the evidence of someone else's sentiment, we do not feel anything; the ideas must be impressed by the imagination into that which is always intimately present to us—ourselves—in order to become sentiments.

If we grant that Humean sympathy works by appropriating emotions, by transforming them from the emotions of another (mere ideas) to our emotions (lively sentiments), we can see how property (or, more precisely, its lack) serves as the invisible link between sympathy and fiction. The body of the other person, although it conveys the original sense data and serves as the basis for all the modes of relationship that supposedly allow sympathetic identification, is also paradoxically imagined to be a barrier. It communicates but it also marks out the sentiments as belonging to somebody else and hence as being simply objective facts. Our conception of the sentiments as appropriate to *that* rather than *this* body must be overcome in the process of sympathy. This proprietary barrier of the other's body is what fiction freely dispenses with; by representing feelings that belong to no other body, fiction actually facilitates the process of sympathy. It bypasses the stage at which the sentiments perceived in other bodies are mere matters of fact and gives us the illusion of immediately appropriable sentiments, free sentiments belonging to nobody and therefore identifiable with ourselves.

In these suppositions, we can see why fictional characters would emerge as universally engaging subjectivities. Because they are unmarked by a proprietary relationship to anyone in the real world, we do not regard them with the "objective" eyes with which Hume claims we view the property of others. Although they lack all actual relation to the reader, which Hume believed was the foundation of sympathy, they similarly lack the impediment of being related to anyone else. Hence, they become a species of utopian common property, potential objects of universal identification. Another way to put this might be to say that since the stories are nobody's, everybody can have an equal interest in them. The questions that clustered around putatively "true" stories in the eighteenth century—is the story libelous? who should be allowed to tell it? whose interest does it serve to tell it this way?—vanish, and a new interest takes their place, a gratuitous and hence sympathetic, sentimental interest.

Fiction, then, stimulates sympathy because, with very few exceptions, it is easier to identify with nobody's story and share nobody's sentiments than to identify with anybody else's story and share anybody else's sentiments. But, paradoxically, we can always claim to be expanding our capacity for sympathy by reading fiction because, after all, if we can sympathize with nobody, then we can sympathize with anybody. Or so it would seem, but such sympathy remains on that level of abstraction where anybody is "nobody in particular" (the very definition of a novel character). Nobody was eligible to be the universally preferred anybody because nobody, unlike somebody, was never anybody *else*.

Hume notes that the quality of one's sympathy for a fictional character differs from that feeling elicited by people we believe to be real. The strength and duration of an impression, he argues, are partly determined by the perceiver's belief in the reality of the object; hence our sympathy with fictional entities should be relatively unstable, for all its intensity. He distinguishes between the "fervors" and "apparent agitations of the mind" that "poetic description" creates and the "firm and solid" impression left by historical narration (p. 631): "We observe . . . that such fictions are connected with nothing that is real. This observation makes us only lend ourselves, so to speak, to the fictions" (pp. 631–32).[62]

62. For other discussions of Hume and eighteenth-century fiction, see Bender, *Imagining the Penitentiary*, pp. 35–40; and John Passmore, *Hume's Intentions* (London: Duckworth, 1980), pp. 99–104.

This remark that fictional characters merely borrow our sympathy without fully claiming it gives us another hint about their peculiar efficacy, their ability to "excite" the mind without producing "that weight" (p. 631) of real entities. The lighter, temporary quality of fictional identification further separates it from the weightier but also therefore more difficult task of sympathizing with others.

Conversely, however, Hume also entertains the idea that merely imaginary objects can arouse peculiarly strong emotional responses. Admitting that the essential mechanism of sympathy, the conversion of a mere idea into an impression and then into an actual bodily sensation, might not rely on the existence of anything outside the individual's imagination, he lists several instances in which, because nobody actually feels the emotions with which one sympathizes (p. 386), the imagination is stimulated to produce sentiments "that arise by a transition from affections, which have no existence" (p. 370).[63] Since sympathy works by making sensations out of ideas, the normal empiricist trajectory from body to mind may be reversed: "The lively idea of any object always approaches its impression; and 'tis certain we may feel sickness and pain from the mere force of imagination, and make a malady real by often thinking of it" (p. 319). That Hume's exposition of sympathy should thus find an illustration in one of the eighteenth century's favorite types of tyrannical selfishness, the hypochondriac, indicates that the deeper one looks into it, the more Humean sympathy renders unreal and irrelevant its ostensible object: somebody else.

A similarly strong sense both of the impediments to sympathizing with other actual people and of the attenuation of otherness as a result of sympathy lies at the heart of the novel's most important formal trait: its overt fictionality. The very specificity and particularity of realist representation, moreover, should be viewed as confirmation, rather than obfuscation, of fiction. Those techniques that make up what Ian Watt called the novel's "formal realism"— its wealth of circumstantial and physical detail, its delineation of characters by specific class, gender, and regional characteristics,

63. Hume is referring here, not to the operations of fiction per se, but to those of the "general rules," which are "established persuasions founded on memory and custom" (p. 632). Although he claims that there is a difference between fictions and general rules, he also admits that he cannot define it (pp. 631–32).

and so forth—are all overtly illusionistic confessions that the particulars of the novel character have no extra-textual existence. The character came into *fictional* existence most fully only when he or she was developed as nobody *in particular;* that is, the particularities had to be fully specified to ensure the felt fictionality of the character. A generalized character would too easily take on allegorical or symbolic reference, just as one rendered in mere "hints" would have been read at the time as a scandalous libel. Thinness of detail almost always indicated specific extra-textual reference. But the more characters were loaded with circumstantial and seemingly insignificant properties, the more the readers were assured that the text was at once assuming and making up for its reference to nobody at all. Roland Barthes has pointed out that the contingent, unmotivated detail was the code of the "real" in fiction, but he did not draw what seems to me an obvious conclusion: that realism was the code of the fictional. The very realism of the new form, therefore, enabled readers to appropriate the stories sympathetically, for readers of fiction could be, to paraphrase Burke, "acquisitive without impertinence."[64]

~

In at least two ways overt fictions, invented narratives about people who never were, became both more strongly marked and more positively valued in the mid-eighteenth century than they had been previously: first, the birth of the author-proprietor, whose property claims might rest on his or her "faculty of invention"; and, second, a new emphasis on "sympathy" in discussions of human nature that made nobody's story especially appealing. The fictionality of the novel thus simultaneously, if somewhat paradoxically, allowed both the author and the reader to be "acquisitive without impertinence." That the story was nobody's made it entirely the author's;

64. Burke claims that the sympathetic interest inspired by art, combined with its representational distance from real people, allows viewers to be "inquisitive without impertinence" (*A Philosophical Enquiry into the Origins of Our Ideas of the Sublime and Beautiful*, ed. J. T. Boulton [New York: Columbia Univ. Press, 1958], p. 53). Burke shares the period's understanding that a consciousness of the difference between representation and reality stimulates interest and emotional response.

that it was nobody's also left it open to the reader's sentimental appropriation.

The sources of this desire for sentimental appropriation cannot be adequately catalogued here. Volumes have been written on the mid-eighteenth-century affective revolution—a term that comprehends such phenomena as changes in family structure, the development of a discourse of "sensibility," the spread of emotionally involving religious revivals, the rise of "humane" reform movements, the articulation of moral sense philosophy, the invention of aesthetics, stricter demands for sexual propriety, and the discovery of specifically female virtues. The growth of commerce, the rise of the urban middle class, the new discursiveness and subjectivity of discipline, the burgeoning of the fiscal-military state, and the growth of the national debt have all been suggested as the underlying "causes," common threads, or discursive "knots" linking these developments.

It is seldom disputed, however, that there was a revolution in sensibility in mid-eighteenth-century England. This section of the chapter connects one part of it, the discourse on sympathy we have already examined, to both the rise of fiction and new forms of feminine subjectivity. Charlotte Lennox's *Female Quixote* serves as my text for analyzing these connections,[65] so I return to Arabella's resistance to fiction and ask why she must learn to sympathize with nobody in order to become a modern young woman, ready for matrimony.

First, I have to demonstrate that Arabella *does* resist fiction, a

65. For critical discussion of Charlotte Lennox and *The Female Quixote*, see Catherine A. Craft, "Reworking Male Models: Aphra Behn's *Fair Vow-Breaker*, Eliza Haywood's *Fantomina*, and Charlotte Lennox's *Female Quixote*," *Modern Language Review* 86 (1991): 821–38; Margaret Doody, "Shakespeare's Novels: Charlotte Lennox Illustrated," *Studies in the Novel* 19 (1987): 296–310; Katherine Sobba Green, *The Courtship Novel, 1740–1820: A Feminized Genre* (Lexington: Univ. Press of Kentucky, 1991), pp. 47–54; Laurie Langbauer, *Women and Romance: The Consolations of Gender in the English Novel* (Ithaca, NY: Cornell Univ. Press, 1989), pp. 62–92; James J. Lynch, "Romance and Realism in Charlotte Lennox's *The Female Quixote*," *Essays in Literature* 14 (1987): 51–63; Deborah Ross, "Mirror, Mirror: The Didactic Dilemma of *The Female Quixote*," *Studies in English Literature* 27 (1986): 455–73; Patricia Meyer Spacks, "The Subtle Sophistry of Desire: Dr. Johnson and *The Female Quixote*," *Modern Philology* 85 (1988): 532–42; Spencer, *The Rise of the Woman Novelist*, pp. 187–92; Dale Spender, *Mothers of the Novel: 100 Good Women Writers before Jane Austen* (London: Pandora, 1986), pp. 194–205; Todd, *The Sign of Angellica*, pp. 152–60; and Leland E. Warren, "Of the Conversation of Women: *The Female Quixote* and the Dream of Perfection," *Studies in Eighteenth-Century Culture* 11 (1982): 367–80.

fact that has not generally been noticed; indeed, most commentators take her to be resisting reality. To be sure, Lennox, like Cervantes, implicitly announces that the "realism" of her own book is superior to that of the romances her heroine has read and is trying to relive. This denigration of romance and promotion of realism has seemed to many critics an attack on fiction in general. In the best of these analyses, Laurie Langbauer contends that Lennox equates romance and fiction and that Arabella "is the ideal [fiction] reader, completely given over to the sway of the text, attesting to the power of romance."[66] Langbauer argues that Lennox's novel tries to dissociate itself from its own fictiveness by attributing it to romance, making romance Arabella's disease, and then curing her of it. She argues further that the novel fails in this project, that "romance" and "novel" ultimately become indistinguishable, and that their final similarity signals "the powerful, subversive forces not just of one genre, romance, but of all writing."[67] Langbauer clinches her argument by pointing out that when Arabella learns romances are "senseless fictions," she gets married and the story ends. Patriarchal reality is thus all along what Arabella has resisted, and romance (read fiction) was her method of resistance.

Langbauer's argument (superficially plausible and useful as it is for launching a detailed description of *The Female Quixote*'s formal traits, stylistic impulses, and interweaving of the issues of gender and genre) nevertheless proceeds from questionable assumptions: that the novel as a genre tries to hide its fictionality; that its realism amounts to a naive claim on the real; that it wants its reader to be like Arabella, to imagine that the persons and incidents had, or have, specific extra-textual referents. Langbauer states the argument in even more general terms: novels typify "phallogocentric" writings of all kinds, which are forever attempting to hide the marks of their textuality. Since Langbauer begins with these ideas, the dependence of the novel on the romance (the explicitly fictional, the excessively textual) in *The Female Quixote* appears to her a hidden code revealing female subversion of the male order of representation.

But if one believes, on the contrary, that the novel is explicitly

66. Langbauer, *Women and Romance*, p. 65.
67. *Women and Romance*, p. 30.

the story of nobody in particular, one might argue that the romance-novel connection, far from subversively exploding the book's surface "reality," simply signals the kind of fiction being read. The reader who did not notice that the engine of the plot is Arabella's determination to translate the mundane events of her life into romance adventures would be unable to comprehend the book as, in Henry Fielding's phrase, "a *regular* story"[68] or, in Johnson's terms, "a comic romance"; that is to say, she would be unable to recognize it as a satirical novel if she missed its structural dependence on the parodied form of romance. The difference between Arabella and the novel reader, the reader of *The Female Quixote*, is that Arabella does not know she is reading fiction and, as we have already seen, does not value fiction per se, whereas the reader of this book can register that she is reading a satire, can get the jokes, only by understanding that she is reading a fiction. The reader's superiority, therefore, lies in a superior grasp of reality that proceeds entirely from an awareness of fiction. This is the awareness Arabella herself resists but that the novel and the novel reader, far from repressing, acknowledge at the outset.

The satirical nature of this novel, therefore, ensures that no contrast between fiction and realism is possible; rather, the contrast, unstable as it is, holds between fantastic and realistic fiction.[69] For *The Female Quixote* cannot define its fictional characteristics without promoting its realism. Most obviously, as its earliest commenders noted, it aims for a high level of what we now call "novelistic" probability.[70] Fielding, for example, praised it for avoiding the incredibility that Cervantes's *Don Quixote* indulged:

> [*Don Quixote*] in many Instances, approaches very near to the Romances which he ridicules. Such are the Stories of Cardenio and

68. *The Covent Garden Journal*, no. 24 (March 24, 1752); rpt. in *The Covent Garden Journal* by Sir Alexander Drawcansir, Knt. Censor of Great Britain, ed. Gerard Edward Jensen, vol. 1 (New Haven, CT: Yale Univ. Press, 1915), p. 281.

69. James J. Lynch makes this argument in "Romance and Realism in Charlotte Lennox's *The Female Quixote*." He claims that the novel enacts and celebrates the conversion of romance conventions into those of the sentimental, rather than the realistic, novel. For another look at the novel's use of "romance elements" and its departure from "realism," see Deborah Ross, "Mirror, Mirror: The Didactic Dilemma of *The Female Quixote*."

70. For a full discussion of the paradoxical relationship between probability and fictionality, see Robert Newsom, *A Likely Story: Probability and Play in Fiction* (New Brunswick, NJ: Rutgers Univ. Press, 1988).

> Dorothea, Ferdinand and Lucinda, &c. In the [*Female Quixote*] their
> [*sic*] is nothing except the Absurdities of the Heroine herself, which
> is carried beyond Common-Life; nor is there any thing even in her
> Character, which the Brain a little distempered may not account for.[71]

For Fielding, the work's high level of probability makes it satirically self-consistent: that is, artful.

The "realism" of this book is not a suppression of fiction but rather a sign that fiction is to be taken for granted; *The Female Quixote* shares with other early novels the attempt to make fiction that which goes without saying. Hence the evidence that could be adduced for fiction's suppression in novels, the apparent lack of reflective self-consciousness, can also be construed as proof of fiction's *givenness* in the form.

The "good divine," the "doctor" who cures Arabella of her resistance during the episode discussed earlier in this chapter, points out that probability and illusionistic realism, in contrast to the romance's "self-evident" absurdity, mark "the Perfection of Fiction" (p. 378). The task of the early novel is to establish fiction as the ground of the reading experience without constantly calling attention to it. The novel places itself on a suppositional ontological plane, where "credit" is only solicited conditionally, on the revived Aristotelian terms not of "belief" but of "suspended *dis*belief." The contract between writer and reader implicit in the very conventions of realism specifies that the reader is to believe the story *as fiction*, to grant a conditional assent, to "lend" herself, as Hume put it, for the period of reading, or as long as the writer keeps the story plausible by "delighting the Imagination without shocking the Judgment."[72] The doctor of *The Female Quixote*, as if glossing this phrase from Lennox's *Shakespeare Illustrated*, specifies the writer's stake in this contract, his or her "expense of invention":

> [T]here can be no Difficulty in framing a Tale, if we are left at Liberty
> to invert all History and Nature for our own Conveniency. When a
> Crime is to be concealed, it is easy to cover it with an imaginary
> Wood. When Virtue is to be rewarded, a Nation with a new Name
> may, without any Expence of Invention, raise her to the Throne.
> When *Ariosto* was told of the Magnificence of his Palaces, he an-
> swered, that the Cost of poetical Architecture was very little; and

71. Newsom, p. 281.
72. *Shakespeare Illustrated*, p. v.

still less is the Cost of Building without Art, than without Materials.
(p. 378)

The probability of an invention is thus the sign of the author's expense of art. There is, then, simply no way to tell the difference between fiction's self-effacement (art) and its fulfillment (art).

As the doctor's words emphasize, Arabella, in resisting fiction, refuses to recognize Authorship, the achievement of "costly," plausible inventions; hence, contrary to Langbauer's assertion, she is not the sort of reader a novelist would desire. To appreciate the new form, the reader had first of all to understand what it was. Arabella's spiritual doctor speaks here in the voice of the Author who must teach the naive reader to recognize and thus properly value the "utmost Effort of the human Mind": the invention of a believable fiction. Such speeches are appropriate to early novels, for the writers of the first genre to mark itself "fiction" had to teach their readers to presuppose and appreciate fictionality, to tell cheap from costly inventions. But this was not an easy task, for the more costly, or artful, the novel, the more the fictionality was supposed to permeate it as the realistic illusion that should have gone unremarked.

Hence the usefulness of the quixotic tale, in which romance served not only as the satirical object but also as the pretext for a metafictional discourse. Such tales allowed for the thematization of fiction without undermining that plausibility which the tale itself denominated the perfection of fiction. Although the romance does, as Langbauer points out, bear the thematic burden of untruth in *The Female Quixote*, its purpose is not to disencumber the novel of the "unreal" but to allow for the new form's self-presentation as the regulation and explicit fulfillment of what had previously been an unruly because *unacknowledged* practice. The Quixote's cure begins not with the renunciation but with the acknowledgment of fiction.

It follows from these observations, however, that in curing Arabella of her resistance to fiction, *The Female Quixote* suggests incompatible views of its own novelty: first, it reveals its participation in the invention of fiction as an explicit category of narrative, thereby acknowledging that fiction was only then in the process of coming into self-conscious being; and second, it pretends to explore the history of fiction, thereby implying that fiction had been around for centuries, just waiting to be recognized. We might, then, agree with Langbauer that the novel deliberately regulates the category of "fiction," but we would have to add that it simultaneously purports to be inventing the category. The critical commonplace—that the novel endeavors to chastise and control fiction—is undeniable, but to conclude that this regulative ethos implies separation from, or ambivalence about, fiction is mistaken. We fall into this mistake frequently because we naively credit only one of *The Female Quixote*'s artful inventions: the story that there was a *fictional* form called romance, which existed prior to the novel's identification of it as its *own* errant ancestor. We ignore the novel's simultaneous, but subtler, claim to be originating the very concept of fiction. Arabella, we should remember, has to learn that there is such a thing—a species of writing that does not "claim to be credited" (p. 376)—so that she can understand why romance is an old, surpassed, imperfect version of it. Inventing fiction and identifying its history, learning to take it for granted and engaging in a metadiscourse about it are equally necessary to her new sanity.

Moreover, once we see that Arabella's sanity lies in her acceptance of fiction, we can get a full view of the novel's generic play, which provides additional evidence that romance is not simply its despised generic scapegoat. Bringing Arabella to sanity was certainly a process of sanitizing the genre of the novel by presenting it as fresh and regular, as well as candid and lucid about its ontological status. By incorporating romance as its explicitly transcended history, furthermore, the novel sanitizes itself in a less obvious way: it creates what we might call a generic "screen memory" of its own absurd early romantic distempers in order to conceal its truly *scandalous* history. *The Female Quixote* makes the novel's dependence on, and close historical alliance with, romance as obvious as possible, insisting on binding the two genres together with the thread of "fiction," in order to make a clean break between the novel and its more immediate "ancestor," the scandalous chronicle. Watching early "realistic novels" confess to, and thereby purge, the peccadilloes of the romance is so "diverting," to use one of Lennox's favorite words, that we forget a fundamental fact: in the early eighteenth century the scandal of the novel was not "nonsensical fiction" but *scandal*.

Eighteenth-century readers noticed that there was a gap in *The*

Female Quixote's tacit history of its own form. Fielding, for example, who always avoided the word "novel" for his own stories and was every bit as solicitous as Lennox to find innocent, fictional, and satirizable ancestors, "cannot omit observing, that . . . the Humour of Romance, which is principally ridiculed in this work, [is] not at present greatly in fashion in this Kingdom."[73] And in 1785, Clara Reeve remarked that *The Female Quixote* "came some thirty or forty years too late. . . . Romances at this time were quite out of fashion, and the press groaned under the weight of Novels, which sprung up like Mushrooms every year."[74] In their discussions of Lennox, neither Fielding nor Reeve specifies just what characterized the "novel" fungus. Elsewhere, however, Fielding does refer explicitly to "the modern novel and Atalantis writers" in the very act of claiming that he has never read them,[75] and Clara Reeve names "Mrs. Behn, Mrs. Manly and Mrs. Heywood" as the writers who dominated popular narrative after the heroic romance and before the realistic novel. As one modern critic has pointed out, the *chroniques scandaleuses* of these writers used "the lofty diction of romance . . . only to heighten the salacious appeal" of "slander and vice," so that "the rhetoric of romance, still genuinely idealistic in La Calprenède, Mlle. de Scudéry, and others, came to be associated with scenes of illicit sexuality."[76] Scandal, therefore, would itself have been understood by contemporary readers as a parody of romance. In writing an explicitly fictional romance parody, Lennox was not only foreshortening the history of the novel to emphasize its innocence but also placing her book in a competitive, antagonistic relationship to the libelous parodies. Hence, although we are diverted from noting that scandal is an eligible forebear of the book we are reading, we are encouraged to note that it dominates the discourse of the novel's despised "fashionable world."

Scandal, therefore, is certainly not absent from *The Female Quixote;* indeed, it is the mode of storytelling that the novel most often contrasts to romance. The contrast, moreover, generally consists in

73. *Covent Garden Journal*, p. 282.
74. *The Progress of Romance* (London, 1785; rpt. New York: Facsimile Text Society, 1930), vol. 2, p. 7.
75. *Joseph Andrews*, ed. Martin C. Battestin (Middletown, CT: Wesleyan Univ. Press, 1967), book 3, chapter 1, p. 187.
76. Dieter Schultz, "'Novel,' 'Romance,' and Popular Fiction in the First Half of the Eighteenth Century," *Studies in Philology* 70 (January 1973): 80 and 90.

ironic inversions that trace the fall of "the lofty diction of romance" from "genuine idealism" into the low service of "vice and slander." One of the book's oft-repeated jokes is its play on the word "adventure," by which Arabella means the high-heroic actions of ladies in defense of their honor and all the other characters mean illicit sexual affairs. Hence, when Arabella asks the women she encounters to relate "adventures," they imagine she is soliciting scandal or accusing them of behaving improperly. Trying to begin an intimacy with her fashionable cousin, Charlotte Glanville, for example, Arabella asks,

> Whence comes it, Cousin, . . . being so young and lovely as you are, that you, questionless, have been engaged in many Adventures, you have never reposed Trust enough in me to favour me with a Recital of them?
>
> Engaged in many Adventures, madam! returned Miss *Glanville*, not liking the Phrase: I believe I have been engaged in as few as your Ladyship.
>
> You are too obliging, returned *Arabella*, who mistook what she said for a Compliment; for since you have more Beauty than I, and have also had more Opportunities of making youself beloved, questionless you have a greater Number of Admirers.
>
> As for Admirers, said Miss *Charlotte*, bridling, I fancy I have had my Share! . . . [B]ut, I assure you, Madam, I have had no Adventures, as you call them, with any of them.
>
> No, really? interrupted *Arabella*, innocently.

Arabella "innocently" goes on to explain that many heroines have been "run away with," citing Scudéry's Mandane (heroine of *The Grand Cyrus*), whom Charlotte takes to be a notorious contemporary and "a *Jew*, by her outlandish Name." Charlotte, moreover, persists in hearing Arabella's chivalric jargon as the language of scandal when the subject of "favours" is raised; Arabella is speaking of the trinkets (scarves, and so forth) that a lady might give her champion, whereas Charlotte takes the word to mean sexual commerce: "You have made no Scruple to own, Madam, said [Miss Glanville], that you think me capable of granting Favours to Lovers, when, Heaven knows, I never granted a Kiss without a great deal of Confusion." Now it is Arabella's turn to be shocked: "I never injured you so much in my Thoughts, as to suppose you ever granted a Favour of so criminal a Nature." And Charlotte is all the more convinced that her cousin has only been trying to verify some scandalous gossip she's heard: "All you have said in vindication of granting Favours, was only to draw me into a Confession of what I have done: How ungenerous was that! (pp. 87–89).

Such comic confusions rest on the knowledge that the euphemistic and ironic language of scandal had changed the meaning of key romantic terms, and that one could no longer hear the rhetoric of romance without construing it as a slanderous jest. Arabella alone, having never lived in the "world," is innocent of the newer genre. Almost all her quixotic mistakes about women proceed from her ignorance of scandal; having elicited a recital of Miss Groves's "adventures," for example, she swiftly reformulates the story according to romantic conventions, leaving the woman who supplied her with the material (who expected to be paid for her trouble) to reflect that her ladyship "seemed so little sensible of the Pleasure of Scandal, as to be wholly ignorant of its nature; and not to know it when it was told her" (p. 77).

The novel's regulation of romance itself necessitates the recognition and rejection of scandal; Arabella must learn to "know it when it [is] told her," and yet remain "so little sensible of [its] Pleasure." Only then will she quit asking to hear the stories of real people. Hence we are given an episode that becomes a discourse on scandal, which precedes and parallels the discourse on fiction. Wishing to engage in "innocent Amusement" at a Bath assembly, Arabella asks Mr. Tinsel to tell her "the Adventures of many Persons whom they were viewing." A notorious scandalmonger, Tinsel is happy to oblige and is only slightly put off when Arabella tries to gather a little audience in imitation of the scenes of interpolated storytelling in the heroic romances, where "Kings, Princes, and Commanders of Armies, thought it was no Waste of their Time . . . to listen many Hours to the Relation of one single History" (p. 274). Mr. Tinsel, momentarily overawed and confused by "the Solemnity with which she requested his Information," finally gives a series of vignettes in exactly the style of *The New Atalantis*, with its insistent deictics ("That Lady was for many Years the Mistress of a young military Nobleman . . . this same haughty Peer"; "Observe that gay, splendid lady"; "one of our great Sea Commanders . . . happen'd to lodge at this Inn"; "Such was the Origin of this fantastick Lady") and rhetorical questions stressing the difference between appearance and reality ("Would one not imagine . . . this fine Lady was a Person of very exalted Rank?" [pp. 275–76.]).

In her disappointment at these short and unedifying portraits, Arabella blurts out the standard definition of scandal: "I know not what to make of the Histories he has been relating. I think they do not deserve that Name, and are rather detached Pieces of Satire on particular Persons, than a serious Relation of Facts" (p. 276). Finally Arabella knows scandal, and explicitly dismisses it for being generally inapplicable ("The Ugliness of Vice . . . ought only to be represented to the Vicious") and in itself blameworthy ("that very Inclination . . . to hear other Peoples Faults, may by those very People, be condemned as one, and afford them the same Kind of ill-natur'd Pleasure you are so desirous of"). With this pronouncement that to seek scandal is to be scandalous, that even to learn from it is to admit one's viciousness, the novel not only chastises but also repels the reader of the *chronique scandaleuse*. The guilty reader is not she who aspires to romance, only wanting to hear "something which may at once improve and delight me; something which may excite my Admiration, engage my Esteem, or influence my Practice,"[77] but rather she who is amused with the emotionally and narratively "detached" relation of "other Peoples Faults." It is the scandalmonger, dealing in "other people's" stories and expecting "to be credited," who serves as the novelist's negative double, not the innocent romance writer, who was merely insufficiently attentive to the distinction between history and fiction.

It is, therefore, a rival genre with a claim on the "real"—scandal—that is disclaimed by the early novelist in the process of owning and regulating fiction. Now that these generic distinctions, connections, and contrasts have been sorted out and we can consequently see that Arabella must both suppress her "impertinent" curiosity about real people and accept the existence of fiction, we can return to my question how such lessons about literary genre make Arabella willing to wed.

77. For a closer look at the competition between writers who followed the "idealistic" practice of the seventeenth-century romancers and those who debased the form into scandal in the 1730s, see William H. McBurney, "Edmund Curll, Mrs. Jane Barker, and the English Novel," *Philological Quarterly* 37 (October 1958): 385–99.

As several critics have noted, Arabella resists marriage because she is busy being true to her books. Her quixotism, like that of her prototype, consists in attempting to prove that the heroic romances are true by living them. Her attempt arises, however, not out of an unquestioning faith in the resemblance between the order of the world and the order of language,[78] but out of the perception of a dissimilarity between the two that might be called internal to reading—a contradiction between what she reads and the fact that she is *reading* it. Arabella, we are told, reads romances because she is "wholly secluded from the World." Consulting her mirror, she sees the same dazzling beauty she has read about, but consulting her experience, she notes a potentially humiliating discrepancy: "[S]he could not comprehend, how any Solitude could be obscure enough to conceal a Beauty like hers from Notice; and thought the Reputation of her Charms sufficient to bring a Crowd of Adorers to demand her of her Father" (pp. 7–8). Her solitude, the very condition that immerses her in romance reading, is rendered incomprehensible by that activity; that Arabella has so much time to read unmolested in itself refutes either what the books *say* or her narcissistic belief that what they say is applicable to *her* life. Since having time and privacy enough to read the books necessarily calls either their truth or their pertinence into question, Arabella's story begins with the irreparable gap that reading itself has made between existence (solitary reading) and its representation (a crowd of suitors).

Although this gap is too fundamental to be ignored, Arabella attempts to overcome it, most obviously by imagining that she is in fact already besieged by lovers (gardeners, casual visitors to the neighborhood) in disguise who are too deferential or deceitful to declare themselves. Hence the gap between what she reads and the fact that she is reading is only apparent. However, when her cousin appears and openly asks her to marry him, her expedient for protecting the truth of the books collapses: if suitors behaved like her cousin, she would never have had any time for reading. He insists on interrupting her solitude and telling her he loves her: "What a horrid Violation this," reflects Arabella, "of all the Laws of

78. See Foucault's discussion of *Don Quixote* in *The Order of Things* (New York: Vintage, 1970), pp. 46–50.

Gallantry and Respect, which decree a Lover to suffer whole Years in Silence" (p. 32). By breaking silence, young Glanville threatens to open the gap in the reading that Arabella had papered over by assuring herself her lovers were there but afraid to call attention to themselves. Thus, to protect the integrity of her reading and her own narcissistic investment in it, Arabella endeavors to live out her youth without ever actually *hearing* a marriage proposal.

She has, moreover, another, subtler, way of avoiding the paradox of reading; she places the romances in an eternal realm, denying the time and effort spent in reading them by expecting everyone she meets to know them perfectly. She behaves as if the books must be universally known, always already read, so that she can forget the fact that calls their "reality" into question: that she, a heroine, has unaccountably been allowed to spend most of her life reading them. Quite a bit of the book's humor turns on Arabella's ridiculous insistence that the romances can be taken for granted: she finds it "inconceivable" that the seamstress she asks to make her a dress in the style of the Princess Julia requires any further directions, and her conversation consists in lengthy glosses on the lives of heroines (always delivered as if the facts were common knowledge) that integrate her auditors' signs of puzzlement or impatience as alternative interpretations. She is generally mortified when she has to tell the stories or refer to the actual books, for such references to their textuality open the gap between the stories and their reading that threatens her role as heroine.

As readers, however, we are never allowed to forget the textuality of the romances. Every time Arabella opens her mouth, we are reminded that she read them "not in the original *French*, but very bad Translations" (p. 7); midway between French and English, her language takes on the ridiculous opacity of *doubled* textuality,[79] which is then comically intensified when her maid tries, as instructed, to repeat her speeches word for word.[80] The more Arabella

---

79. Dorothy Osborne objected to these translations: "I mett with Polexandre and L'Illustre Bassa, both soe disguised that I who am theire old acquaintance hardly knew them, besydes that they were still soe much french in words and Phrases that twas impossible for one that understood not french to make any thing of them" (*The Letters of Dorothy Osborne to William Temple*, ed. G. C. Moore Smith [Oxford: Clarendon Press, 1928], p. 91).

80. "[T]ell him . . . All the Blood in his Body is too little to wash away his Guilt,

tries to suppress the textuality of the romances by actually using their language, the more it asserts itself in the density of puns and other linguistic anomalies.

Early in her relationship with Glanville, Arabella's two strategies for suppressing the gap in reading come into conflict. In an uncharacteristic moment of lucidity, she realizes that her suitor-cousin's deviations from heroic behavior stem from ignorance rather than depravity, and she steps out of her role to call for the scripts that will enforce his silence. But doing this just raises the problem of the reading *experience:*

> For heaven sake, Cousin, [Arabella exclaims,] how have you spent your Time; and to what Studies have you devoted all your Hours, that you could find none to spare for the Perusal of Books from which all useful Knowledge may be drawn; which give us the most shining Examples of Generosity, Courage, Virtue, and Love; which regulate our Actions, form our Manners, [and so forth]? (p. 48)

It soon becomes clear, though, as Glanville confronts the formidable material reality of the romances (the ten volumes of *The Grand Cyrus* alone ran to fifteen thousand pages), that his "spare" time will be insufficient to the task.

> *Arabella* having ordered one of her Women to bring *Cleopatra, Cassandra, Clelia,* and the Grand *Cyrus,* from her Library, *Glanville* no sooner saw the Girl return, sinking under the Weight of those voluminous Romances, but he began to tremble at the Apprehension of his Cousin laying her Commands upon him to read them; and repented of his Complaisance, which exposed him to the cruel Necessity of performing what to him appeared an *Herculean* Labour, or else incurring her Anger by his Refusal. (p. 49)

The episode goes on to stress the opposition between reading and being a romance hero by emphasizing that Glanville's heroic service will be purely textual. He fails in his "Herculean Labour" of reading the prescribed passages (he is preoccupied with Arabella), but he redeems himself by saving these very volumes from destruction at the hands of his uncle, who, enraged at Arabella's refusal of her

---

or to pacify my Indignation" comes out "something about washing in Blood, and you must . . . not appear before the Nation" (p. 350).

cousin, decides to burn the books. The narrator gleefully emphasizes the gap between the textual and heroic:

> [Her father] went out of the Room, leaving her to bewail the Fate of
> so many illustrious Heroes and Heroines, who, by an Effect of a
> more cruel Tyranny than any they had ever experienced before, were
> going to be cast into the merciless Flames; which would, doubtless,
> pay very little Regard to the divine Beauties of the admirable *Clelia,*
> or the heroic Valour of the brave *Orontes;* and the rest of those great
> Princes and Princesses, whose Actions *Arabella* proposed for the
> Model of hers. (p. 55)

In restoring the books, Glanville continues in the same solemn
style: "Assuming . . . a Countenance as sad as he was able, he laid
the Books before her; and told her, he hoped she would excuse his
coming into her Presence without her Permission, since it was only
to restore her those Books, whose Loss she seemed so greatly to
lament" (p. 56). Literal service to the romances can only be mock-
heroic; thus by returning them to Arabella as books, Glanville
reasserts the paradox they contain.[81]

The textuality of the romance—that they must have been read,
that they had to have been written—repeatedly disturbs Arabella,
for it renders the books "historical" in ways that threaten their
"truth." Although she considers them true histories, their truth
does not derive simply from their factuality, from their happening
to have occurred at some time in the past. As Arabella repeatedly
explains, they are peculiarly true because they explain "the Nature
of Things" (p. 320), which is necessarily unchangeable: "Custom
. . . cannot possibly change the Nature of Virtue or Vice: And since
Virtue is the chief Characteristic of a Hero, a Hero in the last Age
will be a Hero in this" (p. 328). Indeed, one of Arabella's most
exasperating traits is the ease with which she converts signs of
textuality into signs of its transcendence. She is not bothered when
the heroines seem always to be eighteen years old, no matter how
many years the narration is supposed to encompass, or when
heroes live or die at the mere command of the heroine. The capacity

---

81. The entire episode, moreover, signals that the book we are reading, unlike
the romance, is not at all threatened by its own textuality, for it is the episode in the
novel that is derived most explicitly from *Don Quixote.*

for perpetual stasis as well as the dependence of being on merely linguistic acts (the novel's most frequent joke) clearly indicate to all the other characters in *The Female Quixote* that the romances are mere fictions: that the characters have no existence apart from the printed page, where they might be forever the same or just as easily drop out of existence at a word. But for Arabella these very "absurdities" constitute the hyper-reality of the stories and characters: "The Empire of Love, said she, like the Empire of Honour, is govern'd by Laws of its own, which have no Dependence upon, or Relation to any other" (p. 320). She concludes that the reality "which . . . may be collected from all the Words and Actions of . . . Heroes" is simply more real than changeable everyday life. Note that she does not speak of "collecting" "the Words and Actions of the Heroes" from books, but rather of collecting "the Nature of Things" and the "independent Sovereignty" of the romantic code of love and honor from the "Words and Actions of the Heroes." For Arabella, the textuality of the romances threatens to demote them to the historically contingent, whereas it is her task to establish them, as well as herself, as historical exempla of the eternally real. Hence she both disguises the nature of her "collecting" (reading) and turns the very signs of the romances' status as written representations into signs of their "independent Sovereignty."

Suppressing both the historical nature of the books and her own temporal being, therefore, keeps the gap internal to reading (between "the Nature of Things" and the actual process through which one knows it) from emerging and threatening Arabella with the possibility of change. Absolute stasis is what her "fidelity" to the books achieves. She cannot hear the legitimate proposal of a suitor, cannot enter the world of courtship and marriage, because to do so would be to admit that there was a time when she did not have suitors and a time when she would cease to be a heroine. All proposals are considered already accomplished and infinitely deferred, just as all stories are imagined to be already told and are *consequently* forever repeated. Convinced that one Mr. Selvin is desperately in love with her but refuses to admit it, indeed denies it, to escape being banished from her presence (denial being an even more transparent sign of love than silence), Arabella commands him to leave the country:

[Y]ou know *Thrasimedes* fell upon the same Strategem [denying his love] to no Purpose. The rigid *Udosia* saw thro' the Disguise, and would not dispense with . . . banishing him from *Rome*, as I do you from *England*—

How, Madam! . . . Pray, how does my staying in *England* affect your Ladyship's Glory?

To answer your Question with another, said Arabella, Pray how did the Stay of *Thrasimedes* in *Rome*, affect the Glory of the Empress *Udosia*?

Mr. *Selvin* was struck dumb with this Speech, for he was not willing to be thought so deficient in the Knowledge of History, as not to be acquainted with the Reasons why *Thrasimedes* should not stay in *Rome*. (pp. 312–13)

The satire here is directed at Selvin, the ignorant man pretending a knowledge of history, who cannot refute Arabella's argument because he does not understand the nature of the books from which her information comes. Because Arabella and Selvin himself both think that he should know the story of Thrasimedes and Udosia, he cannot question its relevance, and Arabella's belief in the universal force of the stories is confirmed. The complete identity of Arabella and Udosia, Selvin and Thrasimedes, Rome and England, their existence on a single ontological and atemporal plane as mere instances of the "Nature of Things," ensures that nothing can actually happen in Arabella's life. Thus a certain naive reverence for "History" verifies her belief in the timelessness of reality and comically delays a comic resolution. All the young men Arabella encounters will be silenced; all will be, to use her favorite word, "questionless."

Only in this way can Arabella close the gap opened up in the very experience of reading the romances, a gap she experiences as a wound to her "Glory." To fill it she denies time, change, and textuality: she has always had lovers; the romances are always already read. Therefore, the first step in curing Arabella and making her willing to marry is to focus her attention on the books as books, as printed works that were written at a particular time and place. Before the stories can be recognized as fictions, their textuality must be established. In the concluding conversation between Arabella and the "doctor," Arabella blunders into the admission that she has read "these books" and begins a discussion of them as books (p. 374). Indeed, in defending herself against the implications of the doctor's claim that such "senseless fictions . . . vitiate the Mind, and Pervert the understanding," she even makes a clear distinction between the romances and herself as their reader; she censures the "License of [the doctor's] Language, which glances from the Books upon the Readers." Of course, it was Arabella, sitting before the mirror in the opening chapter, who literally glanced from the book to its reader and thereby made the narcissistic identification that opened the gap in reading. In acknowledging that she has read the books, Arabella breaks her identification with them, and it is then an easy matter for the doctor to call their truth into question by interrogating the historical conditions of their production: "Your Ladyship knows, I suppose to what Authors these Writings are ascrib'd? . . . And at what Distance, Madam, are the Facts related in them from the Age of the Writer? . . . [B]y what accident . . . did it happen these Records and Monuments were kept universally secret to Mankind till the last Century?" (p. 375). The questions continue until Arabella admits that these stories, which have been demoted from timeless truths to historically produced texts, may indeed be fictional.

The concession to textuality allows for change, for Arabella's marriage to her cousin, and it is for this reason that marriage in *The Female Quixote* is so closely thematically entwined with novelistic fictionality, for both rely on imaginative excursions into the realm not of "the real" but of "the possible." Indeed, at the conclusion of this novel an ability to discern the merely possible is equated with rationality itself; the *form* of the dialogue between Arabella and the doctor, often condemned by critics as an antifictional surrender to the reality principle,[82] can actually be said to have a deep affinity with fiction and thus with the state of mind required for Arabella's marriage. The dialogue is insistently, aggressively, suppositional. It is a lesson in reasoning from grounds that are only provisionally credited; even to begin, Arabella has to promise to behave *as if* she were not a delicate young woman (p. 371). And the deeper the

---

82. See, for example, Lynch, "Romance and Realism in Charlotte Lennox's *The Female Quixote*," p. 61. A number of critics have commented upon the "patriarchal" nature of the concluding dialogue, including Langbauer, *Women and Romance*, p. 81; Patricia Meyer Spacks, "The Subtle Sophistry of Desire: Dr. Johnson and *The Female Quixote*," p. 534; and Leland E. Warren, "Of the Conversion of Women: *The Female Quixote* and the Dream of Perfection," pp. 377–78.

dialogue gets into the issue of fiction, the more it stresses the use of the suppositional: "You grant [the romances], Madam, to be fictions? Sir, interrupted *Arabella*, eagerly, you are again infringing the Laws of Disputation. You are not to confound a Supposition of which I allow you only the present Use, with an unlimited and irrevocable Concession" (pp. 375–76). Although Arabella here is still resisting fiction, she has already "eagerly" embraced the logic on which it is founded: that one can grant the "present use" of a supposition to which one does not attach "unlimited" credit, complete belief.

To "suppose," literally to "place under," is to lay a discursive foundation for a train of thought that need not itself, as the doctor says of fiction, "claim to be credited" (p. 376). This was the conditional state of mind into which eighteenth-century novel heroines were constantly being invited by the question "*Could* you love Mr. ———?" The question "*Do* you love?" could not be posed since a woman was not allowed to have sentiments before being asked. The first step in a marital exchange was thus the *pos*ing of the question about an emotional *poss*ibility. If we can allow ourselves, for a moment, to "glance from the books to the readers," we might speculate that fiction, simply as fiction, helped women reach this state of conditional emotional being by inviting readers to sympathize with characters because they were fictional and then requiring them to cease feeling the transferred emotions upon closing the book because, after all, characters are only fictional. Such a deliberate creation of emotional discontinuity allows for a separate dimension of affective life, one in which emotions were only "practiced," in which the feelings themselves take on the same suppositional, conjectural status as the "nobody" in whom they supposedly originate. Such emotional "practice" would have been especially important for women in an age when the new affective demands of family life came into conflict with the still prevalent belief that women were not to love before they were beloved. It is not, then, surprising that Arabella's practice of suppositional logic, her acknowledgment of fiction, and her acceptance of the match with her cousin should swiftly succeed each other.

By thus linking fiction and family formation, the novel makes the continuous succession of generations seem dependent on suppositional, textual interruptions of continuous female identity. To read a fiction knowingly (that is, sympathetically), it implies, is to seek that very discontinuity in the experience of reading and being that Arabella could not abide. As Johnson explains sympathy in the *Rambler*, it always entails a suspension of disbelief for a defined period; it is hence closely allied with the experience of textuality Arabella suppressed:

> All joy or sorrow for the happiness or calamities of others is produced by an act of the imagination, that realizes the event however ficti-tious, or approximates it however remote, by placing us, for a time, in the condition of him whose fortune we contemplate; so that we feel, while the deception lasts, whatever motions would be excited by the same good or evil happening to ourselves.[83]

For Johnson, the essence of sympathy is the "deception," lasting only *"for a time,"* that we are placed "in the condition" of another; sympathy simply *is* an illusion that comes to an end, and hence reading and ceasing to read novels, which are doubly illusionary because at once fictional and possible, would be particularly salient instances of the general experience of sympathizing. The tempo-rality of reading, its creation of the break in our experience of ourselves that Arabella dreaded and denied, becomes its own glory, and so does our very capacity for "lending" ourselves to an imagi-nary entity.

Like many early novels, *The Female Quixote* parodically represents naive reading as reading that does not know how to stop. One lesson to be learned from such satires is that naive identification is ultimately egotistical. This lesson is especially true in Arabella's case, since, as the doctor declares, "It is impossible to read [ro-mances] without lessening part of that Humility, which by preserv-ing in us a Sense of our Alliance with all human nature, keeps us awake to Tenderness and Sympathy, or without impairing that Compassion which is implanted in us" (p. 381). That is, Arabella's identification with the heroines limits her ability to sympathize with almost everyone else. But the subtler lesson is that Arabella's resistance to the fictionality of fiction gives her no practice in the various modes of having emotions, trying them out, holding them

83. *Rambler*, no. 60, pp. 318–19. For a thorough discussion of Johnson's concep-tions of empathy in reading, see Edward Tomarken, *Samuel Johnson on Shakespeare: The Discipline of Criticism* (Athens: Univ. of Georgia Press, 1991).

in a speculative, tentative, and above all temporary way, without making an "unlimited, irrevocable concession" to them.

Learning to hold and release nobody's sentiments by reading fiction, therefore, could easily have helped women conform their emotional lives to the exigencies of property exchange. The marriageable woman could then become an abstract variable, an emotional potential who occupied many different, but never quite "real," sentimental states in turn. To be sure, this process of temporarily de-realizing one's sentiments might also have been instrumental in shaping (or, more precisely, hollowing out) that generalized subject of exchange, the commercial mind. In the same number of the *Rambler* quoted above, Johnson intimates as much while remarking (in a Humean vein) on the difficulty of sympathy: "[T]he man whose faculties have been engrossed by business, and whose heart never fluttered but at the rise and fall of stocks, wonders how the attention can be seized, or the affections agitated by a tale of love."[84] Here the man of business and the feminine or feminized sentimental reader of love stories are juxtaposed in a way that reveals their abstract similarity: both hearts "flutter" to a set of signs that, although not personally addressed to them, seize and agitate them, inviting or discouraging an investment for a defined term. Each has entered that suppositional mental space where beings who are nobody in particular (the conglomerate shareholders' mind represented by the variation of numbers attached to a stock, and the fictional lovers) provisionally solicit identification. As readers, they both speculate.

The release into the culture of strongly marked overtly suppositional identities, belonging to nobody and hence temporarily appropriate to anybody, therefore, should be seen as one among many modes of facilitating property exchange and investment in the period, of creating the speculative, commercial and sentimental subject. But we should, nevertheless, recall the difference between the masculine and feminine versions of this subject. The commercial man is imagined to undergo spells of suppositional self-suspension in order to invest profitably and increase his property, but representations of property exchange involving women frequently stress that they lose whatever property they had previously owned.

84. Johnson, p. 391.

The Female Quixote is a case in point; as long as Arabella refuses fiction, resists the suppositional, she owns her estate, but when she capitulates to textuality, she becomes the vehicle through which the estate descends from her father to his chosen male heir, her cousin. When Arabella understands the books as mere representations, in other words, she understands her "real-life" function as a representation, as a means of transferring and preserving the property by giving herself away. Thus a woman's practice in sympathizing with nobody was a peculiarly fitting prelude to disposing of, rather than increasing, her own material substance.

~

When fiction was asserted to be at once a form of authorial property and nobody's story, when women were supposedly learning (through the very fictions the female author claimed as property and promoted as freely appropriable) to disclaim property, where did the married woman author stand in relation to her commodities? If fiction had its roots, as I have been arguing, in both the property claims of authors and the sentimental dispossession of women, then Charlotte Lennox, as a married woman author of fiction, was caught in a hopeless contradiction, at once asserting her author's right by her invention and recommending that women trade their property claims for sentimental identifications. But I wish to argue, in this concluding section, that the very contradictions in Lennox's career enable us to focus with peculiar intensity on the general paradoxes of authorial property in the period. Indeed, I hope to show that Lennox was something of an emblematic figure for her male contemporaries, a representation of deserving, dispossessed authorship, who resembled a fictional nobody in her availability for sympathetic appropriation.

In many ways, her situation was like that of other novelists. Since the normal condition of getting a novel published was selling the copyright, with no provision for royalties, the author was usually dispossessed of any legal claim to the text by the time it appeared in print. Moreover, since even quite popular novels were seldom reprinted after the lapse of the original fourteen-year copyright, few novelists could look forward to the resale of the copyright they were legally entitled to make. The Statute of Anne created the sense of a constantly elusive rightful property by giving the author the original copyright, a right that she had to alienate immediately since she normally could not afford to exercise it by printing her own work. Authors in general, we might say, were in the "feminized" position of perpetuating themselves only by renouncing their property.

Moreover, the consciousness of dispossession seems to have been increased by the temporariness of copyright, not only because novelists seldom struck a second bargain and thus felt mocked by the return of a right that had been drained of its marketability, but also because the law encouraged some writers to cherish hopes of bringing out profitable subscription editions of their earlier works. If copyright had been perpetual, if the law had allowed it to be an absolute property that could be alienated forever, Charlotte Lennox, for example, could never have made her repeatedly unsuccessful attempts to republish by subscription: first, an illustrated edition of The Female Quixote (proposals advertised in 1773–74); second, an edition of her collected works (proposals advertised in 1775); and third, a revised edition of Shakespeare Illustrated (proposals advertised in 1793). The proposals for these editions, as we saw earlier in the chapter, invited potential subscribers to help Lennox recoup the profits that should have been hers all along. Such language, not unusual in subscription proposals, contributed mightily to the pathos of authorship in the period. Because of its limited term, therefore, copyright was a commodity one was generally forced to alienate but one that did not simply go away; it regularly came back, and hence it haunted Lennox as an unrealizable potential that only gave her occasions for advertising her impotence.

Both women and authors in the period were frequently presented as doomed to dispossession: they were both identified with, indeed identified by, things that were no longer theirs. Moreover, the female author, especially the married female author, by being doubly dispossessed, could easily serve as a hyperbolic instance of authorial suffering. Charlotte Lennox's marriage seems to have put her in just this category. As we saw at the opening of the chapter, having a husband guaranteed her a certain respectability that allowed her to mix "innocently" in the society of literary London. But the shadowy Alexander Lennox who was employed by the printer William Strahan in 1747,[85] when he married Charlotte Ramsay, was generally understood to be a drain on her resources. Soliciting money from the Royal Literary Fund in 1793, she called him "a husband whose fortune I have made by the sacrifice of my own,"[86] "sacrifice" here probably referring to her decision to seek an office for her husband instead of a pension for herself when she was offered aid by the duke of Newcastle sometime in the early 1760s. According to a contemporary account, Newcastle proposed the pension, but she "very politely declined in favour of her husband, for whom she solicited a place, which the Duke promised to procure him at the first opportunity."[87] A 1760 letter to the duchess of Newcastle, quoted earlier in the chapter, provides additional verification for this story and indicates that Lennox expected her husband's place to free her from the drudgery of hack work:

> I have the comfort to hear from Mr. Stone that Your Grace continues Your favourable intentions with regard to Mr. Lennox, and this hope supports me in my present slavery to the Booksellers, whom I have the more mortification to see adding to their heaps by my labours, which scarce produce me a scanty and precarious subsistence.[88]

Her understanding that she had won her husband's place for him by years of literary labor was also implicit in her gesture of sending her works to the commissioner of customs just after the appointment was made, a gesture the commissioner seems to have considered somewhat indelicate:

> Sr. Wm. Musgrave makes his Compliments to Mrs. Lennox & is much obliged to her for the very agreable present of her writings which he accepts & values for their Intrinsic Merit—He is sorry she sho[uld] think any acknowledgements necessary for the little Distinctions which he may have had it in his power to shew Mr. Lennox

---

85. This information comes from Small, *Charlotte Ramsay Lennox*, p. 14. Alexander Lennox is not mentioned in J. A. Cochrane, *Dr. Johnson's Printer: The Life of William Strahan* (Cambridge: Harvard Univ. Press, 1964), so it is improbable that he held an important position at the printer's.

86. Quoted in Small, p. 59.

87. Anonymous, "Memoirs of Mrs. Lenox," *Edinburgh Weekly Magazine* 58 (October 9, 1783): 35.

88. Quoted in Small, p. 28.

& which are entirely due to the very good Character he has heard of him.[89]

In 1765, Lennox gave birth to a daughter, and there was a four-year gap in her publishing record, suggesting that in the first few years after receiving "the place of tidewaiter in the Customs"[90] her husband did actually support her. But correspondence from the late sixties and early seventies attests both that his income was inadequate and that his place had cost her more than the proffered pension. Known as a Newcastle placeman, Alexander seems to have become a liability in Charlotte Lennox's continuing efforts to obtain patronage from the "fine Ladys" of the new Bedford administration.[91] In the 1790s, the Lennoxes appear to have separated, and Charlotte was given only a small amount of the yearly income she had obtained for her husband. In the last years of her life (1803–04), her husband dead, she became the first regular pensioner of the Royal Literary Fund, which had been established to assist worthy but impecunious authors.[92]

To her contemporaries, therefore, Lennox seemed to have been doubly dispossessed, prevented by both the conditions of the marketplace and the parasitism of her husband from receiving the just rewards of her authorship. Of course, even if Alexander had been frugal and industrious, Charlotte Lennox's properties would

89. Sir William Musgrave to Mrs. Charlotte Lennox, Wednesday, June 5, 1765, published in "The Lennox Collection," ed. Duncan Isles, *Harvard Library Bulletin* 19 (January 1971): 56–57, item 23.

90. Quoted by Duncan Isles in his discussion of these arrangements in "The Lennox Collection," p. 59 n. 121, item 24.

91. In a 1769 letter responding to Lennox's apparent request for advice about dedicating a "performance" of *The Sisters* to a "great personage," James Murray wrote, "My Wife [Countess Gower's sister] has no Interest, for the same reason that the protection of a Noble Lord was withdrawn from you /viz:/ on account of Mr. Lennox having got a Place from the late Duke of Newcastle so all I can say is, that when your performance is to [be] Acted, I shall with pleasure attend it, with as many of my acquaintances as I can prevail upon to go & I most sincerely wish it may meet with the most favourable Reception. . . ." Duncan Isles suggests that Lennox was planning to dedicate a subscription publication of *The Sisters* to the unnamed "great personage," but he uses the word "performance" for both the thing to be dedicated and Mrs. Lennox's benefit night, indicating that the scheme was to get a large sum of money out of an individual who would preside over the third night in a special manner. James Murray to Charlotte Lennox, Wednesday, February 8, 1769, in "The Lennox Collection," pp. 57–60, item 24.

92. Nigel Cross, *The Common Writer: Life in Nineteenth-Century Grub Street* (Cambridge: Cambridge Univ. Press, 1985), p. 170; Cross discusses the earnings of a variety of women writers in this period on pp. 168–74.

technically have been her husband's anyway; she would still, that is, have made his fortune at the expense of her own. She was conscious of this fact when she wrote to Johnson in 1777, announcing that "Mr. Lennox is so desirous of recovering his property out of the hands of the booksellers that he gives me leave to take any measures that shall be judged proper—it will be necessary to have the advice of some gentleman of the law."[93] The property of Mr. Lennox referred to here turns out to be the copyright of his wife's translation of the *Memoirs of Maximilian de Bethune, Duke of Sully*, a standard history, the "copy" of which was still quite valuable more than fourteen years after its original publication. Two previous pirated Scottish editions of the translation had no doubt already stimulated Charlotte Lennox's sense of economic injury. Another letter to Johnson in 1778 makes the situation clearer:

> I saw Mr. Dodsley yesterday, and he told me they had printed another edition of Sully's Memoirs—I apprehend they had no right to do this without my consent, it is more than fourteen years since that book was first published; and about a year ago, I offerd to give them my corrected copy for a reasonable consideration, which Dodsley in the name of the partners refusd—and now they have reprinted it without consulting me although by the late decision concerning literary property[94] the copy is mine.[95]

"The copy is mine" and therefore due for resale; when the booksellers refused to recompense the author for the second sale of her right, Mr. Lennox stepped in with a lawsuit to claim *his* property. Charlotte Lennox then briefly floated the idea of taking her corrected version to a printer and publishing it herself "in numbers":

> I have some reason to hope that I may have success by publishing it in this manner, as the purchase will be so much easier—but I must be speedy . . . it will be necessary I suppose to draw up a little address to the publick explaining my reasons for publishing Sully myself, and in this manner—this favour I earnestly entreat of you [Johnson].[96]

93. Letter reprinted in Small, *Charlotte Ramsay Lennox*, p. 50.
94. Lennox refers to the 1774 decision in the House of Lords against perpetual copyright.
95. Quoted in Small, p. 52.
96. Quoted in Small, p. 52.

Dodsley's partners thus stubbornly maintained their ownership of Charlotte Lennox's property, and against them Mr. Lennox asserted his ownership. Meanwhile, the author hoped for a rival self-published edition and asked Johnson, as usual, to impersonate her authorial voice and address the public, as he had so often before, in her name.

A compromise was finally reached with Dodsley,[97] but the conflict itself is instructive since it so neatly illustrates Lennox's double dispossession as well as the use she seems to have made of it. Lennox's property, when it was unjustly appropriated, could only be reclaimed as her husband's; direct access and control over what was acknowledged by common parlance to be "hers" was obstructed by two different arrangements of estrangement. When we add to this combination Lennox's notorious ne'er-do-well husband, we can begin to see how Charlotte Lennox became the center of a remarkable circle of (mostly male) collaborators and promoters. Her lack of full ownership of herself and her works seems to have multiplied her agents in literary London. The casual way in which she prevails on Johnson to "draw up a little address to the publick explaining my reasons" typifies Lennox's manner of distributing the tasks of her authorship. The publication of "The Lennox Collection" (letters to Lennox from her contemporaries) provides ample evidence of the collaborative nature of many of her productions. Richardson helped her revise *The Female Quixote* and partly negotiated the sale of the copy to Millar; Johnson also negotiated on her behalf, wrote the dedications to many of her works, and may have written the last chapter of *The Female Quixote*. *Shakespeare Illustrated* was assisted by Johnson and John Boyle, the earl of Orrery; both these men and a few others worked on her translation of Pierre Brumoy's *Théâtre des Grecs* (1760); she asked for Garrick's help in revising her plays; the eleven numbers of her *Lady's Magazine* (1760–61) were also by several hands; and in the 1790s we find James Boswell writing proposals for a subscription edition of *Shakespeare Illustrated*. If we include not only people who collaborated on the works but also those who championed her cause with booksellers, patrons, or the public, the list gets much longer. As the editor of

97. For an account of the compromise, see Bloom, *Samuel Johnson in Grub Street*, pp. 230–31.

the "The Lennox Collection" has remarked, "The most unusual aspect of these letters as a literary discovery is . . . that here we see so many eminent men of letters all writing to, and being engaged in the problems of one person—and a relatively obscure person at that."[98]

Lennox's relative obscurity and the extraordinary common exertion made on her behalf by "so many eminent men of letters" seem to me but two sides of the same coin. In dealing with her peers, Lennox frequently stressed her inability to own her works; and since they were never going to be completely hers, she seems to have had little compunction about asking others to share the labor of composing them. Writing to Garrick in 1768, for example, she presents her play, *The Sisters*, as a piece both originally inspired by her correspondent and completely open to his revision: "You will find that I have pursued a hint you gave me some years ago, which has furnished me with one of the most interesting incidents in the whole piece; you may depend upon it that every alteration, and amendment which you judge necessary, will be readily, and thankfully admitted."[99] Indeed, the script seems to have been literally open-ended: "I have not yet written the concluding lines, but that can be done, when the piece has received your corrections." Authorial collaboration, moreover, is to result not so much in a public success as in the collective patronage of her "friends": "[B]y accepting it you will . . . put it in the power of my friends to serve me, in a way which they have often wishd to serve me, and often recommended to me."[100] Lennox's authorship of the play is presented as her friends' idea: a convenient opportunity for them to rally around and pay her what they imagined somebody else (her husband or the booksellers) really owed. This is not to say that Charlotte Lennox was the only author in London who sought either collaboration or occasions, such as subscription editions or author's benefit performances, on which her friends might serve her. We may think of the "Age of Authorship" as a time when writers were individuated with biographies and dignified as proprietors, but the elusive nature of literary property that encouraged Lennox to rely

98. Duncan Isles, "Introduction to The Lennox Collection," *Harvard Library Bulletin* 18 (October 1970): 323.

99. Quoted in Small, p. 36.

100. Quoted in Small, p. 36.

on the kindness of friends, even as she insisted on her rights and complained of her dispossession, led many writers to ignore in practice the principles of authorial self-reliance they proclaimed. Did Lady Vane write the "Memoirs of a Lady of Quality" that occupy the center of *The Adventures of Peregrine Pickle*? Did Sarah Fielding help write chapters 4 and 5 of book 2 of *Joseph Andrews*? Did Johnson write the climactic penultimate chapter of *The Female Quixote*? That scholars continue to debate these questions attests to the general diffuseness of authorship in the period.

What does seem to distinguish "our Charlotte," as Johnson called her, was the skill with which she broadcast her dispossession and thereby invited the investment of time, labor, and money in her career. As an author, in other words, she functioned rather like one of her own fictional characters. Johnson, for example, was required to "stand in her place" whenever he impersonated her in a dedication or introductory address, and he is never more "the author of the *Female Quixote*" than when calling attention to some deficiency in her experience or being: "My *Sex*, my *Age*," he writes for her, "have not given me many Opportunities of mingling in the World."[101] The very lack he mentions here is the occasion for the sympathetic identification that motivates him to write the preface for her. He supplies her need both in the sense that he creates it as a part of her public persona and in the sense that he compensates for it by making it rhetorically effective. Lennox thus became a type of the author of the age in much the same way that nobody became everybody's common relative: by standing for a definitive lack of property. She was celebrated, sympathized with, puffed, pitied, and impersonated because she could never become her own person.

101. *Shakespeare Illustrated*, p. viii.

5

Nobody's Debt

Frances Burney's Universal Obligation

Frances Burney was only fifteen when she started writing to Nobody. Her first "private journal" (1768) begins,[1]

> To whom . . . *must* I dedicate my wonderful, surprising & interesting adventures?—to *whom* dare I reveal my private opinion of my nearest Relations? the secret thoughts of my dearest friends? my own hopes, fears, reflections & dislikes?—Nobody!
>
> To Nobody, then will I write my Journal! since To Nobody can I be wholly unreserved—to Nobody can I reveal every thought, every wish of my Heart, with the most unlimited confidence, the most unremitting sincerity to the end of my Life! For what chance, what accident can end my connections with Nobody? No secret can I conceal from No-body, & to No-body can I be ever unreserved. Disagreement cannot stop our affection, Time itself has no power to end our friendship. The love, the esteem I entertain for Nobody, Nobody's self has not power to destroy. From Nobody I have nothing to fear, ⟨the⟩[2] secrets sacred to friendship, Nobody will not reveal, when the affair is doubtful, Nobody will not look towards the side least favourable.
>
> . . . In your Breast my errors may create pity without exciting contempt; may raise your compassion, without eradicating your love. (1:1–2)

I quote this passage at length to demonstrate how the conceit, which seems at first merely to express Burney's intention of keeping her journal private, proceeds toward general social satire as the writer explores the linguistic paradox of a substantive that overtly

---

1. It was labeled "Old Juvenile private Journal No. 1" by Frances Burney d'Arblay when she edited it many years later. "Private Journal" distinguishes it from the many journal letters Burney wrote for distribution inside the family circle. It is published in *The Early Journals and Letters of Fanny Burney*, vol. 1, 1768–1773, ed. Lars E. Troide (Kingston and Montreal: McGill-Queen's Univ. Press, 1988). Subsequent quotations from this work are cited parenthetically in the text.

2. The editor of *Early Journals* uses angled brackets to indicate uncertain readings.

proclaims the nonexistence of its referent but nevertheless has all the grammatical functions of any proper noun. One can make Nobody the subject of a sentence, as if one were talking about anybody else, but to posit anything of Nobody is to deny that quality in everybody. To delineate Nobody's virtues ("From Nobody I have nothing to fear") is also to cast aspersions on everybody. To declare one's confidence in Nobody's perfect "compassion" is to make a terse joke out of the Humean puzzle discussed in the preceding chapter: sympathy flows most freely when one of the parties to it is nonexistent. Nobody, the juvenile Burney implies, is an especially necessary companion to all properly reserved young females; "to No-body can I be ever unreserved," she writes twice, with minor variations. And the more this necessity is insisted upon in the language of sentimental enthusiasm, the hollower that very language sounds and the more broadly applicable the satire becomes.

Burney's earliest extant writings thus link the ideas of private self-reflection and satire through witty play with the concept of Nobody. The concept, moreover, quickly suggests the idea of an explicitly fictional addressee, marking the easy transition between writing to and writing about Nobody. Since the reader is Nobody, anything can be supposed of her:

> I will suppose you, then, to be my best friend; tho' God forbid you ever should! my dearest companion—& a romantick Girl, for mere oddity may perhaps be more sincere—more *tender*—than if you were a friend [in] propria personae [*sic*]—in as much as imagination often exceeds reality. (1:2)

This move, however, is immediately identified as humorously reversible: "[B]ut why, permit me to ask, must a *female* be made Nobody? Ah! my dear, what were this world good for, *were* Nobody a female?" (1:2). Through the concept of Nobody, Burney clears a linguistic space that can be occupied by a suppositional being; but since this "romantick Girl" stands in the place of Nobody, she represents the very void that made room for her. Moreover, feminine reserve is so deeply implicated in this fiction-making process (by necessitating Nobody in the first place and then defining her ideal qualities),[3] that its reversibility facetiously threatens the very existence of the female.

---

3. Family and friends explicitly told Frances that her journal writing might be a

Nobody helped Burney reinvent the novel, and in this chapter I explore Nobody's social and economic conditions more fully in order to understand how she became so helpful and what sorts of inspiration she provided. First, I briefly outline Nobody's history and identify the gender, class, and literary characteristics that make the fictional Evelina, her intended readers, and her author all into Nobodies. Second, I discuss the Burney family's lack of independent social and economic substance, especially their reliance on both the literary marketplace and a widely ramified patronage network; this double dependence, strikingly figured in the division of literary labor between Frances Burney and her father, made the Burney family itself seem a phenomenon of representation in which the normal patriarchal order was sustained by fictions. Third, I explore the sense of placelessness and universal obligation that attended these circumstances, arguing that Burney's perception of ceaseless circulation and unpayable debt aroused the transcendent ethical aspirations, a new way of longing to be Nobody, that shaped her second novel, *Cecilia*, and that those very aspirations introduced moral self-criticism into the heart of the novel form.

Most of Burney's jokes about Nobody were very old by 1768, dating back at least to the *Odyssey*.[4] The early modern period in northern Europe saw the widespread use of the figure of Nobody in popular social satire, and the tradition lived on longer in England than anywhere else.[5] Richard Burton used the conceit in the *Anatomy of Melancholy* in ways that were typical of a late medieval and Renaissance tradition that would still be evident in Burney's journal 150 years later. Wondering who should *not* be locked up in a madhouse, he remembers that "Nemo is wise at all hours, Nemo is born without faults, Nemo is free from crime, Nemo is content with his lot, Nemo in love is wise, Nemo is good, Nemo's a wise man and perfectly happy and therefore Nicholas Nemo or Monsieur No-body shall go free."[6]

---

dangerous pastime because it left a record of thoughts that a young woman, especially, should keep to herself. See the diary, pp. 18–22.

4. Greta Calmann traces the history of Nobody in "The Picture of Nobody: An Iconographical Study," *Journal of the Warburg and Courtauld Institutes* 23 (1960): 60–104, beginning with the trick Odysseus played when he told the Cyclops his name was Noman, thus causing the monster's fellows to ignore him when he called out that no man was tormenting him.

5. Calmann, pp. 93–104.

6. *Anatomy of Melancholy* (New York, 1951), p. 99; quoted in Calmann, p. 93. For

In the course of the seventeenth and eighteenth centuries, though, Nobody evolved some peculiarly English qualities, which, although not emphasized at the beginning of Burney's private journal, probably kept Nobody's fictional possibilities alive in her imagination during the long gestation of *Evelina*. First, the English word "nobody" allows a pun that was not possible in other European languages, "and by the seventeenth century he is pictured as a manikin composed of head and limbs only, without a trunk."[7] The title page of a 1606 play called *Nobody and Somebody*, for example, represents Nobody as a man with a head, arms, and enormously long pantaloons, starting just under his chin. The figure excuses himself for his lack of fashionable clothes by explaining that he has "no body," thereby emphasizing bodilessness, or minimal materiality, among Nobody's characteristics. This personage became even more grotesquely disembodied when Hogart capped a long iconographic tradition by drawing Nobody as merely a head attached to a pair of calves and feet.[8]

The young Burney invokes Nobody's physical, as well as metaphysical, nonbeing when she praises her addressee's eternal sameness and simultaneously alludes to her impotence: "Time itself has no power to end our friendship. The love, the esteem I entertain for Nobody, No-body's self has not power to destroy." Nobody is thus at once the prototype and reductio ad absurdum of the fictional character; she names a "persona" who is emphatically detached from all that normally defines a "self"—the particulars of time, place, sex, class, and age that no real body can escape—and who therefore cries out for imaginative embellishment.

But in eighteenth-century England Nobody was not a complete cipher, for the name had come to signify a common person, a

---

an account of St. Nemo, the progenitor of Burton's Nicholas, see Calmann, pp. 60–61; and Heinrich Denifle, "Ursprung der Historia des Nemo," *Archiv für Literatur- und Kirchengeschichte des Mittelalters* 4 (1888): 330–48.

7. Calmann, p. 94.

8. Hogarth's drawing of Nobody is the tailpiece of an illustrated text by Ebinezer Forrest titled *An Account of what seemed most remarkable in the five Days Peregrination . . . Imitated in Hudibrasticks by one well acquainted with some of the Travellers, and of the Places here celebrated*. Written and illustrated in 1732, the text went unpublished until the 1770s. The identification of the tailpiece as a portrait of Nobody and that figure's iconographic history in England are given by Charles Mitchell in a twentieth-century edition, *Hogarth's Peregrination*, ed. and introd. Charles Mitchell (Oxford: Clarendon Press, 1952), pp. xix–xxxi.

person of no social consequence. Henry Fielding, for example, defined "No Body" as "All the People in Great Britain, except about 1200."[9] Hogarth also seems to have intended his Nobody to stand for the common man, and "opposed him . . . to the pretentious Somebody."[10] Somebody was used throughout the seventeenth and eighteenth centuries as Nobody's foil; the two figures were common enough, for example, to form a pair in a deck of playing cards and were stock masquerade characters. Somebody was often depicted as nothing but a substantial, well-dressed body, with dwarfed limbs. Often a fop, he "was a person of consequence, whose name was perhaps intentionally suppressed."[11] Hence, just as Nobody might be seen as the prototype of fictional characters, Somebody might be seen as the prototype of scandalous reflections.

Nobody's social profile reminds us that the eighteenth-century preoccupation with reference in representation had always been tied closely to issues of status. If we see Nobody, the addressee of Burney's juvenile journal, as the progenitor of the author's first heroine, therefore, Evelina's social insubstantiality looks all but inevitable; her lack of social status, even social identity, is both an extension and an obfuscation of her fictionality. Her constant teetering on the brink of social nonbeing, the frequency with which she is reminded that she is "a person who is nobody,"[12] even the

9. *The Covent Garden Journal*, no. 4 (January 4, 1752); rpt. in *The Covent Garden Journal* by Sir Alexander Drawcansir, Knt. Censor of Great Britain, ed. Gerard Edward Jensen, vol. 1 (New Haven, CT: Yale Univ. Press, 1915), p. 156.

10. Mitchell, introduction to *Hogarth's Peregrination*, p. xxix.

11. Calmann, p. 93.

12. *Evelina; or, the History of a Young Lady's Entrance into the World*, ed. and introd. Edward A. Bloom and Lillian D. Bloom (Oxford: Oxford Univ. Press, 1982), p. 32. Subsequent quotations from this edition are cited parenthetically in the text. Recent studies of *Evelina* include Joanne Cutting-Gray, *Woman as "Nobody" in the Novels of Fanny Burney* (Gainesville: Univ. Press of Florida, 1992), pp. 9–31; Julia Epstein, *The Iron Pen: Frances Burney and the Politics of Women's Writing* (Bristol: Bristol Classical Press, 1989), pp. 93–122; Irene Fizer, "The Name of the Daughter: Identity and Incest in *Evelina*," in *Refiguring the Father: New Feminist Readings of Patriarchy*, ed. Patricia Yaeger and Elizabeth Kowaleski-Wallace (Carbondale: Southern Illinois Univ. Press, 1989), pp. 78–107; Susan Fraiman, *Unbecoming Women: British Women Writers and the Novel of Development* (New York: Columbia Univ. Press, 1993), pp. 32–58; Judith Lowder Newton, *Women, Power and Subversion: Social Strategies in British Fiction, 1778–1860* (Athens: Univ. of Georgia Press, 1981), pp. 23–54; Toby A. Olshin, "'To Whom I Most Belong': The Role of Family in *Evelina*," *Eighteenth Century Life* n.s. 6:1 (October 1980): 29–42; Ronald Paulson, *Satire and the Novel in Eighteenth-Century England* (New Haven, CT: Yale Univ. Press, 1976), pp. 158–92; Mary Poovey, "Fathers and Daughters: The Trauma of Growing Up Female," in *Men by Women*,

memory of the ease with which her mother, Caroline Evelyn, dwindled in the vacuum of social ostracism into the bodilessness of a mere letter—all this discourse of nonentity indicates the vanishing point, the absence of reference that makes realistic fictional perspective possible and simultaneously seems to give that very absence a referent in the specific social situation of an illegitimate daughter. As is the case in reading *The Female Quixote* or any number of other eighteenth-century novels, therefore, to be mindful that *Evelina* is nobody's story and to be oblivious of the fact are practically the same thing.

To get a full sense of the uses of Nobody in Burney's career, though, we need to note yet another of the figure's contemporary associations, one that brings us back to the implications of writing *for* as well as about Nobody. As Fielding's definition suggests, Nobody was easily interchangeable with Everybody. Indeed, Hogarth used the conceit of writing for Nobody/Everybody to define the situation of the writer whose works were intended for the

ed. Janet Todd, *Women and Literature* n.s. 2 (1981): 39–58; Patricia Meyer Spacks, *Imagining a Self: Autobiography and Novel in Eighteenth-Century England* (Cambridge: Harvard Univ. Press, 1976), pp. 158–92; Susan Staves, "*Evelina*; or, Female Difficulties," *Modern Philology* 73 (1976): 368–81; Kristina Straub, *Divided Fictions: Fanny Burney and Feminine Strategy* (Lexington: Univ. Press of Kentucky, 1987), pp. 23–108; and Jennifer A. Wagner, "Privacy and Anonymity in *Evelina*," in *Fanny Burney's Evelina*, ed. Harold Bloom (New York: Chelsea House, 1988), pp. 99–109.

For recent assessments of Burney's career as a whole, see Margaret Doody, *Frances Burney: The Life in the Works* (New Brunswick, NJ: Rutgers Univ. Press, and Cambridge: Cambridge Univ. Press, 1988); and Lillian D. Bloom and Edward A. Bloom, "Fanny Burney's Novels: The Retreat from Wonder," *Novel* 12 (Spring 1979): 215–35; Rose Marie Cutting, "Defiant Women: The Growth of Feminism in Fanny Burney's Novels," *Studies in English Literature, 1500–1900* 17 (1977): 519–30; Martha G. Brown, "Fanny Burney's 'Feminism': Gender or Genre," in *Fetter'd or Free? British Women Novelists, 1670–1815*, ed. Mary Anne Schofield and Cecilia Macheski (Athens: Ohio Univ. Press, 1986), pp. 29–39; Marjorie Dobbin, "The Novel, Women's Awareness, and Fanny Burney," *English Language Notes* 22 (March 1985): 42–52; Eva Figes, *Sex and Subterfuge: Women Novelists to 1850* (London: Macmillan, 1982), pp. 33–55; Juliet McMaster, "The Silent Angel: Impediments to Female Expression in Frances Burney's Novels," *Studies in the Novel* 21 (1989): 235–52; John J. Richetti, "Voice and Gender in Eighteenth-Century Fiction: Haywood to Burney," *Studies in the Novel* 19 (1987): 263–71; Katharine M. Rogers, "Fanny Burney: The Private Self and the Published Self," *International Journal of Women's Studies* 7:2 (March/April 1984): 110–17; Jane Spencer, *The Rise of the Woman Novelist: From Aphra Behn to Jane Austen* (Oxford: Basil Blackwell, 1986), pp. 95–98; Dale Spender, *Mothers of the Novel: 100 Good Women Writers before Jane Austen* (London: Pandora, 1986), pp. 270–86; Janet Todd, *The Sign of Angellica: Women, Writing and Fiction, 1660–1800* (London: Virago, 1989), pp. 273–87. See also Joseph A. Grau, *Fanny Burney: An Annotated Bibliography* (New York: Garland, 1981).

general public rather than for a patron or coterie. He planned to preface a semiautobiographical book on the arts and artists of England with "The no Dedication":

> Not Dedicated to any Prince in Christendom for fear it might be thought an Idle piece of Arrogance.
> Not Dedicated to any man of quality for fear it might be thought too assuming.
> Not Dedicated to any learned body of Men as either of the universityes, or the Royal Society, for fear it might be thought an uncommon piece of Vanity.
> Not Dedicated to any particular Friend, for fear of offending another,
> Therefore Dedicated to nobody.
> But if for once we may suppose Nobody to be every body, as Every body is often said to be nobody, then is this work Dedicated to every body.[13]

"The no Dedication" has obvious affinities with Johnson's letter to Lord Chesterfield, discussed in the preceding chapter; it announces the author's independence as a corollary of his willingness to rely on a theoretically unlimited multitude of readers. Hogarth, however, draws out the paradox that the larger this crowd grows (the more it equals Everybody), the more its individual members shrink in significance. His joke is ostensibly pointed toward the absurd arrogance of the Somebodies who think almost Everybody is Nobody; nevertheless, the metamorphosis accomplished here reveals the necessary insubstantiality of any particular unit of that aggregate giant the public. When writers like Fielding, Johnson, and Hogarth equated their authorial virtue with their allegiance to this entity, a sense of its problematic ontological status was already well developed.

Indeed, one might argue that the upright author in the market-place of letters was bound to imagine his reader as Nobody in order to tell the truth and avoid flattery. His integrity, as the earl of Shaftesbury claimed in his "Advice to an Author" at the beginning of the century, depended on the reader's de-realization. In an interestingly gendered metaphor, Shaftesbury complained about "the coquetry of a modern author, whose epistles dedicatory, pre-

---

13. Quoted in Mitchell, p. xxxi.

faces, and addresses to the reader are so many affected graces, designed to draw the attention from the subject towards himself." He recommended writing dialogues in which the author would, through a pair of personae, interrogate his own opinions instead of rhetorically embellishing them to cajole and seduce the reader-lover. In true philosophical dialogues, he confidently claimed, "the reader, being no way applied to, stands for nobody."[14]

Writing for Nobody, therefore, was what both the talented literary entrepreneur and the serious, self-effacing philosopher were said to do in the eighteenth century. Keeping a journal addressed to Nobody and publishing a book for Everybody's consumption were thus perhaps in Burney's mind not so much polar opposites as paradoxical counterparts. Nobody clears a space not only for Evelina but also for the unknown and unknowable reader, who must be kept a cipher if the author is to preserve her integrity. Recalling Shaftesbury's chastisement of authorial "coquetry,"[15] moreover, we can speculate that the pressure to make the reader "stand for nobody," to annihilate the addressee in order to escape the censure of carrying on a flirtatious correspondence, might have been even stronger for a female than for a male author. The increasing demands for female modesty during the century might have dovetailed conveniently with the growth of the reading public to blur the distinction between privacy and publication. Paradoxically, the larger and more impersonal the audience became, the more writing for it could be conceived in the same innocent terms as writing only for oneself, that is, as writing for nobody.

This last point brings us back to the most obvious referent of Burney's "Nobody": herself. To say that she writes for Nobody is

14. Anthony, earl of Shaftesbury, "Advice to an Author," in *Characteristics of Men, Manners, Opinions, Times*, ed. John M. Robertson, introd. Stanley Grean (Indianapolis, IN: Bobbs-Merrill, 1964), vol. 1, p. 131.

15. The coquette has an interestingly ambiguous gender in the eighteenth century. She seeks to gratify her vanity by achieving emotional ascendancy over men; she wishes to be loved without loving, and hence she represents the "common" female vice of narcissistic self-preoccupation. However, the very word "coquette," deriving from "coq," reverberates with associations of masculine vainglory. The coquette reverses the "natural" relations of male and female by assuming the role of the preening barnyard rooster surrounded by a flock of admiring men. Hence coquetry is unfeminine. The masculine behavior it mimes, however, is generally regarded as foppish when observed in the salon rather than the barnyard, and hence it is strongly tinged with femininity. Thus coquetry can be imagined as doubly androgynous: it is practiced by women in imitation of effeminate men.

to say that, as she later told a companion, "*my* Journal was *solely* for my own perusal" (*Early Journals*, 1:21). Hence critics have pointed out that the writer becomes Nobody, counting the journal's mode of address as the first of Burney's characteristic authorial self-effacements.[16] It presages, for example, both the emphatic anonymity of *Evelina*'s author and the namelessness of Evelina *as* author: the heroine signs her first letter in this epistolary novel "Evelina ———" and then proceeds to ask, "what other name may I claim?" All of this would seem to point toward a strong association between authorship and blankness or emptiness of reference.

Moreover, the namelessness of Evelina and her creator, which seems to place them at the brink of existence, is thematically linked to their fathers' power to "own" or "disown" them.[17] That is, anonymity is explicitly marked as a daughter's condition. The author's reluctance to identify herself, she contends in the dedicatory poem, addressed "To ——— ———," stems from her refusal to make what might be seen as an illegitimate use of the patronym. She defers to her father as author, characterizing herself as a mere representation:

> Oh author of my being!—far more dear
> To me than light, than nourishment, or rest,
> Hygieia's blessings, Rapture's burning tear,
> Or the life blood that mantles in my breast!
>
> If in my heart the love of Virtue glows,
> 'Twas planted there by an unerring rule;
> From thy example the pure flame arose,
> Thy life, my precept—thy good works, my school.[18]

16. Margaret Doody, for example, links the "Nobody" trope, anonymity, and the general social insignificance of young women: "In her novel, Burney explores the universal adolescent experience of making an entrance into the world as 'nobody,' without an established personality or fixed social self. But Burney explores that experience from the female point of view . . ." (*Frances Burney: The Life in the Works*, p. 41). On Burney's address to "Nobody," see also Cutting-Gray, *Woman as "Nobody" in the Novels of Fanny Burney*, pp. 109–30; Bloom and Bloom, "Fanny Burney's Novels: The Retreat from Wonder"; and Straub, *Divided Fictions*, pp. 160–61.

17. For other interpretations of the significance of Burney's father to her life and work, see Fizer, "The Name of the Daughter: Identity and Incest in *Evelina*"; Elizabeth Kowaleski-Wallace, *Their Fathers' Daughters: Hannah More, Maria Edgeworth, and Patriarchal Complicity* (New York: Oxford Univ. Press, 1991), pp. 9–11, 22–23; Olshin, "'To Whom I Most Belong': The Role of Family in *Evelina*"; and Poovey, "Fathers and Daughters: The Trauma of Growing Up Female."

18. These lines allude to two passages in *Paradise Lost* that Burney may have

That the stanza's fiery language ("light," "burning," "glows, "flame") itself seems to murmur the unwritten name "Burney" only increases our sense of the difficulty of the suppression. As the dedication continues, the author-daughter asserts that her status as her father's work, and therefore as his representation, makes it impossible for her to claim her own work, which must belong ultimately to him. To name herself is to name her father and thereby to interfere in his *self*-representations:

> Could my weak pow'rs thy num'rous virtues trace,
>   By filial love each fear should be repress'd
> The blush of Incapacity I'd chace,
>   And stand, recorder of thy worth, confess'd:
> But since my niggard stars that gift refuse,
>   Concealment is the only boon I claim;
> Obscure be still the unsuccessful Muse,
>   Who cannot raise, but would not sink, your fame.

Here the "burning" life blood—the "spark" of life provided by Dr. Burney—becomes a "blush" at the daughter's comparative weakness as an author. To match her father's authorship would be to replicate the best part of her own "being," but since the poem assumes a diminution in vitality from author to work, from substantive being to mimesis, such a feat is impossible. As imitation the daughter necessarily represents the father imperfectly, and as imitation the writing necessarily represents the daughter imperfectly; hence it is doubly imperfect as a representation of the father. But what else can a daughter do? Unlike a son, a daughter cannot become the "author" of bodies that bear her father's name; she cannot restore the full, warm, breathing substance to the word "Burney," for her legitimate offspring would necessarily bear some

---

conflated in memory. The first is Eve's speech to Adam, which would make the Burneys' relationship embarrassingly sexual: "My Author and Disposer, what thou bidd'st / Unargu'd I obey" (4.635–36). The second is even more problematic, but the linguistic echoes are undeniably strong: "Thou art my Father, thou my author, thou / My being gav'st me" (2.864–65). This is Sin's address to Satan! Yet another source for the lines, almost as weird, is Goneril's flattery of Lear:

> Sir, I love you more than word can wield the matter;
> Dearer than eye-sight, space, and liberty;
> Beyond what can be valued, rich or rare;
> No less than life, with grace, health, beauty, honour.
>   (*King Lear* 1.1.56–59)

I am grateful to Janet Adelman for pointing out these similarities.

other name. In her father's name, she can only come up with cold, pale substitutes, representations twice removed: no bodies. Burney's dedication puts the dutiful daughter in a double bind: she must try to imitate the authorial act in her father's name, but her attempts to pay her life debt through writing must also always be deficient.

By imagining fatherhood as the original act of authorship, therefore, Burney, drawing on an ancient tradition of thought about women, gives herself the secondary ontological status of representation.[19] Her existence, like that of the heroine she has in turn created, is contingent, a mere reflection of an entity at a higher level of reality. The dedication, then, partly answers the question of the fifteen-year-old journal writer—"why . . . must a *female* be made Nobody?"—by showing that females, in relationship to their fathers, start out with a deficit of being. Their deficiency, moreover, stimulates authorship, which paradoxically adds to the daughter's sense of diminishing "life." Thus, as I noted at the beginning of this chapter, female writing about Nobody brings to mind the regrettable precariousness of female existence in general: "what were this world good for, *were* Nobody a female?"

We should not, however, be too quick to associate anonymity entirely with the figure of Nobody, for both the author and the heroine claim by their very "———"s to be related to Somebody. "———," as we have noticed in previous chapters, is the sign of *non*fictional writing, the mark of scandal, the tear in the text that indicates an outside where a referent too important to be named waits to be discovered. In this sense, to go nameless and to be Nobody were opposite conditions. The dedication to *Evelina* tells the reader that there is matter and substance behind the author's unwritten name, just as Evelina's "———" is the first step she makes toward asserting her relationship to her aristocratic father: "———" erases "Anville" and clears a space where "Belmont" will eventually appear.

Authorial anonymity in Burney's early works, therefore, does not indicate a lack of substance without simultaneously calling attention to the significance of the author's patronym by making an issue out of the daughter's right to use it. The dedication claims

---

19. See R. Howard Bloch, *Medieval Misogyny and the Invention of Western Romantic Love* (Chicago: Univ. of Chicago Press, 1991).

that Burney is Somebody's daughter and therefore neither Somebody in her own right nor Nobody. For Evelina, too, "————" is simultaneously the erasure of a name and a line drawn between the status of Nobody (Evelina) and that of Somebody (Belmont), a kind of rope on which the writer suspends herself. Even in the case of the teen-aged journal writer, "Nobody" applies to the writer as reader of her own secrets, and to assert the existence of such secrets is to move toward self-substantiation.

In sum, Burney wrote for, about, and from the point of view of "Nobody," stressing the questionable ontological and/or social status of her characters, her readers, and even herself, but in each case Nobody is transformed into one of her doubles. *Evelina* becomes a book for and about Everybody by Miss Somebody. As critics have pointed out, in her very blankness Evelina becomes a prototype for all young women, a diminutive, modern Eve.[20] And her readers' receptivity to the satirical discourse that supposedly issues from her pen relies on their identifying with her lack of defined being in the world. As we will see in the next section, Burney expected her readers to be nobodies. The shift from the altogether private to the altogether public is thus merely the fluctuation from one meaning of "Nobody" to another.[21]

Nobodiness, therefore, seems to spread out from *Evelina* and touch all parties to the literary exchange, as if fictionality itself were leaking out of the novel and into its surrounding conditions of production and reception.[22] However, as I have specified, the idea of Nobody already informed notions both of the reading public and of the unsubsidized author, so that the fictionality of the text might also be seen as an absorption of the terms in which the literary marketplace was described. It was not surprising that Frances Burney's writings are remarkably saturated with those terms, for discourse about nonentity had special resonance for people who lived off their representations.

20. See for example Eva Figes, *Sex and Subterfuge*, pp. 34–35.
21. Critics have offered various treatments of the relation between public and private in Burney's work; see, for example, Rogers, "Fanny Burney: The Private Self and the Published Self"; Spencer, *The Rise of the Woman Novelist*, 95–98; and Wagner, "Privacy and Anonymity in *Evelina.*"
22. Steven Knapp makes a similar point about eighteenth-century uses of personification, in *Personification and the Sublime: Milton to Coleridge* (Cambridge: Harvard Univ. Press, 1985), chapter 2.

~

Burney's relationship to the literary marketplace differed from that of the other authors we have surveyed because she was born and raised in a "literary" milieu. Aphra Behn, Delarivier Manley, and Charlotte Lennox had all claimed to be the orphaned daughters of military officers, claims on which their status as gentlewomen rested. But the daughter of a man who was a musician, music teacher, composer, and author had few secure social credentials. Authorship was the highest activity to which Burney's father aspired; without it, he was a mere hireling. He had apparently cultivated a gentlemanly demeanor early in life, which made it easy for him to find employers, but for many years his relationship to them was much more that of servant to master than that of artist to patron. He was an apprentice to the composer and orchestra leader Dr. Thomas Arne in 1748, when Fulke Greville, in need of a musician who would be "fit company for a gentleman,"[23] bought his indenture for £300. Through Greville, he made numerous contacts and some lasting friendships with broad-minded gentlefolk, but his status in many of their homes was ambiguous, something between music teacher and guest. The Thrales, for example, paid him a salary of £100 for "dining [at their house] once a week and remaining for the evening, departing as early as he wished in the morning."[24]

When Frances was summoned to meet the Thrales after the appearance of *Evelina* and the revelation of her authorship, she was at first perceived by Hester Thrale not as a lady novelist, but as a performer: "[H]is Daughter is a graceful looking Girl, but 'tis the Grace of an Actress not a Woman of Fashion—how should it?"[25] The Burney family, she pointed out elsewhere, was on display: "[E]very individual of it must write and read & be literary."[26] Their accomplishments were less marks of leisure than of semiprofessional training. Indeed, Frances's understanding of the tasks of authorship came from her exhausting work as amanuensis to her

23. Quoted by Joyce Hemlow in *The History of Fanny Burney* (Oxford: Oxford Univ. Press, 1958), p. 2.
24. Hemlow, p. 70.
25. From *Thraliana*, 1:368; quoted in Doody, p. 59.
26. *Thraliana*, 1:399; quoted in Doody, p. 21.

father. She had to copy all of *Evelina* in a "disguised hand" before sending it out because her own handwriting was already familiar to London compositors. In a sense, then, she was raised to the trade, and authorship could not be imagined in her case as a step down from a previous state of gentility. When we remember that publication was thought of as an upwardly mobile strategy in the Burney family, the anonymity of Frances's first novel might begin to seem downright pretentious. Was she, the daughter of a mere musician and writer, entitled to the anonymity she claimed?

There is no "true" answer to this question, since the response would always be based on the perceiver's relative social position. We should notice, though, that the Burneys' title to the gentility implied by anonymity would not have been universally recognized. Frances Burney's "———" might therefore be said to register not only the individual author's claim to belong to Somebody but also the desire for social recognition and status of a relatively new category of people: those whom Pierre Bourdieu has described as the holders and producers of "cultural capital."[27] The accumulation of such assets in the Burney family was intense: Charles Burney the elder began as an indentured servant; his son Charles ended as a famous classicist and doctor of divinity. Another son rose to be an admiral and authored naval histories. Two of the daughters were accomplished musicians who performed at Dr. Burney's soirées and helped turn the family home into a gathering place for musicians, painters, actors, authors, and patrons. Two other daughters, Sarah Harriet and Frances, did arduous secretarial work for their father and wrote novels. Cultivating talent, polishing performance, making and improving contacts, and collecting and disseminating knowledge were the economic activities of the Burney family, and they were conceived of as contributing to a collective property, a corporate fame. They puffed each other, sought patronage for each other, introduced each other to the right circles, negotiated each other's contracts, and advertised each other's subscriptions. Their accretion of cultural capital and the development

27. See Pierre Bourdieu, *Distinctions: A Social Critique of the Judgement of Taste*, trans. Richard Nice (Cambridge: Harvard Univ. Press, 1984), esp. pp. 1–96, and "Social Space and Symbolic Power," in *In Other Words*, trans. Matthew Adamson (Stanford, CA: Stanford Univ. Press, 1990), pp. 123–39.

of relationships that would make it grow was bound up with their most intimate sentiments and deepest sense of identity. The social significance of the family name, however, was not a given. The family was self-consciously engaged in the project of creating it. They had no rent roles, no pedigrees, no real or invented histories of military or public service; they had only talent and knowledge, copyrights and such "symbolic capital" as Dr. Burney's degree from Oxford and (much later) Frances's place at court. The writings of other families might have been imagined as second-order realities, as accomplishments indicating a (past or present) economic independence, but the writings of the Burneys were the business of their lives.

Once we notice the family's dependence on cultural and symbolic capital, the dedicatory poem of *Evelina* takes on a different significance. The "———," I have suggested, announces what might easily have been disputed at the time: that the author's father is Somebody, a man of substance. The first line of the poem then goes on rather slyly to place, if not to name, him. "Oh author of my being!" may at first appear simply to repeat, with its Miltonic echoes, the familiar author-male, pen-penis metaphors that have so often been the object of feminist analysis. But insofar as those metaphors assume that the ability to father precedes the ability to author, that authorship depends on phallic power, Burney's line potentially upsets the usual order of precedence. When we read it with the Burneys' actual situation in mind, it seems a covert acknowledgment that the father has achieved the authority of a traditional *paterfamilias* through the quite untraditional means of authorship. Indeed, the metaphor collapses into a kind of facetious literalism: Dr. Burney's authorship of his books is the basis of Frances Burney's being because it is her economic provision. Frances's place in her father's household was assured by her employment as his secretary and copyist. In this sense, representation could be said to have preceded substance. Reread as a comment on the specific relationship between Frances Burney and her father, rather than as a comment on daughters and fathers in general, the dedicatory poem hints at a possible reversal of the assumed primacy of "life" over writing, substance over representation. Such a hint in turn destabilizes the very thing the poem so loudly proclaims: the priority of the father over his mere representations, including his daughter.[28]

If Frances Burney's father was Somebody, therefore, he differed from other Somebodies by virtue of the difficulty of distinguishing his substance from his representations. The father, like the daughter, was sometimes on the edge of Nobodiness. That was, perhaps, why the daughter had to be particularly chary (as a "Burneyed" child) of his and her name/fame: they were all her father had. The dedicatory poem, then, was at once pretentious and apt; it may have exaggerated the father's social status, but it simultaneously admitted his "fame" was so fragile and so all-important that he could be materially damaged by his daughter's literary failure. The poem might be read, then, as both a clever piece of puffery and a reminder to us modern readers that aristocratic patriarchal assumptions (even in the revised version used by seventeenth- and eighteenth-century women writers) are inappropriate to cultural capital accumulation. The patriarchal language obscured the father's dependence on representation; the social and economic conditions of the Burneys revealed it. The anxiety underlying the naming of the father in the dedicatory poem to *Evelina* might stem from both an exaggerated sense of the father's loftiness and a recognition of his peculiar vulnerability: a father who lives by the pen can be injured by the pen.

The very appropriateness of authorship to Frances Burney's social milieu, therefore, entailed risks for the fledgling novelist and her family: the risk of exposing the incorporeality of the family's substance. She seems to have believed that the novel was an especially risky genre for a Burney to undertake,[29] but for that very reason she may also have been drawn to it. The explicit fictionality of the form allowed her to explore the theme of nobodiness, but it might also have revealed too much about the author's situation.

The social meanings of genres, however, are not stable, and they cannot be inferred from formal properties alone. A full sense of

28. Others who have discussed *Evelina* as a possible subversion of patriarchal norms include Newton, *Women, Power and Subversion*, pp. 42–50; Figes, *Sex and Subterfuge*, pp. 59–83; and Straub, *Divided Fictions*, pp. 25–26.

29. When her father told her he could not understand why she had published her novel anonymously, why she had anticipated his disapproval, she explained that she thought the form too far below his standards.

why novel authorship was specifically associated with nonentity in this period, and thus why it might have seemed a hazardous departure from the family enterprise, requires a brief description of changes in the production and dissemination of novels in the later decades of the eighteenth century.

It was during this period that novels became the favorite reading matter of that common avatar of Nobody: Everybody. The market in novels during those decades appears to have expanded even faster than the swelling general marketplace in books. Historians of the book trade and of literacy credit this general expansion to a growing population and the extension of the market into the middle ranks of society: the appearance, that is, of the numerous nobody readers discussed earlier. In the preceding chapter, I noted that the middle decades of the century, when the novel was beginning to establish itself, were not a period of growth for the book trade. Indeed, there was a slump in the 1740s, when the total number of publications in England was only 10,000, and the recovery of the 1750s was modest: the 11,794 titles produced in that decade were only 270 more than the number published in the decade 1710–19. Although historians often generalize about the dramatic increase in publications of the second half of the eighteenth century, most of it actually occurred in the last three decades: the 1770s show an increase of 2,400 (approximately a 20 percent increase over the total number of publications of the 1760s); the 1780s again produced a 20 percent increase; and the statistics for the 1790s (which are admittedly questionable) show a whopping 64 percent increase.[30]

Many of the new nobody readers were women, and judging by the rate of increase at which women began publishing in these decades, the expanding market was receptive to female authors of all forms of belles lettres. The number of previously unpublished

30. These numbers come from Michael Crump, "Stranger than Fiction: The Eighteenth-Century True Story," in *Searching the Eighteenth Century: Papers Presented at the Symposium on the Eighteenth Century Short Title Catalogue in 1982*, ed. M. Crump and M. Harris (London: British Library, 1983), pp. 61–62. The number of publications of the 1790s might be greatly inflated by Crump's decision to include all publications dated 1800 by the ESTC, thus creating an eleven-year decade. Moreover, many works dated 1800 by the ESTC might well have been published a few years later. As Crump explains: "I have chosen to combine the final decade with the searches for 1800 because it is ESTC policy to date undated material to the nearest five years and to flag the conjecture with a question mark. This means that a considerable number of works around the end of the century have the date: [1800?]" (p. 61).

women writers was augmented by 50 percent every decade starting in the 1760s.[31] The biggest gains were made among poets and novelists, but writers of religious meditations, authors of collections of letters, autobiographers, and playwrights also increased markedly. In the decade 1760–69, for example, only two new women playwrights were published, whereas between 1770 and 1779, thirteen published for the first time; another thirteen first appeared in the 1780s, and the number of novice women playwrights rose to sixteen in the last decade of the century.[32] Poetry was the genre that attracted the largest share of new women writers in these decades,[33] but the novel was almost as popular a choice. The rate of increase in new women novelists was greater than the overall increase in women writers, matching the figures for increases in the total number of novels published in each decade. In 1770, there were nineteen women novelists; in 1790, there were approximately seventy-five.[34]

Although the new readers were by no means exclusively interested in novels, the genre certainly benefited from their emergence. Or so it would seem from the rate of growth in publications *calling* themselves novels, which is even more striking than the overall expansion of the literary marketplace, especially in the last two decades of the century: the 1770s show a 24 percent increase, the 1780s a 90 percent, and the 1790s a 149 percent increase.[35] These numbers could indicate either an increase in prose fiction or simply an increase in the use of the word "novel" on title pages. In either case, though, they attest to a new acceptance of the term and desire for the form. Despite the frequent attacks on "novels" in the second half of the century,[36] the label was an asset in marketing books. The

31. Judith Phillips Stanton, "Statistical Profile of Women Writing in English from 1660 to 1800," in *Eighteenth-Century Women and the Arts*, ed. Frederick M. Keener and Susan E. Lorsch (New York: Greenwood Press, 1988), esp. pp. 248–51.

32. Stanton, p. 251.

33. Indeed, poetry was the preferred genre for women's first publications all through the second half of the century. In the first half, religious writings in prose dominated. Stanton, pp. 250–51.

34. Cheryl Turner, *Living by the Pen: Women Writers in the Eighteenth Century* (New York: Routledge, 1992), p. 37.

35. Crump, "Stranger than Fiction: The Eighteenth-Century True Story," p. 61.

36. See John Tinnon Taylor, *Early Opposition to the English Novel: The Popular Reaction from 1760 to 1830* (New York: King's Crown Press, 1943); and F. W. Gallaway, "The Conservative Attitude towards Fiction, 1770–1830," *PMLA* 50 (1940): 1041–59. See also Chapter 6 of this book, pp. 273–88.

changing reading habits of upper-class men, their shift to what Johnson called "general and easy reading,"[37] was no doubt partly responsible for the augmented use of the term "novel"; but contemporaries and modern historians agree that the term was most enticing to the new readers: women of all classes, country people, and lower-middle-class townspeople. Indeed, one might argue that the term was designed to demarcate a class of books suitable for these readers.

For example, in 1779, immediately after the Donaldson dispute had been finally settled in the House of Lords and numerous copyrights that had formerly been held de facto in perpetuity became public property, John Cooke began putting out cheap (sixpenny) editions of Fielding, Richardson, Defoe, and others under the rubric "Novelists' Magazine."[38] It would appear, then, that in picking up a lucrative former property for which no copyright money need be paid and marketing it to a rapidly increasing lower-middle-class readership or to young women on small allowances who were actively seeking "novels," Cooke and other booksellers helped retroactively to put Fielding and Richardson in a category the writers themselves had resisted. The cheap editions thus strengthened a classifying and marketing trend that had begun at mid-century when Defoe, Fielding, and Richardson were classified as "novelists" in the catalogues of the circulating libraries.[39] Although novels by no means constituted the majority of volumes in the large circulating libraries, there was a strong belief at the time that the dissemination of fiction among a new class of readers was their raison d'être.

Market expansion and new modes of dissemination thus gave the novel "classics," creating a national "tradition" of prose fiction, which could be considered the common property of everybody who could read. Such a development had contradictory effects on the genre's prestige, both sides of which can be seen in the preface to *Evelina*. The book came out the very year the copyright dispute was settled in favor of the publishers of cheap editions, and Burney

37. Quoted in A. S. Collins, *The Profession of Letters: A Study of the Relation of Author to Patron, Publisher, and Public, 1780–1832* (London: Routledge, 1928), p. 65.
38. Collins, pp. 58–59.
39. K. A. Manley, "London Circulating Library Catalogues of the 1740s," *Library History* 8 (1989): 74–79.

enlisted "Fielding, Richardson, and Smollet" in the preface to raise the rank of "the humble Novelist" (preface, p. 1). But the means by which these writers became undisputed "classic" novelists were also the means by which they were cheapened, and their cheapening attested to the appeal of the whole genre to an undiscriminating audience. Thus Burney jokingly suggests that the word "public" was perhaps too dignified a title for the readers she was likely to get: "The following letters are presented to the public—for such, by novel writers, novel readers will be called" (p. 7). She assumes a tone of decided superiority to novel readers in general:

> Perhaps were it possible to effect the total extirpation of novels, our young ladies in general, and boarding-school damsels in particular, might profit from their annihilation: but since the distemper they have spread seems incurable . . . surely all attempts to contribute to the number of those which may be read . . . at least without injury, ought rather to be encouraged than contemned. (p. 8)

In competing even with the classics for a share of the new downscale market, *Evelina* claims only to be innocuous fare for undiscerning but voracious appetites.

When cheap booksellers, circulating libraries, and new writers like Burney insisted that Fielding and Richardson were, after all, novelists, they consolidated and legitimated the genre, but they simultaneously homogenized what had previously seemed distinct works and lumped the whole under "light" reading fit for the unlearned. In simply becoming a novelist, the author of *Evelina* thus wandered far from the authorial path marked out by her father. Furthermore, she imagined herself to be even more errant, to be writing for the least learned among the new readers. She claimed that she had expected *Evelina's* "only admirers wd be among school girls."[40] Her description of the writing, printing, and dissemination of her first novel shows once again the elision of the difference between writing for oneself and writing for the vulgar: "I had written my little Book simply for my amusement, I printed it . . . merely for a frolic to see how a production of my own would figure in that Author like form . . . [But I] destined [*Evelina*] to no

40. Quoted in Hemlow, *The History of Fanny Burney*, p. 100.

nobler habitation than a circulating library."[41] *Evelina*, she claimed, was intended to have readers rather than buyers; it was destined for people who would consume it without even owning it. The imagined relationship between text and reader here is not only anonymous but also transitory. Such books were intended to be constantly circulating among subscribers, who paid between 10 and 16 shillings per year; finally, tattered and no longer "novel," they were discarded. Often merely "sewn" or half-bound, their physical form declared their ephemeral status.[42]

Burney's readers barely existed in her imagination as individuals; they were diminished in every sense. In another often quoted letter, she describes them as artisanal nonentities:

> I have an exceeding odd sensation, when I consider that it is now in the power of *any* and *every* body to read what I so carefully hoarded even from my best friends, till this last month or two,—and that a work which was so lately lodged, in all privacy of my bureau, may now be seen by every butcher and baker, cobbler and tinker, throughout the three kingdoms.[43]

The place of *Evelina*, then, was really no place because it was every place; it was the state of circulation itself, where it belonged to nobody because its readers were "*any* and *every* body."

In short, to publish a novel, especially one for the circulating libraries, in the late 1770s was to embrace all that was most impermanent and insubstantial about the literary marketplace; it was not to court immortality but to solicit a big audience of little people for a short time. Frances Burney's first book thus appeared in an "Author like form" that differed widely from that of her father's books. Dr. Burney's publications were certainly economic enterprises, but they were by no means intended for those newest additions to the reading public, the Miss Nobodies who frequented the circulating libraries. They were, rather, aimed at discriminating

41. It was widely believed that subscribers to circulating libraries, as one reviewer of *Evelina* remarked, "are seldom in more elevated situations than the middle ranks of life" (quoted in Hemlow, p. 101). There is evidence, however, that circulating libraries were patronized by the upper classes as well.

42. See Hilda M. Hamlyn, "Eighteenth-Century Circulating Libraries in England," *Library* 5th ser. 1 (1946–47): 197–222. See also Raymond Irwin, *The English Library: Sources and History* (London: Allen and Unwin, 1966), chapter 14.

43. Quoted in Hemlow, p. 101.

readers, and they were obvious occasions for exploiting the network of powerful acquaintances the author assiduously developed. He published his first book, *The Present State of Music in France and Italy,* at his own risk, and, according to his admiring daughter, "sent a multitude of them to his particular friends as presents" (*Early Journals,* 1:146–47). By undertaking the gentlemanly pursuit of letters and making presents of his product, Dr. Burney stressed his equality with those gentlemen and ladies who had admitted him to their society; it was an important step in his climb from musician to music teacher to composer and then to "man of letters."[44] The book eventually did make a profit; indeed, it went into a second edition in two years. Whenever Frances mentions it in her journal, though, she refers to the "honour" it brought her father; she pays detailed attention to the ways in which it extended Burney's acquaintance:

> We hear Daily of new Readers & approvers. Mr. Mason has wrote him a very polite Letter upon it desiring to introduce him to Sir James Gray, one of the most accomplished men of the Age, who was so much pleased with my Father's Book, as to beg of Mr. Mason to make them Acquainted.
>
> Dr. Brookes—Husband to the Mrs. Brookes who wrote Lady Julia Mandeville, & many other Books,—has also wrote to praise it. (*Early Journals,* 1:153)

Contacts like these were Dr. Burney's lifeblood: Sir James Gray, a diplomatist and antiquary, gave Burney letters of introduction for his travels through Germany in 1772; Mrs. Brooke (Burney misspelled the name) and her husband became managers of the opera and were therefore important contacts for a composer.

In short, Dr. Burney's writings were directed at the powerful and accomplished people who conferred prestige and preferment, whereas his daughter claimed that her first novel was aimed at an anonymous, undiscriminating crowd.[45] At the beginning of Frances

44. Roger Lonsdale, *Dr. Charles Burney: A Literary Biography* (Oxford: Clarendon Press, 1965), p. viii. For a positive assessment of both Burney's ambitions and his achievements, see Lawrence Lipking, *The Ordering of the Arts in Eighteenth-Century England* (Princeton, NJ: Princeton Univ. Press, 1970), chapter 10.

45. The difference between Frances Burney's intended readership and Dr. Burney's was perhaps like that between the commercial circulating libraries and the proprietary libraries. A typical proprietary library of the late eighteenth century, the Bristol Library (whose borrowing records for the years 1773–84 have been pub-

Burney's career, then, the father and daughter seem to have had almost opposite orientations toward the literary marketplace: Dr. Burney imagined himself to be entertaining and informing a readership of socially and culturally prominent people, whom he aspired to know; Frances Burney, in contrast, described herself as a "popular" entertainer, superior to her unknowable readers. The two Burneys, we might say, at first glance represent two different profiles of the cultural producer: one seeking alliances with people in higher ranks and insisting on his own respectability even when he assumed a subservient posture toward the powerful; the other catering, condescendingly, to a growing middle- and lower-middle-class audience.

These two profiles, though, are attached to the same being: together they make up the Janus-faced figure of authorship at the end of the eighteenth century. In his orientation toward what Bourdieu would call the "dominating classes," Dr. Burney rightly recognized the necessity for an alliance with them that entailed an acknowledgment of his own dependence. Frances Burney's orientation toward the anonymous marketplace, in contrast, was becoming the more normal mode through which cultural producers became, again in Bourdieu's words, "the dominated sector of the dominating classes." *Evelina's* actual reception, however, as opposed to the reception the author had fantasized, shows the prox-

lished), admitted members at the price of a guinea and then charged another guinea for a yearly subscription. Members, who tended to be upper-middle-class and overwhelmingly male, actively helped choose the library's books. Of 198 members in 1798, only five were women. The library offered very little prose fiction, and among those novelists represented, Fielding and Sterne were vastly more popular than Richardson, whose *Pamela* was borrowed less frequently than Hannah More's *Two Legendary Tales*. The Bristol Library owned none of Frances Burney's novels, but three of Charles Burney's works are listed under "Belles Lettres" and were frequently borrowed. Of course, members of the proprietary library might also have subscribed to one of the six commercial circulating libraries in Bristol, and, as Paul Kaufman points out, "the low scores of Richardson and a few other works of fiction and the absence of . . . other novelists, as well as some 18th-century drama and lighter literature can be explained by the borrowing of all these from the circulating libraries" (*Borrowings from the Bristol Library, 1773–1784: A Unique Record of Reading Vogues* [Charlottesville: Bibliographical Society of the Univ. of Virginia, 1960], pp. 132–33). Some of the same readers, then, might have borrowed from both libraries, but the circulating libraries had a much higher percentage of female and lower-income subscribers, and novels were considered the natural fare of such readers. Proprietary libraries in the new industrial towns seem to have carried more novels, including Frances Burney's. See M. Kay Flavell, "A Study of the Liverpool Library, 1758–1790," *British Journal of Eighteenth-Century Studies* 8 (1985): 17–35.

imity of what at first looked like widely different forms of authorship. The novel had its own Cinderella-style success story, a story
very much like that of the novel's heroine. A work of "obscure
birth," which started out among "boarding-school damsels," its
conspicuous merit won it the distinguished admirers the author
claimed she had never expected. Six months after its publication,
according to a letter from Thomas Lowndes, who published it, "the
Great World was sending for *Evelina*," and ladies feared being
"unfashionable for not having read it."[46] Frances Burney's diaries
began to fill up with the names of the accomplished and powerful
people who were reading her novel, just as they had earlier filled
up with the lists of her father's admirers. There was, indeed,
considerable overlap between the two lists, and when her identity
became known, her father's important acquaintances lionized her.

If Burney had once vaguely feared that her address to Nobody
might expose the family's obscure origins and insubstantial foundations, she must have been doubly delighted to find herself
sought after by the very people her father had courted. Indeed,
because she had never sought them, she had an aura of "proud"
independence that her father never cultivated. In her recent biography of Burney, Margaret Doody discusses Hester Thrale's apparent surprise when the newly discovered author rebuffed her attempts to patronize her, to make her gifts of money, and to
"employ" the daughter in the ways she had been used to "employ"
Dr. Burney, receiving entertainment and encomia in return. Dr.
Burney apparently expected to be patronized and acknowledged
his dependence openly; to a Christmas gift from Mrs. Thrale in the
very year of *Evelina*'s publication, he responded:

> Insolvent, yet I ne'er repine
> At Favour heap'd on me & mine,
> And though both numerous & great
> They no remorse or shame create
> For, by the Manner you bestow
> The Hearts acquire so warm a glow
> Of all who benefits receive
> As makes them feel like those who give.[47]

46. Quoted in Hemlow, p. 101.
47. Charles Burney to Hester Thrale, March 8, 177[1?], Rylands MS 545, no. 4.
Quoted in Doody, *Frances Burney: The Life in the Works*, pp. 67–68, where the date is

But his daughter, who was read by everybody and whose next book was expected to make a killing, behaved with more reserve and was soon accepted as an intimate friend by Hester Thrale. In other words, precisely because she was read by all those Nobodies, she could assume an assured place among the Somebodies. As her career progressed, the literary circles she inhabited and her contacts in the fashionable world increasingly determined what and how she published, but her status as a "popular" author, her orientation toward Nobody, actually made her contacts with the powerful seem merely sociable, obscuring their economic significance and her actual relations of dependency. Burney's adherence to Nobody, therefore, paradoxically augmented the family's apparent substance and gave it a more secure social position.

∽

But what was Frances Burney's position? *Evelina,* "unpatronized, unaided, unowned, past through Four Editions in one year,"[48] but this profuse dissemination did little to stabilize the author's position. It was widely known that she had parted with the copyright to the bookseller Thomas Lowndes for twenty guineas ("O, ma'am, what a Book thrown away was that!—all the Trade cry shame on Lowndes"[49]). The book was "unowned" by its author in more than

---

given as March 1778. For numerous instances of Dr. Burney's unembarrassed acceptance of the patronage of the great and his assiduous efforts to please them, see Lonsdale, *Dr. Charles Burney,* esp. chapters 1, 6, and 7.

48. Preface to *Cecilia; or, the Memoirs of an Heiress,* introd. Judy Simons (New York: Penguin Books/Virago Press, 1986). Subsequent quotations from this edition are cited parenthetically in the text.

49. Reportedly said to Hester Thrale by Mr. Bowen, the bookseller at Brighton. The passage continues: "[N]ot, ma'am, that I expected he could have known its worth, because that's out of the question,—but when its profits told him what it was, it's quite scandalous that he should have done nothing!—quite ungentleman like indeed!" (quoted by Hemlow, p. 101). *The Booksellers,* a 1766 poem by Henry Dell, characterizes Lowndes primarily as a publisher of drama and a polemicist in the copyright controversy, although which side he was on is unclear:

Subservient to his interest Lownds has made
The better part of th'dramatic trade,
'Bout property he made a much ado,
But now the point is settled firm and true
'Twas his, 'tis mine, and may belong to you.

Quoted in Terry Belanger, "A Directory of the London Book Trade, 1766," *Publishing History* 1 (1977): 31.

one sense, so her capital was entirely symbolic. She was now perhaps the most famous Burney, but that might only have impressed her with the bubble quality of the family's resources and the difficulty of living by one's wits. If she were to maintain an illusion of dignified independence among her new acquaintances, she had to learn how to collect on the circulation of her fame. Otherwise, as a character in *Cecilia* intimates, her nobodiness could become all too literal: "as to a lady, let her be worth never so much, she's a mere *nobody* . . . , being she knows nothing of business" (p. 857, emphasis mine). That Burney might succeed as a popular writer and yet fail to get anywhere or gain anything of substance was facetiously, but also rather pathetically, indicated by Johnson in 1780:

> [H]e offered to take me with him to Grub Street, to see the ruins of the house[s?] demolished there in the late riots, by a mob that, as he observed, could be no friend to the Muses! . . . "[Y]ou and I, Burney will go together; we have a very good right to go, so we'll visit the mansions of our progenitors, and take up our own freedom together."[50]

As Pat Rogers comments, this ruin was "the only bit of London literary men could call their own."[51] To have arrived at the august heights of being a companion to Samuel Johnson was to share the freehold of a "place" that was being demolished into a metaphor. It was rather emphatically to be no place in particular. Frances Burney found herself, then, like her novel, circulating—"traversing all London amongst the literary and fashionable alike"[52]—while she tried to determine how she might gain a more secure situation.

All of Burney's advisers—Mrs. Thrale, Samuel Johnson, David Garrick, Edmund Burke, her father, and her adopted "Daddy" Crisp—at first agreed that she should capitalize on her initial success with a play. At the end of the eighteenth century, as at the end of the seventeenth, plays were still the most potentially lucrative literary investments, and *Evelina* had amply demonstrated its

50. *Diary and Letters of Madame D'Arblay*, ed. Charlotte Barrett (London: Macmillan, 1904), vol. 1, p. 438 (cited hereafter as *D and L*).

51. Pat Rogers, *Hacks and Dunces: Pope, Swift and Grub Street* (London: Methuen, 1980), p. 118.

52. Quoted in Hemlow, p. 101.

author's talent as a satirist of manners and conversation. Ultimately, though, Dr. Burney and "Daddy" Crisp refused to allow the production of Frances's comedy, *The Witlings* (1779); their reasons merit our attention because they articulate the dilemma faced by the author as she embarked on her second novel.

The trouble with *The Witlings* was that it seemed to be about Somebody, Elizabeth Montagu, in fact, the queen of the bluestockings. As Joyce Hemlow explains, "The butt of the criticisms was not here the jostling vulgarity of the lower middle classes and follies of fops, rakes, and affected young ladies . . . but a surprisingly sharp satire on the affectations of the witlings [minor wits] themselves and especially the *bas bleus*."[53] In short, Burney was lampooning a portion of the very set she had so recently been allowed to join. This scandalous play could be seen as a declaration of her independence, a statement that, unlike her father, she would not be eager to please.[54] Johnson, indeed, seems to have admired it for just this quality, imagining that Frances Burney and Elizabeth Montagu, despite the enormous social and economic gap that divided them, were simply competitors in a battle of wits:

> Down with her, Burney!—down with her!—spare her not!—attack her, fight her, and down with her at once! You are a rising wit, and she is at the top; when I was beginning the world, and was nothing and nobody, the joy of my life was to fire at all the established wits! and then everybody loved to halloo me on.[55]

But, as the nostalgic tone of this passage hints, Johnson mistook the times and their etiquette. The rude, combative days of the 1730s and 1740s (when Johnson was "nobody") had given way to the genteel civility he had himself, as we saw in the last chapter, done so much to promote by attacking the patronage mentality that had encouraged scandal. Perhaps one could still make a living writing scandal and personal satire, but powerful people would no longer pay much for it, and it was certainly not a respectable occupation. Dr. Burney shrewdly assessed the damaging effect such a play might have on the family's credit and suppressed it, insisting that

53. Hemlow, p. 133.

54. Margaret Doody interprets the episode as rebellion against Dr. Burney. See *Frances Burney: The Life in the Works*, pp. 66–98.

55. *D and L*, vol. 1, p. 115.

his daughter return to fiction: "In the Novel Way, there is no danger."[56]

The incident might be said to replicate the dynamic traced in the last two chapters. Frances Burney had to relearn for herself the lesson of the century, that the writer's surest resource was becoming nobody's story. But the incident also brings to light a new phase in the overall process. The world of patronage, of "belonging" to the socially, politically, and economically powerful, had once required scandalous texts from writers. Indeed, we cannot entirely rule out the possibility that Burney, on first entering the world of the wits, anachronistically associated it with personal satire,[57] and, on observing that there was a rivalry between her particular promoter, Hester Thrale, and the more powerful bluestocking Elizabeth Montagu, took her patroness's part. If so, she, like Johnson, mistook the nature of the milieu she had penetrated. What we might call the late eighteenth century's "soft" forms of patronage were inimical to such aggressive partisanship. Writers no longer depended on individuals or even on small groups but on large and relatively diffuse networks of influence. Hence, as Dr. Burney instinctively knew, it was important not to antagonize anyone who had any kind of power. If at mid-century it looked as though the vestiges of patronage and the marketplace might be imagined as opposites, late in the century they were thoroughly interwoven. The only way Frances Burney could keep up and benefit from her acquaintance with Somebody was to continue to write for and about Nobody.

By the time *Cecilia* was begun, therefore, the social orientations of the two Burneys had shifted somewhat: Dr. Burney continued to address himself to Somebody, but his daughter could no longer imagine that she was writing to Nobody alone. Although her father called her "little Burney" in an anonymous piece of puffery in 1782,[58] hers had become the larger and more diverse audience. She had inherited the name, and, despite her father's belittling designation of her, she had become its primary referent in the public mind; thus she was probably more conscious than ever of her

---

56. Unpublished letter from Dr. Burney to Frances Burney, August 29, 1779, quoted in Doody, p. 96.

57. Note all the talk in Burney's crowd about being afraid of her, about assuming she was going to engage in personal satire, as if that was expected.

58. See Doody's discussion of this incident, pp. 99–100.

family's relations of dependence, the limitations imposed by their actual social and economic connections. However, this knowledge did not teach her, to paraphrase Evelina, "to whom she most belonged";[59] instead it taught her that her relationships must be to Everybody simultaneously. Since her acceptance among the dominating classes relied on her successful address to Nobody, her lack of defined "place" became the very condition of her social relations.

This placelessness, this belonging everywhere and therefore nowhere, could also be thought of as a universal obligation. In the period between her first two novels, Frances Burney was living on the credit of her name, a credit she had done much to increase, but a mere credit nevertheless. And credit, of course, implied debt.[60] Burney was obliged to write another novel for the "public," for her father, for the wits and hostesses who had encouraged and patronized her—in short, for Everybody. The daughterly debt she acknowledged in the dedicatory poem to *Evelina* had not been repaid by that novel's success; it had rather been multiplied and dispersed into the world at large. Now that she was "Burney," a stern, impersonal injunction to write emanated from everywhere, but there was no longer even the fleeting illusion that writing would discharge rather than augment it.

As numerous critics have noticed, the change in Burney's status is rather obviously encoded in *Cecilia; or, Memoirs of an Heiress.* Instead of being nameless like Evelina, Cecilia Beverley is overburdened by her name; her uncle's will, which as a condition of her inheriting his estate enjoins that any man she marries take the surname Beverley, welds patronym and property together. In *Evelina*, the sought-after name Belmont, whose use implied her father's

59. "I hardly know, my Lord, I hardly know myself to whom I most belong," Evelina tells Lord Orville when he asks if she is free to dispose herself in marriage (p. 353).

60. That a writer's creditors might own even his unwritten works is advanced by one pamphleteer in 1762 as an absurd consequence of the concept of literary property: "If these works were to become a Property, they would be taken in Execution for Debt. . . . If literary Property consists in the Ideas, the Creditors would have an Interest in all the Ideas of their Debtors. Ideas are in their Nature equally susceptible of Property, whether they exist only in the Brain of the Author, or are by him transmitted to Paper" (*An Enquiry into the Nature and Origin of Literary Property* [London: William Flexney, 1762], p. 35). Literary property thus makes one's mind vulnerable to seizure for debt, according to this writer, and his warning might indicate the state of trepidation and self-estrangement Burney experienced in the long incarceration during which she wrote *Cecilia*.

acknowledgment of her legitimacy, was actually employed by the heroine only once, just after her father's recognition and just before her marriage: "Now then, therefore, for the first—and probably the last time I shall ever own the name, permit me to sign myself, . . . EVELINA BELMONT" (p. 404). The plot culminates in owning the name, but there is no anxiety about keeping it; it is something not only to be traded on but also to be traded in. The plot of *Cecilia*, on the contrary, focuses on whether the heiress can keep her name and her fortune. A name is not something to be achieved and then changed but something to be maintained, perhaps at great expense. For the heiress, moreover, as for the author, the demanding patronym is inextricably entwined with her estate, so much so that the two cannot be told apart.[61]

This seems a relatively simple allegory registering the anxiety and resentment of a writer undertaking her second novel in a dutiful mood, conscious that she had become the chief representative of the family name and was expected both to promote and to cash in on it. The diaries and letters from the period of the novel's writing resonate with these demands. Dr. Burney, for example, wanted the novel produced as quickly as possible so that its publication would coincide with the appearance of the second volume of his own *History of Music* in 1781, and his daughter repeatedly chastised herself for failing to meet the deadline that was calculated to boost the family's fame. The financial issue also permeates the correspondence; in a playful conflation of the author and the heroine, for example, "Daddy" Crisp delivered his admonitions concerning money in the very idiom of Cecilia's miserly guardian, Mr. Briggs: "*'Touch the yellow Boys'—'grow Warm'*—make the Booksellers *come down handsomely—Count the ready—the Chink—*

61. For a discussion of the contrast between the two heroines, see Doody, p. 101; for discussion of the names in *Cecilia*, see Doody, pp. 135–40, and Epstein, *The Iron Pen*, pp. 156–59. Recent interpretations of *Cecilia* may be found in Terry Castle, *Masquerade and Civilization: The Carnivalesque in Eighteenth-Century English Culture and Fiction* (Stanford, CA: Stanford Univ. Press, 1986), pp. 255–89; Cutting-Gray, *Woman as "Nobody" in the Novels of Fanny Burney*, pp. 32–52; Edward Copeland, "Money in the Novels of Fanny Burney," *Studies in the Novel* 8 (1976): 24–37; Jan Fergus, *Jane Austen and the Didactic Novel: "Northanger Abbey," "Sense and Sensibility," and "Pride and Prejudice"* (Totowa, NJ: Barnes and Noble, 1983), pp. 62–72; Epstein, *The Iron Pen*, pp. 155–73; Figes, *Sex and Subterfuge*, pp. 41–45; Kay Rogers, "Deflation of Male Pretensions in Fanny Burney's *Cecilia*," *Women's Studies* 15 (1988): 87–96; and Straub, *Divided Fictions*, pp. 109–51.

do but secure this one point, while it is in your Power, & *all Things else shall be added unto thee.*"[62]

Cecilia, however, is far more than an allegory of Burney's personal anxieties. Indeed, to read it simply as a fictionalization of any particular situation is to ignore its exploration of placelessness and its attempt to generate a universal subjectivity out of that nonsituation. *Cecilia* focuses on one of the major paradoxes of this study with extraordinary intensity: when one tries to explain a text by embedding it in the material particulars of its production, one discovers that those particulars are themselves matters of disembodiment, abstraction, dissemination, and displacement. *Cecilia* becomes an allegory of this paradox by specifying the particulars of the heroine's universalist ethical consciousness; but the particulars are themselves deficiencies or surpluses that are construed as debts. The specific social, economic, and psychological conditions surrounding both Cecilia and *Cecilia*—placelessness, endless circulation, and a sense of general indebtedness—are the circumstances of a universalist subjectivity. Burney's novel is personal only in a paradoxical way: it records the moment when certain conditions of *displacement* conspire to create a generalized ethical subject.

As many critics have noticed, the character of Cecilia differs from that of Evelina by being more than merely innocent.[63] If we can distinguish between Evelina the character and Evelina the narrator, we can say that the character concentrated on maintaining her virginity, safeguarding her reputation, and avoiding "prepossession." Her virtues were almost entirely negative, like the minimal virtue of fiction itself: Evelina and the novel were both good because they were not scandalous. Of course, the narrator Evelina and the novel *Evelina* also provided satirical comedy and conduct-book morality, but the whole did not aspire to be an integrated ethical discourse. *Cecilia*, in contrast, is the first of Burney's moral

---

62. See *D and L*, vol. 2, pp. 98–99, where the quotation is somewhat different; this is from the letter of July 1782, quoted by Doody, p. 159.

63. Julia Epstein, for example, puts Cecilia in a line of philanthropic heroines that includes Clarissa, the heroines of Sarah Scott's *Millenium Hall*, and Dorothea Brooke (*The Iron Pen*, p. 159); Margaret Doody proposes a similar genealogy (p. 127). Kay Rogers characterizes Cecilia as "a young woman who, unlike Evelina, has the internal and external resources to control her own life" ("Deflation of Male Pretensions in Fanny Burney's *Cecilia*," pp. 87–88).

"works."[64] The heroine obviously strives to go beyond Evelina's mere passive goodness, just as the novel as a whole claims ethical significance for fiction.

Granted, then, that Cecilia seems more serious, more intellectually and morally ambitious, than Evelina as a character. That very ambition, however, creates its own blankness. If Evelina ———— was nobody looking for a name (Belmont) and an inheritance, Cecilia Beverley is a name and an inheritance trying to achieve the consciousness of nobody in particular. As soon as she enters the fashionable world of London, where her name and fortune completely define her, she envisions escaping from its petty and insipid routines through impersonal acts of charity:

> Many and various . . . were the scenes which her fancy delineated; now she supported an orphan, now softened the sorrows of a widow, now snatched from iniquity the feeble trembler at poverty, and now rescued from shame the proud struggler with disgrace . . . [S]he regarded herself as an agent of Charity, and already in idea anticipated the rewards of a good and faithful delegate: so animating are the designs of disinterested benevolence! so pure is the bliss of intellectual philanthropy! (p. 52)

The mild irony of the narrator's tone in this passage gently mocks, even as it holds up for admiration, Cecilia's dream of leaving her own story behind and becoming a deus ex machina in myriad other stories. She will no longer be simply another human being, but the "agent" or "delegate" of "Charity." Her ambition is to escape from the particulars of novelistic "character" into the abstraction of allegorical impersonation. But, as the passage wryly hints, such "disinterested benevolence" is alway purest when it is imaginary, disembodied, "intellectual philanthropy." The very moral ambition that makes Cecilia more substantial than Evelina, therefore, impels her toward an ideal form of Nobodiness.

Cecilia's dreams of being nobody in particular and occupying

---

64. Burney began insistently referring to her writings as "works" instead of "novels" during the composition of *Camilla*. See Edward A. Bloom and Lillian L. Bloom, introduction to *Camilla: or, a Picture of Youth* (Oxford: Oxford Univ. Press, 1983), p. x; and *The Journals and Letters of Fanny Burney*, vol. 3, ed. Joyce Hemlow with Patricia Boutilier and Althea Douglas (Oxford: Clarendon Press, 1973), letter 171, pp. 117–18. We might, however, use the distinction to describe the difference between her first two fictions.

nowhere in particular so that she can dispense charity and justice are almost always, as in the passage above, subjected to some form of Johnsonian deflation. Margaret Doody points out that the following passage, for example, counterposes the dream of allegorical disembodiment against the reality of personal connectedness and mortality:[65]

> In her sleep she bestowed riches, and poured plenty upon the land; she humbled the oppressor, she exalted the oppressed; slaves were raised to dignities, captives restored to liberty; beggars saw smiling abundance, and wretchedness was banished the world. From a cloud in which she was supported by angels, Cecilia beheld these wonders; and while enjoying the glorious illusion, she was awakened by her maid, with news that Mrs. Charlton [Cecilia's old friend and companion] was dying!
>
> She started up, and undressed, was running to her apartment,— when the maid, calling to stop her, confessed she was already dead! (pp. 696–97)

Certainly the passage is Johnsonian in the way it chastens Cecilia's vainglorious dream of omniscient and omnipotent benevolence: as she imagines seeing and relieving all suffering, she is actually ignorant of and powerless to prevent the "paralytic stroke" (p. 712) simultaneously being suffered by her friend.

The passage, though, has some features that cannot be explained wholly as an ironic commentary on Cecilia's naive enthusiasm or even her egoism. The dream itself, for instance, has an odd structure. Cecilia sees herself not only righting all wrongs, but also *seeing* herself righting all wrongs. There are two Cecilias in the dream: one who acts, and one who floats above and enjoys watching the acts. This configuration resembles Adam Smith's description of the self-division inherent in moral self-scrutiny:

> When I endeavour to examine my own conduct, when I endeavour to pass sentence upon it, and either to approve or condemn it, it is evident that, in all such cases, I divide myself, as it were, into two persons; and that I, the examiner and judge, represent a different character from that other I, the person whose conduct is examined into and judged of. The first is the spectator, whose sentiments with

regard to my own conduct I endeavour to enter into, by placing myself in his situation, and by considering how it would appear to me, when seen from that particular point of view. The second is the agent, the person whom I properly call myself.[66]

In the dream Cecilia is both the "agent" practicing virtue and the "spectator," who appears in the dream as a deified figure of virtue itself, complete with supporting angels and surrounding clouds. The passage, then, stresses the link between Cecilia's moral ambition and her desire to achieve a vantage point so comprehensive that it would include even herself, a site outside time and space. What Smith calls the impartial spectator's "particular point of view" is revealed in the dream to have no particularity in the spatio-temporal world.

The passage then goes on not only to mock such an ambition as vain, in both senses of the word, but also to reveal its association with death. The Cecilia who floats in the sky is not so much an ironic contrast to the dead Mrs. Charlton as she is the latter's apotheosis. The doubled report of Mrs. Charlton's death, making it seem at once in progress and already accomplished, furthermore, repeats the doubling of Cecilia in the dream, actor and spectator. The suffering/dead Mrs. Charlton resembles the acting/watching Cecilia, aligning the second terms of each pair: death and omniscient beholding. The proximity of death to what the narrator earlier called "intellectual philanthropy" is additionally implied by the pronominal confusion of the quotation's last sentence: "She [Cecilia] started up . . . to her [Mrs. Charlton's] apartment . . . when the maid, calling to stop her [Cecilia], confessed she [Mrs. Charlton] was already dead!" The rapid alternation of pronoun referents unsteadies that of the final "she" who is "already dead."

Repeatedly, then, the novel enforces an awareness that Cecilia's ideal self—the ethical transcendental subject—is hard to distinguish from Nobody. Like *Clarissa* before it and numerous novels to follow, *Cecilia* uses the characterization of the heroine-heiress to transform the paradox of the novelistic imperative—to be Nobody *in particular*—into a moral dilemma. How can one be a moral paragon whose perceptions and actions are altogether disinterested

66. Adam Smith, *Theory of Moral Sentiments*, ed. D. D. Raphael and A. L. Macfie (Oxford: Clarendon Press, 1976), 3.1.6.

if one also has a moral obligation to be in the world where one is blinded and impeded by a mass of particular entanglements? *Cecilia* also converts the paradox of *reading* novels into a corresponding moral problem. Insofar as one identifies with novel heroes and heroines precisely because one knows they are Nobodies, one indulges in a fantasy of one's own potential transcendence of the world. The very moral elevation one experiences in reading a properly uplifting fiction, therefore, is caused by one's imaginary removal from any context of moral action. The heavenly Cecilia who watches herself in the dream sequence is an obvious allegory for the reader's vicarious pleasure as she indulges in the "glorious illusion" that the ideal Nobody (precisely because she *is* Nobody) called "Cecilia" is a version of herself doing splendid things. Burney's language suggests that the moral imagination *by its very nature* perpetually defers the possibility of moral engagement outside the "dream." Even inside the dream, the actions are "beheld" simultaneously, suspending temporality. The narrator also tells us that the Cecilia who watches from the clouds, like the reader, experiences a "promissory enjoyment" (p. 696), which further complicates the temporal sequence and stresses the connection between the pleasures of moral imagining and the deferral/suspension of moral life.

Cecilia, therefore, is a moral heroine, not because she serves as a paragon or pattern of what virtuous females should be, but because she turns the paradox of being a fictional heroine into a moral problem. The novel, moreover, rearticulates what had been the comic predicament of *The Female Quixote* (how can one both read and be?) as a moral dilemma. To imagine "disinterested" benevolence, to identify with the character who strains against particularity, is to receive "promissory enjoyment," a phrase that implies some sort of obligation. *Cecilia*, we will see, persistently suggests that the moral reader does not simply "borrow" fictional personae; she borrows with a promise to repay with interest. Disinterested benevolence actually exacts a usuriously high level of interest. The novel thus becomes a moral work, not by providing some detachable lesson, but by first eliciting the reader's identification with a Nobody, whose very morality is defined by her sense of universal indebtedness, and then further suggesting that the reader's identification is itself a form of borrowing for which he or she should be held accountable.

The inseparability of debt, morality, and identification with Nobody is evident from the outset of *Cecilia*. The heroine's first indulgence in "intellectual philanthropy," for example, is prefaced with this explanation: "A strong sense of DUTY, a fervent desire to ACT RIGHT, were the ruling characteristics of her mind: her affluence she *therefore* considered as a debt contracted with the poor: and her independence, as a tie upon her liberality to pay it with interest" (p. 52, emphasis mine). It is precisely this construction of herself as the universal debtor that stimulates Cecilia's imagination: "Many and various, *then* . . . were the scenes which her fancy delineated" (p. 52). The passage begins with a consciousness of debt and ends with indulgence in promissory enjoyments.

Debt, therefore, is both the condition and the result of morality in the novel. Cecilia begins with the understanding that she owes whatever she owns, and the telos of the novel is to make that proposition literally true. Thus at its climax the heroine actually becomes an item in a pawnshop. Improbable as this climax sounds, it is the logical outcome of a transcendent morality (at once promoted and criticized by its superimposition on the structure of fictional experience) that destroys the distinction between discharging and incurring debts. To be sure, Cecilia is not allowed to run headlong into deficit spending to prove her moral superiority. On the contrary, almost every step of the nearly nine-hundred-page journey to the pawnshop is taken reluctantly. Perhaps no book in the annals of the English novel succeeds as thoroughly as this one in focusing our apprehensive attention on a character's property. We do not often fear for Cecilia, but we are kept in a state of perpetual anxiety about the fate of her money. The heroine very gradually loses her fortune through a series of painful extortions. Nevertheless, each expropriation displays Cecilia's moral consciousness, that is, the consciousness that she is already in debt.[67]

Cecilia is neatly divided into two parts, corresponding to the two components of the Beverley family fortune that Cecilia, as sole survivor, has inherited. The opening of the novel is extraordinarily

---

67. Other interpretations of the role of money in *Cecilia* include Castle, *Masquerade and Civilization,* relating the novel's "shift in emphasis from the erotic to the fiscal" to its "decarnivalization of the masquerade" (p. 161); and Epstein, *The Iron Pen,* which focuses on "money as a medium of exchange for . . . plot and . . . materialist social critique" in *Cecilia* (p. 159).

precise about these matters: her parents, we immediately learn, have left her £10,000, and through her uncle and former guardian, "in whom, by various contingencies, the accumulated possessions of a rising and prosperous family were centered," she has been bequeathed an estate of £3,000 per annum. The only restriction on her ownership of the estate is "that of annexing her name, if she is married, to the disposal of her hand and her riches" (pp. 1–2). One part of her fortune, then, is a direct money legacy from her parents; the first half of the novel tells of the loss of that wealth. The other part, which she loses in the second half of the book, is the landed estate that represents the wealth of all the rest of the Beverley family. These two bequests are quite distinct in the heroine's moral economy. Although the whole is a "debt contracted with the poor," the second is not really imagined to be at her disposal at all. She holds it "sacred" (p. 174) and thinks of herself, in Burke's terms, as its trustee. "But the £10,000 bequeathed me by my father," she announces, "I regard as more peculiarly my own property" (p. 174). It is this property, which is not entirely (but "more peculiarly") her own, that she loses first.

Because the money is more her own, it is in principle easier than the estate to detach from her. As in so many other books surveyed in this study, ownership in *Cecilia* is realized by the disposal of property. Because Cecilia thinks of the £10,000 as "more" hers, she thinks herself "at liberty to dispose of it as I please" (p. 174). But the cunning of the plot is to force Cecilia to part with her money in a way that does *not* please her or anyone else. The plot sternly enforces the idea of a universal debt when the heroine herself would qualify and compromise it. Things are so arranged that Cecilia cannot spend her money as she chooses. First, it is entrusted to a guardian for most of the period covered by the novel's action; and, second, Cecilia prides herself on living frugally so that she can pay her debt to the poor by patronizing worthy objects of charity. Worthy objects, of course, seldom need much, since they are frugal themselves. The deep reason Cecilia cannot spend her money as she pleases, though, is simply that to do so would please her. Whenever Cecilia does manage to give something to worthy poor people, she receives egotistical gratification, a self-satisfying emotional return that is difficult to account for in her own logic of debt. When, for example, she establishes the Hills, a widow's family, in a little shop of their own, she gets in return augmented self-importance:

> Never had the heart of Cecilia felt so light, so gay, so glowing, as after the transaction of this affair: her life had never appeared to her so important, nor her wealth so valuable . . . [T]o view such sights, and have power to say *"These deeds are mine!"* what, to a disposition fraught with tenderness and benevolence, could give purer self-applause, or more exquisite satisfaction? (p. 197)

By localizing her general "debt to the poor" in deserving objects and actually trying to pay it off, Cecilia allows herself to feel pride in the mere discharge of her duty.

The plot, however, imposes a more rigorous regime of obligation, separating ethical action from such gratifications. Cecilia must learn to give her money away with no expectation of any emotional return. The demand comes from no legitimate, indeed from no identifiable, source, and the payment results in no "exquisite satisfaction." The achievement of the first half of the novel is to separate Cecilia from her money, before she legally has it, in a way that seems both ethically imperative and utterly wasteful.

As if impelled by these exigencies, Mr. Harrel, one of Cecilia's three guardians, manages to put Cecilia in debt to usurers for the entire amount of her paternal legacy. In the first of these transactions, she steps in to save Mr. Arnott, Harrel's brother-in-law and the brother of Cecilia's childhood friend, from a severe financial loss. When Cecilia sees Harrel, an incorrigible gambler and spendthrift, imposing upon Arnott's generosity, she immediately interposes and substitutes herself for the victim. At first the plan seems rational because Mr. Arnott would have to "take up money" at a loss to pay Mr. Harrel's debt, whereas Cecilia believes she can simply ask for an advance on her inheritance. It turns out, though, that Mr. Briggs, the guardian who controls her fortune, refuses to advance her money ("Keep it for your husband; get you one soon"), and Cecilia finally feels obliged to go into debt herself: "The heart of Cecilia recoiled at the very mention of a *Jew, and taking up money upon interest;* but impelled strongly by her own generosity to emulate that of Mr. Arnott, she agreed, after some hesitation, to have recourse to this method" (p. 183). Cecilia's imitative action, her "emulation" of Mr. Arnott, is just one link in a chain of debt. To substitute herself for Arnott, who was generously trying to substitute his money for Harrel's, Cecilia must substitute "honest old Aaron's" money for her own, thereby taking Harrel's place as the debtor. Both the ultimate source and the destination of the money are unknown. Harrel claims he must pay his tailor, but we are led to doubt him; and the usurer's money, because it is a usurer's, cannot be said to belong to anybody. The actual scene of Cecilia's generosity, therefore, is precisely the opposite of the spectacle of transcendent goodness she fantasizes: instead of floating above the world and watching the spectacle of her heroic and invulnerable self, she "recoils" from the dimly understood interchange; instead of seeing herself exalted, she is forced to sully herself by "contracting a voluntary debt" (p. 182) and thus changing places with the villain of the piece.

The next two extortions follow the same pattern. Harrel threatens suicide to force her to borrow another £7,500 and then holds his wife hostage until Cecilia signs for yet another £1,000. The Jews become more anonymous and rapacious, and Cecilia's sense of the unworthiness of both the Harrels constantly increases. After dissuading Harrel from suicide by swearing to pay his debts, for example, she found that "every moment she obtained for reflection, augmented her reluctance to parting with so large a sum of money for so worthless an object, and added strength to her resentment for the unjustifiable menaces which had extorted from her such a promise" (p. 262). And after the final signing, Cecilia's sense of desolation is so strong that she doubts she has performed an ethical act at all: "The soothing recompense of succouring benevolence, followed not this gift, nor made amends for this loss: perplexity and uneasiness, regret and resentment, accompanied the donation, and rested upon her mind; she feared she had done wrong" (p. 383.) In the austerely ethical world Cecilia comes to inhabit, there is no "recompense" of any kind for right action, nor is there a simple set of definitive markers that distinguish right from wrong. Mrs. Harrel benefits from Cecilia's generosity because she just happens to be there pressing a claim of childhood friendship that is also purely accidental: "When [Cecilia's] enlightened mind discerned [her] deficiencies, [Mrs. Harrel] had already an interest in her affections" (p. 698).

The recognition of this "interest," this prior condition of debt arising merely from the fortuitous particulars of one's life regardless of the merit of the object, makes Cecilia a moral paragon and complicates her dreams of "disinterested," transcendent morality. This debt, entailed in one's mere being in the world, is literalized by Cecilia's bonds. Simultaneously, however, the demand is presented as bizarrely impersonal and abstract: the heroine has not chosen Mrs. Harrel as a friend, nor is she tied to her by family connections. Indeed, she explicitly cites her duty to her dead family as a reason against borrowing money for the Harrels:

> I have not, it is true, any relations to call me to account, but respect for their memory supplies the place of their authority, and I cannot, in the distribution of the fortune which has devolved to me, forbear sometimes considering how they would have wished it spent, and always remembering that what was acquired by industry and labour, should never be dissipated in idleness and vanity. (p. 373)

But despite this competing sense of duty, Cecilia must give in to the immediate demand for protection presented by her childhood friend, a demand that seems absolute because of its emergency and contingency. The accidental quality of these expropriations, in others words, displaces Cecilia, removes her from such relatively stable particulars as her family identity, and forces her to change places with, to borrow the identity of, the most proximate sufferer.

Cecilia is thus left "holding the bag" for Harrel when he blows his brains out in Vauxhall at the climax of the novel's first half after presenting her with a packet containing "a roll of enormous bills, and a collection of letters from various creditors, threatening the utmost severity of the law, if their demands were longer unanswered" (p. 419). "On a slip of paper which held these together," we are told, "was written, in Mr. Harrel's hand, *To be all paid tonight with a Bullet* (p. 419). Once again Cecilia occupies the vantage point of the dead, from which, "to her no small amazement," she sees reams of detached demands. The dream of being Nobody in particular has become a nightmare.

The substitution of the packet of papers for Harrel's life returns us to the topic of reading. Harrel includes a short account of himself with the bills, as well as one final supplication to Cecilia and Mr. Arnott: "Pray for me." The addressees respond with the appropriate sentiment:

> Wretch as Mr. Harrel appeared, without religion, principle, or hon-
> our, this incoherent letter, evidently written in the desperate moment
> of determined suicide, very much affected both Cecilia and Mr.
> Arnott; and in spite either of abhorrence or resentment, they mu-
> tually shed tears over the address to themselves. (p. 421)

Once the body is out of the way, identification is all the more
imperative and disconnected from worth. Of course, identification
at this point is seemingly risk free, just as it is normally considered
risk free when one sympathizes with fictional nobodies. But the
passage nevertheless locates the roots of Cecilia's indebtedness in
this ready readerly response. Arnott and Cecilia cannot disavow
what the narrator had earlier called "the obligations" of "a general
humanity" (p. 406), and precisely because Harrel had individually
"forfeited all right to [Cecilia's] esteem" (p. 406), he becomes,
especially in his death, an emblem of the minimally human, the
very nobody that can never deserve or repay our sympathetic
interest. Harrel becomes a figure for fiction's necessary default.

There is, moreover, one further link between debt and reading
in this part of the book. When Cecilia first decides to stand in for
Mr. Arnott by paying Harrel's debt, she tries to get £600 from her
guardian Briggs, £400 of which she intends for Harrel, £50 for the
impoverished Mrs. Hill and her family, and £150 to clear her
account with a bookseller. Cecilia's only legal debt in the beginning
is the one she has contracted as a reader. Furthermore, paying this
debt is the only purpose she mentions when she asks for an
advance on her inheritance, so her discussions with her guardians
Mr. Briggs and Mr. Delvile make a firm connection between reading
and going into debt. It is the nature of the outstanding bill that
confirms Mr. Briggs's opposition to paying it: "'Books,' he cried,
'what do you want with books? do no good; all lost time; words
get no cash'" (p. 174). Next she applies to Mr. Delvile, her aristocratic guardian, to override the decision of the miserly Briggs, but
again the nature of the debt is remarked as singularly inappropriate:

> "But what bill at all," cried he, with much surprise, "can a young
> lady have with a bookseller? The Spectator, Tatler, and Guardian,
> would make library sufficient for any female in the kingdom, nor do
> I think it like a gentlewoman to have more. . . . And let me counsel
> you to remember, that a lady, whether so called from birth or only

from fortune, should never degrade herself by being put on a level with writers, and such sort of people." (p. 179)

Briggs's and Delvile's condemnations are meant to contrast their valuations of intellectual life with those of Cecilia and the narrator, who consider "reading" to be the "richest, highest, and noblest source of intellectual enjoyment" (p. 27). Nevertheless, Briggs and Delvile are partly right: reading is intimately connected, especially in the novel's first half, with Cecilia's loss of both fortune and status. As a reminder of the connection between reading and owing, the account with the bookseller remains unsettled until Cecilia reaches her majority; it is a sign of debt in general that carries over from episode to episode.

Cecilia's inability to clear this debt, like the necessity of resorting to usurers, is obviously and insistently linked to her femaleness. That single women, like readers, are just naturally in debt is one of the novel's most fundamental assumptions. Cecilia's three guardians agree on only one matter: that her fortune is property she holds in trust for her future husband. Cecilia may be eccentric in believing that she owes what she owns to the poor, but she concurs with her patriarchal custodians in imagining that she owes it to someone.

In keeping with the pattern set in the first half of the novel, the second half deprives her of her estate by literalizing the idea that a woman must pay for marriage. As in the first half of the novel, moreover, she must pay without receiving any emotional return, without feeling satisfied that her estate has been well disposed of according to her own will. Cecilia's dream of bestowing it on a worthy husband (young Delvile), like her dream of giving her money to deserving objects of charity, is thwarted. The ultimate disposition of the estate, like that of the £10,000, seems almost anonymous. Upon her marriage, she finds herself in debt to a total stranger, one Mr. Eggleston.

Although the entire second half of the book revolves around the clause in her uncle's will that deprives her of the Beverley estate if her husband does not take her name, she returns to that estate after her secret wedding as if she were still its proprietor. Mr. Eggleston's laywer then rudely reminds her that each hour of her married life puts her deeper in debt to this distant relative:

> [W]hen this business comes to be settled, it will be very essential to
> be exact as to the time [of your wedding], even to the very hour; for
> a large income per annum divides into a small one per diem; and if
> your husband keeps his own name, you must not only give up your
> uncle's inheritance from the time of relinquishing yours, but refund
> from the very day of your marriage. . . . You will please, then, to
> recollect, madam, that this sum is every hour increasing. (p. 836)

Moreover, this unconsciously contracted debt, this hourly charge
on her married life, is owed to a stranger who himself does not
bear the Beverley name and who apparently plans to exploit the
estate to pay his sons' debts. It is as if Cecilia suddenly finds herself
in debt to a brood of Harrels, who are themselves in debt to God-
knows-who. Her estate, like her personal fortune, becomes an
abstract debit, a link in a chain of debt with an unspecified origin
and destination.

This happens, moreover, at precisely the moment she loses her
name, for the plot is so arranged as to require either Cecilia or
Mortimer Delvile to be disinherited at the moment of their marriage. The provisions of Cecilia's uncle's will had reversed normal
patriarchal practices by compelling the husband to adopt the wife's
surname, to be folded in to the female line. Of course, Cecilia's
property would still become her husband's, but he would, like a
woman, change his family identity on marrying. Young Delvile's
aristocratic family, though, refuses to endure this humiliation:
"How will the blood of your wronged ancestors," Mrs. Delvile
assures her son, "rise into your guilty cheeks, and how will your
heart throb with secret shame and reproach, when wished joy
upon your marriage by the name of Mr. *Beverley!*" (p. 662). The
severance of "blood" from name here promises a humiliating lack
of control over one's body, a lack of control triggered by the name
Beverley.

It is this humiliating feminization of her son that gives Mrs.
Delvile an excuse to take over Harrel's role as extortionist in the
second half of the book.[68] Mortimer Delvile himself accuses his
mother of extortion when she attempts to convince Cecilia to
renounce him: "I see your intention, I see your dreadful purpose;

---

68. Doody, *Frances Burney: The Life in the Works*, p. 137.

you will work upon the feelings of Miss Beverley, you will extort from her a promise to see me no more!" (p. 664); and Mrs. Delvile reenacts Harrel's suicidal threats and actions when she thinks the young couple will rebel:

> Grief and horror, next to frenzy . . . rose in the face of Mrs. Delvile, who, striking her hand upon her forehead, cried, "My brain is on fire!" and rushed out of the room.
> . . . Delvile . . . hastened eagerly to pursue her: she had only flown into the next parlour; but, upon following her thither, what was his dread and his alarm, when he saw her extended upon the floor, her face, hands, and neck all covered with blood. "Great Heaven!" he exclaimed, prostrating himself by her side, "what is it you have done!—where are you wounded?" (p. 665)

Mrs. Delvile has not actually attempted self-slaughter; she has only burst a blood vessel, as if to illustrate that the Delvile "blood" will not tolerate her son's insubordination (for Mrs. Delvile not only married a Delvile, but was also born one). Nevertheless, the parallel to Harrel's behavior is unmistakable. Mrs. Delvile's bloody face, moreover, is a highly effective threat, and Cecilia eventually resigns her name and property to save the older woman's life, just as she had signed away her paternal fortune under the threat of Harrel's suicide.

Once again, moreover, the individual life she tries to save is a placeholder for a more abstract, indeed unknowable, set of extortionists. Just as Harrel's body eventually dissolved into a bag of bills, Mrs. Delvile's is threatened by inundation with the blood of her ancestors. It is not Mrs. Delvile personally but rather the ancestors who seem to demand Cecilia's sacrifice, and these ancestors are characterized throughout the book by nothing so much as their deadness. "Why all them old grandfathers and aunts you brag of," Briggs rails at Delvile, "mere clay and dirt! fine things to be proud of! a parcel of old mouldy rubbish quite departed this life! raking up bones and dust, nobody knows for what! ought to be ashamed; who cares for dead carcasses? nothing but carrion" (p. 443). Hence, despite Cecilia's admiration for Mrs. Delvile, her attempt to save that lady by giving up her property is merely a response to the echo of a demand that originates, finally, in nobody.

Cecilia, then, must pay the debt of her sex, a debt that no avuncular will could cancel, and she must not pay it to her husband, from whom she might expect some return. The dream of being nobody in particular recurs as a nightmare. Unowned by her father-in-law; separated from her husband, who is tending his mother (in whom the blood of their ancestors continually threatens to "rise up") abroad; and driven from her former estate by the fear of incurring further debts to Eggleston, Cecilia is entirely displaced: "[S]he was now in one moment to appear to the world, an outcast from her own house, yet received into no other! a bride, unclaimed by a husband! an HEIRESS, dispossessed of all wealth!" Indeed, she is not even capable of claiming her new name: "To be first acknowledged as *Mrs. Delvile* in a state so degrading, she could not endure" (p. 848). Such a complete dispossession, one would imagine, would at least bring the relief of canceling all debts, but liability clings to the heroine. A series of accidents in London deprives her of her purse, the contents of her pockets, all indications of her identity, her memory, and her reason. In this state, she runs into an open shop, which just happens to be the establishment of pawnbrokers, and sits down on the floor, literally putting herself in hock. The pawnbrokers duly lock her up and advertise for "Whoever she belongs to" (p. 879) to come and redeem her.

As an item in a pawnshop, Cecilia attains a bizarre fulfillment of the fantasy of freedom from all particulars. Although she is locked up, she exists, like everything else in the shop, in a state that postpones normal property relations, for a pawnshop is where people temporarily suspend their rights to ownership. Things in a pawnshop are peculiarly unowned, inhabiting a transitional state between proprietors. Forfeited, they become the pawnbroker's commodities; redeemed, they return to their original owners; but while they are in hock, they seem to belong to nobody in particular. In this location of estrangement, Cecilia does not even own herself; she experiences what the narrator calls a "temporary . . . alienation of reason" (p. 878). Finally, when she was truly beside herself, "her fancy roved" (p. 879) from one incident of her history to another, just as it had roved during her dream of disembodiment from one scene of charity to another. She no longer has "promissory enjoyment," but while she dreams, the pawnbroker's bill grows longer.

This state of suspended identity, this escape from all particulars, achieved through (and constantly augmenting) debt, marks the climax of Cecilia's adventures. Once she is reclaimed by the Delviles, she gives up her longings for universal benevolence, her belief that owning and owing are the same, so that the novel can finally end. The possibility of closure is provided, moreover, by giving Cecilia a new and highly particular obligation. Mortimer's aunt, "in a fit of sudden enthusiasm" for the heroine, "altered her will, to leave her, and to her sole disposal, the fortune which, almost from his infancy, she had destined for her nephew" (p. 917). The Delvile ancestors give something back to Cecilia, but not as much as they had exacted; she once again has a fortune. And since this fortune has been gained at Mortimer's expense, it once again reverses the sexual norm. However, the fact that the money was originally destined for her husband finally solves the problem of universal debt, for it relieves Cecilia from having to accede to everybody's importunate demands: "She had learnt the error of profusion, even in charity and beneficence; and she had a motive for economy, in her animated affection for Mortimer" (p. 917). Mortimer becomes her saving principle of particularity; if she cannot ever really own her money, she can now at least know to whom it is owed. With this "motive for economy" the book can finally end because it has found a restrictive principle with which to stop the hemorrhage of expense that began with Cecilia's longings for a transcendent ethical position. The generalized being she had aspired to, which was repeatedly linked to death, to Nobody's perspective, is replaced by an "animated" partiality.

Some contemporary readers, however, who expected to find the heroine's moral aspirations rewarded rather than restricted at the end of a novel, complained that *Cecilia* failed to repay their interest by adequately compensating the heroine. They wanted, like Cecilia in her aerial dream, to see justice done, to watch evil characters punished and virtuous ones exalted; but instead the author largely ignores the villains in the end and rewards virtue by diminishing its means and chastening its ambition. Critics complained about the paucity of pleasure in such an ending:

> [H]ad the Eggleston family been represented as more worthy of their good fortune, or had a flaw in the Dean's will enabled Miss Beverley to enter again into possession of her estate, perhaps the conclusion would have left a more pleasing impression on the mind.[69]

69. *The English Review,* quoted in Doody, p. 144.

They also implied that the work's moral was obscured by the failure to give each character his due:

> Cecilia's conduct, in sacrificing so large a fortune to gratify the pride of the Delvile family, is an example which we would by no means wish to propose as an object of imitation for the fair sex, nor do we entirely approve of the conclusion, as we are of the opinion that the pride and ostentation of old Delvile, ought, in justice, to have been punished.[70]

The waste of the heroine's resources was thus seen as a seepage of meaning out of the novel, as well as a dissipation of the reader's investment of time and sympathy. Frances Burney, these critics suggest, had reneged on an implicit contract to provide the reader with an unequivocal emotional payoff. Edmund Burke even "wished the conclusion either more happy or more miserable; 'for in a work of imagination, he said, there is no medium.'"[71] The switch from a general to a restrictive economy of identification, the refusal to be profuse "even in beneficence," comes just at the time when the demands of the reader are at their most clamorous: the end.

Burney had actually considered and expressly rejected these demands when they were earlier voiced by Samuel Crisp and Charles Burney on reading the manuscript. According to Margaret Doody, Frances Burney's two Daddies "tried hard to think of expedients that would preserve Cecilia's estate for her and Mortimer—they were quite tender-hearted at seeing the fictional girl robbed of her treasure."[72] But the author was adamant, and her reply to a letter from Crisp on this subject reveals the connection between her chastening conclusion and the desire to differentiate herself in the literary marketplace:

> I must frankly confess I shall think I have rather written a farce than a serious history, if the whole is to end, like the hack Italian operas, with a jolly chorus that makes all parties good and all parties happy!
> . . .
> You find, my dear daddy, I am prepared to fight a good battle here; but I have thought the matter much over, and if I am made to

70. *Critical Review*, quoted in Doody, p. 144.
71. Quoted in Doody, p. 145.
72. Doody, p. 145.

give up this point, my whole plan is rendered abortive, and the last page of any novel in Mr. Noble's circulating library may serve for the last page of mine, since a marriage, a reconciliation, and some sudden expedient for great riches, concludes them all alike.[73]

To reward Cecilia for her sacrifice, to reward the reader for his, both would be to abort "the whole plan" by rescinding the novel's severe rule: identifying with Nobody must end in default. But, paradoxically, by enforcing this rule the writer herself escapes from the importunate demands of an anonymous public. The reader must learn to cut his losses so that they will not become the writer's. By herself defaulting on "promissory enjoyment" she avoids being a "hack" (the linking of this word with "Italian operas" might have been particularly effective against Dr. Burney) and establishes a principle of particularity that distinguished her novel from all the fungible capitulations to Nobody that circulate through Mr. Noble's library. Unlike Cecilia, the author shows her peculiar worth by not putting herself in Nobody's place.

$\sim$

Despite complaints about the ending, *Cecilia* was a huge popular success. A first edition of two thousand copies sold rapidly. Booksellers had difficulty keeping it in stock, and "the circulating library people . . . had it bespoken by old customers for months to come."[74] It did not, however, make Frances Burney financially independent. Apparently she was not specifically consulted about the sale of the copyright, which her father contracted to Payne and Cadell for £250 while she was away at Chessington. Thomas Payne was closely associated with the family, and Dr. Burney had obviously not driven a hard bargain with him, although there was apparently an informal agreement that Payne might pay an additional £50 "if the work answer'd." Dr. Johnson calculated that "honest Tom Payne," as the Burneys called him, must have made a profit of £500 in the first four months of sales, July to October 1782.[75] Frances Burney's letters record her growing realization that she had not

73. Quoted in Doody, p. 145.
74. Quoted in Hemlow, *The History of Fanny Burney*, p. 151.
75. The information on these transactions is all drawn from Hemlow, pp. 149–51.

been able to cash in on her enormous authorial credit: "Miss Cholmondeley told me she understood I have behaved like a poor *simple thing* again, & had a Father *no wiser than myself!*[76] Burney's "pretty spill" from *Cecilia* was invested in the three-per-cents, that is, appropriately, in the national debt; it paid her a mere pittance annually.

Dr. Burney casually, indeed unconsciously, sacrificed his daughter's individual financial interest to what he probably saw as the family's corporate good. Payne had been his own publisher, and his son James was courting Payne's daughter Sally; "Old Payne's" friendship was a valuable family asset, and sending him a profitable book would only improve and solidify their connection. The incident reveals, once again, the discrepancy between Dr. Burney's orientation toward networks of influence and patronage and his daughter's orientation toward an anonymous marketplace. As we have seen, there was a paradoxical complementarity to these orientations early in Frances Burney's career, but after *Cecilia* their incompatibility became increasingly apparent.

Dr. Burney was relatively indifferent to the cash value of his daughter's copyright because he was not ambitious for her financial independence. His ambition, rather, was to extend the family's honor and social reach through her authorship, and this ambition was completely fulfilled when Frances was offered a place at court as Second Keeper of the Queen's Robes. She would have a maid and footman and be paid a salary of £200 a year; her duty would be to assist at the queen's toilette. Her father was delighted at this proposal of "a place solicited by thousands and thousands of women of Fashion and Rank"[77] and even more excited by the prospect, as Joyce Hemlow remarks, "of organ-posts for himself, ships for James, schools, degrees, and dioceses for Charles."[78] The daughter dreaded to disappoint such high hopes: "I see him so much delighted at the prospect of an establishment he looks upon as so honourable . . . [B]ut what can make *me* amends for all I shall forfeit?"

The sad story of all Frances "forfeited" to the Burney family

---

76. Quoted in Hemlow, p. 151.
77. Quoted in Hemlow, p. 196.
78. Hemlow, p. 197.

interest during her five years in court has been frequently retold. She never was able to command much patronage; she had little time to herself; she was separated from her friends and kin alike and subjected to the stultifying routine of a royal domesticity that was at once deadeningly conventional and, as George III's insanity deepened, pathological. Her career as a novelist was suspended during these years, although she did write several tragic plays while attached to the royal household. Even the £200 salary, which should have made her some amends, seems to have been a source of oppression:

> If you will not laugh at me too much, I will also acknowledge that I liked Mr. Mathias all the more for observing him as awkward and embarrassed how to present me my salary as I felt myself in receiving it.
>
> There is something, after all, in money, by itself money, that I can never take possession of it without a secret feeling of something like degradation: money in its effects, and its produce, creates far different and more pleasant sensations. But here it made me feel so like— what I am, in short—a servant! We are all servants, to be sure, in the red book, but still—[79]

The source of degradation here is mysterious; the phrase "money, by itself money" directs our attention to the physical stuff, with its odd lack of substance, which is immediately opposed to "money in its effects, and its produce." In that moment of receiving bank notes, before their anonymous potency has been traded for particular things, the author seems to feel her own substance disappear; she becomes just another servant. "Money, by itself money" at once specifies too little and too much. To Burney's mind, it simultaneously denies her individuality and recalls the family history by conjuring the "place" where her father's career began, that of a servant.

When Burney, after exhausting the possibilities of patronage for her family, resigned her place in the royal household, she was given a pension of £100 per year, an adequate income for a single gentlewoman. But in 1793 she married an impoverished French émigré, M. d'Arblay, who had been adjutant general to Lafayette, had been imprisoned in Nivelles, and had escaped with nothing

79. *D and L*, vol. 3, pp. 142–43.

but his life: "Et me voilà, madame, réduit à rien, hormis un peu d'argent comptant, et encore très peu."[80] At first they lived on Burney's income—£100 from the pension, and £20 per annum from the invested revenue from *Cecilia*—but inflation, the failure in production of one of the tragedies she had written while serving as Second Keeper of the Queen's Robes, and the birth of a son sent her back to her surest resource, the novel.[81]

This time she was determined to ensure the highest income possible by subscription publication. Like Cecilia, she now had "a motive for economy" in her husband and son. Echoing and reinforcing her own sentiments, her brother Charles composed a slogan to guide his negotiations with the booksellers: "What Evelina . . . does now for the Son of Lowndes, & what Cecilia does for the Son of Payne, let your third work do for the Son of its Authour."[82] At the beginning of the saga of the publication of *Camilla*, we might say, Frances Burney was in the position Cecilia attained at the end of her story: she was liberated from a sense of obligation to Everybody and Nobody. She was finally free to pursue her self-interest in the form of cash. As if to mark the discontinuity represented by this policy, she associates herself with the usurious instrument of Cecilia's indebtedness, asking Charles to use "Jewish callousness"[83] in his dealings with the booksellers. Charles, in fact, proved a trustworthy agent, but she once again found herself at variance with the Burney family's collective needs. She wanted to publish by subscription, retaining the copyright and employing the bookseller who bid the highest amount for the project. Her family and friends all approved and enthusiastically joined in the subscription plan, for it demonstrated the extraordinary effectiveness of their extensive network of influence. But her father thought it was rude to deal so impersonally with the booksellers; moreover, her brother

80. Quoted in Hemlow, p. 229.

81. "For my own part I can only say, & solicit, & urge to my Fanny to *print, print, print!*—Here is a ressource [*sic*]—a certainty of removing present difficulties" (quoted in Bloom and Bloom, introduction to *Camilla*, p. xii; and in *The Journals and Letters of Fanny Burney*, vol. 2, ed. Joyce Hemlow and Althea Douglas [Oxford: Clarendon Press, 1972], letter 101, June 9, 1793, p. 148).

82. Quoted in Bloom and Bloom, introduction to *Camilla*, p. xviii; and in *The Journals and Letters of Fanny Burney*, vol. 3, letter 179, July 15, 1795, p. 140.

83. Quoted in Bloom and Bloom, introduction to *Camilla*, p. xvii; and in *The Journals and Letters of Fanny Burney*, vol. 3, letter 174, July 5, 1795, p. 126.

James pushed the claims of his father-in-law, Payne. But Frances steadfastly pleaded the needs of her new family, especially her "bambino," over the interests of her original family. Marriage and motherhood had, ironically, given her a new sense of ownership in her works at the very moment when, legally, she had lost them. *Camilla* was her "*Brain* work as much fair & *individual* property, as any other possession in either art or nature,"[84] she wrote to her brother Charles when defending her decision to sell the job to the highest bidding bookseller no matter who he was. The author finally had a family of her own to defend her against the patronage network of the family that had previously owned her.

She could, moreover, keep this new family *particular*; her sense of responsibility to them did not perpetually ramify out into "Everybody" or dissolve into "Nobody." M. d'Arblay's status as a French exile ensured the separation of the two families (the Burneys could make nothing of d'Arblay) and sustained Frances's illusion that she was the "individual" to whom her "*Brain* work" belonged. The letters between Frances and her "agent," Charles, make no mention of d'Arblay or his wishes; the general is referred to simply, in his own word, as the book's "copiste." Even the siblings' debate about maintaining or selling the copyright after the subscriptions had been collected is oddly silent on the topic of the legal owner. Indeed, an 1812 letter from d'Arblay indicates that he did not know the copyright to *Camilla* ever had been sold.[85] In arguing whether or not to sell it, an argument sparked by her marriage, all parties seem to have forgotten that because of her marriage it was not hers to sell. In becoming Madame d'Arblay, then, Frances Burney acquired both an alibi for asserting her individual economic interests in opposition to the Burneys' collective wishes and a docile, foreign husband who, "réduit à rien," apparently pressed no claims of his own.

Temporarily this arrangement gave her a location. With part of the approximately £2,000 she earned from *Camilla*, she and d'Arblay built Camilla Cottage, which was to have been both their home and their son's legacy. The name of the cottage stressed that one could turn cultural capital into a material structure, that through

84. *The Journals and Letters of Fanny Burney*, vol. 3, letter 176, July 7, 1795, p. 130.
85. Quoted in Bloom and Bloom, p. xxiv.

the magic of the marketplace, properly exploited, one could write oneself into one's own stable and heritable place. But the stability proved short-lived. For a variety of complicated reasons, the d'Arblays spent most of the Napoleonic period in France, and eventually they lost Camilla Cottage when the land under it was sold.

Hence the transition from Burney to d'Arblay, which seemed at first to offer a stabilizing particularity, actually inaugurated a new set of displacements. Moreover, the marriage to d'Arblay recapitulated the author's association with Nobody. Like Dr. Burney, d'Arblay combined Nobody and Somebody, since he was a déclassé French nobleman "réduit à rien." Dr. Burney had started out as the Nobody that d'Arblay was on the brink of becoming. It was as if Frances Burney had been attracted to d'Arblay because he provided the heritage that her own father lacked, but a heritage that had been reduced simply to a name. This "rien," furthermore, put the author more at Nobody's disposal than she had ever been before. She was now completely intent on writing a novel that would sell, and the result was a marked decline in the quality of her work. *Camilla* was a great financial success, but it did not succeed with critics because it was hastily written and designed to please every taste. It tried, for example, to capitalize on the new craze for Gothic,[86] was excessive in its melodrama and trite in its conduct-book moralizing, and concluded with precisely the sort of payoffs Frances Burney had denounced as bribes when she defaulted at the end of *Cecilia*. In short, this capitulation to what the author apparently believed were the demands of her anonymous public actually produced a book that the public found disappointing. It sold on the basis of her reputation, but that reputation was also diminished by it. She had finally cashed in her credit with her readers, but only by devaluing her own paper.

In a sense, Burney continued to live off the credit of her first two novels for the rest of her life. Even the place that Napoleon gave d'Arblay when the couple lived in France was, the general thought, really just a tribute to "le mari de Cecilia," *Cecilia* being one of the emperor's favorite novels. She never wrote another truly popular work, although both *Camilla* and *The Wanderer* made money. However, because the criticisms of these later works belied their sales,

---

86. See Bloom and Bloom on this point, p. xx.

because readers complained of having been disappointed in their expectations, the author continued to owe what she owned. The more she wrote, the more she sold, the deeper in debt she was to a public who continually complained that she was not making good on her earlier promise. The Nobodies who had taken such pleasure in her fictions gradually declined, it seemed, into nobody at all.

6

The Changeling's Debt
Maria Edgeworth's Productive Fictions

One might expect Maria Edgeworth not to have had the same feelings of indebtedness that plagued Frances Burney. Unlike the Burneys, the Edgeworths were gentry. Far from belonging nowhere, they lived in a town in Ireland called "Edgeworthstown," where the family had been installed since the time of Elizabeth. Maria Edgeworth, moreover, composed her first works for publication with her father's full approval, and she thought of their literary relationship as a "partnership." She had, furthermore, a far more fully developed rationale than Frances Burney's for explaining the role of fiction in the general economy of literature. And to top off all these advantages, she had been taught to believe in the "productivist" economic theories of the political economists, who stressed that human labor created value, and she applied their ideas to her own work as an author.

We might expect these various factors to combine into an optimism about staying out of debt, and many of Edgeworth's explicit statements fulfill that expectation. In an 1836 letter, for example, she declared, "I have always thought it disgracefully mean in literary manufacturers to trade upon their name and to put off ill-finished works upon credit. That is what I never will do."[1] In the same letter she explained that she relied on market forces themselves (as embodied in the booksellers) to keep her from living off her authorial credit: "The Booksellers, the publisher are the only advisers to be depended upon because both their interest and their

1. Letter to Rachel Mordecai Lazarus, April 15, 1836, in *The Education of the Heart: The Correspondence of Rachel Mordecai Lazarus and Maria Edgeworth*, ed. Edgar E. MacDonald (Chapel Hill: Univ. of North Carolina Press, 1977), p. 276.

knowledge of the facts by which they should judge of the *public* taste and feelings enable them to judge and advise well."[2]

This belief in the free market's ability to stimulate efficient production and hence promote the general good is fundamental to Edgeworth's works. Indeed, one modern critic, after acknowledging Edgeworth's pioneering role in the development of children's literature, the regional novel, and the novel of manners, concludes, "Her outstanding and epoch-making feat, however, is that she introduced the newly-developed science of political economy into literature, assimilating it not only to her personal beliefs, but also to her artistic purposes."[3] The very concept of virtuous action, for example, changes subtly as Edgeworth's tales stress that the landed gentry should not dispense charity but should rather engage in fair and productive business dealings. Everyone, including the hero, should refrain from interference with the smooth functioning of the benevolent free market. As Edgeworth explained in *Professional Education*, which was published under her father's name in 1808:

> The knowledge of the value and price of land, of the rents which tenants are able to pay, of the causes which affect the rise and fall of rents, is absolutely necessary to a good landlord: he deals in land as tradesmen deal in different commodities; his tenants are his customers; he should therefore know precisely the value of what he is to sell, and of what they are to purchase, that he may neither be a dupe nor an extortioner.[4]

Noblesse oblige in her works requires deference to the invisible hand of the marketplace. "[E]ven if the study of political economy were only to teach country gentlemen to refrain from rash interference," *Professional Education* asserts, "it would be of material service" (p. 290).

Indeed, one of the most oft-repeated plots of Maria Edgeworth's tales is the "embourgeoisement" of the hero: a young man is educated out of his fashionable disdain for business, takes charge

2. Pp. 275–76.

3. Ria Omasreiter, "Maria Edgeworth's Tales: A Contribution to the Science of Happiness," in *Functions of Literature: Essays Presented to Erwin Wolff on His Sixtieth Birthday*, ed. Ulrich Broich, Theo Stemmler, and Gerd Stratmann (Tübingen: M. Niemeyer, 1984), p. 207.

4. *Essays on Professional Education* by R. L. Edgeworth, Esq. (London, 1812), p. 290. Subsequent quotations from this edition are cited parenthetically in the text.

of his own affairs, and learns to accept economic reality, even when it violates his generous impulses or his "sensibility." The unpracticed Lord Glenthorn in *Ennui*, for example, generously raises his laborers' wages only to find that the people work less "when they could with less work have money enough to support them."[5] He thereby learns to allow wages to find their own level, just as he learns not to overpopulate his estate by giving a "reward" for childbearing or to encourage a false "independence" by persuading his tenants to make at home things that they could, his enlightened agent assures him, more cheaply buy. The free marketplace, when disencumbered of middlemen, monopolies, protective taxes, and artificially inflated rents, the narrators of the tales often explain, promotes and regulates the highest possible level of production.

This was the creed by which the Edgeworths ran their own estate. For example, they engaged no middlemen outside the family, and hence the work of overseeing the estate and representing the landlord often fell to the children, especially Maria. From the time she was fourteen, according to her stepmother's *Memoir*,

> Her father employed her as an agent and accountant; an employment in which she showed marvellous acuteness and patience; it not only gave her habits of business and accuracy, but let her into a familiarity with the modes of thought and terms of expression among the people which she could in no other way have acquired. The exactness of arithmetical calculations far from disgusting her by its dryness, was agreeable to the honesty of her mind, and the apparently monotonous business of adding up columns of accounts was a pleasure to her, so much did she like to make her totals agree and complete her admirably kept account books.[6]

By keeping a steady watch over her father's economic affairs, Maria Edgeworth believed she was improving the productivity of the land and promoting the industry and prosperity of the tenants. A sharp eye to the family's self-interest and a fastidious attention to income

5. *Ennui*, in vol. 4 of *The Novels of Maria Edgeworth in Twelve Volumes* (London, 1893), p. 66. Subsequent quotations from this edition are cited parenthetically in the text.

6. Mrs. [Frances] Edgeworth, *A Memoir of Maria Edgeworth, with a Selection from Her Letters* (Privately printed, 1867), vol. 1, pp. 14–15; quoted in Marilyn Butler, *Maria Edgeworth: A Literary Biography* (Oxford: Clarendon Press, 1972), pp. 89–90.

and expenditure were thus early incorporated into her sense of filial and class duty. All sorts of morality lay in well-kept accounts.

But could this classical economic liberalism really be applied to literary production? If a landlord was merely a businessman dealing in land, was an author merely a businesswoman dealing in texts? Like the letter quoted earlier, many of Maria Edgeworth's comments on authorship conform, at least on the surface, to her general optimism about the efficiency and morality of the marketplace: market forces should stimulate the production of high-quality literary commodities, over which the writer had assiduously labored. Upright economic dealings were inherently moral, and hence no "feminine" or genteel reticence about money matters can be found in Edgeworth's letters, no fear of being "degraded" by the marketplace. Her business correspondence is neither pathetic, like Charlotte Lennox's, nor ambivalent, like Frances Burney's. Until his death in 1817, Richard Lovell Edgeworth handled their correspondence with their publishers, first Joseph Johnson and then his nephews and heirs, John Miles and Rowland Hunter. After Richard Lovell's death, though, Maria dealt with Hunter herself. When she became convinced that he was mismanaging her affairs, she matter-of-factly proposed that they end their association.[7] Later, she asked John Gibson Lockhart, Walter Scott's son-in-law, to be her agent in negotiating with publishers. Lockhart did an excellent job for her, so when he and Richard Bentley suggested that her 1833 novel, *Helen*, be published in three volumes rather than the two that she had requested, she accepted their judgment along with an extra £200 for the third volume (she had already received £900 for the copyright): "You find that I did not swear and kick but behaved like a reasonable woman & a lady moreover & pockets my £200 with a very good grace."[8]

Edgeworth's argument with Bentley and Lockhart about *Helen*, however, points to deep inconsistencies in her thinking about the literary marketplace. She hoped to publish *Helen* in two volumes rather than three because she wanted the public to know that "far from having stretched a single page or a single sentence to *make out*

---

7. Butler, p. 491.
8. Maria Edgeworth to Honora Edgeworth, November 2, 1833; quoted in Butler, p. 465.

a third volume—I have cut away as much as ever I could—cut it to the quick."[9] Edgeworth frequently expressed this fear of appearing to write too much and too easily. For example, in the letter with which I began this chapter, she cites overproduction as the normal weakness of literary manufacturers:

> I have written so much that I ought to fear falling into the common fault from which even my admired and admirable friend Sir Walter Scott could not, did not escape. Perhaps he was forced on by his desire to fulfil his engagements with his creditors, but as I have no reason of that kind to urge me to write I should be inexcusable if I were to *overdo*.[10]

Statements like this one indicate that Edgeworth was not as firmly convinced about the efficacy of the literary marketplace as she sometimes proclaimed, for the market could create literary excess, especially if one were, like Scott, overdependent on it. The marketplace, therefore, was not self-sufficient; it would not necessarily eliminate authorial debt: to pay his creditors, Scott "put off ill-finished work upon credit"; he borrowed on his literary reputation. In contrast, a writer like Maria Edgeworth, whose income came from outside the literary marketplace, could best be counted on to act like a truly conscientious manufacturer. Although in this letter she expressed her belief that the booksellers are the most reliable sources of information about the literary marketplace because they are financially interested, she also admitted that her relative financial independence was what allowed her to turn out a "finished" product.

Moreover, the threat of debt was not entirely squelched even by the author's economic independence, for Edgeworth was obviously anxious that her very liberty would make her all the more culpable if she failed to honor the public's faith in her, if she defaulted on her implicit contract by overproducing. Although Scott might have been forced by financial necessity to write novels that were little more than overdrafts against his reputation, Edgeworth's very leisure might just as easily, she claimed, have led to the excess she considered a form of debt. Hence, the best chance one had of being a truly conscientious literary businesswoman, independence of the

9. Letter to Honora Edgeworth, November 2, 1833; quoted in Butler, p. 465.
10. Letter to Rachel Mordecai Lazarus, April 15, 1836, p. 275.

marketplace, also put one in constant danger of imposing on the public.

To escape from this danger, one had to depart radically from productivist economic principles by almost disregarding the author's time when assessing the "thrift" of a literary work. A fear of overproduction led Edgeworth to imagine the efficient adjustment of literary means to ends almost entirely from the reader's point of view, assuming that the writer could afford to spend her time in unremunerated labor. Just as Maria's estate accounts never took account of the time required to make them, the labor of her writing was never charged against the "economy" of her works. Indeed lavish, rather than efficient, labor was one of Maria Edgeworth's hallmarks as a craftswoman. Richard Lovell, for example, repeatedly assures the public in his prefaces to Maria's novels that "she does not write negligently,"[11] that in preparing her work for the public she is never "careless or presuming" (*Ennui*, p. vii). "I can assert that twice as many pages were written for these volumes as are now printed," he proudly announces in the preface to *Harrington* and *Ormond*. The labor of composing and revising is frequently stressed along with its resulting conciseness, the saturation of each page with meaning.

Richard Lovell is calling attention in such testimonials to what is commonly called the "economical" quality of his daughter's prose. But the question obtrudes itself: economical for whom? Certainly not for the writer, whose burden of labor—to produce the ease with which the reader is able to extract the meaning—must be imagined as excessive. Indeed, as Lockhart explained when arguing that *Helen* be printed in three volumes, the impression of conciseness did not pay; if the novel was not as long as most three-volume works, it should still appear to be as long. Hence, although Edgeworth eventually "pockets my £200," she still insisted that the appearance of length belied the real thrift of her style. Precisely in stressing her labor, then, Edgeworth turned herself as conscientious manufacturer-author into a new sort of

---

11. "To the Reader," *Harrington*, in vol. 9 of *The Novels of Maria Edgeworth in Twelve Volumes* (London, 1893), p. v. Subsequent quotations from this edition are cited parenthetically in the text.

Lady Bountiful, for only a surplus derived from some source outside the book trade could account for her plentiful pains.

In short, the use of the manufacturing metaphor calls attention to a potential conflict between the very notions of economic and literary value, for labor figures differently in the calculation of each. For example, when Richard Lovell stresses the labor that goes into the works by assuring the reader "that twice as many pages were written for these volumes as are now printed," the almost comical naïveté of the remark might lead one to doubt the applicability of the labor theory of value, the theory that lies at the heart of economic productivism, to intellectual creation. Does the amount of creative or editorial labor expended on a book really correlate with its value? Does a low ratio of words to ideas ensure that the reader will reap a greater intellectual profit per page? Does such a boast not assume that the writing is significant to begin with? What standards of significance should be used? Can the literary marketplace itself provide one?

Maria Edgeworth was willing to answer these questions, but the answers are not integrated into her speculations on the literary marketplace per se. To explain what qualities made a book valuable, she turned from literary economics to the role of literature in the economic reform of nations. In conformity with her economic liberalism, she often affirmed that a good book was one that made its readers more "productive" members of society. But then, what exactly did "productive" mean? Did it simply mean "laborious," or did it also mean, as it would have for the political economists, "commercially profitable"? Since we have just seen that in the work of the author herself "laboriousness" and "commercial profitability" were often in conflict, how is the result of a literary enterprise to be assessed? What productivity in the reader would repay the (commercially unprofitable) pains expended by the author? Edgeworth's theory of fiction, which I examine later in the chapter, addresses these questions, but the theory itself was plagued by a constant sense that literature would always exceed its productive uses.

Indeed, the more the literary work was regarded as a "finished" commodity, complete and self-enclosed, the less useful it might seem as a plan for a productive life. This tension can be felt even when Edgeworth discusses the books of the political economists themselves. She explained, for example, in *Professional Education*,

> Smith's Wealth of Nations is the best book to open [a young land-lord's] views, and to give him clear ideas. While he reads, he should be warned not to take any thing for granted; not to believe, that, because he is perusing an author of high authority, he must therefore resign his understanding implicitly. No—the object is to induce him to think and reason for himself, not to make him get by rote the opinions or words of any author; that would be only to make him a *talking copy* of a book. (p. 297)

The point is not just that a book must be read to be "finished," but that it must be read in a particular, critical, manner that works against its "finished" quality. A good book is an odd sort of tool that can only be useful if it inspires skepticism about itself, for its passive absorption would merely make a representation of a representation, a *"talking copy* of a book." This passage taps into Edgeworth's worry that books might become divorced from realities and merely proliferate signs.[12] The political economists themselves often expressed a similar suspicion of representation and a fear of its autonomy: accounts, money, indeed the whole symbolic apparatus that allowed the market to function was believed to be necessary but subordinate to the value-creating operations of material production, and Edgeworth often seems to yearn for a literature that would also be subservient, rather than supplemental, to those ends. Hence, to make a landlord who could encourage productive tenants, even the *Wealth of Nations* must be treated as a provisional, tentative work, not as something complete and valuable in itself, but as a conditional thing to be constantly tested

---

12. Edgeworth's *Letters for Literary Ladies,* for example, opens with an epistolary exchange between two gentlemen on the subject of women writers. The gentleman correspondent in favor of literary ladies distinguishes between mere "books in circulation" and "produce of intrinsic worth," noting that women's writing might fall into either category:

> If [women writers] merely increased the number of books in circulation, you might declaim against them with success; but when they add to the general fund of . . . knowledge, you cannot with any show of justice prohibit their labours: there can be no danger that the market should ever be overstocked with produce of intrinsic worth.

Letters for Literary Ladies: to which is added, An Essay on the Noble Science of Self-Justification (London, 1814), p. 82. Subsequent quotations from this edition are cited parenthetically in the text.

against reality. Edgeworth's very productivism, therefore, made her hesitate to accord any texts the independent ontological status that would completely qualify them as "finished works."

In general, political economy might be said to have promoted a new fastidiousness in distinguishing between fundamental and secondary phenomena, between, for example, real wealth (e.g., vendible commodities) and its representations (e.g., money, writing).[13] Although it may have encouraged all sorts of industriousness, it also distinguished between kinds of labor, rendering a very large number of activities "unproductive." Consider, for example, Adam Smith's discussion of "unproductive" employments:

> The labour of some of the most respectable orders in the society is, like that of menial servants, unproductive of any value, and does not fix or realise itself in any permanent subject or vendible commodity, which endures after that labour is past, and for which an equal quantity of labour could afterwards be procured. The Sovereign, for example, with all the officers both of justice and war who serve under him, the whole army and navy, are unproductive labourers. . . . In the same class must be ranked, some of the gravest and most important, and some of the most frivolous professions: churchmen, lawyers, physicians, men of letters of all kinds; players, buffoons, musicians, opera-singers, opera-dancers, etc.[14]

Theoretically it was not the work per se that made these jobs unproductive but their usual failure, Smith tells us, to produce profits for a manufacturer; Smith constantly, however, confounds

---

13. In an ingenious reading of Marx on commodity fetishism, Moishe Postone has traced this distinction to the commodity form itself, which

> appears "doubled" as money (the manifest form of value) and as the commodity (the manifest form of use-value). Although the commodity is a social form expressing both value and use-value, the effect of this externalization is that the commodity appears only as its use-value dimension, as purely material and "thingly." Money, on the other hand, then appears as . . . the manifestation of the purely abstract, rather than as the externalized manifest form of the value dimension of the commodity itself. The form of materialized social relations specific to capitalism appears on the level of the analysis as the opposition between money, as abstract, and "thingly" nature.

Hence, representation in productivist ideology is always prone to disavowal and vulnerable as a scapegoat for problems in the economy. "Anti-Semitism and National Socialism," in *Germans and Jews since the Holocaust: The Changing Situation in West Germany*, ed. Anson Rabinbach and Jack Zipes (New York: Holmes and Meier, 1986), p. 308.

14. *The Wealth of Nations*, introd. Edwin R. A. Seligman (New York: E. P. Dutton, 1970), vol. 1, p. 295.

the unprofitableness of these laborers with their lack of a concrete, material product. Lack of profit and lack of material substance were theoretically separable,[15] but the early political economists seldom made the distinction. Presumably, Smith lists the labor of "men of letters of all kinds" under the rubric "unproductive," even though it frequently issues in vendible commodities called books, because the part of the commodity men of letters create is not, in Smith's view, the material stuff, but the books' intangible meanings. In other words, the writer is concerned with the book as a representation, rather than as a material object, and is therefore disqualified from the ranks of productive laborers. Simply to be working, therefore, was not enough; the political economist himself, for example, might be constantly writing and sending texts off for publication and yet still be "unproductive" according to his own definition.[16] The very political economy that inspired Edgeworth's industriousness, therefore, also led her to doubt that her work was truly productive.

In short, Edgeworth was as nervous about the possibility that her authorship was a kind of deficit spending as Frances Burney had been, and her nervousness seems to have arisen from the very factors I listed earlier as likely securities against feeling indebted. Her adherence to classical political economy, we have just seen, created a double bind: if her texts were regarded as ends in themselves, as primary realities, they could take on a dangerous illusion of autonomy; if they were recognized as mere representations, they were not, strictly speaking, the fruits of truly "productive" labor. Hence, productivism was itself a source of anxiety; the rest of this chapter demonstrates that it interacted with the other main facts of

15. Ricardo separated them more rigorously than Smith, and Marx devoted long sections of his notes on political economy, published as *The Theory of Surplus Value*, to defining the difference between productive and unproductive labor in ways that would make the materiality of the labor or the product irrelevant.

16. Furthermore, despite Smith's characterization of much unproductive labor as "noble and useful" (p. 295), within a few pages the terminology of "unproductive and productive" gives way to that of "idle and industrious." Hence what started off as a neutral economic category differentiating kinds of labor blends in to a moral distinction between those who do not work and those who do. See p. 299: "[The rent of land and the profit of stock] might both maintain indifferently either productive or unproductive hands. They seem, however to have some predilection for the latter. The expense of a great lord feeds generally more idle than industrious people. . . ."

Edgeworth's intellectual life—her literary partnership with her father, her convictions about fiction, her membership in the Anglo-Irish gentry—to multiply the ways in which a female author might find herself living on credit. Like Frances Burney, Maria Edgeworth wrote out of a deep sense of obligation, which her participation in the literary marketplace promised to discharge but actually continually augmented. Also like Burney, though, she kept writing because of her sense of indebtedness; the debt itself, we might say, was paradoxically productive.

~

The lesson Maria Edgeworth learned from political economy—that her product was probably ontologically insufficient, merely epiphenomenal—was reiterated in her "partnership" with her father. The literary relationship between the two Edgeworths was, surprisingly, predicated on the traditional split between thought and writing, a secularized version of the religious division between the spirit and the letter of the Word. Such a basis is surprising because the Edgeworths were certainly not traditionalists; indeed, they famously advocated an educational system that stressed individual liberty, regardless of the child's gender. And yet they seem to have participated equally in the process of dividing and gendering their intellectual labor so as to relegate Maria to a subordinate role.

That Maria was seen as the lesser author was all the stranger since their collaboration stemmed from Richard Lovell's inability to write either legible or polished prose. His correspondents, for example, complained that they could not read his handwriting and that his letters were abrupt and inelegant. Far from denying these charges, he wove them into an account of his excessive vitality, declaring himself better suited to communicating "by living voice than by dead letter."[17] Maria, with her neat hand and patient, sedentary habits, should write for him.[18] This "partnership," as she

17. Butler, *Maria Edgeworth: A Literary Biography*, p. 128.
18. As Butler notes, only one modern critic has reproduced this view of the relationship between the Edgeworths uncritically. See Desmond Clarke, *The Ingenious Mr. Edgeworth* (London: Oldbourne, 1965), p. 102. Other treatments of the relationship include Butler; Patrick Murray, *Maria Edgeworth: A Study of the Novelist* (Cork: Mercier Press, 1971); James Newcomer, *Maria Edgeworth*, Irish Writers Series (Lewisburg, PA: Bucknell Univ. Press, 1973); Elizabeth Kowaleski-Wallace, *Their*

called it, never involved anything as simple as dictation; although she claimed that the original ideas were her father's, she acknowledged that the compositions themselves were her own. Nevertheless, Edgeworthian authorship was consciously thought by both partners to be the daughter's execution of the father's intentions.

The relation between the fatherly spirit and the daughterly letter, however, was prone to attenuation, especially when the fatherly intention took the form of a single word assigned as topic and the daughterly realization was a narrative. In 1780, when Maria was a girl at school, Richard Lovell instructed her to "send me a tale, about the length of a 'Spectator,' upon the subject of GENEROSITY; it must be taken from History or Romance, and must be sent the day se'night after you receive this, and I beg you will take some pains about it."[19] When the story was finished, it was judged by both Maria's father and her uncle to be "an excellent story, and extremely well written." "But," the uncle wondered, "where's the Generosity?" That question, her stepmother recalled, "became a sort of proverb with her afterwards."[20] In the author's mind, it seemed to link the justification of her fictional tales to their adequate illustration of a prior Idea in her father's mind. The demand for "Generosity" from the girl was a reminder of what she owed her father strictly on the grounds of her biological generation.[21] And this obligation to be generous with her "pains" in elaborating and elucidating the paternal Idea was increased by her father's generosity in supplying topics. The trick, of course, was to embellish the Idea in narrative without obscuring it; the father's Generosity, his generative spirit, had to be visible through the literal trappings of the tale.

But even when Richard Lovell did not assign the topics, Maria's writing was still conceived as the fulfillment of his intention, since

---

Fathers' Daughters: Hannah More, Maria Edgeworth, and Patriarchal Complicity (New York: Oxford Univ. Press, 1991), esp. pp. 95–99. For an account of the relationship between Edgeworth and her stepmother, see Mitzi Myers, "The Dilemmas of Gender as Double-Voiced Narrative; or, Maria Edgeworth Mothers the Bildungsroman," in *The Idea of the Novel in the Eighteenth Century*, ed. Robert W. Uphaus (East Lansing, MI: Colleagues Press, 1988), pp. 67–96.

19. Frances Edgeworth, *A Memoir of Maria Edgeworth*, p. 8.
20. Frances Edgeworth, *A Memoir of Maria Edgeworth*, p. 8.
21. This writing assignment followed Richard Lovell Edgeworth's instructions in the same letter about sending a work-bag, which Maria had made, to her aunt.

he had a continuous notion that his daughter should write. Whatever she wrote, she seemed convinced, was therefore a result of his authorship and a further manifestation of his generosity. "In fact," Maria claimed, "my father never thought of becoming an author, till he felt sufficient motive, in the wish to encourage and assist me to finish 'Practical Education' [an early title for *Harry and Lucy*, which was published as part 1 of *Early Lessons* in 1801]. All his literary ambition then and ever was for me."[22]

Such a claim can be squared with the historical fact that what came out in Richard Lovell's name was actually written by Maria only if we understand that she regarded her father's lending his name to a publication as but another instance of his "generosity." For example, when Maria began work on *Professional Education*, she expressed her usual sense of gratitude to her father for telling her what to write about:

> I am now laying myself out for wisdom, for my father has excited my ambition to write a *useful* essay upon professional education: he has pointed out to me that to be a mere writer of pretty stories & novellettes would be unworthy of his partner, pupil & daughter & I have been so touched by his eloquence or his kindness or all together, that I have thrown aside all thoughts of pretty stories, & put myself into a course of solid reading.[23]

When two years later Maria told the same correspondent that the book she had been laboriously writing all that time was to appear under her father's name only, she merely expressed wonder and anxiety about being entrusted with his reputation (which was largely her own creation):

> I am well repaid for all the labor it has cost me by seeing that my father is pleased with it & thinks it a *proof of affection* & gratitude—I cannot help however looking forward to its publication & fate with an anxiety & an apprehension that I never felt before in the same degree—for consider my father's credit is entirely at stake![24]

22. *Memoirs of Richard Lovell Edgeworth, Esq. Begun by Himself, and Concluded by His Daughter, Maria Edgeworth*, 3rd ed. (London: Bentley, 1844), p. 439.
23. Maria Edgeworth to Sophie Ruxton, February 26, 1805; quoted in Butler, p. 210.
24. Maria Edgeworth to Sophie Ruxton, January 23, 1808; quoted in Butler, p. 210.

These letters succinctly state the grounds of Maria's constant condition of debt to her father. When she writes fiction, she is "unworthy" of him ("[W]here's the Generosity?"); when she writes the kind of nonfiction that he might have written himself, even though her pains are recognized as proofs of gratitude, she nevertheless owes him the idea; and the further attribution of authorship to her father, far from canceling the debt, only increases it by putting all his "credit" into her hands. The whole cycle then, predictably, began again when Maria brought out the first three volumes of the *Tales of Fashionable Life* in 1809, which her father claimed in his preface were written "to illustrate *Professional Education*," a book publicly attributed to him, once again opening the gap between fatherly ideas and daughterly fictional illustrations.

The inadequacy of the letter to the spirit, the condition of owing in which it constantly finds itself, was thus the dynamic principle animating the "partnership" between Maria Edgeworth and her father. The nonchalance of Richard Lovell's various "appropriations" indicates that he assumed, as she assumed, that her pen was always naturally at his disposal. In writing to a friend about a pamphlet he was planning, for example, he uses the pronouns "I," "we," and "she" practically interchangeably: "I have a remedy in my power . . . I mean an appeal to the English public—. . . . We, that is to say Maria (who is always meant by we, when writing is in question) have notes taken during every part of the transaction— which are interesting & which she can make entertaining."[25] Even when works appeared under Maria Edgeworth's name, as all her fiction did, she asked her father to endorse them in prefaces, and these short statements often reclaimed the fictions by remarking, as in the preface to *Tales of Fashionable Life*, their merely illustrative status.

These endorsements ultimately earned Richard Lovell a reputation as an egregious egotist, and scholars are still arguing about his moral right to appropriate her work. My task here, though, is not to judge the Edgeworths, but to understand the dynamic that kept Maria writing. Certainly it was "patriarchal" in the sense that both parties to the interaction imagined the daughter's time and energy to be largely at her father's disposal. To have a clever unmarried

25. Quoted in Butler, *Maria Edgeworth: A Literary Biography*, pp. 139–40.

daughter was to have a ghostwriter, as well as an accountant and estate agent, perpetually at one's service. Her time, energy, education, and talents were, after all, otherwise unemployable. These "patriarchal" assumptions, though, not only increased Maria's productivity but also allowed her to conceive of her "author-self"[26] as the expression of a conglomerate being larger than her individual self. Maria Edgeworth had two authorial personae—Maria Edgeworth the fiction writer and Richard Lovell Edgeworth the educator—both of them her father's gifts.

The constant sense of obligation, therefore, was indistinguishable from a sense of expanded, even grandiose, authorship. If Richard Lovell had rigorously separated their intellectual labors and strictly given his daughter credit for every word she wrote, Maria would no longer have had the power to produce her father's "author-self." They seem to have tacitly decided early in their "partnership" that there was to be no strict settlement of accounts between them lest the animating principle of obligation be reduced to a mere calculation of normal debts and payments. In 1791, when her father gave her £500 upon his departure for England, leaving her behind as his estate manager, for example, he later wrote, apparently in response to her embarrassment about the money, to reassure her that he had not intended it as a monetary compensation for her labor:

> *I never meant payment!*
> As to the sentimental part of your letter—a Father may oblige or be obliged by a grown up daughter. . . .
> You were obliged to me whilst I hazarded my affairs & gave up time in teaching you Business.
> I have been obliged by your attention to my affairs for so many years after you had learn'd the Business—The Quantum of Obligation on either side I shall never enquire—not from the fear of finding myself in the lighter scale of the balance but from knowing & feeling that all obligation ceases the moment it is computed by the Giver—[27]

The self-characterization of Richard Lovell here as "the Giver" casually conflates "giving" money because he is obliged with "giv-

26. She uses the term "authorship self" in correspondence with the Ruxtons.
27. Richard Lovell Edgeworth to Maria Edgeworth, August 17, 1791; quoted in Butler, p. 102.

ing" yet another obligation. Paying Maria would have been treating her like an employee; instead her father "obliges" her simply by letting her do his business at his own "hazard." Paying her would have been un*generous* and would therefore have eroded the obligation that set her about her father's business.

And as the letter continues, it becomes clear that the Giver's ultimate gift is the bond of obligation itself. This bond, moreover, hints that the father and daughter might each be both debtor and creditor. Paying Maria would have implied that the father could "requite" the daughter, that the spirit could be "quit" of the letter, and therefore that the daughter-debtor had lost the power to oblige the "Giver" continuously. Richard Lovell reassured his daughter that the £500 was no such announcement of his own independence: "I am therefore under no apprehension of losing you," he declared, "& you may *sew* my name again to my Bond."[28] Because she belongs to him, she holds his bond.

But we should note that Maria can only hold this bond if she acts as the scribe, the maker or restorer of the letters of her father's name. Her father's command to "sew my name" might be read in two ways. It could be an image of embroidery, which invokes both Maria's femininity and the peculiarly binding fastness of the signature.[29] But since he is asking her to sew his name "again" to his bond, the sentence might imply that the signature of the imaginary bond might have been metaphorically torn from it, perhaps as a result of the misunderstood £500, for a bond was formerly canceled by having its signature ripped off.[30] If we interpret the sentence in this way, Maria is being given the task of repairing a make-believe document, which she herself must have rent, by reattaching her father's name to it. In either case, Maria has the care of the physical signature that binds them, and the most generous thing her father can do is allow her to attach it to some document. Out of her sense of obligation for this generosity, she continues to write.

28. Quoted in Butler, p. 103.
29. Richard Lovell assigned Maria embroidery jobs when she was a child, just as he assigned her writing tasks. In two of his letters of 1780, for example, instructions about embroidery precede his directions about writing. See Frances Edgeworth, *A Memoir of Maria Edgeworth*, pp. 5–9.
30. I am grateful to Stephen Greenblatt for this suggestion.

~

As several of the passages I have quoted indicate, the gendered distinction between the letter and the spirit extended to the Edgeworths' notions about genres. The fictions were published under Maria's name because they were believed to partake more of the letter than the spirit: the *Tales of Fashionable Life*, for example, were exemplary instances of the more abstract principles of *Professional Education*. The fictions, Maria Edgeworth continually stated, were to the treatises as particulars are to generalities, examples to precepts, illustrations to ideas, material signifiers to immaterial thoughts.

The tales, that is, were considered secondary; they owed their very raison d'être to the principles they illustrated. Like their acknowledged author, therefore, they came into the world indebted. Their debt, moreover, was augmented by their necessarily exceeding the messages they conveyed, thereby calling attention to their superfluity in the economy they imagined. The story must always exceed the moral, just as the sugar that makes a medicine palatable is always an accessory to the drug. Hence although Edgeworth's metaphors for her fictions frequently stressed that she added nothing to the substance of her father's thought, they can never wholly obscure the tales' supplementary nature. "In the lighter works [i.e. the novels]," she wrote to Francis Jeffrey in 1806, ". . . I have only repeated the same [i.e. her father's] opinions in other forms. . . . A certain quantity of bullion was given to me and I coined it into as many pieces as I thought would be convenient for popular taste."[31] Repeating and coining in this quotation are difficult ideas to reconcile; when one coins bullion, one does not make a copy of it but rather gives it a different material form. However, if one repeats opinions, especially opinions that have already been circulated in written form, one is necessarily duplicating the "originals."

The coining metaphor, though, emphasizes the disseminating function of the tales, linking the fiction more closely than the nonfiction to both print itself and the literary marketplace. The

31. Quoted in Butler, p. 272.

implication is that the father's riches can only be put into circulation by the particularizing activity of the daughter. I will return to the implications of Maria's sense of herself as the disseminator of her father's riches when I discuss her revision of the Jessica plot from *The Merchant of Venice*. At this stage in the argument, though, I want to note that the coining metaphor, in addition to attaching dissemination to the particularity of fiction, also effects a paradoxical transposition of the relationship between matter and idea. The metaphor equates stories with the forms that a certain material mass, the bullion, can be made to take. Here the fatherly ideas seem to be a "raw matter" on which the daughter's imagination imprints particular forms. The implied image on the coin is material in that it is available to the senses of sight and touch, but it is ideational in that it refers to something beyond both itself and the gold. The gold only becomes "convenient" for general use, then, by the addition of heterogeneous ideas: the images of the fictions themselves.

If Maria Edgeworth habitually wrote of the relation between her tales and her father's theories as that of illustration to idea or material letter to meaning, her own metaphors, especially those inspired by political economy, also reversed these terms, identifying the father's contribution as the material substance and the daughter's as the superadded form: "[A]ll the general ideas originated with him, the illustrating and manufacturing them, if I may use the expression, was mine."[32] The manufacturing metaphor, like that of coining, makes the father's general ideas the *material* that is being worked into a usable and commodifiable form. Thus when she is employing rather old-fashioned idealist-patriarchal images, she casts her father's ideas as the originary spirit and her own fictions as their illustrative signifiers, whereas when she uses a more materialist vocabulary, her father's ideas become the palpable substance and her own fictions are the mere formal vehicles through which they circulate. To be sure, the reference to "manufacturing" places her on the very brink of claiming that her labor is the source of the texts' value, but she undercuts any such implication by nervously pointing out the mere figurativeness of the word ("if I may use the expression"). Thus whether she uses an idealist

32. Quoted in Butler, p. 171.

or materialist vocabulary, she manages always to cast herself and fiction in a secondary role as the "accidents" of a paternal "substance." Either her fictions are too material, too particular and concrete, or they are not material, not substantial, enough.

This double denigration of fiction was not unique to Maria Edgeworth. Indeed Edgeworth was merely taking as her starting point the two most common charges against fiction in the late eighteenth and early nineteenth centuries: that it was an excessively particularizing genre, which interfered with rational generalization because it encouraged emotional responses to individual stories, and that it achieved this very concreteness of effect by having no "real" substance, by being nobody's actual story. Edgeworth's first publication, *Letters for Literary Ladies* (1795),[33] was itself an antifictional tale that rehearsed these very charges. The discussion of this work that follows examines the relation between Edgeworth's fictional practice and the antifictional discourse in which she participated. It returns us, moreover, to what I have called the "productive" ambitions of her writing, for the aptly named *Letters* raises the issue of fiction as part of an inquiry into how books produce productive people. In the second section of Edgeworth's tripartite book, the one on which I focus, women are regarded primarily as readers, rather than "manufacturers," of literature, and the overriding concern is to identify the sort of reading that would create stable, reliable domestic women, who could in turn raise useful, productive children.

A general worry about women's personal stability, and whether literature promotes or retards it, permeates the fictional correspondence between the two young ladies that makes up the second series of *Letters for Literary Ladies*. According to the studious Carolyn, the proper sort of reading for women fortifies the rational faculties and imparts information about the world, allowing women to practice self-control and prepare for their pedagogical role. They are, however, often more strongly attracted to the improper sort, indulged in by the frivolous Julia, which encourages unrestrained and diffuse sensibility and fails to increase one's fund of knowledge. The first sort leads to an ever sharper self-definition; the second produces a desire for vicarious pleasure and a lack of

33. The first edition was anonymous; the second, in 1799, was signed.

singular identity. The right sort of reading is epitomized by philosophy, the wrong sort by the novel.

Novels are counterproductive, Carolyn argues, because they elicit deep emotional responses to nobody, to mere figments of the imagination. Novels encourage feeling simply for the sake of feeling and despite the obvious absence of an object. Women who indulge in this species of sentimental activity suffer from both overstimulation and depletion of the passions. They are too ready to spend their emotional energy on nonentities and then too exhausted to respond to real people. As Carolyn explains to the fiction-besotted Julia:

> You ask why exercise does not increase sensibility, and why sympathy with imaginary distress will not also increase the disposition to sympathize with what is real?—Because pity should, I think, always be associated with the active desire to relieve. If it be suffered to become a *passive sensation*, it is a *useless weakness*, not a virtue. The species of reading you speak of must be hurtful, even in this respect, to the mind, as it indulges all the luxury of woe in sympathy with fictitious distress, without requiring the exertion which reality demands: besides, universal experience proves to us that habit, so far from increasing insensibility [*sic*], absolutely destroys it, by familiarising it with objects of compassion. (p. 134)

Fiction, then, is the prototype of an antiproductive literature; it is uneconomical both in its representational excess and in its weakening of the desire to act effectively in the world.

But these are the very qualities that attract Julia to novels; she is enthralled by fiction's seemingly unique power of allowing her to maintain myriad emotional possibilities without ever committing herself, and this habit becomes so strong that she cannot sustain a single emotional obligation. Finally, as Carolyn had predicted, Julia's own life comes to seem unreal to her, *"as tedious as a 'twice-told tale,'"* and she separates from her husband.

·Julia's story, until her separation from her husband, is a fairly typical depiction of a woman suffering from what the physician Alexander Crichton, in his *Inquiry into the Nature and Origins of Mental Derangement* (1799), was soon to call "disproportionate activity of the representative faculties."[34] According to Crichton and

---

34. Alexander Crichton, *Inquiry into the Nature and Origins of Mental Derangement*

several other influential medical writers, "the faculty of fiction too frequently exercised" aroused "strong passions" and led to unsteadiness of character and other nervous disorders. The medical literature on this point echoed, moreover, several decades' worth of attacks on the novel, all centering on the genre's peculiar emotional power over women and the disruption of their domestic lives. The following quotation from a 1795 periodical is typical:

> I have actually seen mothers, in miserable garrets, *crying for the imaginary distress of an heroine*, while their children were crying for bread: and the mistress of a family losing hours over a novel in the parlour, while her maids, in emulation of the example, were similarly employed in the kitchen. I have seen a scullion-wench with a dish-clout in one hand, and a novel in the other, sobbing o'er the sorrows of a *Julia* or a *Jemima*.[35]

These substitutions of merely "representative" or "imaginary" involvements for the real concerns of domestic life, "this identifying propensity"[36] of the novel that made women forget who they really were, caused widespread complaint in the late eighteenth century, complaint that bears a closer investigation here because of the peculiar way Edgeworth inflects it.

Edgeworth and Crichton agree that it was not (as various twentieth-century commentators seem to assume) cheap fiction, or romantic fiction, or even women's fiction, but fiction per se that caused convulsions of the passions and fracturing of the personality.[37] That is, these and other attacks on the novel assume not only that it is absurd to waste emotions on imaginary people but also that imaginary people have an unusually strong emotional appeal. The attacks, therefore, develop the same postulate of a link between fiction, property, and emotion that was explored in the last two chapters: the sentiments of fictional characters were believed to be especially appropriable *because* they belonged to nobody.

(London, 1799), vol. 2, pp. 10–11. I am grateful to Thomas Laqueur for bringing this passage to my attention.

35. *Sylph*, no. 5 (October 6, 1795): 35. For this and numerous similar quotations, see John Tinnon Taylor, *Early Opposition to the English Novel: The Popular Reaction from 1760 to 1830* (New York: King's Crown Press, 1943), p. 53 and passim.

36. *Eclectic Review* 8 (June 1812): 606.

37. For a thorough discussion of late eighteenth-century attacks on women's reading, see Peter de Bolla, *The Discourse of the Sublime: Readings in History, Aesthetics and the Subject* (Oxford: Basil Blackwell, 1989), chapter 10.

By the time Edgeworth embarked on her novelistic career, though, those links had been arranged in a pathological sequence, whereas earlier they had seemed a healthy solution to the problem of scandal. The task for novelists of the 1750s had been to convince readers that their characters truly were fictional in order to suppress scandal and facilitate a sentimental response. At mid-century, the novel still needed to be cleansed of its association with libelous criminality, and the gratuitous sympathy one felt for the characters could be seen as a token of the genre's new innocence. Innocent fiction, fiction devoid of scandalous reference, after all, could not fail to be sentimental, since the emotion felt for a person the reader knew never existed was ipso facto *excessive*, and yet the reader was believed to feel it *because* that character never existed.

But the very ease with which readers identified with fictional characters soon became a different kind of scandal in its own right. After "novel" had come to designate "fiction" exclusively, caveats about the genre substituted depictions of sentimental readers, like Edgeworth's Julia, for the previously satirized naive readers, like Lennox's Arabella. The utter appropriability of the fictional character's sentiments, the fact that nobody "owned" them, became the very thing that made feeling them in some sense *in*appropriate. The poor woman deaf to her hungry children and the scullery maid with a dish cloth in one hand and a novel in the other are exaggerated emblems of the inappropriate involvement with nobody's story. Eighty years earlier the chambermaid with a copy of Manley's *New Atalantis* was also a disturbing figure, but not because she was sympathizing with a satirized heroine like Hilaria; if she had happened to reproduce such a heroine's vices, she was more likely to be accused of impudence than of unsuitable and hysterical sentimental identification.

This nervousness about feeling emotions that are not, properly speaking, one's own does not seem to have been anticipated by the mid-eighteenth-century purveyors of fiction. Writers like Charlotte Lennox and Samuel Johnson implied that the universal expropriation of nobody's sentiments would be offset by their provisional and temporary quality. Normal readers, they suggested, would just naturally stop identifying with characters when they closed their books, and such temporal discontinuity would accustom them to provisional mental states. Moreover, as I suggested in Chapter 4, the novel might therefore have played an important role in teaching readers to experiment with conditional emotional states, to feel things tentatively and temporarily. This emphasis on experimental emotional states in the mid-century works of writers like Lennox and Johnson, however, came into conflict with the growing belief in fiction's peculiar emotional surplus. The sentimental reader came to be portrayed not as an affective speculator, capable of entering and abandoning emotions, but as an emotional addict, craving fictional identification and powerless to disengage from it. "Nobody" had created a monstrous mirror image: the novel reader was a body inhabited by many sentiments, but none of them was her own.

By the end of the century, then, the novel was associated with prodigality, waste, and the loss of private property in at least three ways. First, it represented nobody and was therefore ipso facto incapable of establishing an economical proportion between words and represented entities. Second, in representing nobody, the novel acquired a peculiar emotional charge that wasted the reader's energy and made her incapable of work. Third, that emotional charge severed the reader from what might properly belong to her, her most intimate affective ties, thereby disrupting the personal identity on which property was founded.

Why, given the number and gravity of these charges against fiction, would a productivist like Maria Edgeworth even attempt to redeem it? One obvious answer is the popularity of the form at the turn of the century.[38] *Letters for Literary Ladies*, moreover, suggests several others. Like many fictional warnings against fiction in the period, it depicts sentimental reading as pathological in order to recommend a different kind of fiction, one that would absolutely ensure what the earlier writers had too optimistically assumed would follow from merely closing the book periodically. Edgeworth rehearsed the charges against the novel to contrast that genre with her own tales, which were shorter, supposedly more probable, and far less emotionally extravagant. The moral tales,[39] which explicitly

38. In addition to the sources cited in Chapter 5, see J. M. S. Tompkins, *The Popular Novel in England* (Lincoln: Univ. Press of Nebraska, 1961).
39. Edgeworth preferred the term "moral tale" to "novel." In the 1801 "Advertizement" to *Belinda*, she dissociated her work from the latter category: "The following work is offered to the public as a Moral Tale—the author not wishing to

construct their "nobodies" as examples of general principles, aspire to generate only enough emotional identification to keep the reader reading. Moreover, the tales produce emotion while simultaneously preparing readers to disavow it.

Thus *Letters*, for example, provides short exercises in the skills of emotional involvement *and* extrication, thereby putting fiction to work to teach nonsentimental reading habits and to train reasonable, resilient, and agile personalities. In one such exercise, Carolyn suggests that Julia should engage in a fictional experiment to help her decide whom to marry:

> [B]efore you can decide which of the two would make you the happiest in life, you must determine what kind of life you may wish to lead; for my brother, though he might make you very happy in domestic life, would not make the Countess of V—— happy; nor would Lord V—— make Mrs. Percy happy. They must be two different women, with different habits, and different wishes; so that you must divide yourself, my dear Julia . . . into two selves; I do not say into a bad and a good self; choose some other epithets to distinguish them, but distinct they must be—so let them now declare and decide their pretensions; and let the victor have not only the honours of the triumph, but all the prerogatives of victory. Let the subdued be subdued for life—Let the victor take every precaution which policy can dictate, to prevent the possibility of future contests with the vanquished. (pp. 141–42)

---

acknowledge a novel." See Elizabeth Harden, *Maria Edgeworth*, Twayne's English Authors Series (Boston, 1984), p. 62, for a discussion of the distinction. See also Butler, *Maria Edgeworth: A Literary Biography*, pp. 302–05. Despite her rejection of the label, however, reviewers and critics continue, quite rightly, to assess Edgeworth's contribution to the English novel. Harden, Butler, and Newcomer are the most thorough recent studies. For an early and influential statement of Maria Edgeworth's transitional importance for the English novel, see Ernest Baker, *The English Novel*, vol. 6, *Edgeworth, Austen, Scott* (London: Witherby, 1935), pp. 11–56. For Edgeworth's contributions to specific novelistic developments (besides the regional novel, which I will deal with separately), see also Kowaleski-Wallace, chapter 4; Mitzi Myers, "Dilemmas of Gender as Double-Voiced Narrative; or, Maria Edgeworth Mothers the Bildungsroman," and "Quixotes, Orphans, and Subjectivity: Maria Edgeworth's Georgian Heroinism and the (En)gendering of Young Adult Fiction," *Lion and the Unicorn* 13 (1989): 21–40; Janet Egleson Dunleavy, "Maria Edgeworth and the Novel of Manners," in *Reading and Writing Women's Lives: A Study of the Novel of Manners*, ed. Bege K. Bowers and Barbara Brothers (Ann Arbor: Univ. of Michigan Press, 1990), pp. 49–65; and Twila Yates Papy, "A Near-Miss on the Psychological Novel: Maria Edgeworth's *Harrington*," in *Fetter'd or Free? British Women Novelists, 1670–1815*, ed. Mary Anne Schofield and Cecilia Macheski (Athens: Ohio Univ. Press, 1986), pp. 359–69.

Julia is to invent two persons, Mrs. Percy and Lady V——, for the express purpose of deciding not only whom to become but also whom not to become. She must, then, have the ability both to continue a fictional identification by becoming one of her projected characters and to conquer absolutely such an identification with the other character. Oddly, the "vanquished" does not simply disappear; the potential, unrealized self is merely "subdued for life," held in a prison of eternal provisionality.

Passages such as these show Edgeworth's commitment to what we might call a "productivist" account of the self; there is no unproblematically given personality against which false and fictional identities might be simply contrasted. Carolyn does advise Julia to "examine your own mind carefully" to determine "what is really and truly essential to your happiness" (p. 143), as if a true self is to be revealed as well as created in the fictional exercise. But a natural self-division is the condition that necessitates such a practice of self-reflection through fictional projections. If Julia's lack of unity is partly caused by sentimental novel reading, it can only be overcome by extending the provisional thinking of fiction into the habits of daily life. Julia must cease to be the mere passive consumer of other people's imaginings; instead, she must provide her own stock of characters and match each against a "self" that is not given but rather consciously made.

To be sure, Maria Edgeworth considered such a practice universally necessary because she believed Hume's claim that everyone's self is an imaginary construction. "The identity [sameness over time] which we attribute to the mind of man," wrote Hume, "is a fictitious one,"[40] and Edgeworth frequently echoed this sentence. Since identity is a continuity of consciousness that can be neither experienced nor demonstrated, to claim it or to claim other things (for example, property) in the name of it, Edgeworth believed, was to construct a fiction, but a fiction that both is your property and legitimizes your property. The relationship between this sort of continuous, lived fiction that enabled property and the discontinuous literary fictions that were nobody's property is a recurrent motif in Edgeworth's tales.

40. *A Treatise of Human Nature*, ed. L. A. Selby-Bigge (Oxford: Clarendon Press, 1968), p. 259.

In *Letters for Literary Ladies*, though, its special application to women is stressed. Women, unlike men, must keep a number of different suppositional self-characterizations in stock, Julia implies, because their identities cannot be fixed until relatively late in life, at the moment of marriage.[41] The lived experience of the self for a young woman, then, is a special imaginary enterprise, one that must constantly monitor itself to make sure that the pleasures of suppositional identification are not intense. For the woman might find that the man she prefers does not offer marriage or that she has more than one attractive suitor. In either case, the marriageable woman must practice putting the sympathetic machinery, as Hume described it, into reverse, turning dangerously vivacious impressions back into mere affectless ideas by extricating them from her notion of herself. Edgeworth tried, therefore, to develop a fiction that would make the processes of identification and de-identification amenable to conscious control, that would teach women to break off the sympathetic connection especially in its most pleasurable moments.

Letters for Literary Ladies, for example, is one long didactic interruption of the story of Julia's life. Most of the story is never actually told; we merely infer it from the general reflections that briefly cite it as an instance. Although *Letters* is the most extreme example of Edgeworth's suppression of fictional identification, her subsequent domestic tales are also punctuated by similar discursive intrusions. The expressed purpose of these interpolations is to run the sentimental machinery backward, converting feeling into principle and impression into idea. Such a reversal of the sentimental urge would not only ensure an "economical" fiction—a story with very little remainder, with minimal representational or emotional surplus over the moral—but also ingrain the habits of responsiveness and control necessary to a consistent, albeit self-revising, individual.

Edgeworth's belief in self-production and revision, therefore, motivated both her critique of fiction and her use of it. Unlike conservative opponents of the novel, she never admonished women simply to obey or stoically accept their given lot. Rather, within what she thought of as "reasonable" social boundaries, she

41. In contrast, *Professional Education* argues that boys be put on a professional track as early as the age of six!

recommended that women be educated to make rational decisions about their lives based on a Benthamite calculation of pains and pleasures. Nobody's helpfulness in making such calculations, in teaching women to speculate, was obvious to Edgeworth. But equally obvious was Nobody's power to substitute mere play in her own hall of mirrors for the disciplined self-reflection that would allow revision. Nobody could not simply be wished away; she had to be organized into a different fictional regime.

An ability to form and break identifications, however, was not the whole of Edgeworth's projected reformation. The cognitive potential of fiction as well as its affective power attracted her. From the 1740s to the end of the century, a standard defense of the novel had invoked its ability to portray types rather than individuals. In *Joseph Andrews*, for example, Fielding had underscored fiction's peculiar ability to avoid the scandal inherent in the satire of individuals while maintaining, indeed increasing, the effectiveness of satire aimed at general types:

> I question not but several of my readers will know the lawyer in the stage-coach the moment they hear his voice. . . . To prevent, there-fore, any such malicious applications, I declare here, once for all, I describe not men, but manners; not an individual, but a species. . . . [The depiction of the lawyer] is calculated for much more general and noble purposes; not to expose one pitiful wretch to the small and contemptible circle of his acquaintance; but to hold the glass to thousands in their closets, that they may contemplate their defor-mity, and endeavor to reduce it, and thus by suffering private mortification may avoid public shame. This places the boundary between, and distinguishes the satirist from the libeler: for the former privately corrects the fault for the benefit of the person, like a parent; the latter publicly exposes the person himself, as an example to others, like an executioner.[42]

A fictional character, because it refers to nobody in particular, refers to everybody of a certain "species." One could say, then, that novelistic depiction, far from being representationally excessive, is peculiarly economical—a neoclassical consideration that no doubt informs Fielding's argument in this passage. Even more significant, though, is fiction's cognitive effect: when readers are prevented

---

42. *Joseph Andrews*, ed. Martin C. Battestin (Middletown, CT: Wesleyan Univ. Press, 1967), p. 189.

from seeing somebody else in the textual reflection (that is, when they understand that they are reading fiction), they become capable of seeing themselves. Self-knowledge, in this case a knowledge of selfishness, is achieved by a reader's identification with a character taken to be typical because of his fictionality. The resulting chastisement is, therefore, benignly private, for the reader refers the representation to him- or herself as a solitary exercise. Libelous satire, on the other hand, had publicly exposed living examples, thereby merely discouraging certain forms of behavior. Fielding's satirist has a nobler aim: to give readers the habits of quiet self-reflection and rational self-improvement. These aims could be met only by a referential generality that superseded nonfictional, individual reference.

Fielding's distinction between public execution (libel) and private, parental, correction (fiction) certainly gives weight to the claims of recent critics, writing in the wake of Foucault, that fiction is associated with specifically modern modes of discipline, modes that differentiate themselves from crude or "inhumane" public punishments. The complete Fielding passage, though, stresses that the novel relies for its disciplinary impact on the reader's understanding that she is reading fiction; because the story refers to nobody, it can easily refer to her. Typification *as a sign of fictionality* is thus the specific formal trait upon which the novel supported its claim to be a benign instrument of self-discipline, at once regulating, normalizing, and individuating its readers.

Maria Edgeworth was obviously attracted to this use of fiction. In a late work, she reiterated Fielding's reasoning, arguing that true stories should never be integrated into fictional works because the truth is too often atypical. The striking facts in life "are out of the common course of events, [and] are for this very reason unfit for the moral purposes as well as for the dramatic effect of fiction."[43] History, biography, and journalism draw on exceptional events; when these "uncommon facts" are introduced into fiction, "the reader stops to question the probability of the narrative, [and] the illusion and the dramatic effect are at once destroyed."[44] Edgeworth here makes the common eighteenth-century argument that the

43. *Memoirs of Richard Lovell Edgeworth*, p. 445.
44. *Memoirs of Richard Lovell Edgeworth*, p. 445.

really extraordinary and incredible belong to the factual genres, whereas the realistically commonplace and probable are the properties and signs of fiction. This is the formal trait that makes fiction especially productive of moral reform, for "[i]n proportion as events are extraordinary, they are unsafe and useless as foundations for prudential reasoning."[45]

Edgeworth went beyond Fielding, however, by implying that the whole enterprise of self-production depends on fictional typification. In tale after tale, she demonstrated that one cannot have a self without knowing and consciously imitating a generalized "type."[46] And since these ordinary representatives are most often found in fiction, it is there that one must look for a life pattern. This notion that self-creation and revision entail the typification of the individual, indeed that the self is an instance or "reflection" of a type, roots Edgeworth's productivism deeply in the novelistic imagination.

The conclusion of *Letters for Literary Ladies* can be used to illustrate this racination. At its end Julia, like numerous sentimental novel addicts before her, dies in disgrace. Her downfall is attributed, however, not to a habit of identification and imitation, but to the lack of such a habit. What sinks Julia is her inability to move from the particulars of her own story to typifying generalizations about it, and then back again. At first merely mired in a series of particulars (which, incidentally, we are not allowed to share), she gradually loses the thread of her own story. An impatience with the effort of continuous self-creation and revision sets in, and she begins to espouse a philosophical nihilism, characterizing particularity itself as *nothing*. "To an enlarged mind," she reasons, "accustomed to consider the universe as one vast *whole*, the conduct of that little animated atom, that inconsiderable part[icle] of *self*, must be too insignificant to fix or merit attention. It was nothing" (p. 166). "[I]t might be *nothing* compared to the great *whole*," Carolyn responds, "but it was *every thing* to the individual" (pp. 166–67).

Julia has failed to create an intelligible "self," although Carolyn has been urging her to that effort throughout their correspondence.

---

45. *Memoirs of Richard Lovell Edgeworth*, p. 445.
46. For another discussion of the role of Edgeworth's novels in the process of self-creation, see Dunleavy, "Maria Edgeworth and the Novel of Manners."

A self, Carolyn frequently argues, is something an individual makes by paying a certain kind of attention, which Carolyn calls "reflective," to her own experience. To "reflect," as Carolyn uses the word, is to produce continuity through generalization. One's life, to have a recognizable, coherent shape, must conform to a pattern or type. For instance, when earlier Carolyn urged Julia to imagine two prospective selves, Mrs. Percy and Lady V——, she explicitly used them as examples of "the domestic woman" and "the fashionable lady" respectively. Julia's fundamental mistake was not her failure to adhere to the man she married but her inability to adhere to the type she chose. To give meaning to her particularity, to make it a comprehensible *"something,"* would have meant living her life as an example of a general category. Her failure to become a type has left her particularity with no point of reference besides the "universal whole," in comparison to which she can only see herself as a mere "nothing." Predictably, she fades into the "nothing" with which she identifies by dying; since she has failed, through an undisciplined reading of novels, to achieve novelistic exemplarity, there is nothing left for her to do.

Also predictably, though, her death gives her back her capacity to typify; her story becomes that of the typical female reader who uses fiction to become a succession of nobodies instead of using it as a reflective aid to self-construction. Carolyn tells Julia's daughter the story of her mother's disastrous slide from emotional indulgence to existential crisis as a cautionary example. Julia's story will be the Fieldingesque mirror that her daughter (as well as the reader who stands in her place) will use to reflect philosophically on her own literary habits.

One cannot, therefore, avoid such stories; producing oneself always involves some sort of imaginative doubling, a positive or negative encounter with a "typical" hypothetical self. Typicality is the productive and economical aspect of fiction; it reveals that the character is nobody in order to stress that he might be anybody. Just as Carolyn tells Julia to imagine herself as two potential wives, the reader of *Letters for Literary Ladies* is forced to imagine herself as two potential readers. She can either read reflectively, like Carolyn, and thereby become more and more herself, or she can read hysterically, like Julia, and become more and more fragmented. *Letters*, therefore, not only emphasizes the typicality of the characters but also demonstrates that self-creation depends on one's ability to make productive use of imaginary types.[47]

Edgeworth's use of fiction to chastise novel readers, then, was not a bald contradiction but an experiment in the novel form as well as a treatise on its potential uses. Her novels, the experiment promised, would require reflection rather than emotional substitution; hence they would consolidate rather than deplete identity. The novel would enter into the production of normative people by providing the patterns to be imitated or avoided. To function effectively, of course, the patterns have to be recognized for what they are: hypothetical paper representations, not ready-to-wear goods. She uses the clothes-making metaphor to stress the utterly different materials of fiction and fact: "[M]ost literary manufacturers practically know how dangerous it is to put a patch of truth into a work of fiction. The truth is too strong for the fiction, and on all sides pulls it asunder."[48] Fiction's fragility thus sets it apart as peculiarly papery stuff; it does not wear well. But this quality is precisely what gives it general applicability. Edgeworth's image of the literary manufacturer resigned to working in insubstantial material underscores her awareness that fiction is provisional. Her use of the manufacturing metaphor, indeed, always seems to complicate the productivist beliefs that motivate it; here it calls attention to the very limited way in which fiction, as Edgeworth conceived of it, might ever be said to be "finished work."

Despite Edgeworth's efforts to integrate fiction into a new productivist moral economy, therefore, *Letters for Literary Ladies* puts off revealing what the literary lady's product is ultimately supposed to be. Fiction provides the pattern, but for what? For the woman

---

47. Mitzi Myers comes to a similar conclusion in her analysis of Edgeworth's quixotic tale, *Angelina:*

> Rather than neatly dichotomizing Angelina's heroinely reading and real life . . . , the tale demonstrates that the protagonist achieves the heroism of mature female subjectivity by working through heroinism in an ongoing process that is not complete by story's end—and cannot be complete in life. . . . Subjectivity, the ways culture offers to define and express concepts of self, is not a given within, but a site or place where different discourses (and thus selves) are tried on for size.

"Quixotes, Orphans, and Subjectivity: Maria Edgeworth's Georgian Heroinism and the (En)gendering of Young Adult Fiction," p. 29.

48. *Memoirs of Richard Lovell Edgeworth,* p. 445.

who produces, through revision, her domestic self. Moreover, the actual "productive" work this woman does is simply to reproduce her self-production: that is, Carolyn spends her time teaching her own and Julia's daughters to read in the same reflective and self-improving way that she does. Domesticity is equated in this work with a certain kind of reading, and what mainly gets typified is the very act of self-typification.[49] Moreover, since the typical and the novelistic were virtually synonymous, making oneself exemplary threatened to collapse the distinction between persons and representations. The more one was required to make oneself, the more "fictional" one was likely to become.

~

The Edgeworths' commitment to economic liberalism was partly inspired by their Anglo-Irishness. They were somewhat disaffected members of the "middle nation," or "Ascendancy"—those Protestants who expropriated the estates of vanquished Catholic landlords in the sixteenth, seventeenth, and eighteenth centuries—and they seem to have had a stronger sense than most landlords of the arbitrariness of their right. Richard Lovell wrote in 1792, "I am now [possessed] of . . . landed property by the right of Conquest—[That] right has hitherto been sufficient for the common purposes & common sense of mankind—Upon [what] foundation is another question."[50] Edgeworth's suspicion that his property right was based on a conventionally acceptable but nevertheless questionable foundation was in keeping with his philosophical radicalism, and his doubts probably reinforced his commitment to the productivist ideology he frequently used to justify his tenure. Representing themselves as honest, progressive business people, whose property rights were bound up with their willingness to invest, experi-

---

49. My argument here is opposed to that of Kowaleski-Wallace, who claims that Maria Edgeworth's domestic ideology relies heavily on an idea of woman's "nature." See *Their Fathers' Daughters*, pp. 109–37. For two additional treatments of Maria Edgeworth and the woman question, see Colin B. Atkinson and Jo Atkinson, "Maria Edgeworth, *Belinda*, and Women's Rights," *Eire-Ireland: A Journal of Irish Studies* 19:4 (1984): 94–118; and Gary Kelly, "Amelia Opie, Lady Caroline Lamb, and Maria Edgeworth: Official and Unofficial Ideology," *Ariel: A Review of International English Literature* 12:4 (1981): 3–24.

50. To Mrs. Ruxton, December 13, 1792; quoted in Butler, *Maria Edgeworth: A Literary Biography*, p. 112.

ment with new agricultural methods, and generally stimulate production, the Edgeworths avoided the legitimacy issue. Turning
away from what they perceived as the shaky historical grounds of
their tenure, they justified themselves on the basis of their present
actions. And they recommended that their peers do the same, that
they identify with the Irish nation as a whole, practice sectarian
liberality, forget their oppressive "rights" of conquest, and simply
get on with the work of improving the commonweal.

It is fitting, therefore, that the plot of self-production should be
a staple of Maria Edgeworth's Irish tales, for the "middle nation,"
in her view, was a largely unrealized entity. Most of her Anglo-
Irish heroes are heir to a confused identity. Because the Ascendancy
seemed insufficiently justified by history, those born of it are in-
determinate at the outset of the tales. Many of them are unsure of
their nationality. Like the women in *Letters for Literary Ladies*, Anglo-
Irishmen seem to suffer from an internal doubleness: like women
who must "change" their identities through marriage, the Anglo-
Irish have "changed" theirs by "adopting" another nation.

Femaleness and Anglo-Irishness are thus both opportunities for
self-production, and, as we saw in the last section, that process is
logically open-ended. What the Irish tales display even more prominently than *Letters* did, however, is that successful self-creation
(the progressive movement toward a coherent "type") depends on
the perpetuation of someone else's incoherence. Ireland was not
just a remote and picturesque part of the kingdom that Edgeworth
exploited as an exotic setting for her tales; it was also thought to be
the site of a general identity problem that gave it a special affinity
to fiction. Anglo-Irish national and personal identity was difficult
to sustain not only because it was hyphenated but also because
one of its terms was "Irish." Edgeworth implied, especially in her
turn-of-the-century works, that Anglo-Irish instabilities, as well as
possibilities for self-creation, could be traced to an intrinsic *Irish*
changeableness. The Anglo-Irish protagonists of Edgeworth's novels are doubled characters, national changelings, and they are also
people who find themselves (in both senses of that phrase) in a
disorienting relationship to a creature Edgeworth seemed to imagine could never be quite himself: the Irishman.

As the virtual inventor of the regional novel,[51] Edgeworth wrote

51. Walter Scott may have been the first to credit Edgeworth with the invention

a great deal about the Irish, but nothing she wrote explores what she understood as the precariousness of the Irish personality better than *The Essay on Irish Bulls* (1802). In her continuation of her father's memoirs, she attributed the plan of the book to him, and it was published under both their names, although the actual writing seems to have been entirely Maria's. She recalled that "under the semblance of attack, he wished to shew the English public the eloquence, wit, and talents of the lower classes of people in Ireland."[52] This description makes the book sound more consistently ironic than it actually is; in fact, it achieves neither a constant "semblance of attack" nor a uniform demonstration of "eloquence, wit, and talents." But it explores the relationship of personal identity, language, and property, all tenuous possessions of the Irishman.

In the *Essay*, the Irishman exists in a state of ontological extremity that might be seen as the comic version of Julia's experience of herself as "nothing." The Irishman, however, is brought to this state not by the way he reads but by the way he talks; he talks himself into nothingness by an idiosyncratic form of wit called the "bull," which is the *Essay*'s main subject. One of the book's first examples of a bull seems rather slight, but the essayists (the point of view is first-person plural) make a great deal out of it: "'I hate that woman,' said a gentleman, looking at one who had been his nurse, 'I hate that woman, for she changed me at nurse.'"[53] This bull is analyzed as the apogee of linguistic absurdity, for through

---

of the genre in which they both wrote. In the 1829 preface to the *Waverley Novels*, he acknowledged her as precedent and inspiration: "Without being so presumptuous as to hope to emulate the rich humour, pathetic tenderness, and admirable tact which pervade the works of my accomplished friend, I felt that something might be attempted for my own country, of the same kind with that which Miss Edgeworth so fortunately achieved for Ireland" (*Waverley* [New York, 1923], p. xxii). Thomas Flanagan's judgment that *Castle Rackrent* was the first Irish novel is generally accepted. See *The Irish Novelists, 1800–1850* (New York: Columbia Univ. Press, 1959), p. 100. See also Natalie Schroeder, "Regina Maria Roche and the Early Nineteenth-Century Irish Novel," *Eire-Ireland: a Journal of Irish Studies*, 19:2 (1984): 116–30; Gregory A. Schirmer, "Tales from the Big House and Cabin: The Nineteenth Century," in *The Irish Short Story: A Critical History*, ed. James F. Kilroy (Boston: Twayne, 1984), pp. 21–44; and Klaus Lubbers, "Author and Audience in the Early Nineteenth Century," in *Literature and the Changing Ireland*, ed. Peter Connolly (Totowa, NJ: Barnes and Noble, 1982), pp. 25–36.

52. *Memoirs of Richard Lovell Edgeworth*, p. 439.

53. *Essay on Irish Bulls* (London, 1815), p. 16. Subsequent quotations from this edition are cited parenthetically in the text.

these words the speaker has come close to self-eradication, under-mining "even . . . his personal identity" (p. 16). In claiming to be a *changeling*, the essayists reason, the gentleman insists he is not himself. But he lays claim to no alternative identity; he does not indicate that he was exchanged for someone else. Hence there is no true self behind the deception; his identity simply *is* a deception.

As soon as the absurd depths of this joke have been plumbed, though, the essayists set out to make sense of it. The gentleman's bull turns out to be not just a representative piece of Irish nonsense but also a serious metaphysical possibility. The Irishman has stum-bled onto a theme dear to English empiricist philosophers, and his claim merely to have been changed, the *Essay* points out, accords with Locke's statement that "personal identity consists not in the identity of substance, but in the identity of consciousness" (p. 17). Since no one remembers his own infancy, everyone might be said to have been changed in the cradle. Personal discontinuity, the essayists conclude, is universal, and only the naif can pretend "to understand what is meant by the common words *I*, or *me*" (p. 17). The Irish blunderer and the able metaphysician are equally adept at questioning the grounds on which one can claim to be oneself.

After this philosophical defense of the bull, which already begins to dilute its Irishness, the *Essay* proceeds to a literary defense, in the course of which it links the changeling bull both to early fiction and to the impossibility of determining literary property. Arguing that the bull has a long and distinguished history, the essayists find the joke in so many literary works that they cannot tell who is plagiarizing whom. Their most famous example is Sancho Panza's response, when asked if Don Quixote is the same as the hero of *Don Quixote*: "The very same, my lady, and I am that very squire of his, who is mentioned, or ought to be mentioned in that history, unless they have changed me in the cradle" (p. 19). In the second book of *Don Quixote*, the changeling joke is one of Cervantes' many elaborate tropes on the fictionality of his characters, and the Edge-worths' citation of it creates an association between the Irishman and Sancho Panza, an early instance of a novelistic Nobody.

And yet Cervantes, they claim, is not the bull's real parent, and several earlier versions are identified. Finally, at the end of a lengthy investigation into the origin of this joke about the impossibility of determining origins, the essay concludes that it cannot be anyone's "rightful property" (p. 20). Fittingly, this joke, in which the speaker refuses to take credit for himself, cannot itself be credited to anyone. From whom could it be said to emanate if it is the very act by which the speaker disavows himself? The discussion thus implies that when language calls personal identity into question, property of all kinds, but literary property in particular, is soon at issue.

Irish language, then, unsettles the speaker's identity so deeply that his very Irishness is called into question and yet persists in the linguistic anomalies themselves. Example after example of the Irish bull contains some absurd proclamation undercutting the normal assumptions of identity. "I am a committee" (p. 34), declares the Irish rebel under questioning. "Every man [will be] his own wash-erwoman" (p. 28), promises an Irish advertisement for washing machines. Ultimately, the Irishman of the *Essay* seems to be a walking self-contradiction, constantly eradicating, dividing, or feminizing himself in language that is not exactly his, even though he is characterized by it.

Moreover, the Irishman's property is not just theoretically threat-ened by this self-defeating language; the *Essay* is mordantly candid about the usefulness of such jokes to the Anglo-Irish elite. We are told, for example, of a poor Irish-speaking haymaker who came to a court of law with some petition about his land rights. Knowing scarcely any English, he began his testimony with "My lord, I am a poor widow" (p. 41). "It was sufficient," remark the essayists, "to throw a grave judge and jury into convulsions of laughter. . . . It is of a thousand times more consequence to have the laugh than the argument on our side. . . . [W]e have the laugh . . . : let us keep it by all means" (pp. 41–42). Thus the *Essay* places the Irish joke explicitly in the context of colonial property relations. The joke may potentially confound the whole notion of property, but since it is always made by the Irishman against himself, it can easily be used by the Anglo-Irish to laugh out of court the property claims of the blundering natives. Here the joke is obviously an aid to expropriation.

We must, however, distinguish between the joke and the text through which it circulates. After all, the heavy irony of the quoted passage ("It is of . . . more consequence to have the laugh than the argument on our side. . . . [L]et us keep [the laugh] by all means") calls the relation between language and speakers into question on yet another level and temporarily points the joke back toward the Anglo-Irish; the ironic essayists here expose the rule of laughter as oppressive and unjust, a source, it would seem, of the grievances that turn individuals into "committees." This very irony, moreover, as another instance of the disavowal of one's own language, could be said to imitate the self-dispossession of the Irish speakers. Consequently, in passages like this one, the essayists identify themselves with the Irish, whose identity is constantly crumbling. Although they characterize themselves as Anglo-Irish, their book does not simply endorse what it represents as Ascendancy expropriation.

Neither, however, can it be said to disown the rulers' laughter. Rather the *Essay*'s irony, inconsistent as it is, merely multiplies the objects of mirth. The comic Irishman, moreover, is certainly most often on display, and it is clearly an English audience that is supposed to be amused. Through this regional joke book, Irish nonidentity becomes a vendible commodity. Hence the essayists are, in this sense, capitalizing on the Irishman's language of self-dispossession, but not in the usual Anglo-Irish way. They do not claim the Irishman's property; instead they merely circulate what could never have been legitimate property in the first place. The essayists even profit from their position as mere retailers of Irish language, stressing that the jokes are not their own inventions. How could they be if they are authentic Irish bulls?

The Anglo-Irish writers, therefore, no more "own" the language they sell than the Irish can be said to have "owned" it, but the writers gain from their flaunted lack of ownership, whereas the speakers of the bulls are imagined to be fragmented and deprived. It might be said that the writers share a propertylessness with the natives, but that they repair and even aggrandize themselves by calling the lack "Irish" and alienating it in the marketplace.

In this respect, the authors of the *Essay on Irish Bulls* resemble the "Editor" of *Castle Rackrent* (1800), another purveyor of comic Irishness.[54] Indeed, the *Essay* significantly illuminates the tale by

54. This analysis of Irish bulls in *Castle Rackrent*, first written for an MLA panel at the 1986 convention, was published as "Fictional Women and Real Estate in Maria Edgeworth's *Castle Rackrent*," *Nineteenth-Century Contexts* 12:1 (Spring 1988): 11–19. Just prior to its publication, Coilin Owens, "Irish Bulls in *Castle Rackrent*," appeared in *Family Chronicles: Maria Edgeworth's Castle Rackrent*, ed. Coilin Owens (Totowa, NJ:

exploring the absurdity and utility of the changeling Irishman. If we read the earlier tale bearing in mind the themes of the later *Essay*, for example, the cheerful prediction of Irish nonidentity in its preface, credited to Richard Lovell, looks familiar:

> There is a time when individuals can bear to be rallied for their past follies and absurdities, after they have acquired new habits and a new consciousness. Nations as well as individuals gradually lose attachment to their identity, and the present generation is amused rather than offended by the ridicule that is thrown upon their ancestors. . . .
>
> When Ireland loses her identity by an union with Great Britain, she will look back with a smile of good-humoured complacency on the Sir Kits and Sir Condys of her former existence.[55]

The year of the publication of *Castle Rackrent*, 1800, was also the year the Act of Union was passed, dissolving the Irish Parliament and wiping out Ireland's existence as a separate political entity. Here the union strikingly recalls the figure of the changeling Irishman in the *Essay*: after the union, Ireland is expected to "lose attachment" to its identity, to be "changed." A "new consciousness" will render Ireland no longer itself. The Act of Union, the passage suggests, was a consequential Irish bull, through which the Irish Parliament denied its own legitimacy and dispossessed itself. The eventual result and sign of such a change will be that the formerly Irish recognize the ridiculousness of the people they once were but no longer are. Unlike the Irish gentleman in the bull, these future former Irishmen will hold no grudge against anyone for having "changed" them, and their laughter at their own dispossession will convince everyone of their complete complicity.

Barnes and Noble, 1987), pp. 70–78. Owens cites much of the same evidence to a very different end: that of demonstrating Thady's deviousness. Other analyses of *Castle Rackrent* include Anthony Mortimer, "*Castle Rackrent* and Its Historical Contexts," *Etudes Irlandaises* 9 (1984): 107–23; and Bernard Escarbelt, "'We Lifts Him Up': Fait de langue et effet de style dans *Castle Rackrent*," *Etudes Irlandaises* 10 (1985): 25–30. For background on the novel, see also Tom Dunne, *Maria Edgeworth and the Colonial Mind* (Dublin: National Univ. of Ireland, 1985); and W. J. McCormack, *Ascendancy and Tradition in Irish Literary History, 1793–1939* (Oxford: Clarendon Press, 1985).

55. *Castle Rackrent; an Hibernian Tale, Taken from Facts, and from the Manners of the Irish Squires, before the Year 1782*, ed. and introd. George Watson (Oxford: Oxford Univ. Press, 1980), p. 5. Subsequent quotations from this edition are cited parenthetically in the text.

As soon as we enter the story, though, this jolly outcome of the changeling story begins to seem implausible. For the Sir Kits and Sir Condys, whose stories *Castle Rackrent* tells, were already changelings, yet they seem unable to fully inhabit a "new consciousness." Indeed, the founding of the Rackrent family on nonidentity seems to be the source of its difficulties. "*The* family," as the narrator and family retainer Thady Quirk calls it, was brought into being by the incomplete loss of its "Irish" identity and the crossing of two fictional constructs, one legal and the other mythic. As Thady explains,

> The family of the Rackrents is, I am proud to say, one of the most ancient in the kingdom.—Every body knows this is not the old family name, which was O'Shaughlin, related to the Kings of Ireland. . . . The estate came . . . into *the* family, upon one condition, which Sir Patrick O'Shaughlin at the time took sadly to bear, they say, but thought better of it afterwards, seeing how large a stake depended upon it, that he should, by Act of Parliament, take and bear the sirname and arms of Rackrent. (p. 9)

Here we have, in miniature, the eighteenth-century version of the "union" of Ireland with England, in which (under the Penal Laws) the Catholic (and in this version, Celtic) aristocracy was required to change itself to Anglo-Irish, adopting the name, the allegiances, and (implied but unmentioned in the passage) the religion of the Protestant Ascendancy. The O'Shaughlins, whose legitimacy for the Irish narrator rests on the myth of an ancient Irish feudal order, only possess their legal identity and estate by renouncing their Irish name, that is, by apparently disavowing their identity as an ancient Irish family. This official dispossession from their lineage is the very condition on which they hold their property. Hence they are, like the man in the bull, unable to identify anyone for whom they have been changed.

However, as in the case of the fiction-addicted Julia in *Letters for Literary Ladies*, an imaginary alternative self lives on, goading Sir Patrick to imitate the extravagant hospitality of feudal Irish lords. Sir Patrick finally bankrupts and then kills himself attempting to inhabit this mythic past. The incident that ends his story is an emblem of self-dispossession: his body is seized for debt at his own funeral. And even this seizure, we are led to suspect, is a sham instigated not by the creditors but by the heir, who, "on account of this affront to the body," refused "to pay a shilling of the debts."

This first story displays the pattern of *Castle Rackrent*, in which owning is constantly seen to rest on the action of disowning and, conversely, the claiming of continuity is exposed as a fictional activity that results in dispossession. The next Rackrent, Sir Murtagh, is obsessed with bringing lawsuits to gain more property, but, even when he wins them, they cost him more than he gains. He dies in a dispute over money with his stingy wife. His younger brother, Sir Kit, a profligate gambler, also loses a dispute with this Jewish wife over her property and is killed in a duel.

It is in Sir Condy's story, though, which takes up the majority of the book, that the changeling bull is most elaborately worked out. Sir Condy comes from an obscure branch of the family, but at a young age Thady had already filled his head with "stories of the family and the blood from which he was sprung, and how he might look forward, if the *then* present man should die without childer, to being at the head of the Castle Rackrent estate" (p. 39). Indeed, Sir Condy is a creation of his peasant neighbors, who "always told him he was a great likeness of Sir Patrick, which made him first have an ambition to take after him, as far as his fortune should allow" (p. 40). But by the time he inherits the estate, he has no fortune at all, since for years he had been borrowing from his future tenants on the collateral of his expectations. "He could not command a penny of his first year's income," Thady laments, "which, and keeping no accounts, and the great sight of company he did, with many other causes too numerous to mention, was the origin of his distresses" (p. 41). On the very expectation of being a second Sir Patrick, then, Sir Condy almost wipes out his estate before he even comes into it.

The legacy of "*the* family" now consists mainly of mortgages, but Sir Condy is determined that it should once again be composed of heroic stories. Indeed, he completely dispossesses himself to carry on what he thinks of as the traditions of Sir Patrick. Under these conditions, an identity can never be had for the having of it. The absurdity of his position is made most apparent by the last extended bull of the story: "Thady [says Sir Condy after having been forced to leave the Castle] . . . I've a notion I shall not be long for this world any how, and I've a great fancy to see my own funeral afore I die" (p. 81). Sir Condy's identification with Sir Patrick has reached its final conclusion: he now imagines himself to be the *dead* hero, and Thady encourages the association, exclaiming that Sir Condy's would be "as great a funeral as ever Sir Patrick O'Shaughlin's was" (p. 81).

Hoping to hear stories about himself, stories like those of Sir Patrick on which Thady had raised him, Sir Condy pretends to die and invites the country to his wake. The wake *is* nearly the death of Condy, for he almost smothers under the greatcoats of the visitors, casually tossed on his supposed corpse, and concludes that, after all, there is not much to live for, "not finding there had been such a great talk about himself after his death as he had always expected to hear" (p. 83). When he actually dies trying to reenact one of the drinking feats of the mythical Sir Patrick, the irony is doubled because Sir Patrick had also died trying to reenact one of his own mythical feats.

Like Julia's story in *Letters for Literary Ladies*, then, Sir Condy's also comes to be a "twice-told tale." In *Castle Rackrent*, however, the telling itself, Thady's narration, is both an instrument of Condy's self-division and an intricate instance of self-contradictory Irish language. As critics have noticed, the last of the Rackrents is Thady's creature, an imitation Sir Patrick produced by the servant who is supposed to "belong" to the family. Thady's language and Condy's dispossession are continually linked by the plot. For example, Thady's love of praising his master prompts him to show a stranger over the estate; the man turns out to be the agent of Condy's creditors sent to make an inventory of his assets. As Thomas Flanagan has pointed out, Thady can never realize the causal relation between his own talk and the family's downfall because his sense of himself seems to rely entirely on the idea that he is of service to an ancient Irish clan.[56] *Castle Rackrent* thus depicts the indigenous Irish gentry as prey to the same peasantry it exploits and impoverishes. On this view, the changeling gentry and common folk are locked in a mutually self-destructive relationship that makes both parties willing to trade their material substance for the pageant of a purely Irish past.

---

56. *The Irish Novelists, 1800–1850*, p. 69. For arguments against Flanagan's view, see the following note.

This pattern, however, is certainly complicated by the narrative's largest structural irony: in the end we learn that Thady is not just the faithful family retainer he constantly claims to be but also the father of Castle Rackrent's new proprietor, the lawyer Jason Quirk. Thady professes to hate the passage of the estate into his own son's hands and appears vastly to prefer the illusion of "*the* family's" glory to the possession of the actual property. Our final knowledge that the Rackrents have been not only unwittingly undercut but also purposely supplanted by the Quirks, though, sheds a different light back over the narrative we have just read. What had originally seemed like a series of mere bulls, comically self-betraying statements, begins to look suspicious. It is clear from the outset that the narrative is ironic. When Thady tells us, for example, that "[Sir Condy] was very ill used by the government about a place that was promised him and never given, after his supporting them against his conscience very honorably" (p. 61), reader and implied author are supposed to share a wink, over Thady's head, at the Irish oxymoron "against his conscience very honorably." But some critics have claimed that this is not the final level of irony; the reader who takes Thady as merely blundering rather than crafty has himself been fooled. The revelations of the ending should, these critics contend, at least plant the suspicion that Thady's ostensible "defense" of the family was all along an ironic detraction designed to justify, "under semblance of attack," Jason Quirk's expropriation.[57]

The attempt to stabilize *Castle Rackrent's* irony by giving it such a final and decisive twist, however, blunts its impact. The interpretation that puts the two Quirks in a conscious conspiracy, making Thady either merely treacherous or simply the hero of a local revolution, overlooks a richer possibility: that it does not matter whether Thady is loyal or not because he is so cloven in his language that he will generally bring about a result opposite to his intentions, if he should happen to have any. Thady Quirk can no more control his son than he can control his language. Indeed, the family name warns us against trying to make any unified sense out of these characters: a "quirk" is not only an oddity or trick, but also

---

57. See both Coilin Owens ("Irish Bulls in *Castle Rackrent*") and James Newcomer ("*Castle Rackrent:* The Disingenuous Thady Quirk," in *Family Chronicles*, pp. 79–85) for versions of this argument.

a twist or flourish in writing, a pure graphic excess that means nothing in itself. The doubleness of the Quirks, therefore, is partly a sign of sheer linguistic excess and nonsense: a mirroring in the plot of the doubleness of Thady's language. But it is also a useful excess for the Anglo-Irish writer, because it allows her to disown the whole process of dispossession: the dispossession of the Irish landlords is attributed to the mere quirkiness of the Irish themselves, their failure to achieve and sustain a unified, singular self. The Irish Quirks are thus the "meaningless" flourishes of her own signature; they are among the marks that distinguish her from her commodity at the same time that they designate it as hers.

So far I have argued that the internally riven Irishman parallels the fiction-reading woman, Julia, in *Letters for Literary Ladies*. Both are incoherently imitative and eventually come to "nothing." As conspicuous failures at self-production and self-representation, they appear to be convenient foils for those who succeed at such enterprises: the philosophically inclined domestic woman and the implied Anglo-Irish authors. Additionally, Irishness and promiscuous literary identification both absorb the anxieties generated by Edgeworth's own productive model of the self, which, as we have seen, relies heavily on representation and imitation. The self-production Edgeworth envisions requires these figures of doubleness, receptacles of the incoherence implicit in the actual process of self-creation. But, as we have seen in *Castle Rackrent*, in Edgeworth's fiction generally these remainders of the self seldom behave like docile scapegoats and trot off quietly into the wilderness. Instead, they endure to submit claims against the protagonist, to accuse him of being a changeling; hence their necessity to the process of becoming somebody is kept before the reader's mind.

Edgeworth's later substantial "Irish" tales, *The Absentee, Ormond*, and *Ennui*, feature Anglo-Irish protagonists in whom we can see several of the features already identified. For example, all the heroes experience a plurality of identities in the process of self-making. Of these tales, however, the one that most clearly demonstrates the usefulness of a specifically Irish double in both unsettling and reestablishing Anglo-Irish selfhood is *Ennui*. The hero of *Ennui* is an actual changeling who passes through Irishness as through a crucible of "nothingness" in his progress toward selfhood. Unlike either the speaker of the changeling bull or Sir Patrick, however, Lord Glenthorn (né Donoghoe) can identify the person he was exchanged for: his Irish nurse's apparent son, Christy Donoghoe (né Lord Glenthorn). Many critics have regarded the changeling plot of *Ennui* as an awkward device to force a crisis in the career of the putative nobleman,[58] who is presented as the victim of a faulty education. Others have seen it as expressing an unconscious recognition of the illegitimacy of Anglo-Irish rule.[59] And in fact the device does reveal both the machinery of fiction and the arbitrariness of property rights. But these revelations are presented as basic to the "professional education" of the landholding class. In other words, through the very willfulness of the changeling plot of *Ennui*, Edgeworth demonstrates the "fictional" status of the self and its properties, denaturalizing both, so as to shift the grounds of entitlement from birth to merit.

Let me turn first to the ways in which the changeling plot is linked to fiction. Several chapters into the tale, one of the characters, the witty Lady Geraldine, remarks that although the (then) Earl of Glenthorn is thought to be Somebody, "I think somebody is nobody" (p. 86). This remark agrees with the first-person narrator's judgment of his own youthful self: an aristocratic upbringing had made him selfishly indolent and disdainful of all sorts of "business," characteristics that in turn prevented his personality from solidifying into anything definite. Ignorant and purposeless, Glenthorn is "nobody" in the first part of the book because he is

58. Although Marilyn Butler points out that *Ennui* inaugurated "a new style of sociological realism," she joins the consensus in disparaging the changeling plot: "It has a most improbable plot, in which the hero turns out not to be the man he thinks he is, the wealthy Earl of Glenthorn, but a peasant's son who was changed at nurse" (p. 365).

59. Robert Tracy, for example, notes that the end of *Ennui* resembles the end of *Castle Rackrent* in that former Irish peasants become the proprietors of the estates in both stories.

> Once again an Anglo-Irish estate has fallen into Irish hands; the process is more honorable than in *Castle Rackrent*, but the result is similar—the Anglo-Irish have failed to hold on to what they had. In its tortuous way the plot undercuts all the sensible advice about fair dealing and prudence which the didactic portion of the book offers so freely. Good husbandry is not enough, it seems. The plot suggests that some other vaguely defined legitimacy is needed: . . . an unhyphenated Irish identity, which the hero half embodies, half evades.

"Maria Edgeworth and Lady Morgan: Legality versus Legitimacy," *Nineteenth-Century Literature* 40 (1985): 6.

unrealized and unsituated; he fails to cohere around some central core of continuous traits; as the narrator repeatedly tells us, the young man has no "interests." He has, in other words, no character.

Glenthorn's lack of character would seem to disqualify him as a fictional Nobody, since, as I have maintained throughout this study, the Nobody of the novel is generally recognizable by the very fullness of its representation. Glenthorn's lack of character, though, rather than indicating that *Ennui* is no fiction, instead implies something like an empty starting place for fictionalizing and self-making. Composed almost entirely of the absence of properties, the young Glenthorn spends the first half of the book in a melancholy stupor while the narrator itemizes all the occurrences, sights, and adventures that failed to make an impression on him. The tale emphasizes the hero's ontological delicacy from the outset; by the third chapter, for example, he is intending to commit suicide, and his favorite pastime is to lose consciousness in a nice long nap. Indeed, he only overhears Lady Geraldine's remark about his no-bodiness because he had thrown himself "on a sofa, and never stirred or spoke the remainder of the night," thereby convincing everyone that he was asleep. The young Lord Glenthorn, therefore, is not so much a character, a Nobody-in-particular, as the mere possibility of a Nobody, a space where a character might emerge. Occupying the name, title, and property of someone called Glenthorn, he is a placeholder, a conspicuously not-yet-there Nobody.

Glenthorn's state is a rather obvious metaphor for the absenteeism of Anglo-Irish landlords; indeed, he tends to be "absent" even when he is on his estate, since he leaves the bulk of the business to an agent, interfering only sporadically and, often, ineffectually. The tale, though, pushes beyond the absentee metaphor to suggest that the secure possession of Ireland by the Anglo-Irish depends on the wholesale re-creation of the landowners. In *Ennui* this re-creation, in turn, depends on the protagonist's sudden awareness that in fact he is the mere possibility of a character. The woman he believed was his nurse reveals that she is his mother, who "changed" him in the cradle for the real heir to the Glenthorn estate, now the village blacksmith. Recognizing that he is at an existential crossroads ("To be or not to be Lord Glenthorn," he muses), the protagonist turns over the estate to the blacksmith, takes his "real" name, and sets out to acquire an identity.

The moment of exchanging name and station with Christy Donoghoe is the degree-zero of the protagonist's self-production. Stripped of almost everything but a name, he must now decide what type of person to become: "But how," the narrator muses, "was I to distinguish myself?" Knowing the necessity of creating a personal identity by deciding what sort of person he will be, the protagonist is granted an uncanny awareness of his fictionality. Hence, those critics who have complained that this plot lays bare the mechanism of fiction are certainly right. Indeed, the narrator and various characters anticipate this criticism by remarking the "novelistic" (as in "fantastic") quality of the episode: "Changed at nurse! One hears of such things in novels, but, in real life, I absolutely cannot believe it" (p. 213); and again, "If, among those who may be tempted to peruse my history, there should be any mere novel-readers, let me advise them to throw the book aside at the commencement of this chapter; for I have no more wonderful incidents to relate, no more changes at nurse, no more sudden turns of fortune" (p. 223).

These bits of self-mockery may indicate Maria Edgeworth's discomfort at breaking her own rule of recording only "ordinary" and "typical" events in her tales, but they also point to the metafictional function of the changeling plot, which not only acknowledges artifice but also depicts a moment when identity is not given and self-typification must be willfully accomplished. In this sense, the changeling plot merely reveals the workings of the fictional machinery in "ordinary" self-production, a normalization that allows it to issue in epigrammatic statements, like those spouted by Lord Y——, who befriends and tutors Glenthorn/Donoghoe after the "change": "We are the artificers of our own fortune" (p. 221). Even the former blacksmith is inspired to point the productivist moral of the changeling plot in a well-honed sentence: "Any man, you see, may be made a Lord; but a gentleman, a man must make himself" (p. 202). One tendency of the tale, then, is to make the changeling plot ordinary, to stress, as the essayists in *Irish Bulls* had done, that none of us can "retrograde" in memory to the time of infancy, that consequently there is "no continuity of identity between the infant and the man" (*Bulls*, p. 18), and that individuals must decide whom they are going to be. The epigram, in all its conclusive polish, is the linguistic sign of this normalization.

The tale, however, has a countervailing tendency as well. Despite the epigrams and Glenthorn/Donoghoe's determined immersion in the study of the law, the narrator lingers over his continued "confusion of identity" (*Bulls*, p. 18). And the sign of this confusion is the return of the bull. Forced by his new poverty to act as his own valet, the narrator reports, "I once caught myself saying of myself, 'That careless blockhead has forgot my nightcap'" (p. 206). The blundering confusion of master and servant recalls both one of the *Essay's* bulls, "Every man his own washerwoman," and an earlier incident in the life of the protagonist, when an Irish serving man (who later turned out to be treacherous) "first caught my notice by a strange answer to a very simple question. I asked, 'What noise is that I hear?' 'My lard,' said he, 'it is only the singing in my ears; I have had it these six months'" (p. 139). To be suddenly plunged into Irishness is thus to be bizarrely merged with the class of one's former servants, divested of singularity, and characterized (or de-characterized) by the natives' own linguistic incoherence: "For some time," the narrator confides, "I was liable to make odd blunders about my own identity" (p. 206).

Moreover, even after Glenthorn/Donoghoe has embarked on his new career, he is frequently overwhelmed by a sense of his internal plurality:

> When I found myself surrounded with books, and reading assiduously day and night, I could scarcely believe in my own identity; I could scarcely imagine that I was the same person, who, but a few months before this time, lolled upon a sofa half the day, and found it an intolerable labour to read or think for half an hour together. (pp. 224–25)

That the narrative loiters around these moments of disorientation and even, as in this passage, associates them with books suggests an admission that Edgeworth's recipes for self-improvement generate an excess that cannot be incorporated into the self-made man's singular identity. The passage, that is, suggests a relationship between being aware of one's changeling status and being a reader, between experiencing internal incoherence and making a self.

But this is not the hero's final situation. After succeeding in the law, he is obliged to "take and bear the name and arms" (p. 244) of his new wife, Cecilia Delamere (incidentally the heir at law to the

Glenthorn estate), just as Sir Patrick O'Shaughlin once found it convenient to "take and bear the sirname and arms of Rackrent" (*CR*, p. 9). In other words, once he has made himself a new gentleman, he seems to put away his peasant-Irish name along with the "confusion of identity" that accompanied the period of transition. And here the narrative, written by "Delamere," seems to end.

In *Ennui*, however, as in *Castle Rackrent*, Irishness cannot be so easily dispensed with. An afterword is appended to the seemingly complete story. It begins with a letter from one "Christy Donoghoe," a being we supposed no longer in existence, who announces that he is "as good as dead" (p. 247). This letter from the graveyard of defunct names turns out to be from the person who was born Earl of Glenthorn, but who has reverted to *his* Irishness. It informs the hero, Delamere, that the rightful earl is abdicating because he is unfit to manage either his own family or the estate. In a drunken stupor, his son, Johnny, has burned down the castle, so the blacksmith/earl has resolved to "go back to my forge, and, by the help of God, forget at my work what has passed" (p. 247). "I write this," he explains, "to beg you, being married, of which I give you joy, to Miss Delamere, that is the *hare* at law, will take possession of all immediately" (p. 246–47). The fact that Christy cannot refer to the estate's legal heir without committing a pair of bulls—the hero cannot *be* married to *Miss* Delamere, and, although she is bland and timid, she isn't really a *hare*—reminds us that Christy's "change," unlike Delamere's, has left him even more comically "nonsensical" than ever.

Thus, although Irishness is a stage superseded by the hero, its maintenance in the blacksmith seems crucial to the book's overall economy: there must be a Christy Donoghoe. He endures not just to absorb the strain of the hero's Irish birth but also to refigure his earlier ontological precariousness. As the youthful "Glenthorn" had seemed ever on the verge of existence (indeed, like Condy Rackrent, the hero at one point suffers himself to be thought dead so that he can hear what is said by his survivors), now it is "Christy" who is "good as dead," and yet, just barely, still there. Moreover, "Christy" now seeks the very forgetfulness for which the narrator, remarking that he had been too lazy to form distinct memories, frequently apologized in the course of the tale. If "Glenthorn" was only the possibility of a character at the outset, "Christy Donoghoe" signifies the impossibility of a character in the end. Like the discarded potential self that Carolyn in *Letters for Literary Ladies* advised Julia to keep locked up, "Christy Donoghoe" will live "subdued for life" on the estate of Glenthorn-Donoghoe-Delamere. Unlike O'Shaughlin-Rackrent, Glenthorn-Donoghoe-Delamere will probably not "relapse" when he reinhabits Glenthorn Castle, because his Irishness has been externalized and will soon be buried in the person of his foster brother.

In analyzing Edgeworth's regional fiction, I have traced the patterns that emerged when the productivist idea of the self met the demands of a hyphenated nationality. I have stressed that Edgeworth depicts the plural or ill-defined identities of Anglo-Irishmen as opportunities for self-creation. Little about them is "given" at the outset; indeed, they generally need to decide even such basic characteristics as their national affiliation. Like women, who normally lack a continuous patrilineal singularity and must decide as adults what family they will belong to, the Anglo-Irishmen's very lack of a singular nationality gives them the plasticity necessary to define themselves. Thus the "identity confusions" of Edgeworth's Anglo-Irish heroes are created and represented as so many occasions for self-generation.

But the very blankness and confusion are themselves so strongly represented and firmly associated with fictionality and Irishness, respectively, that they are retained in the narratives even after the protagonists have supposedly transcended them. Incoherent beings are, in short, both the conditions and the by-products of Edgeworthian self-making; and their tendency to be Irish in the end, either by birth or upbringing, justifies the subordination of the Irish to the Anglo-Irish by figuring it as the overcoming of incoherence by coherence. The status quo is thus vindicated not as a natural order but as a dynamic, productive process.

At the same time, however, the mutual dependence and radical interpenetration of the two groups is acknowledged. Like the other binary pairs discussed in this chapter—father/daughter, general/particular, form/matter, spirit/letter, type/instance, fictional/real—the Anglo-Irish/Irish distinction is constantly destabilized by the productivism that inspires it. For example, in the story of the changeling pair Glenthorn/Donoghoe and Donoghoe/Glenthorn, the chiasmic pattern is obviously troubling enough to prompt the author to rename her self-made man anew—Delamere. But this differentiating term, deriving from his wife, only introduces a new discontinuity in the very assertion of the hero's final consistency. The selfhood thus produced can never seem entirely homogeneous and fixed. But fixity, the tales seem to proclaim, is not a desirable or even a possible trait of the productive self. In this section I have explained the connections between such a model of the self-in-process, its explicitly fictional elements, and its colonial situation.

~

This chapter began with an analysis of the complicated genealogical, literary, economic, and emotional exchanges between Edgeworths *père* and *fille*. In explaining why Maria's productivist ideas prevented her from overcoming the sense of indebtedness that plagued her as well as many other writers of the eighteenth century, I invoked her authorial "identity confusion." She seems to have imagined that her very being was an effect of her father's permitting her to write for him. "Where should I be without my father?" she wrote to a friend in 1805 when her father was seriously ill; "I should sink into that *nothing* from which he has raised me."[60] Maria's disbelief in her independent existence—her self-characterization as a mere nothing, a creature temporarily given reality by being made the letter of her father's idea—is reminiscent of both Julia, whose "self" was "nothing," and the gentleman in the Irish bull who did not know "what is meant by the common words *I*, or *me*." Maria imagined that she, too, would some day inhabit the ontological twilight zone of the leftover double, or the dead letter. But Maria's case is even worse than those of the fiction-reading woman and the changeling Irishman because the means by which she has been made something—writing—is also the means by which she sinks into nothing. Since the transient illusion of her being derived from writing, and since she thought writing derived from her father, her very productivity as a writer was proof of how much her father had done for her; hence, the more she wrote, the more indebted

60. Quoted in Butler, *Maria Edgeworth: A Literary Biography,* p. 207.

and deficient she felt. To pay her daughterly debt, the debt of the letter to the spirit, she *"should* sink into . . . *nothing."*

In this final section of the chapter, where I analyze her 1817 tale *Harrington,* I want to return to the relation between daughter-debtor and father-creditor to explore a later stage. In the last years of Richard Lovell's life, his daughter seems to have glimpsed the resemblance between paternal creditors, whom one cannot pay back, and those villains of the productive marketplace, usurers. She began to sense that her constant protestations of debt could be read as so many accusations against her father. A desire to save her father from the defamation of living off his *interest* in his daughter, I hypothesize, is accomplished through the writer's reclamation of the Jewish patriarch, partly a figure for her own father-creditor, in *Harrington.*

Harrington, however, is more than just a personal parable; it can also be read as an allegory about national groups that are out of place, inhabiting lands not their own by long descent but nevertheless contributing to the commonweal. In other words, the Jews in *Harrington* are inverted renderings of the Anglo-Irish; to identify with these economic "middlemen" and transform them from rag-pickers and usurers into cosmopolitan financiers is simultaneously to brighten the image of the "middle nation" to which Edgeworth belonged.

Harrington, in short, confronts the problem of the Edgeworths' surplus (the accumulated remainders of patriarchy, representation, and colonialism) through the figure of the Jew, the traditional scapegoat for accumulation and indebtedness. This unprecedented identification with the Jewish creditor, however, seems to have touched something deep and unruly in Edgeworth's political imagination, and *Harrington* consequently presents a veritable phantasmagoria of bizarre inversions of common Edgeworthian patterns. The usual productivist economy of signs, highly unstable (as we have seen) even when under little pressure, becomes a topsy-turvy chaos in this tale.

Richard Lovell's preface to the volume of *Tales of Fashionable Life* containing *Harrington* and *Ormond* was the last he wrote. It was dated May 31, 1817 (his seventy-third birthday), and he died a few weeks later. In addition to informing the reader of Maria's industry—"twice as many pages were written for these volumes as are now printed"—it gives us two other bits of information. First, it registers critics' complaints about him:

> I have been reprehended by some of the public critics for the *notices* which I have annexed to my daughter's works. As I do not know their reasons for this reprehension, I cannot submit even to their respectable authority. I trust, however, the British public will sympathize with what a father feels for a daughter's literary success, particularly as this father and daughter have written various works in partnership. (p. v)

The prefatory notice also tells the story of the origin of *Harrington:*

> *Harrington* was occasioned by an extremely well-written letter, which Miss Edgeworth received from America, from a Jewish lady, complaining of the illiberality with which the Jewish nation had been treated in some of Miss Edgeworth's works. (p. v)

The preface thus calls attention to two, seemingly unrelated, acts of defamation: his daughter's obnoxious portraits of usurious Jewish creditors, especially in *The Absentee,* and the critics' charge that Richard Lovell took too much credit for his daughter's accomplishments. The preface indicates that *Harrington* will make amends for Maria's libel against the Jews, and, implying that the charge against Richard Lovell is equally unfounded (even while pretending ignorance of its exact nature), the author of the preface both excuses himself by invoking natural paternal pride, with which the public should "sympathize," and compounds his appropriation by reminding us of the Edgeworths' literary "partnership."

Richard Lovell thus implies a parallel between himself and the Jewish nation, both accused of inflating their estimates of what other people owe them. Maria has been the accuser of the Jews; but who has accused Richard Lovell? Surely not Maria? Not, anyway, at first glance. Richard Lovell's declining years were marked by a number of public and private protests against his way of putting himself forward. The correspondence of several literary men, discussing the Edgeworths' visit to London in 1813, attests that Richard Lovell was a social liability for Maria:

> Much as I should like to have become acquainted with her [Maria] the thing was impossible without taking her Papa into the bargain. . . . There was a degree of Irish impudence superadded to philo-

sophical and literary conceit, and a loquacity that prevents anyone being heard but itself which I ner met in any creature to the same degree. He fairly talked down and vanquished all but the stoutest Lion-fanciers of the Bluestocking.[61]

This opinion was stated even earlier by the Irish solicitor general, Charles Kendal Bushe, who complained about Richard Lovell's proprietary patriarchal disposition toward Maria and her works:

He talks a great deal and very pleasantly and loves to exhibit and perhaps obtrude what he wou'd be so justifiably vain of (his daughter and her works) if you did not trace that pride to his predominant Egotism, and see that he admires her because she is *his* child, and her works because they are *his* grandchildren.[62]

Bushe went so far as to suggest that Maria had some vague awareness of the unfavorable impression her father made: "She seems to have studied her father's foibles for two purposes, to avoid them and never to appear to see them."[63]

But whether or not she knew in 1810 or 1813 that others regarded her father as a usurper of the credit and attention that were rightfully hers, she could not have ignored the explicit attack made on Richard Lovell's supposed literary interference by Sydney Smith in his *Edinburgh Review* article on Maria's novel *Patronage*. Here the charge that the daughter owed nothing but the defects of her fiction to her father, which has often been repeated, was first made in print. Playing wittily on the novel's own condemnation of patronage and paternal interference, the reviewer complains that

Surely some heavy spirit has occasionally guided her pen,—has obtruded its ponderous *patronage* on her book,—has swelled the bulk of the work, but taken from its characteristic delicacy,—and has distilled its poppies [papas?] upon pages, which we are compelled to allow are *now and then* prosing and tedious.[64]

Marilyn Butler has argued strenuously and convincingly against the judgment that Richard Lovell was responsible for the prosing didacticism of the fiction. But the validity of the charge interests

61. J. B. S. Morritt to Sir Walter Scott, June 29, 1813; quoted in Butler, p. 231.
62. Charles Kendal Bushe, letter of August 16, 1810; quoted in Butler, pp. 212–13.
63. Charles Kendal Bushe; quoted in Butler, p. 213.
64. *Edinburgh Review* 22 (1814): 433.

me less than its sources, one of which must have been the authorial self-presentations of the Edgeworths. Maria's incessant references to her debt to her father, her insistence that she had no serious ideas of her own, that only the fables were hers, whereas the concepts were his, combined with her father's complete authorial appropriation of *Professional Education* and his statement that the *Tales of Fashionable Life* were its illustrations, would have convinced most readers that Richard Lovell held the didactic reins on his daughter's creative imagination. Richard Lovell's prefaces would have been all the more repugnant as the assumptions of Romantic aesthetics spread; hence it is not surprising that Lord Byron and Thomas Moore took a strongly unfavorable view of Richard Lovell even before Sydney Smith expressed it.[65] In this case, moreover, there is an alliance between Romanticism and free-market productivism. For example, Sydney Smith's review juxtaposes the free-market antipatriarchalism of *Patronage* itself with what both Edgeworths had presented as the patriarchal practice of their authorship:[66] the father controls what the daughter creates. *Harrington* was written in the years just after this review appeared, a period during which, as Marilyn Butler remarks, "Maria was forced to face up to one of the most painful facts of her late life—that the father whom she idolized was barely known or actively disliked in literary London," whereas she was lionized.[67] She must also have had to face up to her own share of responsibility for her father's unpopularity. Had she not presented them as debtor and creditor, thereby insinuating that she was a sort of hostage to her father? When she undertook *Harrington*, therefore, in a state of contrition for having accused the Jews of being a usurious nation, might she not also have wanted to expiate her guilt for unwittingly casting her father in the role of an unsatisfiable creditor?

Much about the tale argues for this subtext. First, on the most superficial level of the plot, we should note that the eponymous hero and narrator learns to sympathize with the Jews by watching two young people, first the peddler Jacob, and then the gentlewoman Berenice Montenero, attempting to protect and support

65. See Butler, p. 230.
66. The same juxtaposition, by the way, was made, far more playfully, by Richard Lovell in his preface to *Patronage*.
67. Butler, p. 231.

their fathers. Harrington's boyhood conversion from anti-Semitism to philo-Semitism begins with the sentence "Jew as he is, you see he has some feeling about his father" (p. 31). And it is also Berenice's "feeling about her father" that attracts Harrington when he watches her deepening consternation at a performance of *The Merchant of Venice*. Her father later explains that Berenice was raised in a small town in America and "was, therefore, ill prepared . . . for European prepossessions; and with her feeling heart and strong affection for those she loves, no wonder that she has often suffered, *especially on my account*, since we came to England" (p. 84). Berenice is early presented as an anti-Jessica, a daughter who refuses to betray and abandon her Jewish father. Hence filial sentiment is the route to the humanization of the Jews; before he can sympathize with these previously shadowy and frightening figures, Harrington must first imagine them to be beloved fathers.

The private allegory, however, manifests itself in subtler ways as well. It comes out as a nervousness in the text about the general applicability of Harrington's story. Contemporary critics worried about the same thing, noting that *Harrington* does not really try to convince the reader that anti-Semitism is a significant social problem in England. Francis Jeffrey, reviewing the work in 1817, typically criticizes what he sees as its objective lack of general significance: "[W]e really cannot help thinking that it was as little worth her while to provide a corrective for gentlemen who have an antipathy to Jews . . . as it would be for an eminent physician to compound an infallible plaster for scratches on the first joint of the little finger exclusively."[68] In these remarks, Jeffrey is merely following the lead of the tale itself, which all too often makes the Jewish Question seem like a private obsession.

The hero, Harrington, happens, quite by accident, to have a personal identity constructed almost completely out of his encounters with Jews. His boyhood acquaintance and ultimate rival, for example, cannot help

> rallying me a little . . . upon the constancy of my Israelitish taste, and the perfect continuance of my identity.
>
> "I left you, Harrington, and I find you, after four years' absence, intent upon a Jew; boy and man you are one and the same." (p. 49)

68. *Edinburgh Review* 28 (1817): 393.

This "continuance of identity" (always an abnormal and question-able state in Edgeworth's self-revising heroes) is emphatically not associated with stability in Harrington. Instead, it resembles a fixation; resulting from a series of bizarre accidents, it is described as a "susceptibility," almost indistinguishable from "nervous dis-ease." To be "intent upon a Jew" is by no means an unambiguous virtue in this tale.

The presentation of the hero's preoccupation as accidental, ec-centric, and perhaps even diseased, I am suggesting, might attest to the author's suspicion that she, too, has an inexplicable private stake in exonerating the Jews, that she is aware that her intimate interest creates an emotional intensity that exceeds the "objective correlative" of the implied social reality. I would also like to suggest, though, that by making Harrington's excessive and "susceptible" psyche the "setting" of the tale, Edgeworth gains access to the phantasmic dimensions of anti-Semitism and philo-Semitism. If Harrington (and, by implication, the author) seem to have inflated the significance of the Jews, by the tale's end we understand that such an inflation is normal, perhaps even inevitable, since the Jews can never be just themselves.[69]

Harrington's strange and defining preoccupation with the Jews begins with his earliest memory; in a powerfully evocative passage, which I will quote at length, he describes his first sight of a Jewish old-clothes man:

> When I was a little boy of about six years old, I was standing with a maid-servant in the balcony of one of the upper rooms of my father's house in London. . . . It was dusk, and I was growing sleepy, but my attention was wakened by a . . . wonder. . . . I saw star after star of light appear in quick succession, at a certain height and distance, and in a regular line, approaching nearer and nearer. . . . Presently the figure of the lamplighter with his blazing torch in one hand, and his ladder in the other, became visible. . . . I saw him fix and mount his ladder with his little black pot swinging from his arm, and his red smoking torch waving with astonishing velocity, as he ran up and down the ladder. Just when he reached the ground, being then within a few yards of our house, his torch flared on the face and

69. Michael Ragussis's excellent article on this novel also stresses its preoccu-pation with representation and its revisions or deconstructions of previous repre-sentations of the figure of the Jew. See "Representation, Conversion, and Literary Form: *Harrington* and the Novel of Jewish Identity," *Critical Inquiry* 16 (Autumn 1989): 113–43.

figure of an old man with a long white beard and a dark visage, who, holding a great bag slung over one shoulder, walked slowly on, repeating in a low, abrupt, mysterious tone, the cry of "Old clothes! Old clothes! Old clothes!" I could not understand the words he said, but as he looked up at our balcony he saw me—smiled—and I remember thinking that he had a good-natured countenance. The maid nodded to him; he stood still, and at the same instant she seized upon me, exclaiming, "Time for you to come off to bed, master Harrington."

I resisted, and clinging to the rails, began kicking and roaring.

"If you don't come quietly this minute, master Harrington," said she, "I'll call to Simon the Jew there," pointing to him, "and he shall come up and carry you away in his great bag."

The old man's eyes were upon me; and to my fancy the look of his eyes and his whole face had changed in an instant. (pp. 1–2)

I quote the passage almost in full because it typifies *Harrington*'s method of introducing anti-Semitism as part of a private psychodrama. The liminality of the scene, its situation between infancy and childhood, waking and sleeping, fantasy and reality, makes the old-clothes man the embodiment of uncanniness. First appearing in a blaze of a light, which seconds before was thought to be a star, and intoning an incomprehensible language, the Jew seems a figure for ontological uncertainty. Moreover, any "reality" he might possess in the split second between his manifestation and the nursemaid's threat is instantly obliterated by Harrington's terror of disappearing into the "great bag." Immediately after the world's disenchantment (those are lamps, not stars), mortality looms up, embodied in the wandering Jew and his bag. Harrington's self-awareness and this figure of death, this scapegoat for the archaic outrage of the child's possible disappearance from the world, are so intimately intertwined that, the story suggests, they can never be wholly separated. Maturation for Harrington will involve transfiguring the Jew, revising his meanings, while remaining "intent" upon him.

Throughout the revisions—from old-clothes man, to peddler, to merchant, to scholar, to gentleman—however, the book systematically maintains the uncanniness of the Jews; they never stray far from the borderland between reality and fantasy. The multiplication of Jewish characters in the story as a whole resembles their bizarre proliferation in the opening pages, when young Harrington's terror itself augments their number in the following way. The nursemaid's use of the old-clothes man as a threat eventually creates such hysteria in the child that his mother pays Simon the old-clothes man a yearly fee to stay away from the house: "The bounty acted directly as an encouragement to ply the profitable trade, and 'Old clothes! Old clothes!' was heard again punctually under my window; and another and another Jew, each more hideous than the former succeeded in the walk" (pp. 12–13). These, the narrator assures us, were not really Jews at all but "good Christian beggars, dressed up and daubed" to be paid by the servants to go away. Soon the "Jews" are everywhere:

> If I went out with a servant to walk, a Jew followed me; if I went in the carriage with my mother, a Jew was at the coach-door when I got in, or when I got out: or if we stopped but five minutes at a shop, while my mother went in, and I was left alone, a Jew's head was at the carriage window, at the side next me; if I moved to the other side, it was at the other side; if I pulled up the glass, which I never could do fast enough, the Jew's head was there opposite to me, fixed as in a frame. (p. 13)

The passage so thoroughly confuses the Jew, the Christian beggar dressed as a Jew, and (in the final image) the framed picture of the Jew, that Harrington's early life takes on the same uncanny character as the people he fears. The world begins to conform itself to his fantasies, and although we are given a naturalistic explanation for this conformity, the descriptions fully participate in his childish amazement.

After a while, Harrington also becomes a creature of this theatrical twilight zone between being and representation. Terrified by his nursemaid's stories but also sworn to silence by her about the source of his fears, he becomes a sensation in London for possessing an inborn nervous antipathy to the Jews:

> I saw myself surrounded by grown-up wise people, who were accounting [in] different ways for that of which I alone knew the real, secret, simple cause. They were all, without my intending it, my dupes. Yet when I felt that I had them in my power, I did not deceive them much, not much more than I deceived myself. . . . I went no farther than affectation and exaggeration, which it was in such circumstances scarcely possible for me to avoid; for I really often did not know the difference between my own feelings and the descriptions I heard given of what I felt. (p. 9)

Locked in an identity-defining antipathy with a people who are not quite real, the child loses a sense of the difference between himself and his "descriptions"; he becomes a creature of representation, too.

Even after Harrington's conversion from anti-Semitism to philo-Semitism, the ontological status of the Jews remains uncertain and continues to unsettle his sense of his own reality. Indeed, he falls in love with Berenice Montenero while in just such a state of disorder, which is brought about by watching Macklin, the great eighteenth-century actor who revived the part of Shakespeare's Shylock. The theater becomes a place where the difference between seeing the representation of a Jew and seeing a Jew, between sympathizing with a Jew and being a Jew entirely breaks down. Harrington, placed so that he can watch both the stage and Berenice in the next box, is assailed by various "susceptibilities":

> At every stroke, characteristic of the skilful actor, or the master poet, I felt a strange mixture of admiration and regret. I almost wished that Shakspeare had not written, or Macklin had not acted, the part so powerfully: my imagination formed such a strong conception of the pain the Jewess was feeling, and my inverted sympathy, if I may so call it, so overpowered my direct and natural feelings, that at every fresh development of the Jew's villainy I shrunk as though I had myself been a Jew. (p. 75)

This de-realization of both the Jews and the hero who is "intent" upon them, this blurring of the boundaries between individual characters and between "real" people and representations, emphasizes the fantastic quality of Harrington's obsession. It gives a decidedly modern, psychologically sophisticated, cast to Edgeworth's analysis of anti-Semitism by allowing her to probe the imagination for its sources. Indeed, early in the narrative Harrington explains that his own case illustrates the need, following the suggestions of Bacon and Hume, to examine such fantasies for their collective import by tracing "the history of the power and influence of the imagination, not only upon the mind and body of the imaginant, but upon those of other people" (p. 11).

Harrington's very abnormality, then, accords with the tale's emphasis, not on the Jews, but on their representations. From the folktales of child theft and murder, the blood libel spoken by the nursemaid, to Shakespeare's charges of vengefulness, to accusations of usury and deceit made by Harrington's father, the book traces the history of anti-Semitic representations right up to the present, into the works of Maria Edgeworth herself:

> I have met with books by authors professing candour and toleration—books written expressly for the rising generation, called, if I mistake not, Moral Tales for Young People; and even in these, wherever the Jews are introduced, I find that they are invariably represented as being of a mean, avaricious, unprincipled, treacherous character . . . [Such representations] certainly acted most powerfully and injuriously, strengthening the erroneous association of ideas I had accidentally formed, and confirming my childish prejudice by what I then thought the indisputable authority of *printed books.* (pp. 16–17)

In this strange moment, when Harrington accuses his maker of having had a bad influence on him, the reader cannot help remembering that Harrington himself is imaginary, even as the moment itself promises a reform of the imagination.

The reform, though, never gets beyond the Jew's figurativeness, the necessity that he *mean* something, even if he means the negation of what he was thought to mean. Mr. Montenero, the sympathetic Sephardic hero, is a one-man antidefamation league. His main role in the novel is to disabuse people of their anti-Jewish prejudices. In Harrington's first conversation with him, for example, Montenero insists on setting the record straight about Shylock. He continually alludes to the "true" story from which Shakespeare borrowed, and Harrington, not knowing what Montenero's point is, responds with "general apologies" and bows of "general acquiescence," but Montenero "saw [the] evasion, and would not let me off so easily" (p. 83). Montenero will not stop talking about Shylock until the *counter-story* has been told: "In the *true* story, from which Shakespeare took the plot of 'The Merchant of Venice,' it was a Christian who acted the part of the Jew, and the Jew that of the Christian; it was a Christian who insisted upon having the pound of flesh from next the Jew's heart." This eager insistence to state the truth as the *reverse* of the generally believed makes Montenero's own phrasing confusingly dependent on the stereotypes it denies: "it was a Christian who acted *the part of the Jew.*" Since Montenero had previously said that Shakespeare was using rather than creating the stereotype, "the part of the Jew" cannot refer simply to the part of Shylock; rather, it is a way of naming a behavior, conventionally called "Jewish," just as the behavior of the "real" Jew can only be explained by calling it "the part of the Christian." The antidefamatory concentration, therefore, merely strengthens our sense that the"parts" abide regardless of who plays them, that anti-Semitism is simply an arbitrary and conventional (although certainly also harmful) sign system, and that to detach what "Jew" means from what individual Jews are requires that Jews themselves become obsessed with their representations.

Montenero's obsessive policing of the borderland between realities and representations is presented as a form of hard-won mastery. The narrator tells us that Montenero had, at one time, lived in dread of the "opinions of others" (p. 103). Like his daughter Berenice and young Harrington, he had himself suffered from a morbid "susceptibility," a "great natural sensibility" that registered how much his people were vilified and loathed (p. 103). But in his maturity, we learn, he has subdued his feelings by taking up arms against the offensive representations. Montenero is a great collector of paintings (an odd occupation for a Sephardic gentleman, given the Jewish taboo on icons), and in one of the tale's most striking vignettes, he buys at public auction a work that depicts "the drawing the teeth of the Jew, by order of some one of our most merciful lords the kings—John, Richard, or Edward" (p. 126). The painting is so gruesome that Harrington has a fit when he sees it: "I started back, exclaiming with vehement gestures, 'I cannot bear it! I cannot bear that picture!'" (p. 128). Montenero's contrasting coolness allows him to buy the painting and then ceremoniously destroy it. Becoming, the narrator stresses, an Inquisitional executioner in reverse, he cuts it to pieces while intoning, "So perish all that can keep alive feelings of hatred and vengeance between Jews and Christians!" (p. 133). He then sends for his friend Jacob, who had been burned out of a shop in Gibraltar by anti-Semitic rioters, "to be present at the burning of this picture" (p. 133). This "*auto da fé,*" as the narrator calls it, is thus a ritual purging through symbolic repetition of the very violence it depicts.

The point of such episodes seems to be that Montenero has gained mastery over the symbolic order. Unlike the mob, who thought poor Jacob was the Wandering Jew, Montenero, it appears, knows the difference between burning a person and burning a representation. But he also knows that the dissemination of certain representations can lead to the burning of people, and hence he is intent on controlling symbolic exchange.

However, the depictions of his control themselves verge on anti-Semitic stereotypes. In the incident of the painting, for example, he tells the group gathered at his house to witness the auto-da-fé that his friend Jacob "put it in my power to prevent this horrid representation from being seen and sold in every print-shop in London. Jacob, who goes everywhere, and *sees* wherever he goes, observed this picture at a broker's shop" (p. 133), where an engraver was bidding for it. Thus Jacob and Montenero conspire to prevent the copying and dissemination of the depiction. This story easily conforms to anti-Semitic fantasies about the disproportionate power of the Jews over symbolic systems, their omnipresence, and their financial ability to monopolize commodities.

To reform the order of representation, then, Montenero is given all the powers normally attributed to conspiratorial manipulators of signs in general and economic markets in particular. Far from denying links between Jews and such economic and representational power, *Harrington* emphasizes them. For example, the story makes sure that we understand that Montenero's wealth takes symbolic and labile forms, which the tale goes out of its way to identify with both the market in art and paper credit. Montenero, for example, saves Mr. Harrington's credit by promising to sell a few of his paintings for £60,000. Indeed, to be on Montenero's side is to embrace rather than to fear the commercial value of art and the instruments of modern financial credit. These last are proudly proclaimed to be Jewish inventions: "'You know,' said [Montenero], 'that we Jews were the first inventors of bills of exchange and bank-notes—we were originally the bankers and brokers of the world'" (p. 120). He then goes on to explain the connection between geographic mobility and the invention of paper credit:

> The persecutions even to which the Jews were exposed—the tyranny which drove us from place to place, and from country to country, at a moment's or without a moment's warning, compelled us, by necessity, to the invention of a happy expedient, by which we could convert all our property into a scrap of paper, that could be carried

unseen in a pocket-book, or conveyed in a letter unsuspected. (p. 120)

A sense of the happiness of this expedient colors the narrator's view of the bank and the mint, which he visits with the Monteneros, and where he is "delighted" to see "the spirit of order operating like predestination, compelling the will of man to act necessarily and continually with the precision of mechanism. I had beheld human creatures, called clerks, turned nearly into arithmetical machines" (p. 119). In these descriptions of the beginnings and ends of credit, we learn that what began as the convenient dematerialization of property to allow for its reappearance in a different place has issued in the figurative disappearance of human beings themselves, their absorption into the clockwork of a mechanical providence, even their ultimate replacement by a machine, "which indefatigably weighs, accepts, rejects, disposes of the coin, which a mimic hand perpetually presents" (p. 119).

The bank and the mint are emblems of "precise" valuation, the sort found in perfectly fungible coins weighed by unerringly objective machines. Theirs is certainly an order of representation purged of human prejudice, but only by being purged of human beings. This submission to a "mechanical providence" that makes all people equal and then finally makes them disappear seems to be the other side of the coin of Montenero's humanism. Despite its sterility, though, the imagery of bodily disappearance and detachable limbs is also eerily reminiscent of Harrington's infantile fantasy that he would vanish into Simon the Jew's "great bag," "that bag, in which I fancied were mangled limbs of children—it opened to receive me" (p. 4).

Montenero's ways of reforming the symbolic order, cornering the market on artistic representation and creating ever more precise and automatic financial instruments, are thus never free from the anti-Semitic images they were designed to counter. But my point in stressing these continuities is not to condemn Maria Edgeworth for her lingering anti-Semitism. It is, rather, to suggest that *Harrington* demonstrates in a peculiarly paradoxical form the double bind of Edgeworth's productivist realism: how can one maintain a clear distinction between realities and representations and simultaneously assert the reality-shaping power of representations? By giving us a Jewish money-man whom we must credit, Edgeworth deprives herself of her usual figure for faulty, inflated accounting;[70] indeed, her past use of the Jews becomes itself the emblem of faulty representation. She thus suggests that anti-Semitism arises, in part, from the desire of productivist imaginations like her own, which cannot bear to countenance the inflationary and inflammatory potential of their own productions.[71]

In *Harrington*, she thus explicitly renounces one of her former mechanisms for subduing or expelling the imagination's fecundity. To be sure, she does create another deceitful villain in Lord Mowbray, who takes "the utmost pains to work on [Harrington's] imagination" (p. 252). But Montenero is not simply contrasted to Mowbray. For, as we have seen, to sympathize with Montenero is to indulge in fantasies of control through symbolic manipulation, and his desire to control representations seems to require a constant involvement with them, almost a willingness to take them as his primary reality, which further collapses the distinction by which falsehood can be identified.

Harrington, therefore, never gets far from the uncanny landscape of its opening, which serves as a stage for the performance of Maria Edgeworth's preoccupations. Thus it is appropriate that this tale's almost surrealistic climax (if such an episodic work can be said to have one climax) both recapitulates and collapses several of the pairs of opposites explored in this chapter—representations and things, debt and credit, letter and substance, fiction and truth, Irish and Anglo-Irish, daughter and father, Jew and Gentile. In this climax, London is once again dotted with "wondrous" fires, like the gaslight "stars" of the hero's first memory, but this time they

---

70. See, for example, Mordicai the coachmaker in *The Absentee*.
71. Moishe Postone, in "Anti-Semitism and National Socialism," makes a similar point about the origins of modern anti-Semitism when he attributes it to the need to split capitalism into a "good" materialism and a "bad" abstraction:

> [C]oncrete labor . . . appear[s] as a purely material, creative process, separable from capitalist social relations. On the logical level of capital, the "double character" (labor process and valorization process) allows industrial production to appear as a purely material, creative process, separable from capital. . . . Capital itself—or what is understood as the negative aspect of capitalism— is understood only in terms of the manifest form of its abstract dimension: finance and interest capital. (p. 310)

are buildings set ablaze by the Gordon rioters: "Newgate . . . [was] in a blaze; that night, the Fleet, and the King's Bench, and the Popish chapels, were on fire, and the glare of the conflagration reached the skies" (p. 186). This time public history itself has been taken over by uncontrolled imaginings. The "populace" of London, not just one helpless little boy, has its imagination excited by "ridiculous reports" that inspire "absurd terrors." Instead of loathing Simon the Jew, the mob, Harrington tells us, is after the pope and any supposed papists who happen to be in London. Although the narrator here, unlike the narrator of the opening scene, has no difficulty distinguishing between true and false reports, this scene nevertheless uses the riot as a milieu in which things lose their solid reality.

Fire is the riot's most powerful de-realizing element: in this episode, as in several others depicting the persecution of the Jews, it is used as a symbol of passionate anarchy. But the repeated threat of fire in the book also seems linked to its de-materializing power, to its destruction of matter, without distinction. The accumulation of fires—the "roasting" of young Jacob by the schoolboys, the destruction of his patron's Gibraltar business, the burning of the painting, the references to the Spanish Inquisition's autos-da-fé, and finally the torching of those bastions of state power, the prisons—gives the impression that anything can be burned, that matter is all the same in this regard. When the Monteneros are under attack from the mob, for example, they hide both their paintings and "the females" in the same place, indicating once again the indistinction of paintings and bodies, which now seem made of the same vulnerable stuff. Indeed, one of the females is so terrified that she has "stiffened" into a "frightful rigidity . . . with a ghastly face, and eyes fixed" and must therefore be carried, like the paintings, to a safe place. The Gordon Riots, therefore, are more than merely a means to find a "real" and deplorable "objective correlative" for Harrington's earlier intolerance and to generalize the problem of anti-Semitism into that of religious prejudice; the particular mode of destruction in the riots creates a category of matter, mere matter, in which all things seem equally real just as they are on the verge of disappearing.

This is not, however, the only threat the riot poses to our ability to differentiate between things and representations. In a move that is supposed to highlight the utter arbitrariness of mob thinking, the crowd abruptly becomes anti-Semitic:

> Without any conceivable reason, suddenly a cry was raised against the Jews: unfortunately, Jews rhymed to shoes: these words were hitched into a rhyme, and the cry was "No Jews, no wooden shoes!" Thus without any natural, civil, religious, moral, or political connexion, the poor Jews came in remainder to the ancient anti-Gallican antipathy felt by English feet and English fancies against the French wooden shoes. (p. 186)

What Harrington describes, though, is not just irrationality but the frighteningly independent automatism of language, whose mere sounds in this incident take the lead over both reason and imagination. But if the crowd is in the grip of the signifier, so too is the very sentence in which it is described, which, though not devoid of sense, seems driven by a phonic, this time alliterative, association ("antipathy felt by English feet and English fancies").

The story, moreover, continues to unfold according to the "logic" of rhymes, which ushers in, of all things, an Irishwoman. When the mob is about to attack Montenero's house, an Irish orange seller (who had previously received Montenero's charity) comes to the rescue, explaining, "They call you a Levite, don't they? then I, the widow Levy, has a good right to advise ye" (p. 187). The Irishwoman spews bulls throughout the episode, as if to emphasize that language and sense are touching at odd angles: "Jew as you have this day the misfortune to be, you're the best Christian any way ever I happened on!" (p. 187). And she seems fond of Montenero partly because "jew" is a piece of her favorite term of endearment, "jewel." "Jewel" is what she calls him throughout the scene until the pun finally seems to burst out of her: "Oh! if he isn't a jewel of a Jew!" (p. 195).

This comic Irishwoman, said to be trusted by the leaders of an *anti-Catholic* riot (men who do not suspect her of being "a little bit of a Cat'olick myself"), who appears on the flimsiest of plot pretexts in the midst of a scene of high drama, might herself be thought of as an eruption of the utterly arbitrary. However, she is hardly a meaningless figure; contemporary reviewers saw Mrs. Levy as Maria Edgeworth's "signature" character, the bit of Irishness that linked this tale with her others. That Montenero has such a "guard-

ian angel," moreover, links him with Edgeworth's Anglo-Irish heroes, especially those, like Glenthorn, who are threatened by an
angry "populous" and saved by a loyal Irish servant. Since it was
well known that Richard Lovell himself had been menaced by both
Catholic and Protestant mobs during the uprising of 1798, Montenero's association with him in this incident would perhaps have
been apparent to contemporary readers. That association also suggests a general similarity between the Anglo-Irish and the Jews;
both are "nations" out of place. Both could be and were called
interlopers and parasites. Indeed, Maria Edgeworth's earlier anti-
Semitism might have been a mechanism for unloading the guilt not
only of representation but also of colonialism onto a convenient
surrogate.[72] In *Harrington*, though, both the Irishwoman and the
gentleman are "outlandish" (p. 188), as Mrs. Levy says, so the
distinction between native and colonizer is neutralized.

If we look even more carefully at Mrs. Levy, we can see that she
both raises and neutralizes another of Edgeworth's problematic
distinctions, that of the daughter-debtor and father-creditor. She
resembles the debt-ridden daughter in several ways. Mrs. Levy,
like the crowd she tries to outwit, gives herself up to the resemblances of the sounds of words. Hence, Maria Edgeworth characterizes Mrs. Levy as she had characterized herself, as more intimately connected to the "letter" than to the "idea" of an utterance.
Mrs. Levy's language, like Edgeworth's own, though, is certainly
not all nonsense; instead, it is often fictional. The widow prides
herself on her stories and alibis, her quick-witted departures from
strict truthfulness:- "[He] could think of noting [*sic*] at all but the
truth to tell," she exclaims when describing the failure of a messen-
ger to get through the mob; her own mode of diverting the crowd
is that of a storyteller:

> [T]here she sat on the steps quite at ease, smoking her pipe or wiping
> and *polishing* her oranges. As parties of the rioters came up, she
> would parley and jest with them, and by alternate wit and humour,
> and blunder, and bravado, and flattery, and *fabling*, divert their spirit
> of mischief, and forward them to distant enterprise. (p. 188, em-
> phases in the original)

72. That the Jews in *The Absentee* are the ultimate beneficiaries of the Anglo-Irish
gentry's defection to London is a transparent attempt to displace Anglo-Irish guilt.

When the mob finally becomes too unruly for her management, Mrs. Levy's *"fabling"* allows her to take Mr. Montenero's message to the military. In other words, her puns, rhymes, nonsense, and fictions, although they may seem merely entertaining and may sometimes even derive from "the pleasure of telling a few superfluous lies" (p. 188), all finally serve to get the patriarch's message through and restore order.

The relationship between Mrs. Levy and the Levite, therefore, resembles that between the two Edgeworths as Maria herself had seemingly always imagined it. The widow, we are told, has long been "patronized" by Montenero; he supplies her with the fruit she polishes and sells. Note that "polishing" and "fabling" are both emphasized in the quotation, as if they were paired in the writer's mind. Like Maria, she glosses and circulates the substance the patriarch provides. Moreover, Montenero entrusts the Irishwoman with his message, and, by carrying the letter on her person, she takes it through to its destination. But she can get it through only because of her inventive fictionalizing. Hence the message must rely on an errant, circuitous medium.

We must, however, also see that since this patriarch cannot himself be said to be separable from representation, the distinctions between father and daughter, debtor and creditor are not securely in place when this episode begins. Indeed, both traditionally and in this specific tale, the Irishwoman and the Jew can both be said to be figures for the letter. Mrs. Levy's very appearance, trundling across the square to a great London house in her "outlandish" black cape and hat, resembles that of Simon the Jew in the opening scene, a resemblance that the illustrator of the 1893 edition seems to have noted in his paired pictures of the two figures. Thus although the Levy-Levite relationship looks like the relationship, so familiar in Edgeworth's lexicon, of daughter-letter-debtor to father-idea-creditor, the similarity between the two terms is what dominates in these depictions.

The Levy-Levite pair, then, metaphorically release the tension inherent in a string of Edgeworthian dichotomies: between Irish and Anglo-Irish, daughter and father, letter and idea, debtor and creditor. But this release is not quite enough to exonerate the father; his justification is incomplete until the daughter in the tale, Berenice, finishes rewriting the Jessica plot and thereby reverses, at least in part, the dynamics of the family debt. Berenice, it turns out, gratuitously took on the role of "the Jewess" to align her fortunes with her father's; she is really a Protestant, whose mother was the daughter of an English ambassador to Spain, but she refused to have this fact publicly known because she does not want to be accepted by anyone who might be prejudiced against her father. Berenice completely inverts the actions of Shakespeare's Jessica; she escapes from gentile society to her father's house, and, instead of embracing Christianity, she temporarily hides hers. "Berenice is not a Jewess," Montenero announces in the last scene; the daughter does not derive her substance from her father, but she *pretends to* out of a sense of loyalty. This final twist of the plot, which most of *Harrington*'s critics have found either inexplicable or highly offensive, might be explained as an allegory of Edgeworth's authorship.[73] She has indeed claimed to represent her father, but now that he is being accused of bending her imaginary works to his purposes, she wants to make it clear that she has represented him gratuitously. There is the generosity! The obligation, if there is one, is mainly his.

Where does all this leave us in relation to productivism? At the beginning of this chapter, I claimed that the Edgeworths' "productivism" was not a solution to the problem of literary debt but was instead an ideology that intensified the problem, especially when combined with patriarchal and antinovelistic assumptions in the culture at large. Did *Harrington*'s systematic blurring of the distinction between debtor and creditor and all the other related binarisms destroy the productivist rationale for Edgeworth's authorship? It certainly did not curtail her use of the manufacturing metaphor; after all, the quotation that begins this chapter is from a letter of 1836. But we might conclude from the two adult fictions written after *Harrington* that the author was no longer anxiously demon-

73. Michael Ragussis sees Berenice's last-minute Christianity as another variant of the conversion plot, connecting it with a long line of similar Christian transformations of Jewish characters. Ragussis's argument is deeply insightful, but it does not attend to the revision of the father-daughter relationship. By labeling Berenice's religion the sole "sign of Edgeworth's submission to the ruling ideology" ("Representation, Conversion, and Literary Form," p. 135), he echoes Rachel Mordecai's contemporary complaint: "[I]n one event I was disappointed: Berenice is not a Jewess" (Mordecai to Maria Edgeworth, October 28, 1817; printed in *The Education of the Heart*, p. 16).

strating how the reader would profit from her works. Richard Lovell, in his preface to *Harrington* and *Ormond*, for example, points out that "The moral of [*Ormond*] does not immediately appear, for the author has taken peculiar care that it should not obtrude itself upon the reader" (p. vi). This lack of an obtrusive moral, moreover, seems associated with the disappearance of the pushy father, for Richard Lovell goes on to ask the reader's pardon for "this intrusion," concluding with "I bid you farewell for ever" (p. vi). Carefully obscuring the moral both protected Richard Lovell from charges of interference and made it difficult to tell the difference between the "letter" of fiction and the "spirit" of general principles. Hence, although Edgeworth never abandoned her ideological commitment to productivism, after *Harrington* she seems to have suppressed its didactic implications.

Her new desire not to "obtrude" her morals brings her more fully into the nineteenth century, when novelists were comparatively unconcerned about justifying fiction per se. The difficulty of distinguishing between the letter and the spirit was, indeed, soon to become the hallmark of serious novels. Hence, although the vast majority of Maria Edgeworth's tales and novels clearly belong to the turn of the century, when significant fictions were expected to have strong theses, her career also demonstrates the fading of those expectations. Edgeworth's desire to ground her fictions in clear and distinct general principles was nurtured by her peculiar late eighteenth-century blend of patriarchalism and productivism; perhaps later forms of realism belonged to a society that, for a variety of reasons, found solace in creating and managing its symbolic debts by imagining more autonomous daughters and a more permeable boundary between a fiction's "interest" and its "principle."

If in *Harrington* Edgeworth wrote her way out of her didacticism and her anxiety about debt, however, she seems also to have written her way out of the desire to write. Her sense of obligation was clearly the productive force in her career, and she apparently no longer felt it keenly after her father's symbolic exoneration and actual death. Hence, she did not write as much. However, since these later works were "gratis," Edgeworth considered the money earned from them "peculiarly" her own. Instead of considering it part of the estate's revenue, she spent it on traveling and on gifts to friends and relatives. There is only one exception to this pattern, one late use of copyright money that fit the old pattern of filial obligation: "With Comic Dramas £300 I had the pleasure of paying a debt of my father's to Catherine Billamore [the housekeeper]. He left to me the privilege of paying his personal debts of which this was the only one I ever heard of."[74] The somewhat wistful tone here suggests that she wished her father had left her more debts to pay.[75]

~

Nobody has many stories. In this book I have outlined only a few, concentrating on those in which nobodiness is peculiarly weighty in order to explore the "nothing" that economic exchange, "woman," and literary representation, especially fiction, had in common. I have tried to convince the reader that the apparent negativity in the rhetoric of these women writers—their emphasis on disembodiment, dispossession, and debt—points not to disabling self-doubts but to an important source of their creativity, a fertile emptiness at the heart of eighteenth-century authorship. As I look back over this study, though, I am struck by its incompleteness. I might have discussed other, lesser-known novelists who would have given a very different impression of female authorship in the period. I might have spent more time on women playwrights and poets, or I could have given a fuller picture of the major women novelists, especially at the end of the century; I might have included Ann Radcliffe, Mary Wollstonecraft, or Elizabeth Inchbald. But I console myself with the thought that there is no "whole story" to be told, only other partial ones. And those will have to be somebody else's stories.

74. Quoted in Butler, *Maria Edgeworth: A Literary Biography,* p. 493.
75. Helen, the heroine of her last novel, might be seen as a figure for this wish; she heroically pays her foster father's personal debts out of her own fortune.

Index

Printed in the United States
45802LVS00003B/152

7257